# BOWHILL

## The House, its People and its Paintings

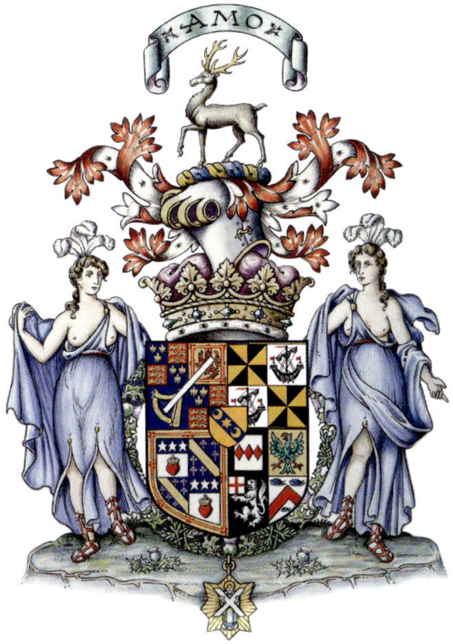


*To the memory of*
*Jane, Duchess of Buccleuch and Queensberry*
*1929–2011*

Richard, Duke of Buccleuch and Queensberry

Edited by John Montagu Douglas Scott

Photographs by Fritz von der Schulenburg

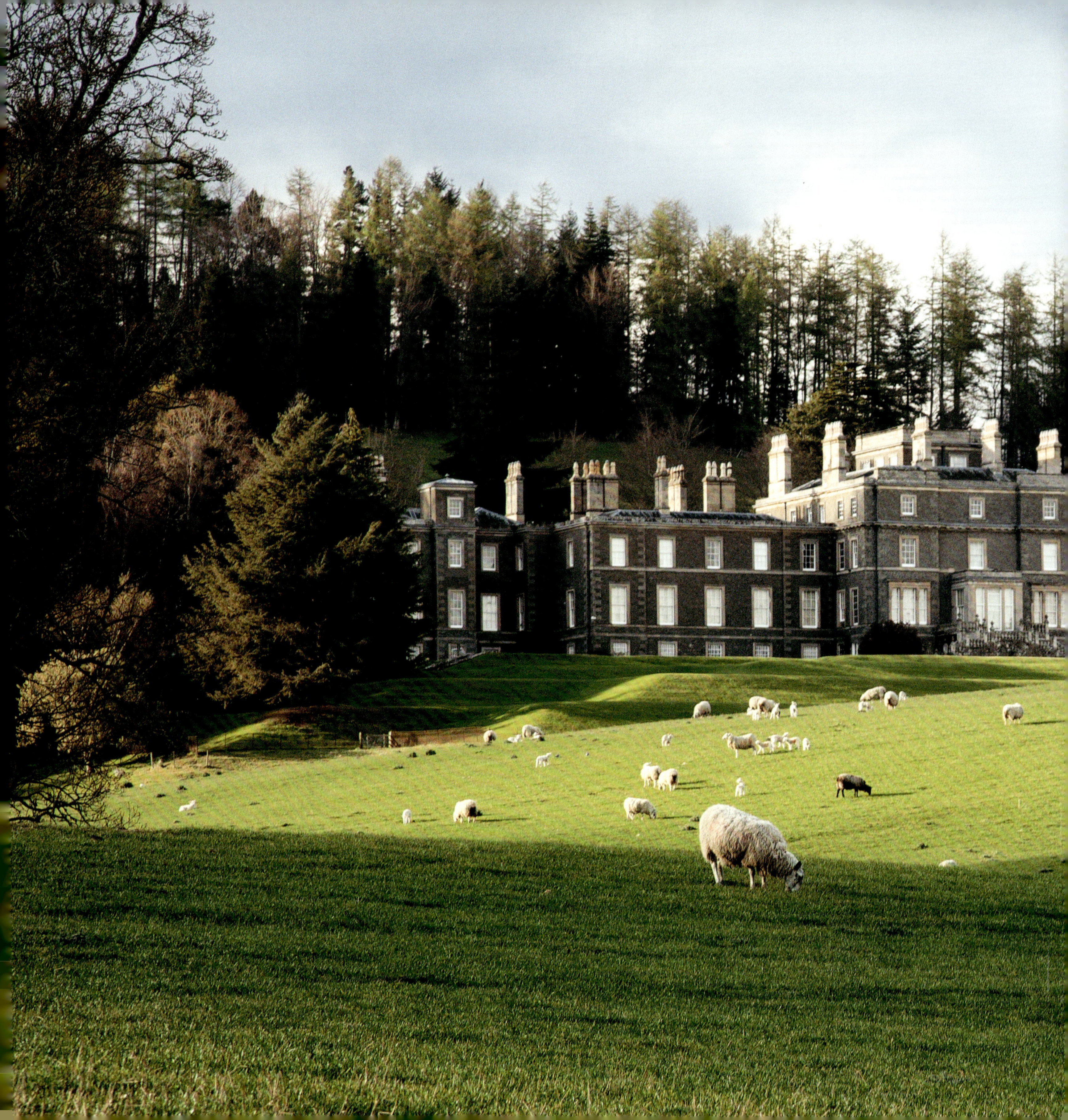

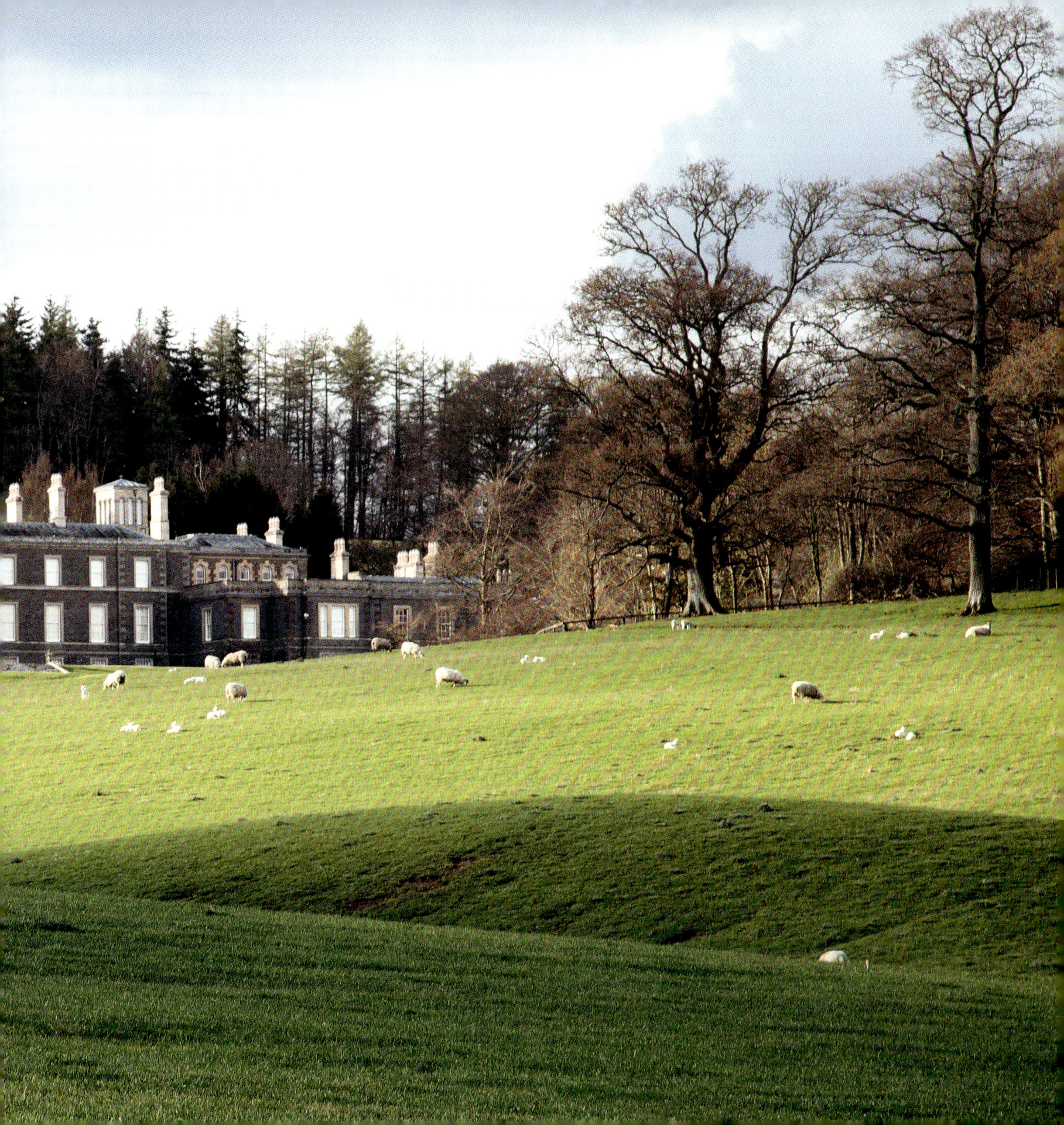

# Preface

With its simple form and dark greywacke stone, its great mass spread along a plain grassy platform above the Ettrick Valley, Bowhill might be thought to verge on the austere, even the institutional. For the approaching visitor there is no hint of a family whose ties thread for centuries back through the histories of Scotland and England, little to encourage hope that rich and varied art collections might lie within, or even that these solid stones might have resonated with festivities and celebrations, the setting for warm sentiments and deeper emotions.

Bowhill is a most deceptive house. For the main branch of my family, the Scotts of Buccleuch, it is the closest we have to a spiritual home, in the heart of Scott country just a few miles from the small cleuch, or ravine, in the Rankil Burn from which our title originated. It manages to be a spiritual home notwithstanding its relatively recent origins – what we see now is a product of the 19th century, begun seriously in 1812 and only finished in the 1870s. Thus it did not bear witness to centuries of almost perpetual conflict and lawlessness, the days of the Border reivers, from the 12th century onwards, when the Scotts accumulated and consolidated their territories and influence, centuries that only ended when Scotland's King James VI ascended the throne of England in 1603 as James I, succeeding Queen Elizabeth. Nor was it the scene of the family's fleet-footed reinvention of itself in an increasingly civilised and sophisticated social and political environment, marrying in the 17th century into the Stuart royal dynasty, and emerging in the 18th century as key figures in the politics and economics of Scotland in the age of the Enlightenment.

Paradoxically, it was as an escape from the spotlight, a place of retreat from the burdens of responsibility in Edinburgh or London, that Bowhill blossomed. 'Talk not, think not of politics, go to the Hills and converse with the Spirit of the Fell,' wrote Charles, 4th Duke of Buccleuch, to his friend and kinsman Sir Walter Scott, and as soon as he inherited he set about making this possible.

It was probably the nearest he could get to our 21st-century notion of a remote second home, a place to enjoy the country life of hunting, fishing and rough shooting. Even as it grew in scale to cope with the patterns and demands of Victorian social life and entertainment, it was fitted out for comfort rather than as a showcase for great art. The 1910 picture catalogue is almost apologetic about the lack of interesting paintings. But by then the nation was on the brink of huge change. A devastating world war would cause unimaginable loss of life. The balance of power in Britain would be transformed, with Asquith's Liberal government in 1911 effectively stripping the hereditary peerage of its political power and embarking on a new era of heavy, and ultimately penal, taxation that would put paid to many of the old families.

Even for a family as powerfully positioned as the Scotts, bolstered as they had been by marriage ties that had added the lands, houses and collections of the Douglases, Dukes of Queensberry, and the Montagus in England, the 20th century was to bring immense change. Two of the principal family seats were given up in quick succession: Montagu House on the Thames in Whitehall reverted to the Crown, and Dalkeith outside Edinburgh was mothballed by 1925. Thus humble Bowhill became the repository of part of one of the finest art collections in Europe.

Bowhill has taken time to adapt. In the intervening decades it has suffered the vicissitudes of dry rot, and been provided with a new roof. My grandparents, and my parents, reordered and redecorated and brought colour and style. It is still most definitely a family home but it is also contributing to the wider life of the Borders community – as a place for quiet recreation, and by drawing on its deep literary connections with Walter Scott and James Hogg. Its little theatre is a local institution, and more recently Bowhill has become part of the Borders Book Festival, at which each year my wife and I present one of the UK's major literary prizes, The Walter Scott Prize for Historical Fiction. There is now also a junior version, and much more is in the pipeline.

This book represents just a snapshot, for the most part through the observant eye of the photographer Fritz von der Schulenburg. It does not purport to be a guide in the traditional sense but instead gives a glimpse of an intriguing house and those associated with it.

Richard, Duke of Buccleuch and Queensberry, KT

PREVIOUS PAGES *Bowhill House, seen from the Lower Loch at lambing time, stands serene but austere. Formal terraces give way to tree-enclosed parkland*
ABOVE RIGHT *The central block dates from 1812, the wings from the 1830s and the final additions (on the right) from the 1870s*
RIGHT *The moors above the house, once part of the Ettrick Forest*

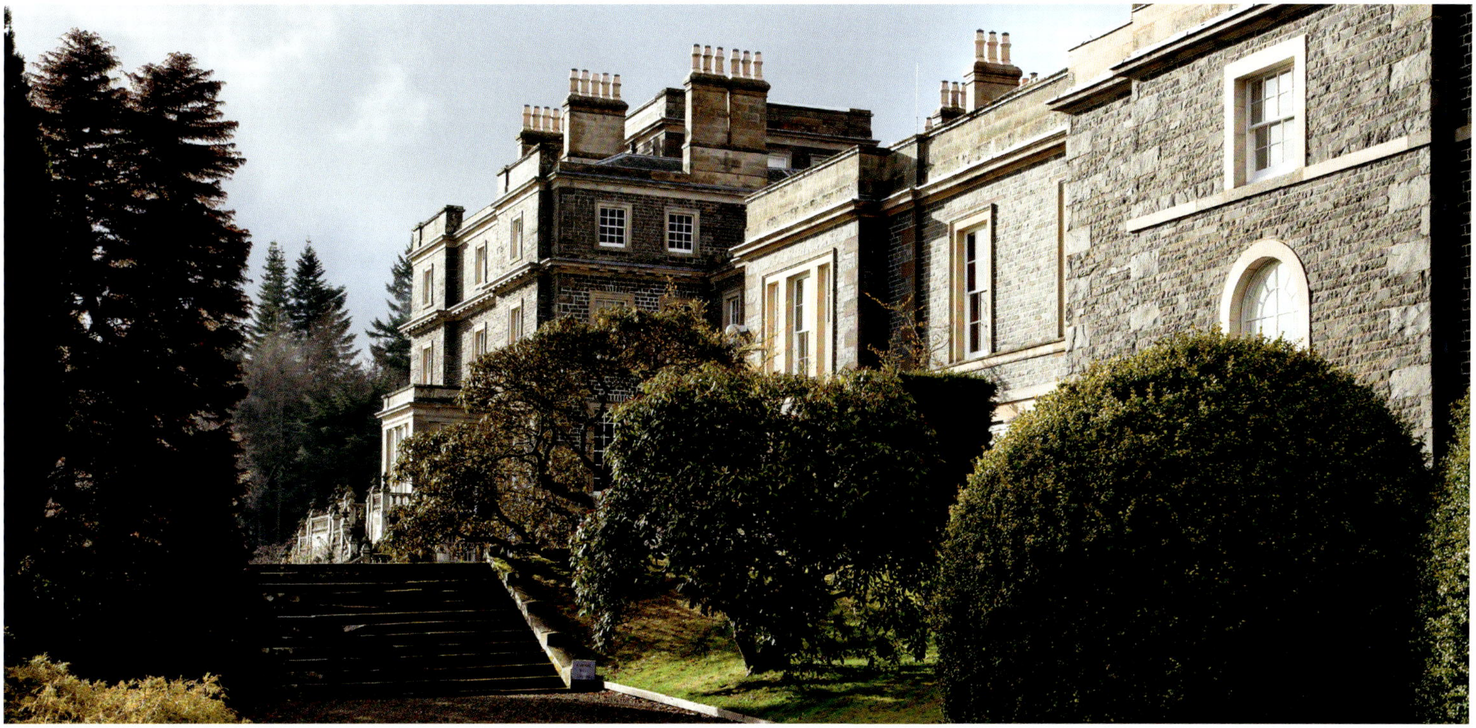

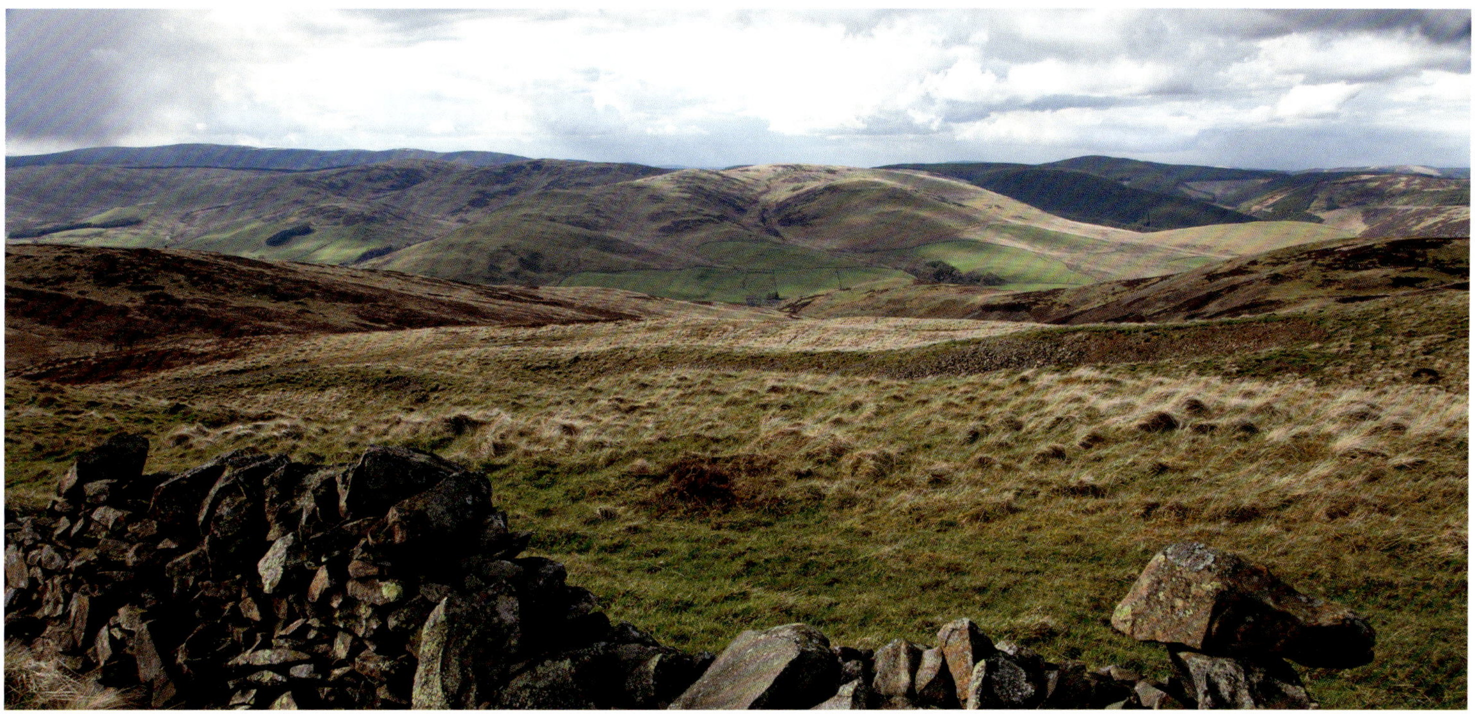

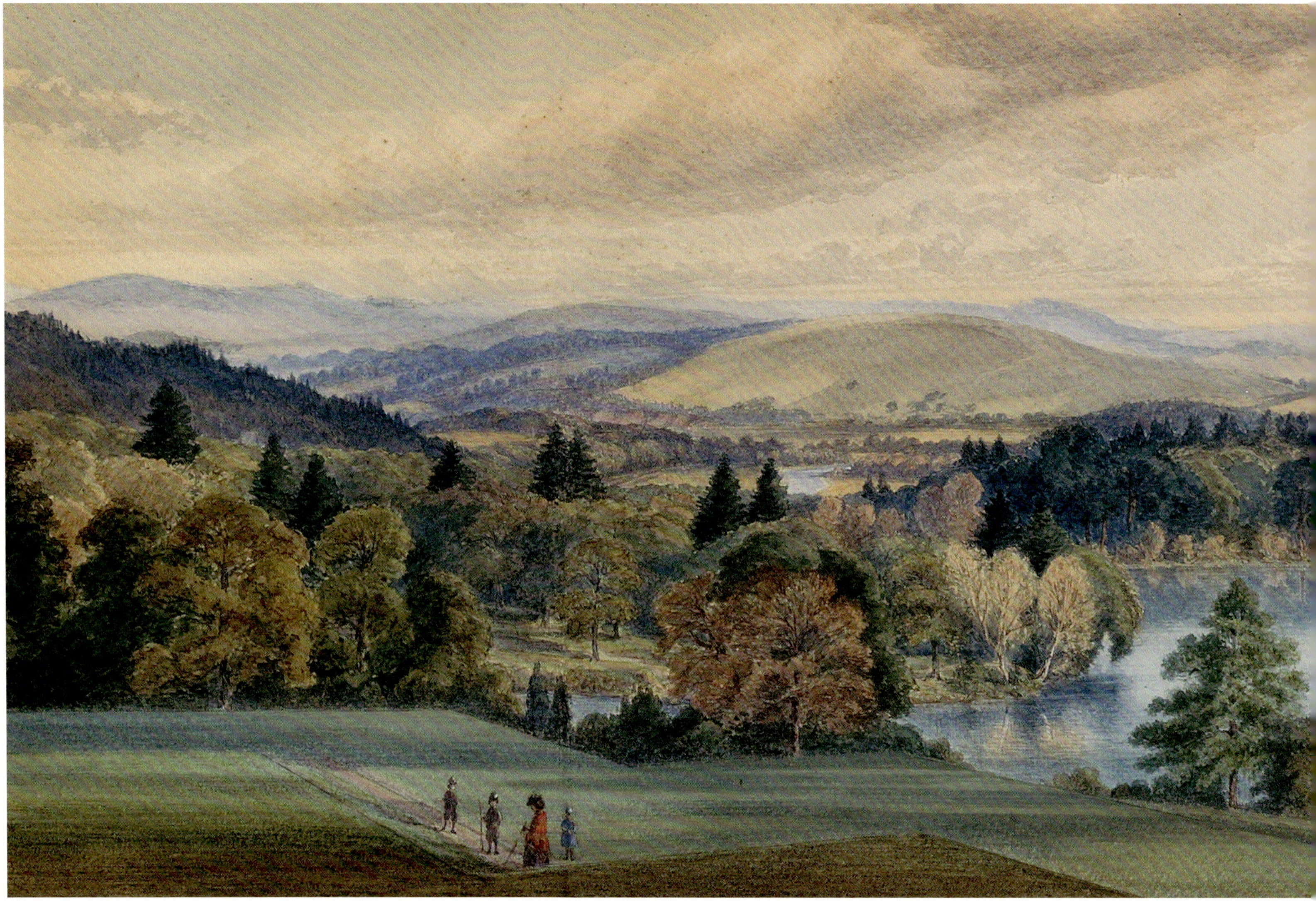

ABOVE *The Upper Loch at Bowhill with the Ettrick beyond, by Lord Henry Scott, c.1870* OVERLEAF *Where valleys meet: a frosty view across the Ettrick and Yarrow Valleys*

# Contents

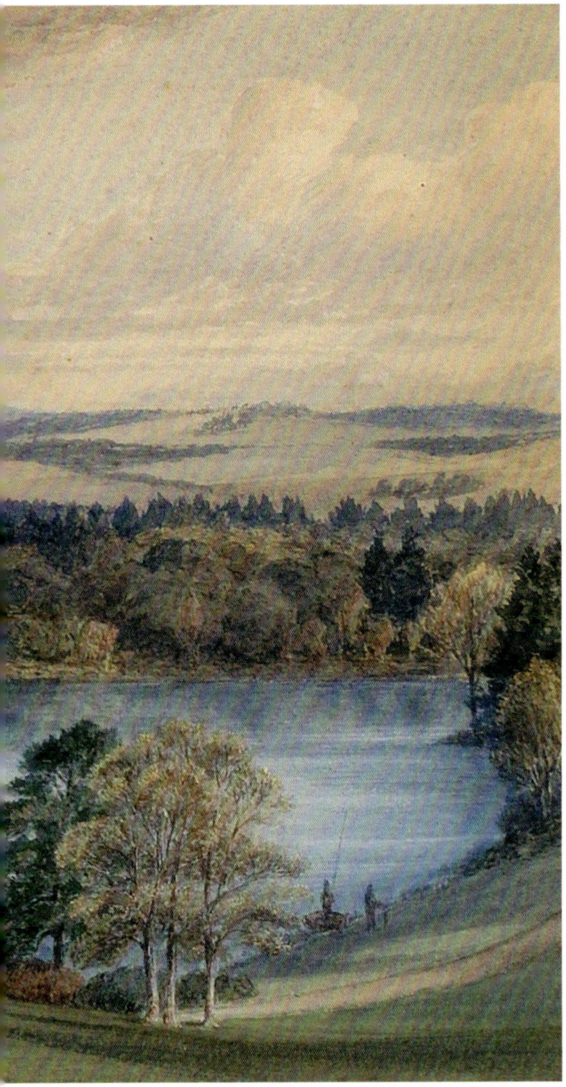

## The Family

The buck that earned the family its name 10

Marriage to the dashing son of Charles II 12

Dalkeith Palace 15

'The Lay of the Last Minstrel' 16

From the Enlightenment to the Victorian age 18

Walter Francis and his Duchess: the partnership that transformed Bowhill 22

The collectors in the family 23

The Victorian house with a Georgian spirit 26

The 20th century 28

## The House

The Outer and Inner Halls 32

The Saloon 40

The Staircase Hall 48

The Library 54

The Drawing Room 58

The Morning Room 68

The Dining Room 72

The Billiard Room 82

The Smoking Room 88

The East Passage 94

The Dalkeith Bedroom 96

The Walter Scott Room 98

The Old Chapel 104

The Buccleuch Miniatures 108

The Boudoir 112

The Archive Room 124

The Exhibition Room 126

The Old Kitchen 130

The Gardens 134

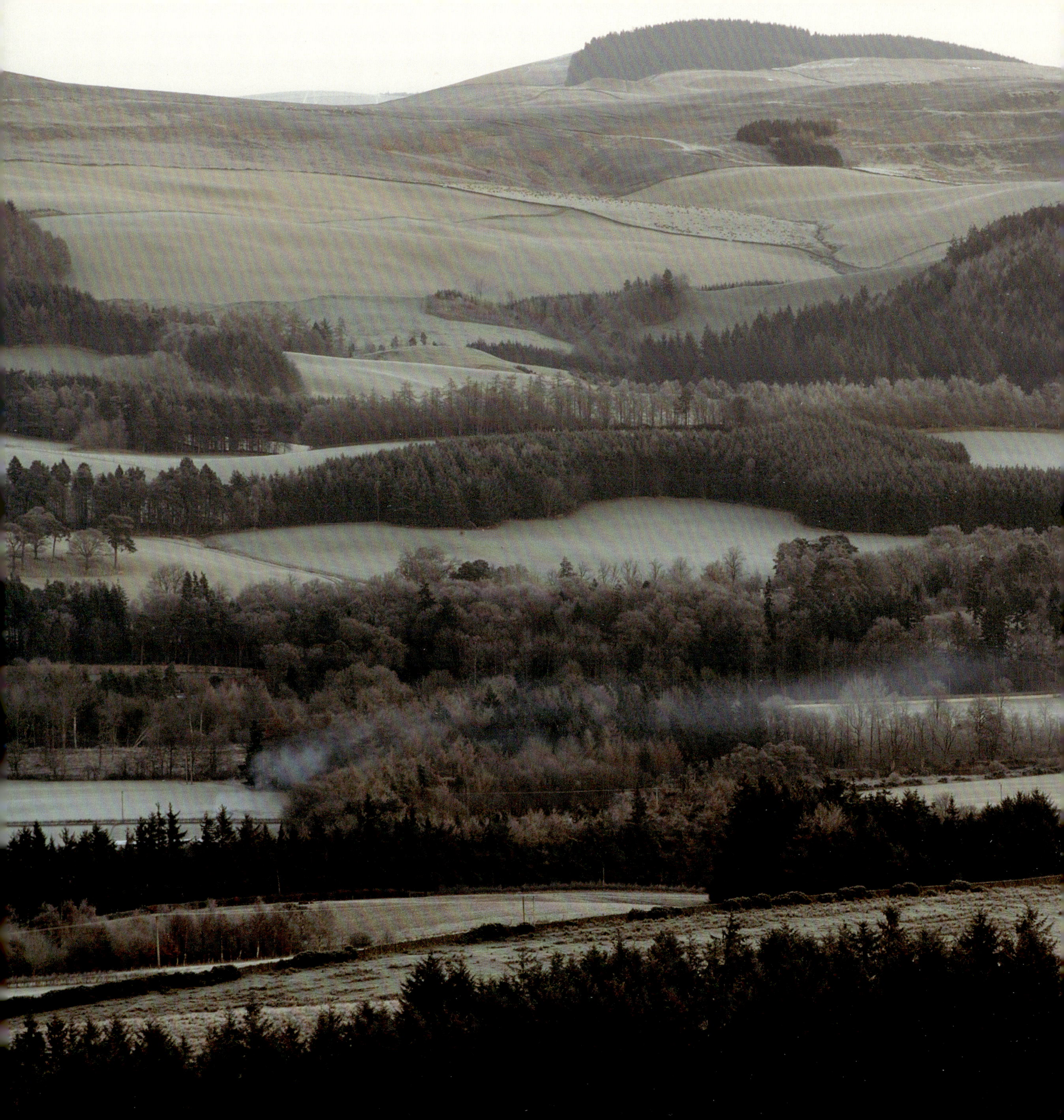

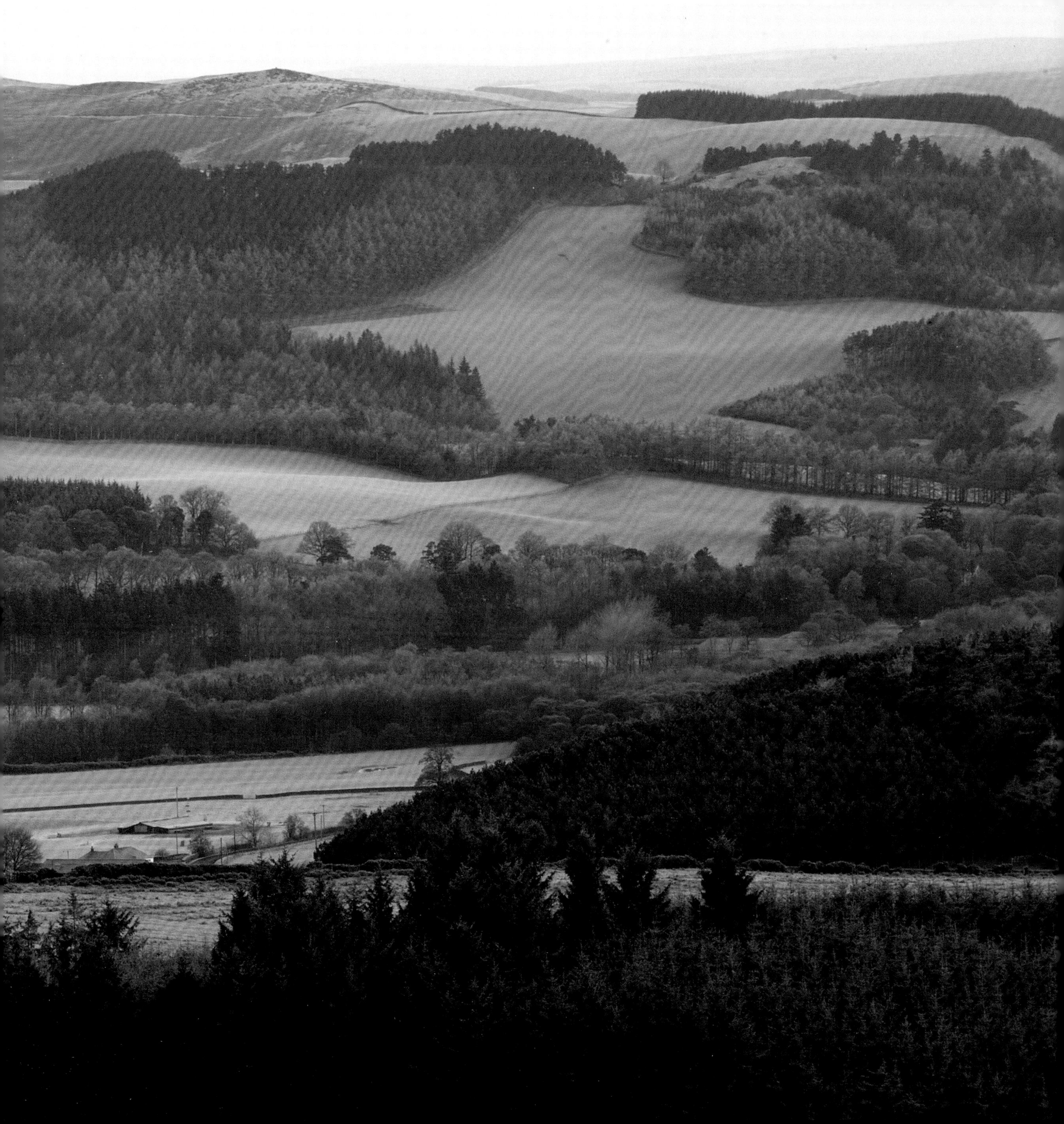

BOWHILL

# The Family

*Stretching back over almost a thousand years, the history of the Scotts sees them transformed from forest dwellers to Border reivers and romantic heroes, then into one of the most influential families in the land*

## The buck that earned the family its name

It is reckoned that there are over 500,000 people with the surname Scott spread across the globe, and there are many branches of the family, each with its own tales and traditions. Originally concentrated in Galloway in southwest Scotland, somewhere in the mists of time they seem to have moved across the country.

The first written record of a Scott with ancestral connections to the Buccleuch line, living in nearby Peeblesshire, occurs in a charter document dated 1116. Legend has it that it was even earlier, in the 10th century, that in a ravine of the Rankil Burn known as Buck Cleuch, where the stags gathered, young John Scott seized the antlers of a charging stag and threw it over his shoulder, thereby saving the life of King Kenneth III (967–1005) and earning the patronymic Scott of Buccleuch. Sir William Fraser's history of the family, however, argues that it is with Richard Scott (c.1265–1320) that the first solid evidence of settlement of the Rankil Burn is to be found.

Little is left of the once extensive Ettrick Forest, a favourite hunting ground of the Scottish kings, who used Newark Castle, a mile to the north of present-day Bowhill, as their base. The Scotts were for generations Rangers of the Forest and benefited directly when it was divided up in the 1550s. For at least two centuries before that, however, they had been accumulating lands in the valleys of the Teviot, Yarrow and Ettrick rivers, all tributaries of the Tweed. They also spread west over the watershed to Eskdale and Liddesdale, creating a defensive network of estates with a series of fortified peel towers, like chicks round the mother hen, that encircled Branxholme Castle near

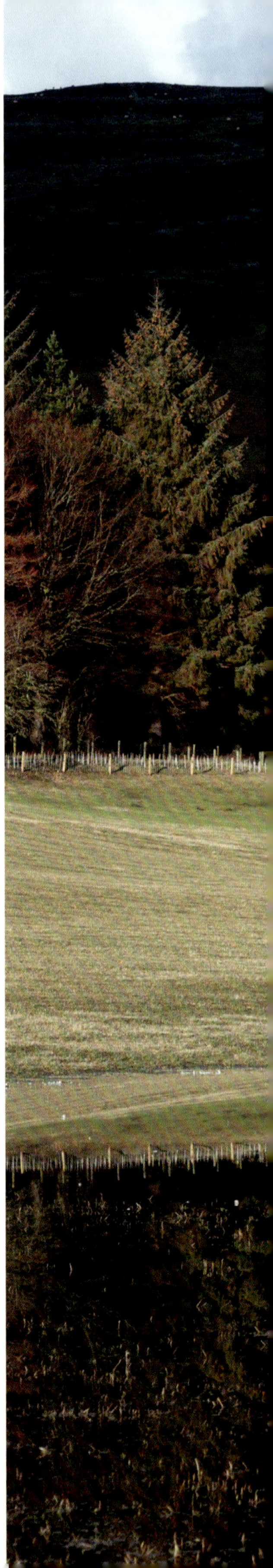

NEWARK CASTLE
*'Behold a ruin hoary! The shattered front of Newark's Towers, Renowned in Border story,' wrote Wordsworth about this 15th-century peel tower a mile from Bowhill. Newark belonged to the Earls of Douglas from 1423 until 1473, when it became a royal hunting seat. Sir Walter Scott of Buccleuch was made Keeper of Newark in 1543, after Mary Queen of Scots came to the throne. It was burnt down by the English five years later*

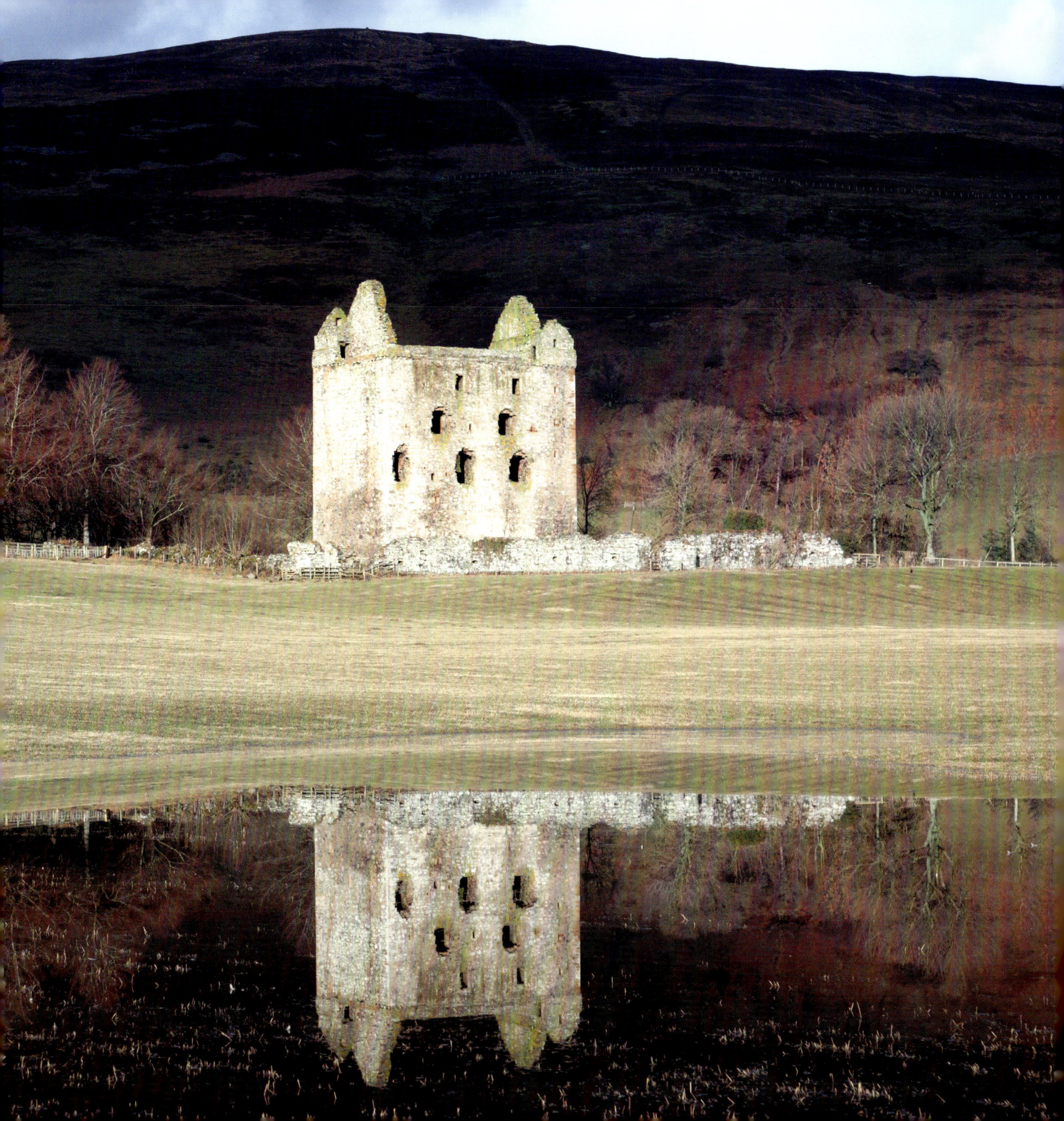

Hawick, the main family fortress of the time.

These were centuries of regular border fighting between the English and the Scots and almost as much fighting between the various competing clans on either side of the border. The Border reivers knew their country intimately, and their legendary skill at driving off other people's cattle was the stuff of many a ballad. It is said that when the Lady of Buccleuch felt food supplies were running low she would serve her husband his spurs on a plate as a reminder of his duty to replenish the larder.

Periodically both English and Scottish monarchs sought to exert control over these lawless border lands. The Scottish kings appointed Wardens of the Marches, generally from the more powerful of the leading families: the Scotts of Buccleuch were regularly Wardens of the Middle March. This still could not prevent family feuding, which ran for generations. The Scotts and the Kerrs of Fernihurst, themselves Wardens of the Marches, had a particularly bitter relationship. Murders were committed on both sides, in spite of which they periodically intermarried – and continued to do so into the 19th and 20th centuries, the present Duke and Duchess of Buccleuch being the most recent example.

In an attempt to make life more tolerable for those on the border, there were rules of engagement, including days of truce. The capture and incarceration in Carlisle Castle of Kinmont Willie, a well-known brigand, in flagrant contradiction of the rules of fair play, resulted in one of the most renowned of the cross-border confrontations. Sir Walter Scott of Buccleuch, known as 'Bold Buccleuch', led a daring rescue party that infiltrated the English fortress and whisked Kinmont Willie to safety north of the border. The infuriated Queen Elizabeth I is said to have remarked with grudging admiration that 'with 10,000 such men our brothers in Scotland might shake the firmest throne in Europe'.

In the end the Scots were forced to surrender Sir Walter, who spent some years in exile, at one time attending the University of Pavia in Lombardy, from which time snippets of rather average Italian love poetry of his own composition survive.

In a sense this is an early harbinger of the transformation of the Scotts of Buccleuch from a frontier warrior breed to leading participants in the new politics of union and a fast-developing society. Bold Buccleuch was made 1st Lord Scott of Buccleuch in 1606 by James I of England and VI of Scotland, his son becoming the 1st Earl of Buccleuch in 1619. The Earl's granddaughter in turn rose to the rank of Duchess in 1663, when she married Charles II's son James, and the dukedoms of Monmouth and Buccleuch were created simultaneously.

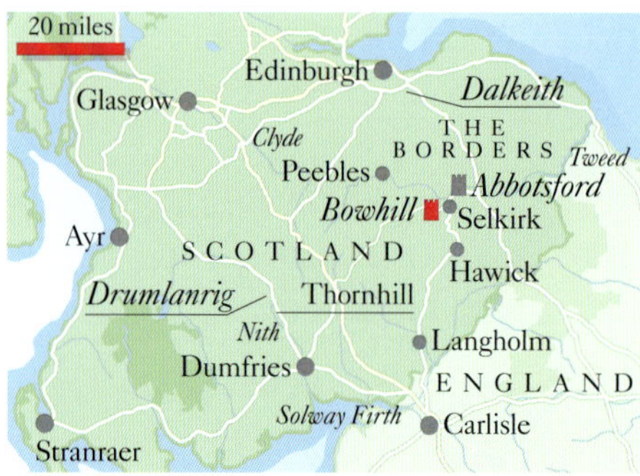


*Bowhill lies close to the heartland of the Scott family, whose estates include Dalkeith and stretch south past Langholm to the English border. Marriage to the Douglas family brought them Drumlanrig and substantial Dumfriesshire estates*

# Marriage to the dashing son of Charles II

The extraordinary endurance of Anna Scott, Duchess of Buccleuch, must have owed something to the fortitude developed in her complex childhood. Born in the era of Cromwell and the Civil War, witness to the Stuart Restoration, the Glorious Revolution, the reigns of two Hanoverian kings, not to speak of the execution of her first husband, she died in 1732, aged almost 82.

Ignored in her childhood until the death of her heiress elder sister, Anna soon became the focus of much scheming, not least by her mother and stepfather, no doubt with the best of intentions. It was at once her fortune and her misfortune that at the age of 12 she was married in the Chapel Royal, in May 1663, to James Crofts, the eldest but illegitimate son of Charles II. Recently snatched from the clutches of his out-of-control mother, Lucy Walter, James was to become his father's favourite. It is difficult to judge whether true love blossomed between the young couple, though by all reports Anna was attractive enough and an agile dancer until she had an awkward fall and remained lame for the rest of her life.

Created the 1st Duke and Duchess of Monmouth and Buccleuch, they lived almost entirely in England, in Whitehall and at Moor Park, just north of London. Perhaps the only excursion to her native land was made by her husband, a competent and brave general,

RIGHT SIR GODFREY KNELLER (1646–1723)
**James, Duke of Monmouth and Buccleuch (1649–85), painted in 1673**
*Anna Scott's glamorous first husband, Charles II's eldest, illegitimate, son, who was executed in 1685*

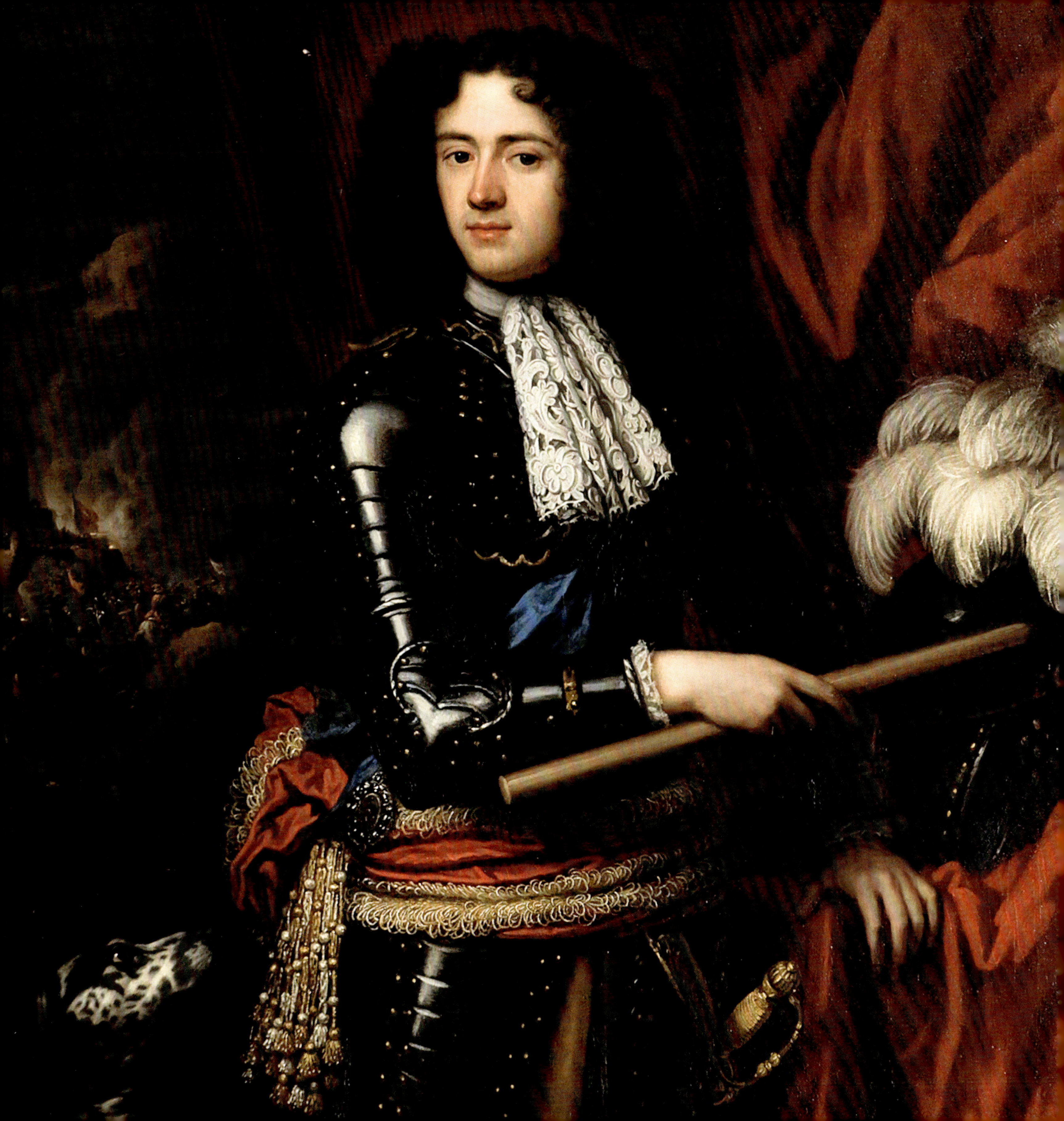

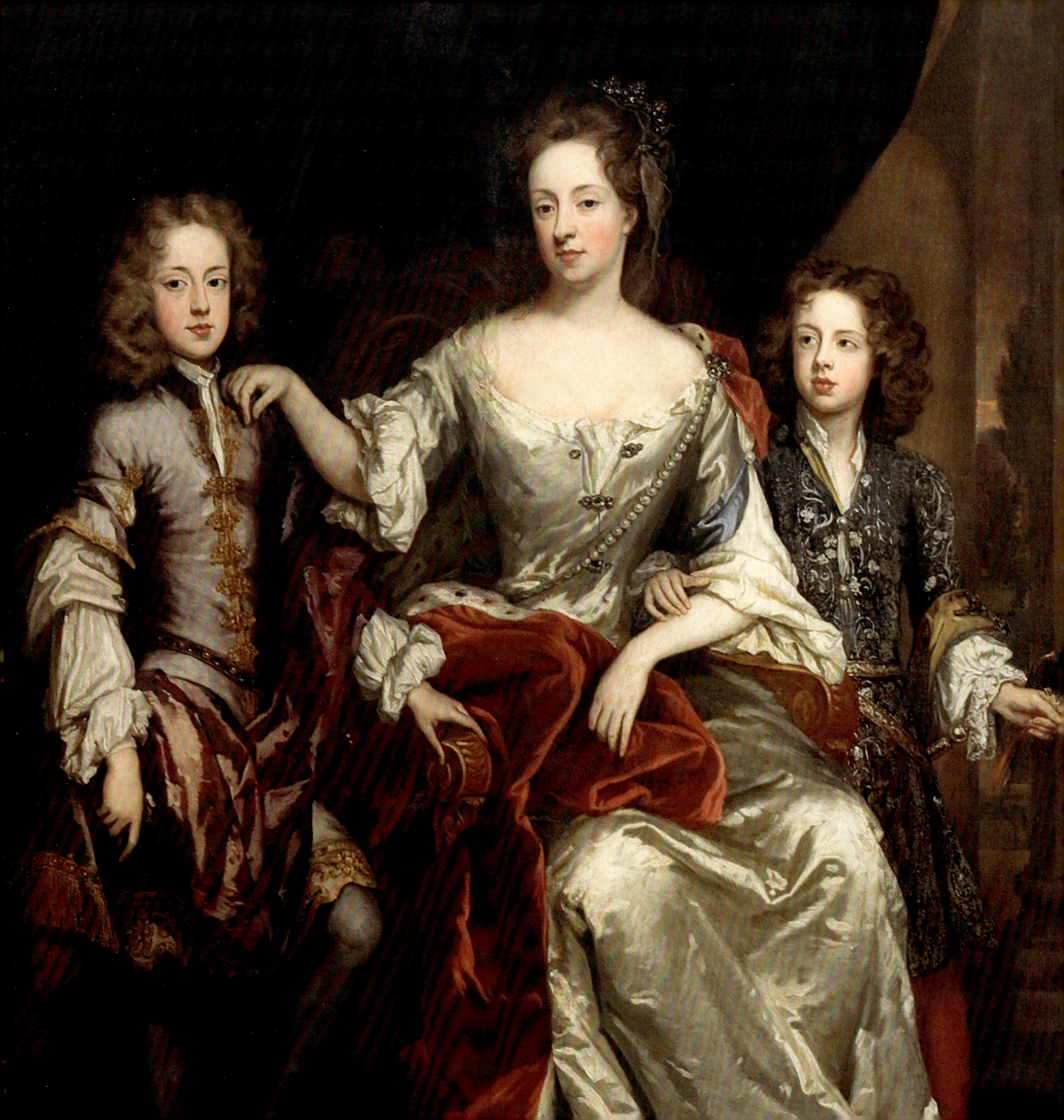

when he commanded the royal army at the Battle of Bothwell Bridge in 1679 (page 105).

Charles lavished money and gifts on his son, but relations became strained even before the King's death in 1683. The religious divide was already apparent, and the succession of the avowedly Catholic James II was to result in open rebellion, with Monmouth the standard-bearer of the Protestant cause. It ended rapidly in defeat at Sedgemoor in July 1685 and equally swiftly in Monmouth's execution on Tower Hill. Although imprisoned for a time, Anna was skilful enough to have ensured the survival of the Buccleuch title and lands.

Anna later married Charles, Lord Cornwallis, and had further children, but in 1700 she returned north to Scotland and began the process of transforming her birthplace and the principal family seat, Dalkeith, from a medieval castle into the palace it became.

Anna outlived her husband by 47 years, her sons by 20. One suspects that her dominance made life difficult for Francis, her grandson and heir as 2nd Duke. Something of an eccentric, he took as his second wife a washerwoman, Alice Powell. When he died in 1752 he, in turn, had outlived his own son.

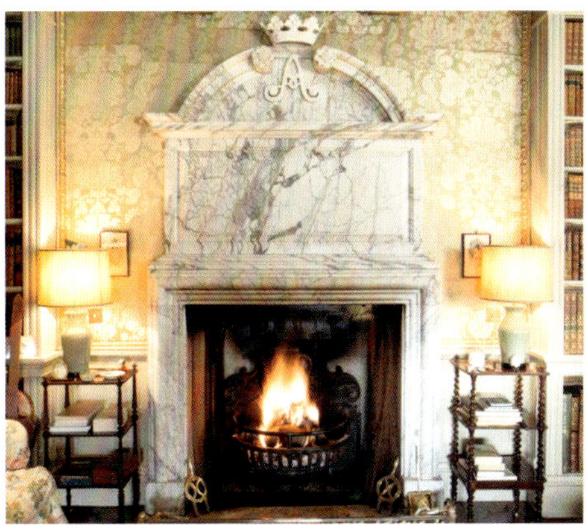

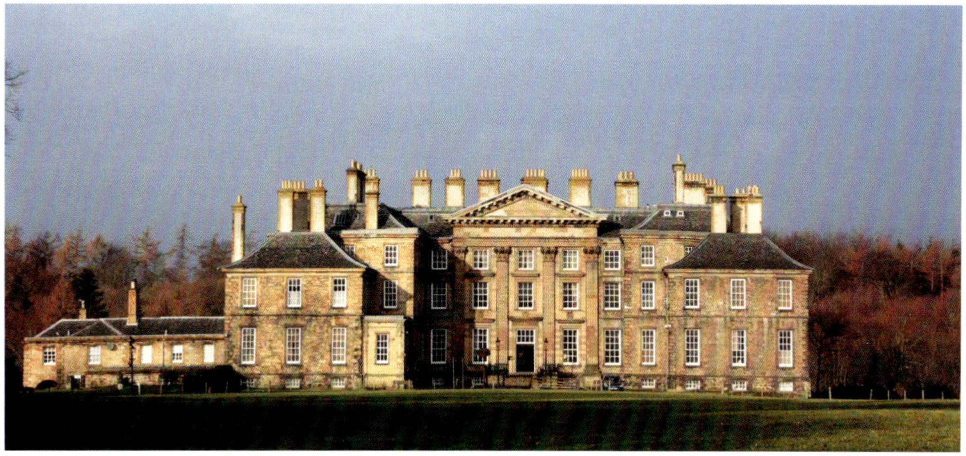

## Dalkeith Palace

Until the 1920s the principal seat of the Montagu Douglas Scott family in Scotland was Dalkeith. Just to the south of Edinburgh, on the edge of a prosperous market town five miles from the sea, it is wonderfully situated, overlooking a bend of the northern section of the River Esk, which flows through an idyllic parkland setting, captured in the 1760s and 1770s in huge canvases by the landscape artist George Barret.

Dalkeith as it stands today was the creation of Anna Scott, Monmouth's widow, who employed James Smith, Scotland's leading architect, using as her model Het Loo, William of Orange's palace in Holland. No expense was spared. Deal, oak, velvet hangings and huge quantities of marble were imported. Grinling Gibbons supplied at least ten carved chimneypieces. It was undoubtedly a more appropriate setting for the treasures that now find their home in relatively austere Bowhill.

In the century that followed Anna's death, the Dalkeith estate was further developed, with a remarkable bridge by Robert Adam and a fine stable block. Fortunately, the dramatic neo-Jacobean makeover planned by William Burn in the 1830s never got beyond the stage of an elaborate model.

OPPOSITE
SIR GODFREY KNELLER (1646–1723)
**Anna, Duchess of Monmouth and Buccleuch (1651–1732), with her sons, James, Earl of Dalkeith, and Lord Henry Scott, later Earl of Deloraine**
*Anna Scott – Countess of Buccleuch in her own right before her royal marriage – held on to the title of Duchess of Buccleuch but lost the title of Duchess of Monmouth after her husband's execution in 1685. She is seen here wearing peeress's robes, her right hand resting on the shoulder of her elder son, the Earl of Dalkeith. She had seven children with Monmouth*

ABOVE *Between 1702 and 1711, Anna transformed Dalkeith from a rudimentary castle to a palace. The architect was the pioneer of Scottish Palladian architecture, James Smith. Bought from the Douglases, Earls of Morton, before the Civil War by her father, Francis, 2nd Earl of Buccleuch, Dalkeith would be the principal family home until the First World War. It is now used as the campus in Scotland of the University of Wisconsin*

LEFT *Anna's monogram and coronet appear on the elegant marble fireplace in the Library at Bowhill, originally made for Dalkeith*

# *'The Lay of the Last Minstrel'*

By Sir Walter Scott

*Buccleuch women are central to this epic poem, which propelled Scott to fame in 1805. He was inspired by Harriet, wife of the 4th Duke; the minstrel of the title addresses his tale to Anna, Duchess of Buccleuch – wife of the executed Duke of Monmouth – and tells the story of her forebear Lady Margaret Scott of Buccleuch. In these opening verses, the minstrel arrives at Newark Castle, a Buccleuch stronghold*

*The way was long, the wind was cold,*
*The Minstrel was infirm and old;*
*His wither'd cheek, and tresses gray,*
*Seem'd to have known a better day;*
*The harp, his sole remaining joy,*
*Was carried by an orphan boy.*
*The last of all the Bards was he,*
*Who sung of Border chivalry;*
*For, welladay! their date was fled,*
*His tuneful brethren all were dead;*
*And he, neglected and oppress'd,*
*Wish'd to be with them, and at rest.*
*No more on prancing palfrey borne,*
*He caroll'd, light as lark at morn;*
*No longer courted and caress'd,*
*High placed in hall, a welcome guest,*
*He pour'd, to lord and lady gay,*
*The unpremeditated lay:*
*Old times were changed, old manners gone;*
*A stranger filled the Stuarts' throne;*
*The bigots of the iron time*
*Had call'd his harmless art a crime.*
*A wandering Harper, scorn'd and poor,*
*He begg'd his bread from door to door.*
*And tuned, to please a peasant's ear,*
*The harp, a king had loved to hear.*

*He pass'd where Newark's stately tower*
*Looks out from Yarrow's birchen bower:*
*The Minstrel gazed with wishful eye –*
*No humbler resting-place was nigh,*
*With hesitating step at last,*
*The embattled portal arch he pass'd,*
*Whose ponderous grate and massy bar*
*Had oft roll'd back the tide of war,*
*But never closed the iron door*
*Against the desolate and poor.*
*The Duchess marked his weary pace,*
*His timid mien, and reverend face,*
*And bade her page the menials tell,*
*That they should tend the old man well:*
*For she had known adversity,*
*Though born in such a high degree;*
*In pride of power, in beauty's bloom,*
*Had wept o'er Monmouth's bloody tomb!*

*When kindness had his wants supplied,*
*And the old man was gratified,*
*Began to rise his minstrel pride:*
*And he began to talk anon,*
*Of good Earl Francis, dead and gone,*
*And of Earl Walter, rest him, God!*
*A braver ne'er to battle rode;*
*And how full many a tale he knew,*
*Of the old warriors of Buccleuch:*
*And, would the noble Duchess deign*
*To listen to an old man's strain,*
*Though stiff his hand, his voice though weak,*
*He thought even yet, the sooth to speak,*
*That, if she loved the harp to hear,*
*He could make music to her ear.*

*The humble boon was soon obtain'd;*
*The Aged Minstrel audience gain'd.*
*But, when he reach'd the room of state,*
*Where she, with all her ladies, sate,*
*Perchance he wished his boon denied:*
*For, when to tune his harp he tried,*
*His trembling hand had lost the ease,*
*Which marks security to please;*
*And scenes, long past, of joy and pain,*
*Came wildering o'er his aged brain –*
*He tried to tune his harp in vain!*
*The pitying Duchess praised its chime,*
*And gave him heart, and gave him time,*
*Till every string's according glee*
*Was blended into harmony.*
*And then, he said, he would full fain*
*He could recall an ancient strain,*
*He never thought to sing again.*
*It was not framed for village churls,*
*But for high dames and mighty earls;*
*He had play'd it to King Charles the good,*
*When he kept court in Holyrood,*
*And much he wish'd yet fear'd to try*
*The long-forgotten melody.*
*Amid the strings his fingers stray'd,*
*And an uncertain warbling made,*
*And oft he shook his hoary head.*
*But when he caught the measure wild,*
*The old man raised his face, and smiled;*
*And lighten'd up his faded eye,*
*With all a poet's ecstasy!*
*In varying cadence, soft or strong,*
*He swept the sounding chords along:*
*The present scene, the future lot,*
*His toils, his wants, were all forgot:*
*Cold diffidence, and age's frost,*
*In the full tide of song were lost;*
*Each blank in faithless memory void,*
*The poet's glowing thought supplied;*
*And while his harp responsive rung,*
*'Twas thus the Latest Minstrel sung…*

Right Newark Castle, by the Rev. John Thomson of Duddingston (1778–1840). Scott championed his work, and this was one of the first paintings to hang at Bowhill

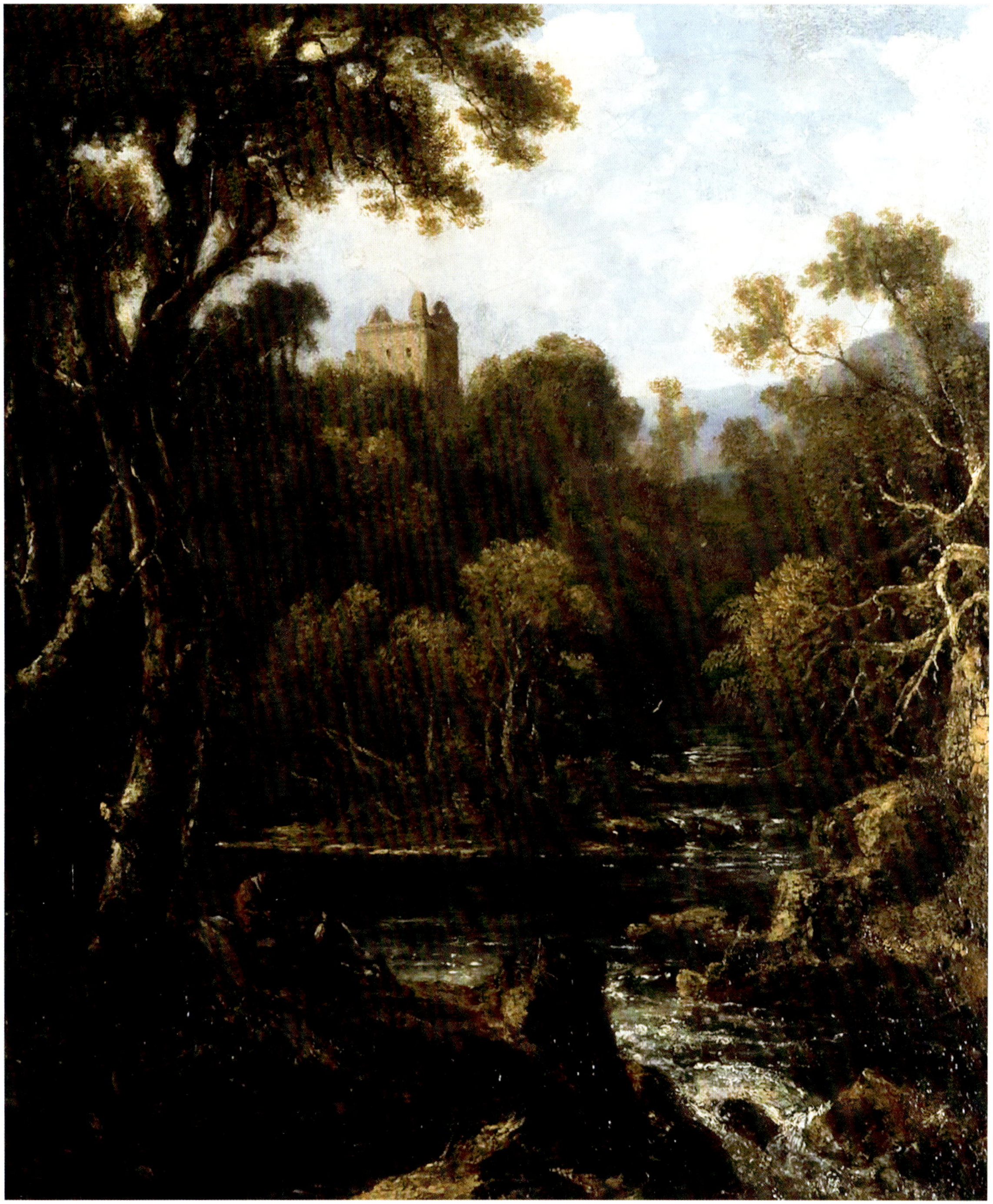

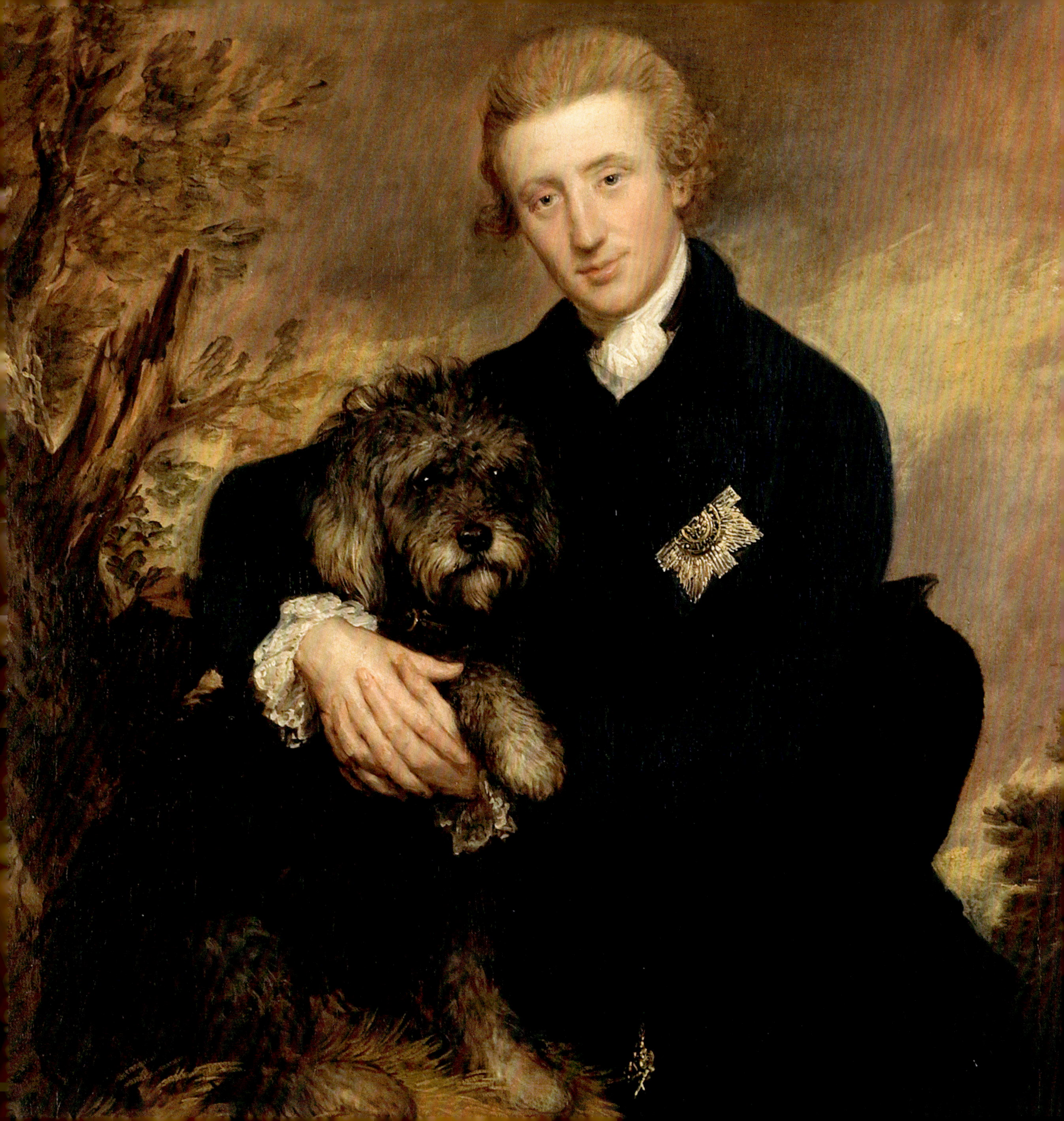

# From the Enlightenment to the Victorian age

*Bowhill started life as a modest Georgian villa bought for political reasons. The art collection was consolidated when Henry, the enlightened 3rd Duke, and his wife, Elizabeth, united the three great families of Montagu, Douglas and Scott. They left it to later generations to transform Bowhill into a huge mansion and add great treasures to the collection*

Gainsborough's portrait of Henry, 3rd Duke of Buccleuch, in the relaxed pose and dress of a country gentleman, his hands clasped round a rather shaggy dog, a Dandie Dinmont, belies the exceptional ability and influence of this young man.

Henry was just five when he succeeded to the title, and by the time of his death half a century later, his inheritance had been greatly enlarged, in terms of both titles and territories. Through his wife, Elizabeth Montagu – seen here in a portrait by Reynolds with her first daughter and the same Dandie Dinmont (on the right) – came landholdings in Northamptonshire, Hampshire and Lancashire and great houses in and around London. Through his grandmother came the dukedom of Queensberry, Drumlanrig Castle and many thousands of acres of southwest Scotland. His mother, Lady Caroline Campbell, was the daughter and heiress of the Duke of Argyll.

Following the death of Henry's father, Francis, Earl of Dalkeith, Lady Caroline had married Charles Townshend, an English politician who became Chancellor of the Exchequer. Townshend proved an invaluable stepfather to the young Duke, persuading the great economist Adam Smith to resign his position at the University of Glasgow and become tutor to Henry. Together they set off in 1765 on a tour of Europe that was to take them to meet many of the most eminent thinkers in France and on to Geneva to meet Voltaire.

It was the start of a lifelong friendship that involved Smith spending considerable time with the ducal family and receiving a substantial pension until his death in 1790. His influence on the Duke was crucial in persuading him as a young married man that he should make his life in Scotland rather than London and that he should develop and improve his estates. Dalkeith, being just outside Edinburgh, was a hub of ideas and

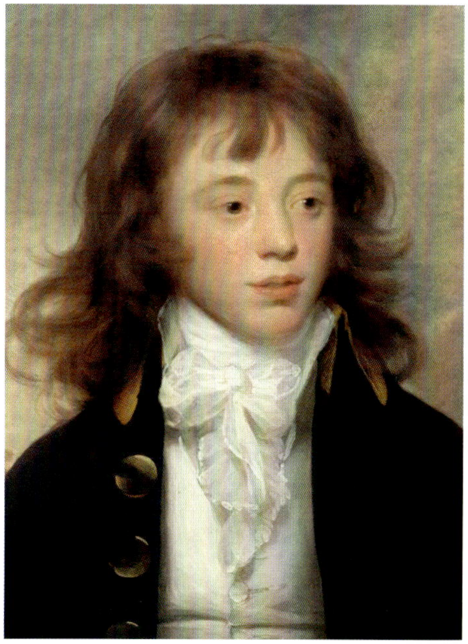

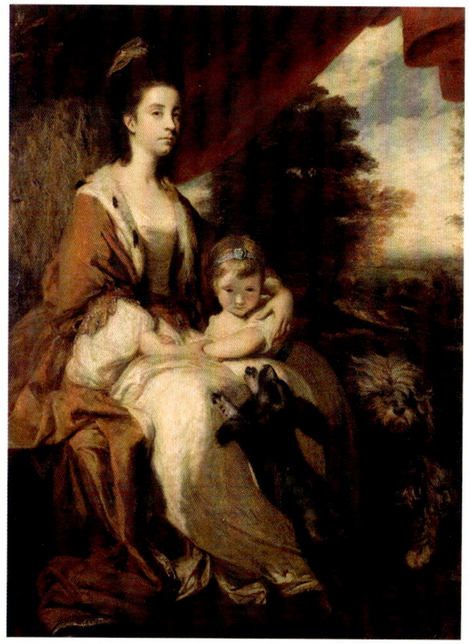

Opposite Thomas Gainsborough (1727–88)
**Henry, 3rd Duke of Buccleuch and 5th Duke of Queensberry (1746–1812), 1770**
*Henry, aged 24, is seen here with his Dandie Dinmont*

Above left Sir William Beechey (1753–1839)
**Charles, Earl of Dalkeith, the future 4th Duke**
*The 3rd Duke's son was the first to build at Bowhill*

Above right Sir Joshua Reynolds (1723–92)
**Elizabeth, Duchess of Buccleuch (1743–1827), and her daughter Lady Mary Scott**
*Charles's mother inherited the Montagu fortune*

new thinking and in 1783, at Smith's encouragement, Henry became the first president of what was to become Scotland's leading learned body, the newly formed Royal Society of Edinburgh.

Nevertheless, he was essentially a rather shy and modest man. He exerted political influence as a close ally of the Tory leader Henry Dundas, 1st Viscount Melville, but preferred to do so behind the scenes. Nor did everything turn to gold – Henry got his fingers badly burnt in the crash of the Ayr Bank in 1772. But he and his wife are remembered for creating an era that enriched the family heritage with cultural activity of many kinds – collecting, artistic patronage and music in particular flourished, epitomised by Danloux's portrait of the couple with their children in the park at Dalkeith in front of Robert Adam's bridge (opposite).

It was to Henry, the 3rd Duke, that the young Walter Scott first looked as his clan chief. His first great success, in 1798, *The Minstrelsy of the Scottish Border*, is dedicated to Henry. But Scott's friendship was to be closest with his contemporary, Charles, the 4th Duke, whose wife, Harriet, was one of his muses and the inspiration for his epic narrative poem *The Lay of the Last Minstrel*.

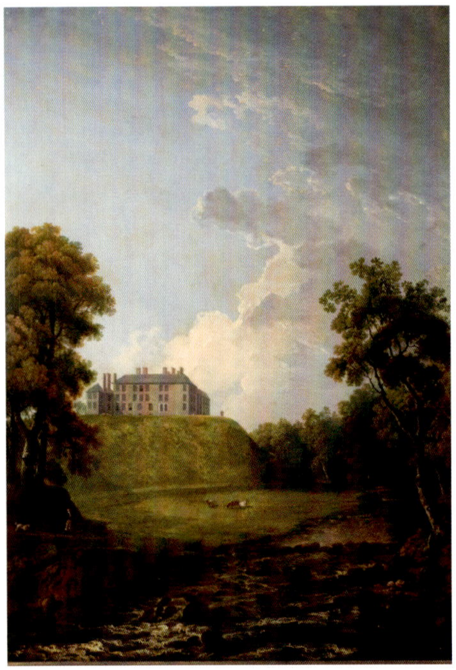

We forget, two centuries on, what a phenomenon Sir Walter Scott was: the publishing sensation of his day, inventor of the historical novel, the world's first bestseller, inspirer of innumerable writers and composers – of everything from high opera to America's *Hail to the Chief* – and linchpin of the nascent Scottish tourist industry. As his fortunes prospered, a few miles downstream beyond Selkirk, Scott created his hugely influential home and estate at Abbotsford, the foundation stone of Scottish baronial architecture.

Tragically, Harriet died only 18 months after her husband became duke. In the correspondence between him and Scott we have a sense of their shared shock and desolation. Indeed throughout their close friendship they appear to have been kindred spirits on every front. Barely five years later, in 1819, Charles too died.

It was a sign of the family closeness that Sir Walter Scott was appointed, along with Charles's brother, Lord Montagu, as guardian of the 13-year-old 5th Duke. Kindly wisdom and concern radiates from their correspondence and from Scott's *Journal*. It was a relationship the young Walter Francis clearly cherished, and he was to repay it in a small but moving way when Scott found himself bankrupted in 1826 by the failure of his publisher, Constable. Among treasured items sold by the creditors was Scott's favourite painting of himself as a young man by Sir Henry Raeburn (page 99). It was only when he was led into the Library on a visit to Dalkeith one day that Scott discovered the young Duke had secretly bought the portrait.

OPPOSITE
HENRI-PIERRE DANLOUX (1753–1809)
**Henry, 3rd Duke of Buccleuch, with his wife, Elizabeth Montagu, and family in the grounds of Dalkeith, 1798**
*This intimate conversation piece shows the family of the 3rd Duke and Duchess in the woods below the Robert Adam bridge at Dalkeith. Duke Henry, now in his 50s, stands beside his wife. His younger son, the red-headed Henry, Lord Montagu, can be seen in profile on the far left.*

*All the daughters would make good marriages. Sketching in the foreground is Lady Caroline Scott, the subject of 'Winter', Reynolds's famous portrait of a little girl (page 75), later Marchioness of Queensberry. Sitting on the ground next to her mother is Harriet, who became Marchioness of Lothian. Playing the harp is Elizabeth, who is about to marry Alexander, 10th Earl of Home.*

*In a blue bonnet on the far right is Mary, at the time the only sister who was married. Her husband, James Stopford, Earl of Courtown, stands arm in arm with her brother Charles, Earl of Dalkeith, the future 4th Duke, who looks out at the viewer on the far right of the painting. Mary places a hand on the shoulder of Charles's wife, Harriet (in a yellow dress). It was Harriet who urged Scott to write 'The Lay of the Last Minstrel'*

LEFT GEORGE BARRET (1730–1784)
**View of Dalkeith Park with the River Esk**
*Barret, a Dublin-born landscape painter and Royal Academician, was commissioned by the 3rd Duke to paint the series of four views of the park at Dalkeith that now hang in the Saloon at Bowhill. The exceptional landscaping is currently being restored*

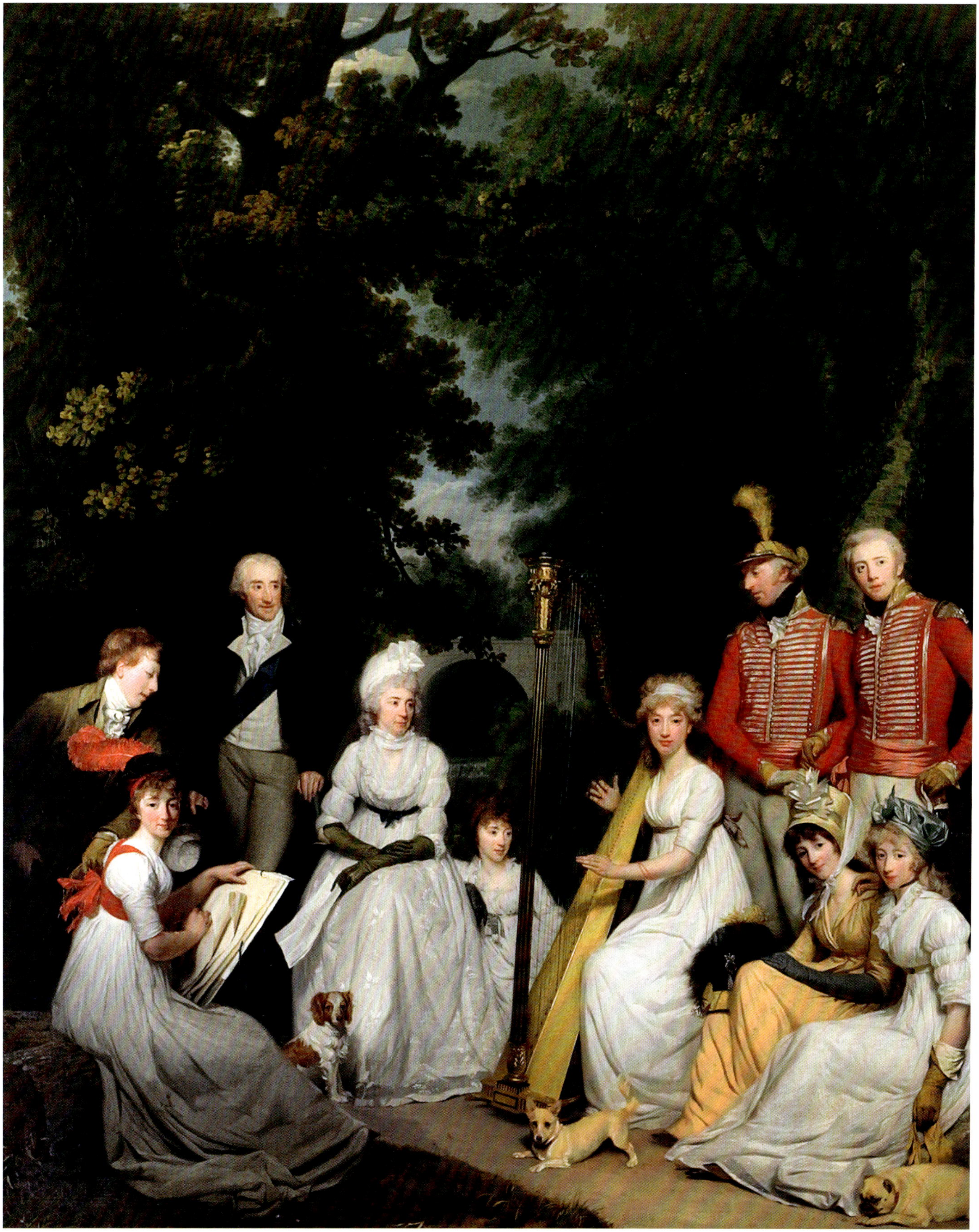

# The partnership that transformed Bowhill

Walter Francis, the 5th Duke, was married in 1828 to Lady Charlotte Anne Thynne, daughter of the Marquess of Bath, a choice very much approved of by Sir Walter Scott. It was to prove an extraordinary partnership, enduring 56 years until his death in 1884. They were intimately bound up with the transformations of the Victorian era and very much part of the court circle – Charlotte Anne was Mistress of the Robes to Queen Victoria, and he was one of the commissioners of the Great Exhibition of 1852.

Not surprisingly, Walter Francis was a progressive manager of the traditional family landed estates, but this was the age of coal and the railways, and he took advantage of both. He was also commercially minded enough to develop a new harbour for Edinburgh at Granton; the statue by Sir Joseph Boehm erected in a prime place

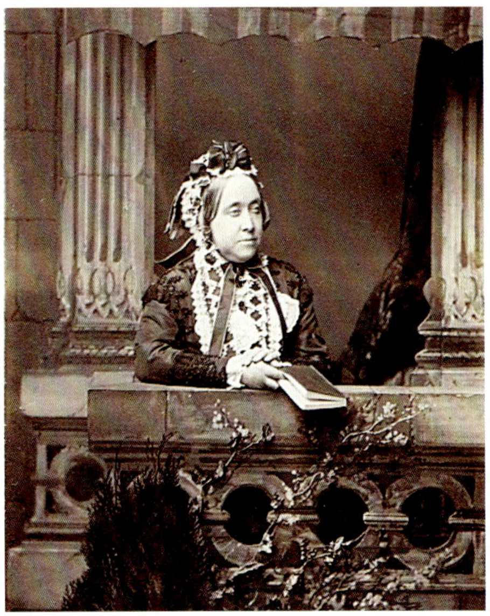

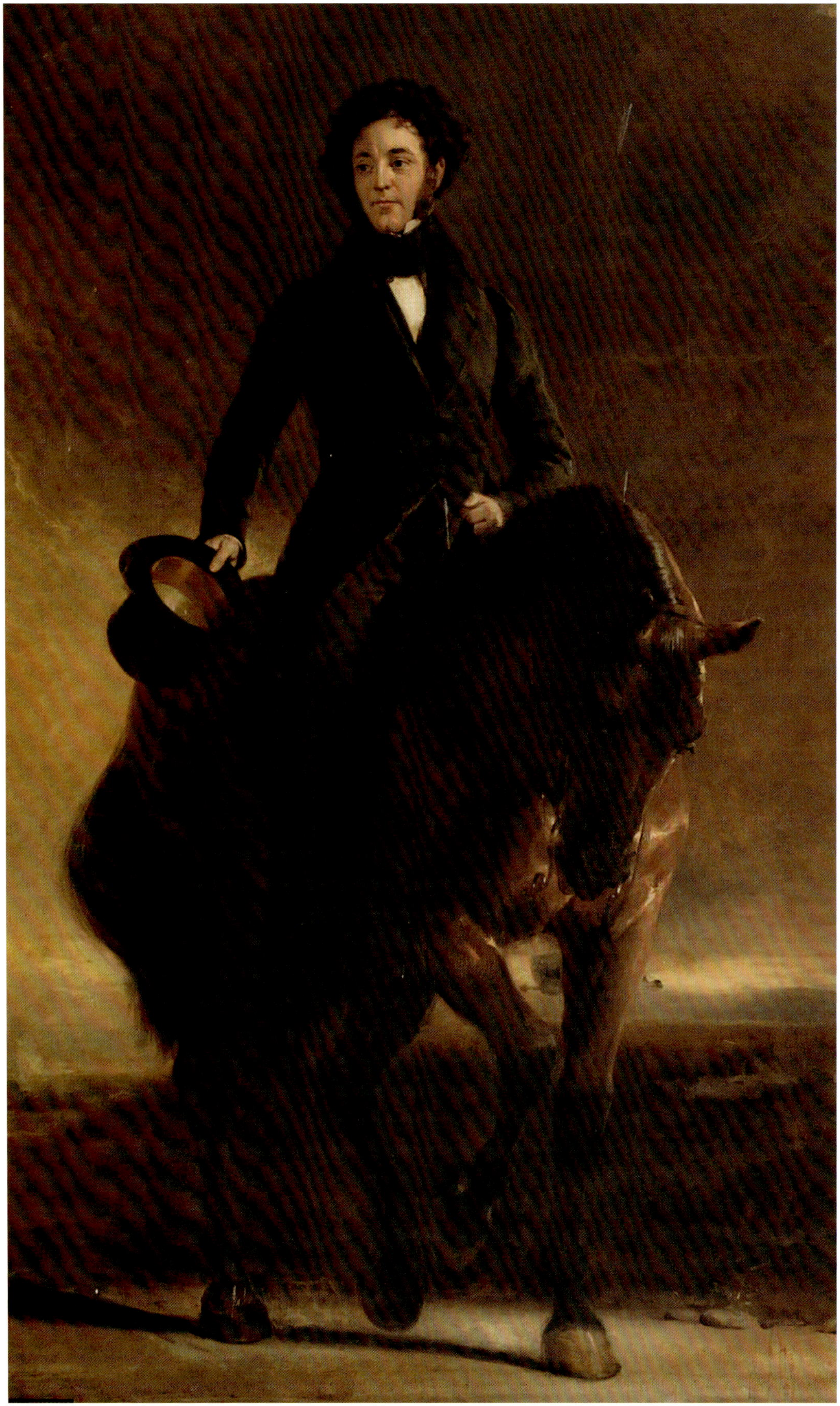

outside St Giles' Cathedral was testament to the city's regard for him.

We have much still to discover about him and his wife. Their many homes and interests often kept them apart but she was an inveterate letter writer. Casual research reveals a deeply affectionate but frank relationship. For all his good works, she considered him at times too concerned with his first love, the countryside and its pursuits. In a letter in 1850 she writes: 'It is a sad life to rise up early and go to bed late for nothing but hunting. How can we expect the children to think of other matters when sport is the chief subject of conversation?' The impact such honesty had is movingly expressed in his words as he lay dying. 'Char, how dearly I have loved you, but I should never have loved you as I did, had I not respected you more.'

Their love for each other was particularly tested by the religious divide that developed. They were both High Church supporters, but in 1850 Charlotte Anne, who had been hugely influenced by Cardinal Newman, converted to Roman Catholicism. Together the Duke and Duchess supported the building of numerous churches, including chapels at their own homes, but the deep nature of the fissure is illustrated by Charlotte Anne's burial in the Roman Catholic St David's Church at Dalkeith rather than beside her husband in the grounds of Dalkeith.

The expansion of Bowhill is very much their story. They were great patrons of the architect William Burn, who tried to encourage them into numerous other projects, including the transformation of Dalkeith mercifully not proceeded with. He did succeed in getting the attractive Montagu House by the Thames (right), part of the Montagu inheritance, knocked down in 1859 and rebuilt in the French Renaissance manner.

They were also prodigious collectors, and that is saying something given the footsteps they were following in.

LEFT SIR JOHN WATSON GORDON (1788–1864)
**Walter Francis, 5th Duke of Buccleuch and 7th Duke of Queensberry (1806–84)**
*The eight-foot-tall portrait of the progressive and much-loved Victorian who expanded Bowhill*

FAR LEFT **Charlotte Anne, Duchess of Buccleuch and Queensberry (1811–95)**
*The 5th Duke's wife, photographed in the 1860s*

BELOW WILLIAM BURN (1789–1870)
*Burn's 1830s model for a new Dalkeith, which would have meant tearing down the present house*

BOTTOM SAMUEL SCOTT (1702–72)
**Montagu House on the Thames**
*The Buccleuchs' residence in Whitehall before Burn was commissioned to rebuild it in 1859*

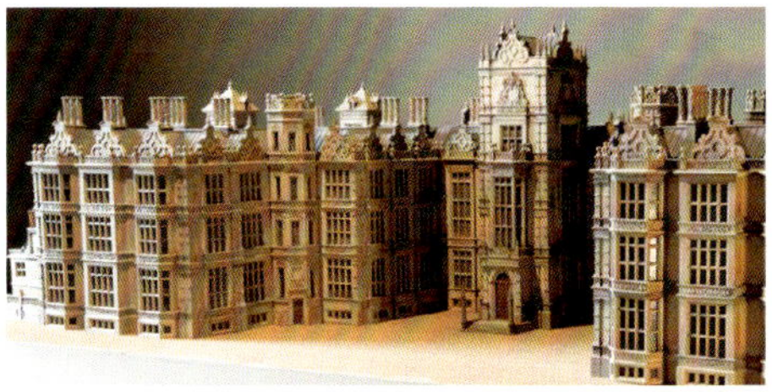

## The collectors in the family

Both Walter Francis and Charlotte Anne, whose family home was at Longleat in Wiltshire, had been brought up amid remarkable art collections, and it is interesting to reflect how far this conditioned their own tastes as collectors. European and in particular French styles predominated in both the Scott and Montagu inheritances, with Louis XIV and Louis XV furniture already featuring strongly. Perhaps it is not surprising, then, that in the 1830s, the decade after their marriage, they became avid buyers of still more furniture of the same kind, particularly through the London dealer EH Baldock.

They acquired many remarkable pieces, such as the Duchesse de Bourgogne's side tables in the Drawing Room, but since the overall decorative effect was also important to them, they appear to have been equally happy filling gaps with altered or fabricated pieces

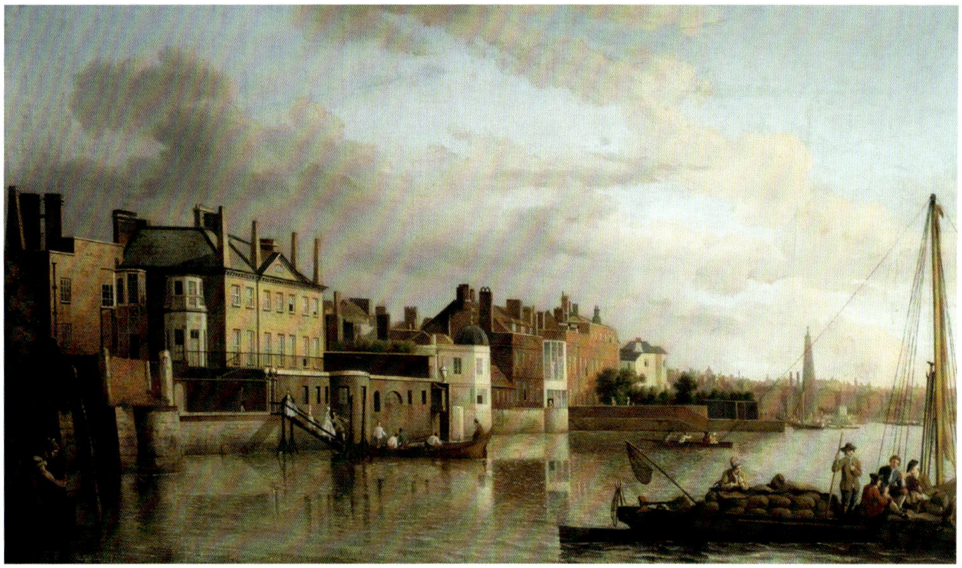

that we would nowadays consider pastiches. This is well illustrated by the Sèvres porcelain collection built up rapidly over 18 months, which contains exceptional early pieces but also conceits such as the green and white plates initialled 'DB', which were created for the 5th Duke of Buccleuch but could purport to have been made for Madame du Barry half a century earlier. In her day the 3rd Duke's parents-in-law – George, Duke of Montagu, and his wife – had been regular visitors to Paris.

Starting in the 1750s, the Montagus bought some of the collection's key pictures, including Leonardo's *Madonna of the Yarnwinder* and the two fine Vernet landscapes. It was also then that their son, James Brudenell, Marquis of Monthermer, the most ardent of the family's Grand Tourists, was in Italy, where he spent the best part of a decade.

One of the earliest to visit the newly discovered ruins of Paestum in the south, Monthermer commissioned Antonio Joli to paint them and other familiar scenes around Naples. Later, in Venice, he acquired works by Francesco Guardi and others.

One might have expected the Canaletto at Bowhill, showing the back of the Montagu family's house in Whitehall in London, to be a Montagu inheritance. In fact it was acquired by Walter Francis in 1839. One has the sense of it at once filling a gap and being familiar.

Walter Francis and Charlotte Anne's collecting could at times be described as obsessive – the Sèvres has been mentioned already – and the same could be said about their approach to portrait miniatures. These they collected throughout their lives, and the invoices from Colnaghi, their dealer, show them being bought by the score. Today more than 800 remain in the collection, and the 16th- and 17th-century English miniatures are particularly renowned (page 108).

Necessity, too, played a part in their collecting. The silver that goes with grand entertaining – candelabra, serving dishes and plates, teapots, decorative tableware – was all purchased in large quantities, for the most part through the silversmith Robert Garrard.

By the end of the 19th century the collecting gene and indeed the wherewithal to support it seem to have faded, and it was only in portraiture that the tradition was maintained.

THE BUCCLEUCH MADONNA
LEONARDO DA VINCI AND ASSISTANT
**The Madonna of the Yarnwinder**
*Acquired by the Duke and Duchess of Montagu in Paris at the Duc de Tallard's sale in 1756, the picture hung in Montagu House, London, until the last century, when it famously travelled around with the Duke of the day to his various great houses. Stolen from Drumlanrig Castle in 2003, it was recovered four years later and is currently on loan to the National Gallery of Scotland. One of two versions of a subject Leonardo was known to have been working on circa 1500, it was included in the 2011/12 Leonardo exhibition at the National Gallery in London. It is now accepted that Leonardo painted the figures and the foreground rocks. The landscape is contemporary or slightly later*

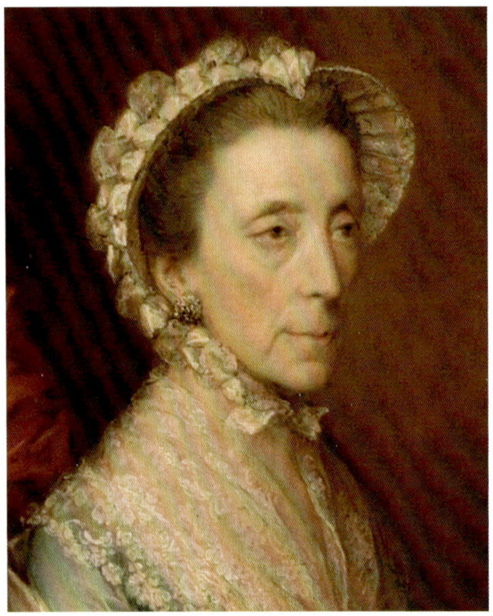

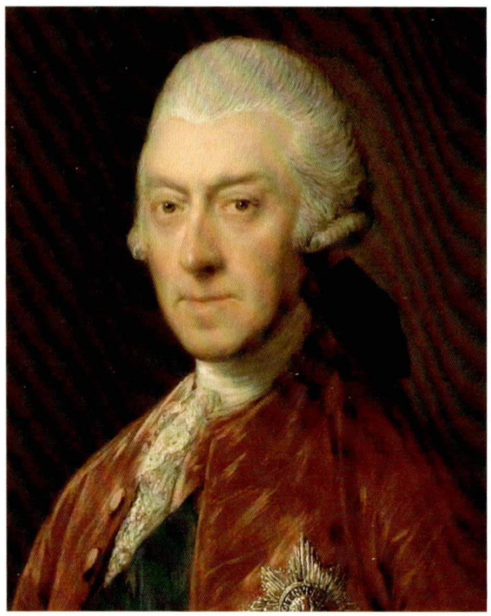

FAR LEFT AND LEFT
THOMAS GAINSBOROUGH (1727–88)
**Mary, Duchess of Montagu, and George, 3rd Duke of Montagu, 1768**
*Mary, Duchess of Montagu (1711–75), was the second daughter and principal heiress of John, 2nd Duke of Montagu. In 1730 she married her neighbour, George Brudenell, 4th Earl of Cardigan (1712–90), and in 1766 the Montagu dukedom was revived for him. The couple were energetic collectors. Their daughter Elizabeth married Henry, 3rd Duke of Buccleuch, and became the Montagu heiress after her brother's death in 1770*

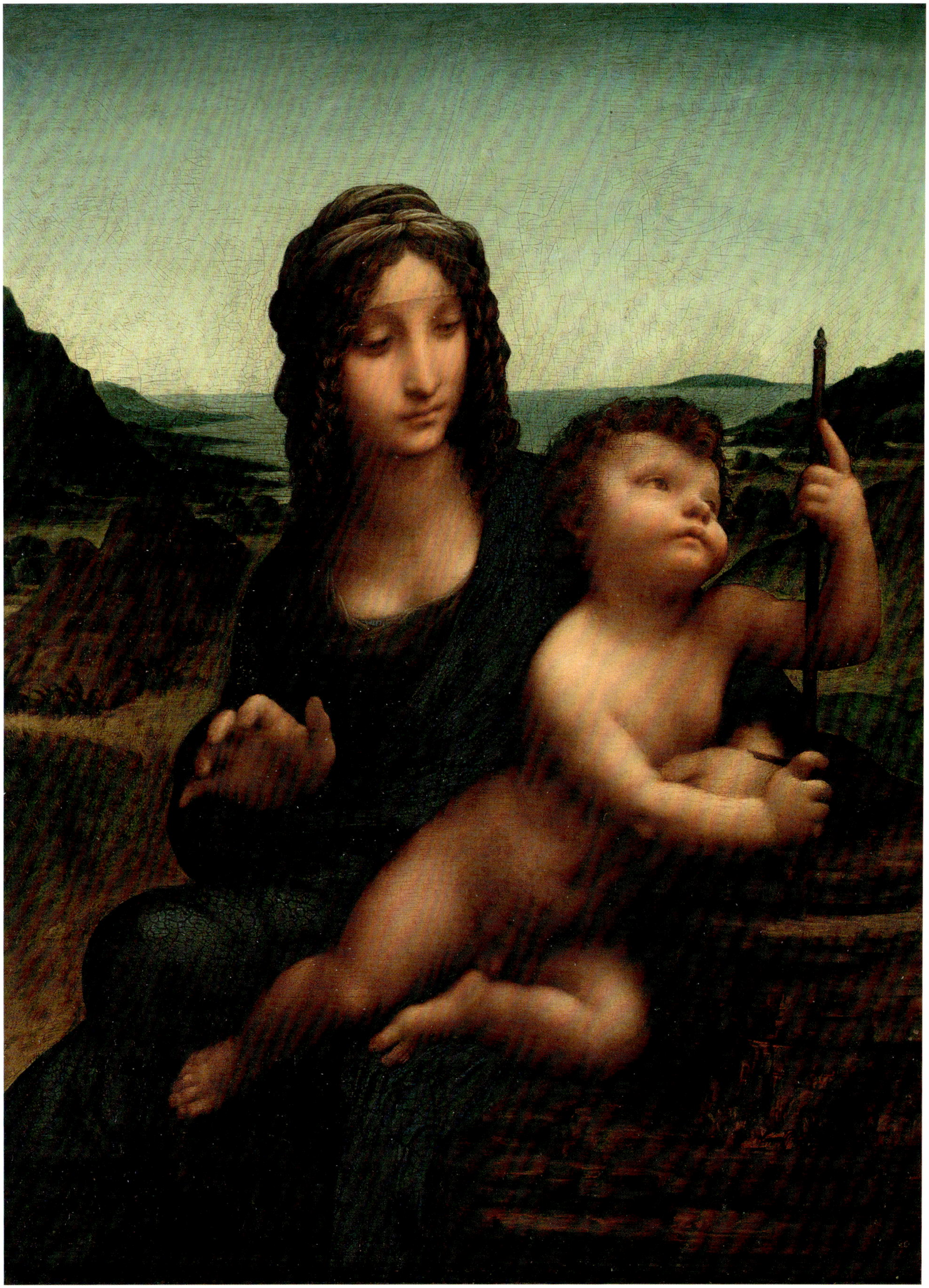

# The Victorian house with a Georgian spirit

Although nowadays as a family we value Bowhill for its geographic proximity to the roots of the Scott family, in 1745 Francis, 2nd Duke of Buccleuch, had more pragmatic reasons for buying back the small estate that had been sold some 50 years before. His second son, Lord Charles Scott, needed such a property if he was to qualify to stand as a Member of Parliament in Selkirkshire, and a full price of £2,214.3s.8d. was therefore offered. Unfortunately neither the Duke nor Lord Charles lived to complete the sale and it fell to the guardians of the new Duke Henry, then only five, to complete the bargain, which they did with evident reluctance. There is no indication that Henry ever occupied the simple early-Georgian house that came with the estate. It was his son Charles who began to develop it shortly before he became 4th Duke in 1812.

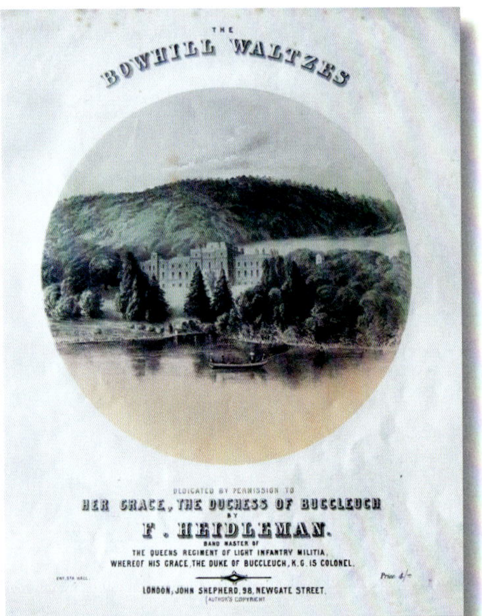


With remarkable speed his architect, William Atkinson (1774/5–1839), a pupil of James Wyatt, was able to build on to the south side a classical villa with three bays, which was ready for occupation by the autumn of 1814. It must have been apparent almost at once that more space would be required, and the accounts show significant expenditure every year until the Duke's early death in 1819, when everything came to a halt. By then, however, the Dining Room and the Library had been completed.

When, more than a decade later, work was restarted, it was to be in the hands of a new architect, William Burn (1789–1870), who for five decades was the 5th Duke's preferred architect over a broad range of projects, including half a dozen churches. Burn's approach at Bowhill, with one notable exception, was what one might call evolutionary, respectful both of the simpler Georgian spirit and of the work of his predecessor, Atkinson, elongating and expanding what was already there. The exception and in some ways the master stroke was to relocate the entrance from the south side of the building to the North Front, thus freeing up the south for the principal private rooms, overlooking the landscape which William Sawrey Gilpin, the 'Picturesque Improver', was now brought in to help design.

Writing about Bowhill in *Country Life* in 1975, John Cornforth noted that the house was transformed from being essentially Georgian to one that satisfied Victorian standards of specialised planning, 'but I think it is the strong element of Georgian survival that makes it such an agreeable house'. For an almost contemporary view of Victorian standards, *The Gentleman's House* by Robert Kerr, published in 1864, provides a helpful if mannered guide: 'an unswerving adherence to the common comforts of residence, a strict and careful adherence to the minutiae of the habits of the gentry, and an avoidance of every sort of ostentation'.

Bowhill certainly lives up to this description, with its long, wide service corridors, its strategic placing of the Duchess's Boudoir apartment at the opposite end to the gentlemen's Smoking Room, its equally strategic positioning of the nurseries directly above the parents, connected by a winding staircase, and its capacious areas for cooking, laundry and storage – all hidden behind its plain external faces. Burn's skill as a master planner is apparent throughout, and it was to bring him a huge clientele across the land.

In its interior decoration Bowhill is a house of contrasts, and these have been accentuated over the years. Many of the bedrooms are simple in their appeal and practical. They could be in any country house. By contrast, in the main reception rooms, even today when so many of the fabrics have faded, when the rich dark woodwork has been painted over and, as in the Saloon, much of its detailing removed, there is still a sense of magnificence and colour, of complex gilded plasterwork ceilings, rich and painstakingly embroidered damask curtains.

TOP RIGHT *These drawings show Bowhill's south elevation and the three-bay classical villa added by the 4th Duke's architect, William Atkinson, in 1812. It now contains the Drawing Room and Morning Room. By 1819, he had added wings for the Library and the Dining Room*

RIGHT *From Georgian villa in 1812 to stately home in 1915. William Burn, the 5th Duke's architect, further elongated the house and replaced the front door on the South Front with large sash windows, but he kept Atkinson's unadorned style*

LEFT *Waltzes for the Duchess: music by Heidleman, bandmaster of the Edinburgh, or Queen's Regiment of Light Infantry Militia, of which the 5th Duke was Colonel*

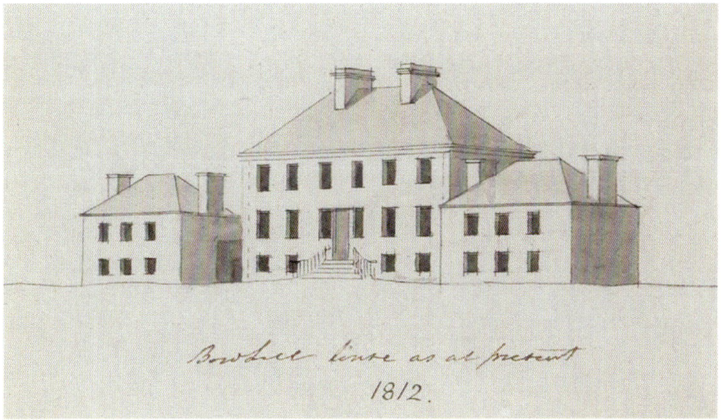
Bowhill house as at present
1812.

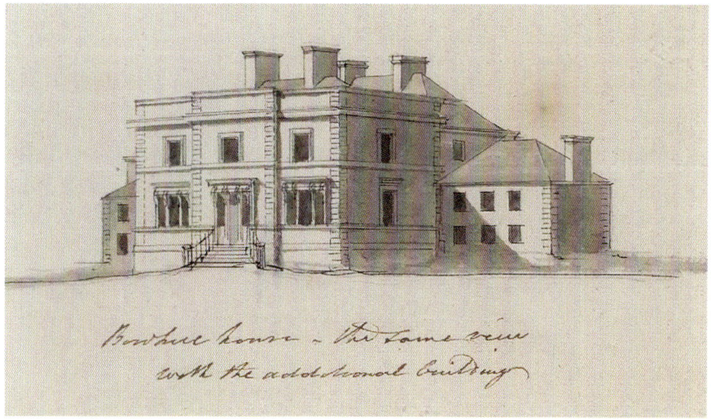
Bowhill house – the same view
with the additional building

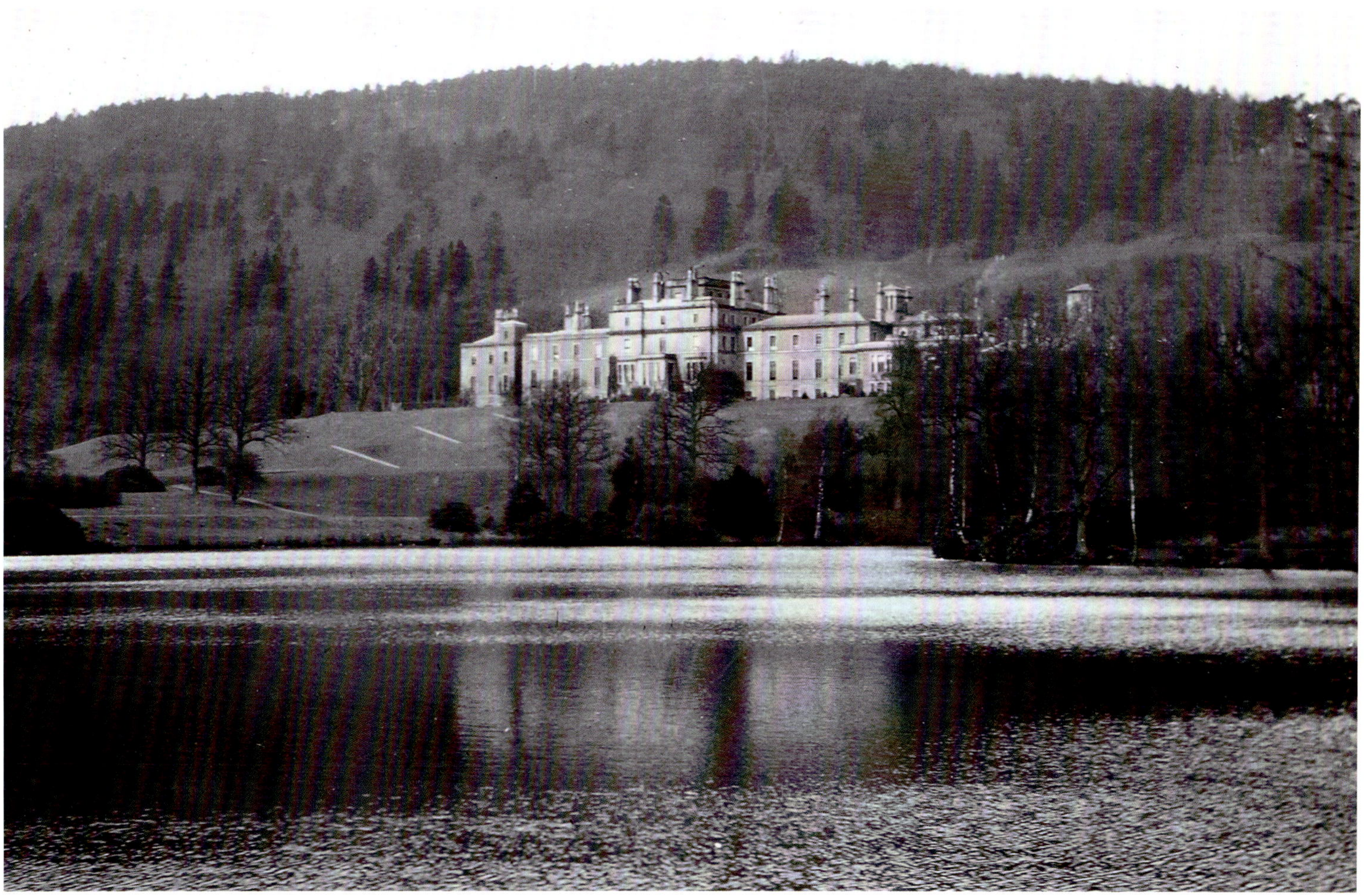

# The 20th century

At the start of the 20th century, inventories of furniture and paintings emphasise the modest nature of Bowhill compared to the principal seat at Dalkeith. In the 1920s everything was reversed. The 6th Duke died in 1914, and in the First World War the house was used as a military hospital. As the family returned, the decision was made to close Dalkeith and there was a huge influx of fine objects and paintings to Bowhill.

The photograph albums testify that it was a much-enjoyed family home: the eight children of the 7th Duke and his wife, Margaret, returned regularly even as they grew up and got married. Walter, the eldest son, who was to become 8th Duke, lived at Eildon Hall a few miles away, until his father died in 1935, when he inherited Bowhill, just before his sister Alice's marriage to HRH The Duke of Gloucester, uncle of the present Queen.

During the Second World War the house was again occupied by the Army, and one has a sense from correspondence of it being in a pretty miserable state. The ravages of dry rot made everything even more difficult, and it is a relief that substantial parts were not simply knocked down, as happened to so many great houses. Its renaissance was started by the 8th Duke and his wife, Molly, and continued with ever greater vigour by the 9th Duke and his wife, Jane, who introduced much-needed colour. They also undertook the colossal task of replacing the entire roof, greatly reducing the likelihood of dry rot.

Bowhill has played a growing part in the artistic life of the Scottish Borders. Recitals are held in the Drawing Room and the Old Chapel. The Little Theatre, opened in the old larder, is used for theatrical performances and concerts and was for 28 years home to the Rowan Tree Theatre Company founded by Lady Steel. More recently, the house has become linked with the Borders Book Festival and the Walter Scott Prize for Historical Fiction. Nevertheless, Bowhill retains its spirit and atmosphere as a family home.

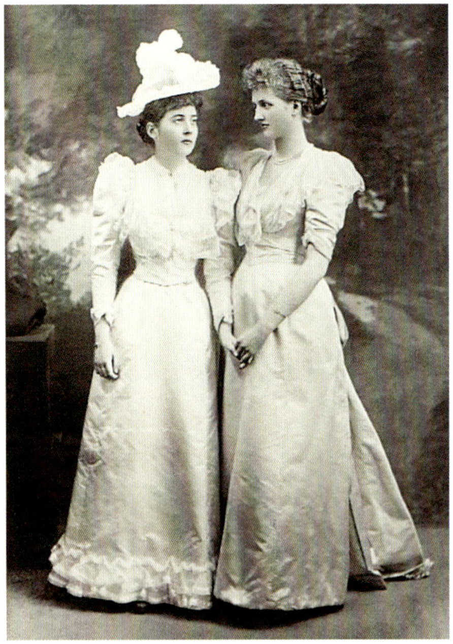

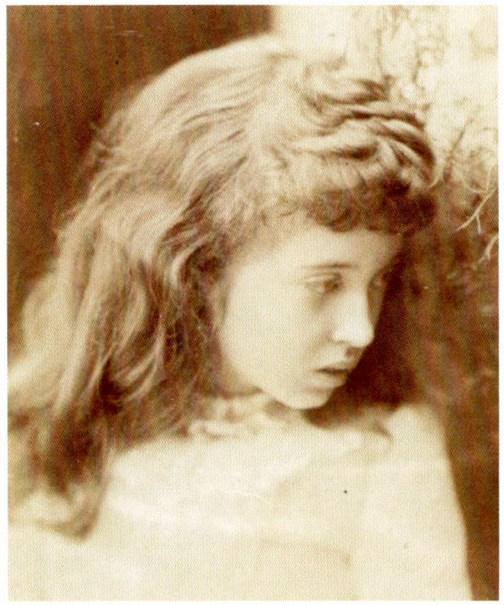

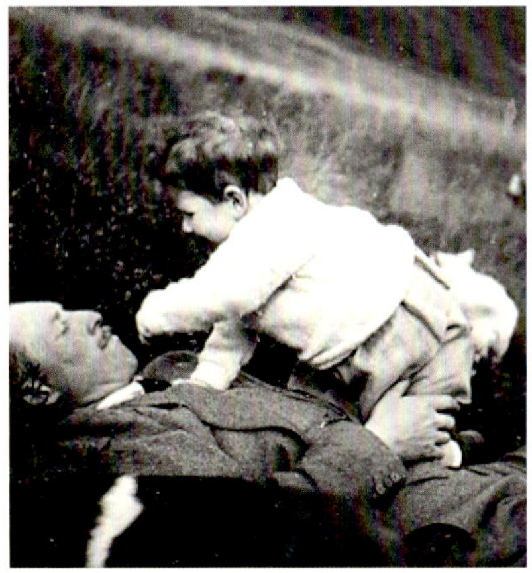

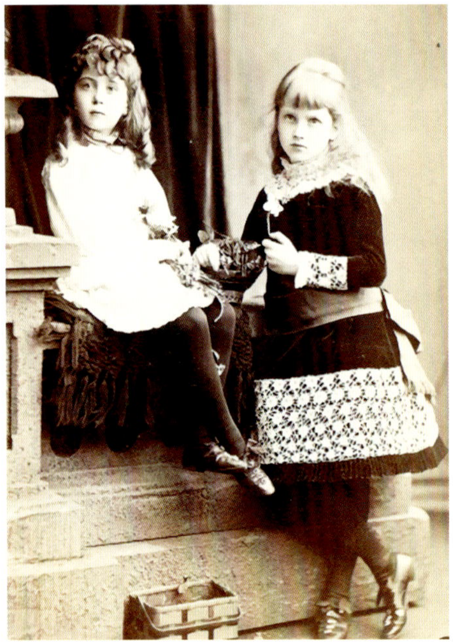

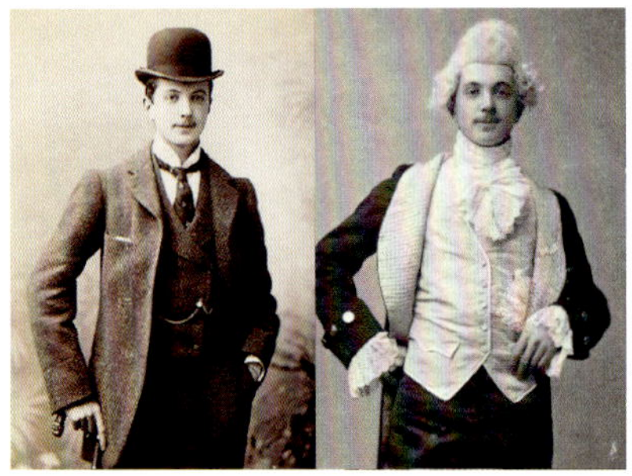

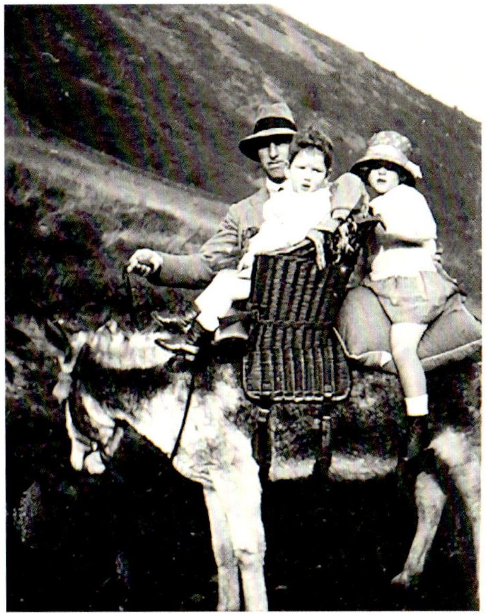

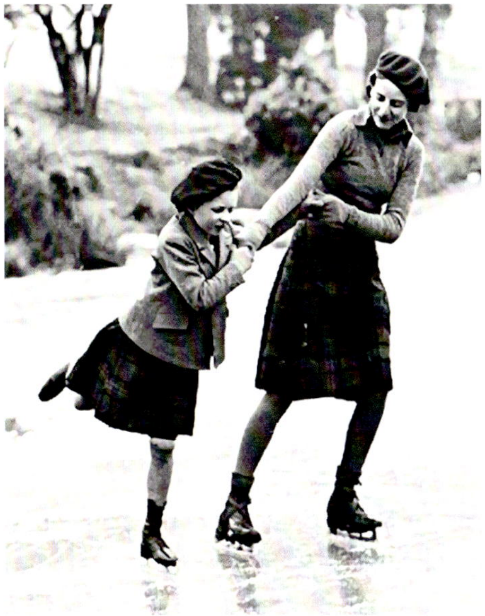

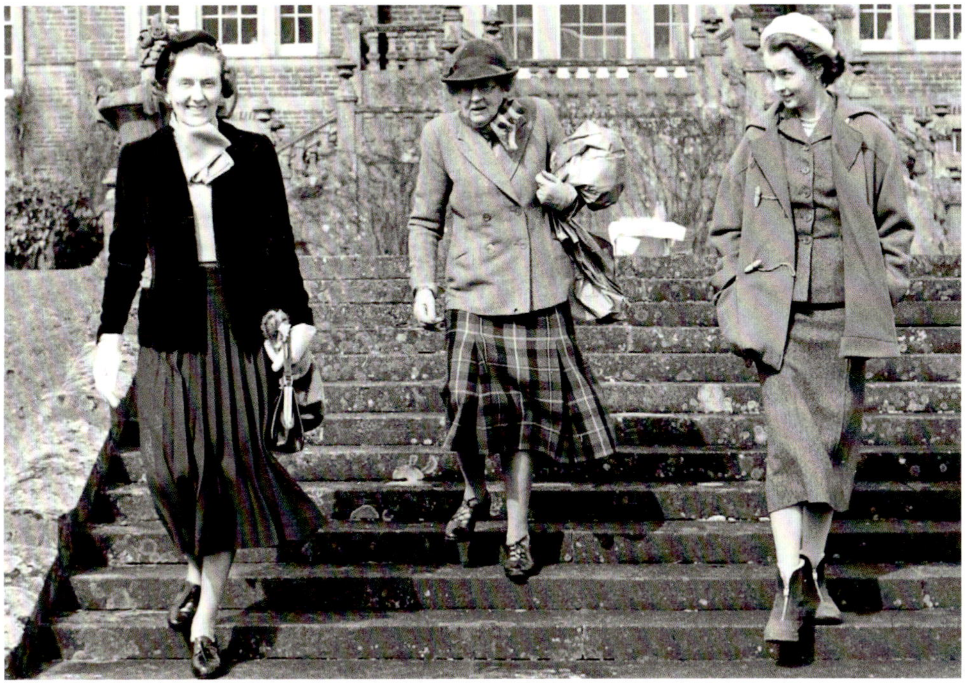

FAMILY LIFE IN THE BORDERS
*Photograph albums stretching back to the early 1860s reflect all aspects of family life. Children feature extensively, posed and at play*

THIS PAGE, TOP ROW
*Autumn 1925 (far left): on the Eildon Hills, near Bowhill, Johnnie, Lord Eskdaill, and his sister Elizabeth perch on a donkey, watched over by their father, Walter, the future 8th Duke. Eildon Hall was the traditional home of the heir. Walter inherited Bowhill in 1935*

*Winter 1934 (left): the present Duke's aunts, Elizabeth (later Duchess of Northumberland) and Caroline (who married the politician and author Ian Gilmour, later Lord Gilmour of Craigmillar), skate on the Upper Loch*

LEFT *Molly Buccleuch, wife of Duke Walter (on the left), and her daughter-in-law Jane (mother of the present Duke) accompany Lady Constance Cairns, the 7th Duke's sister, down the steps at Bowhill in 1955*

OPPOSITE *Lady Constance, known as Aunt Connie, appears in three more photographs here: as a child (top right) in 1882, again as a child with her sister Katie (bottom left), and with Katie a decade later, in an elaborate hat (top left).*

*Her brother Herbert Montagu Douglas Scott is seen in 1893 as a bewigged 18th-century courtier (bottom right). He went on to become chairman of Rolls-Royce. Bowhill still has a wonderful collection of fancy dress costumes.*

*In the photograph above him, Duke Walter, lying in the heather on the Eildon Hills, holds aloft his son Johnnie, the future 9th Duke*

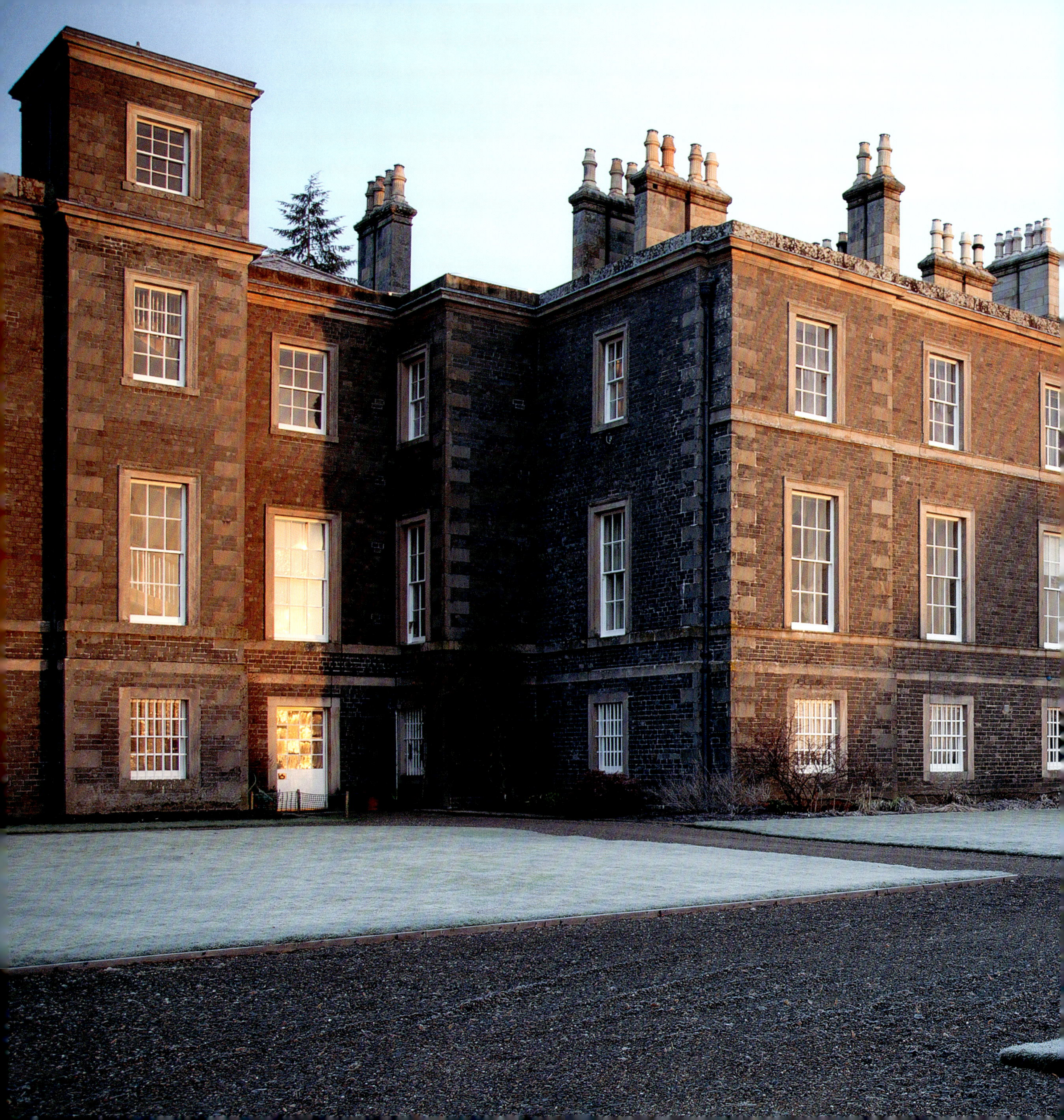

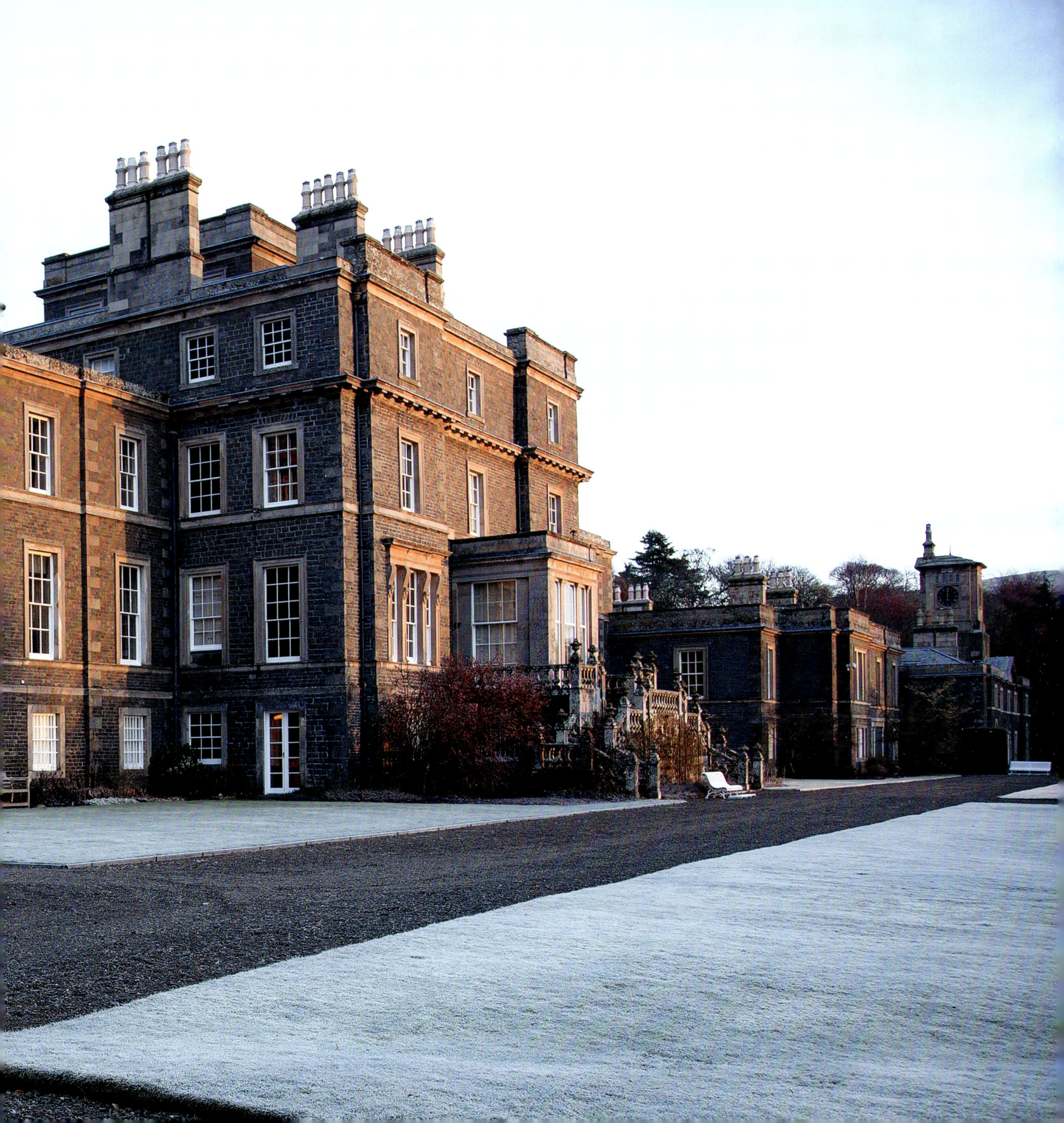

BOWHILL

# The House

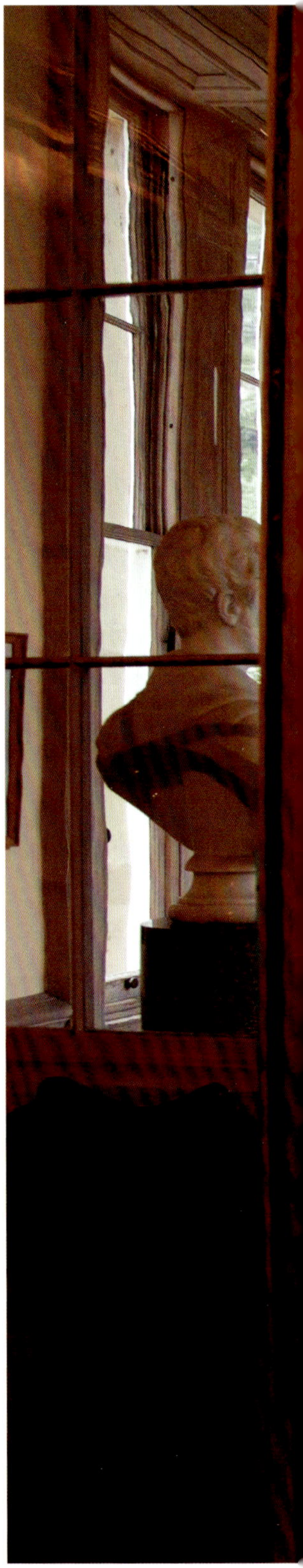

## The Outer and Inner Halls

*Bowhill was built for country life rather than ostentation. It only became a grand house after the First World War. The entrance halls give no clue to the treasures beyond*

Busts of Walter Francis, 5th Duke of Buccleuch, and his wife, Charlotte Anne, greet the arriving visitor, and his large portrait dominates the Inner Hall. Together the couple fashioned Bowhill as a comfortable family retreat in the heart of the countryside. The paintings in the Inner Hall reflect the 5th Duke's passion for fox hunting. From 1831 his pack of hounds, known as the Duke of Buccleuch's, were housed in new kennels established a few miles away at St Boswells.

A scattering of old fishing rods and granite curling stones and a 19th-century child's carriage reflect a love of outdoor life, as do today's toboggans, Wellington boots and jackets. Note the William IV mahogany bootjacks with insets in their bases to ease the removal of boots with spurs.

A pair of grand mirrors, supplied by Mayhew and Ince in 1769, help lighten the Inner Hall and, along with the George III folio cabinets with their inset marble maps of Gibraltar, give an early taste of the richer furnishings brought to the house after the First World War.

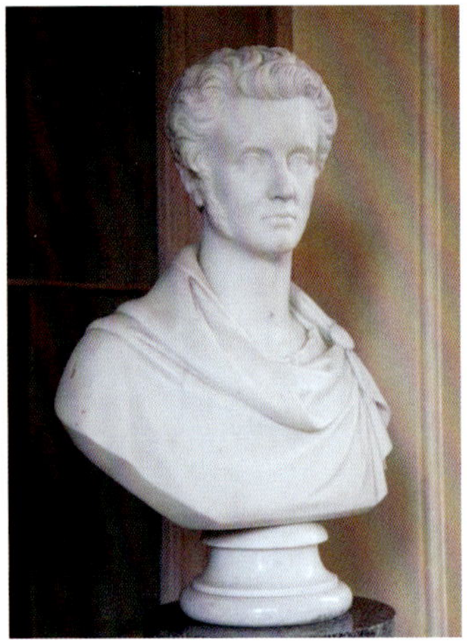

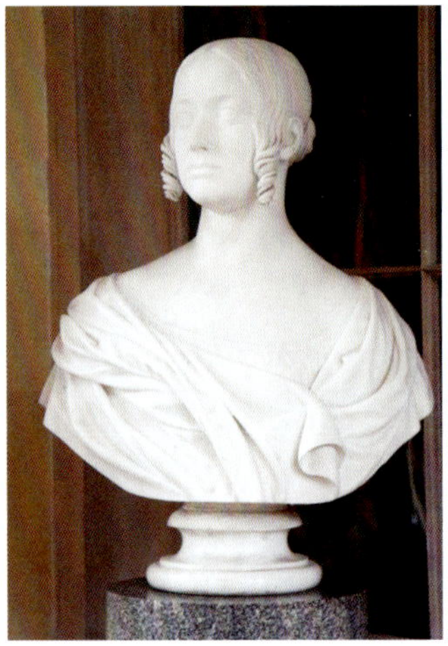

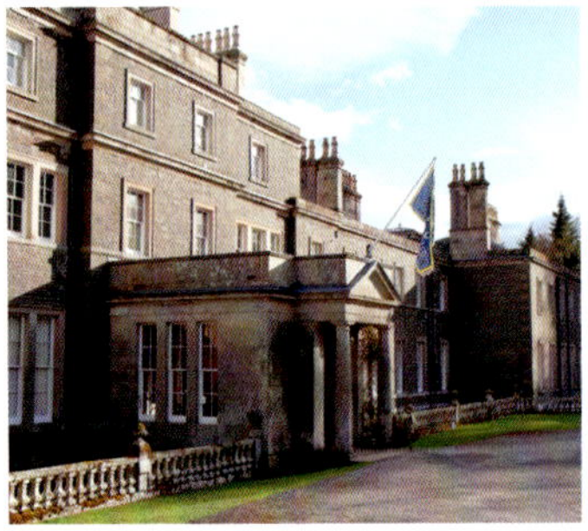

ABOVE *Busts of Walter Francis, the 5th Duke, by Thomas Campbell (1834) and of his wife, Charlotte Anne, by Sir John Steell (1845)*
LEFT *The Scotts' Bellendean banner flies over the front door at Bowhill*
RIGHT *The Outer Hall has limed oak doors, an inlaid stone floor – and Wellington boots. A plaque records Bowhill's wartime use as a hospital*

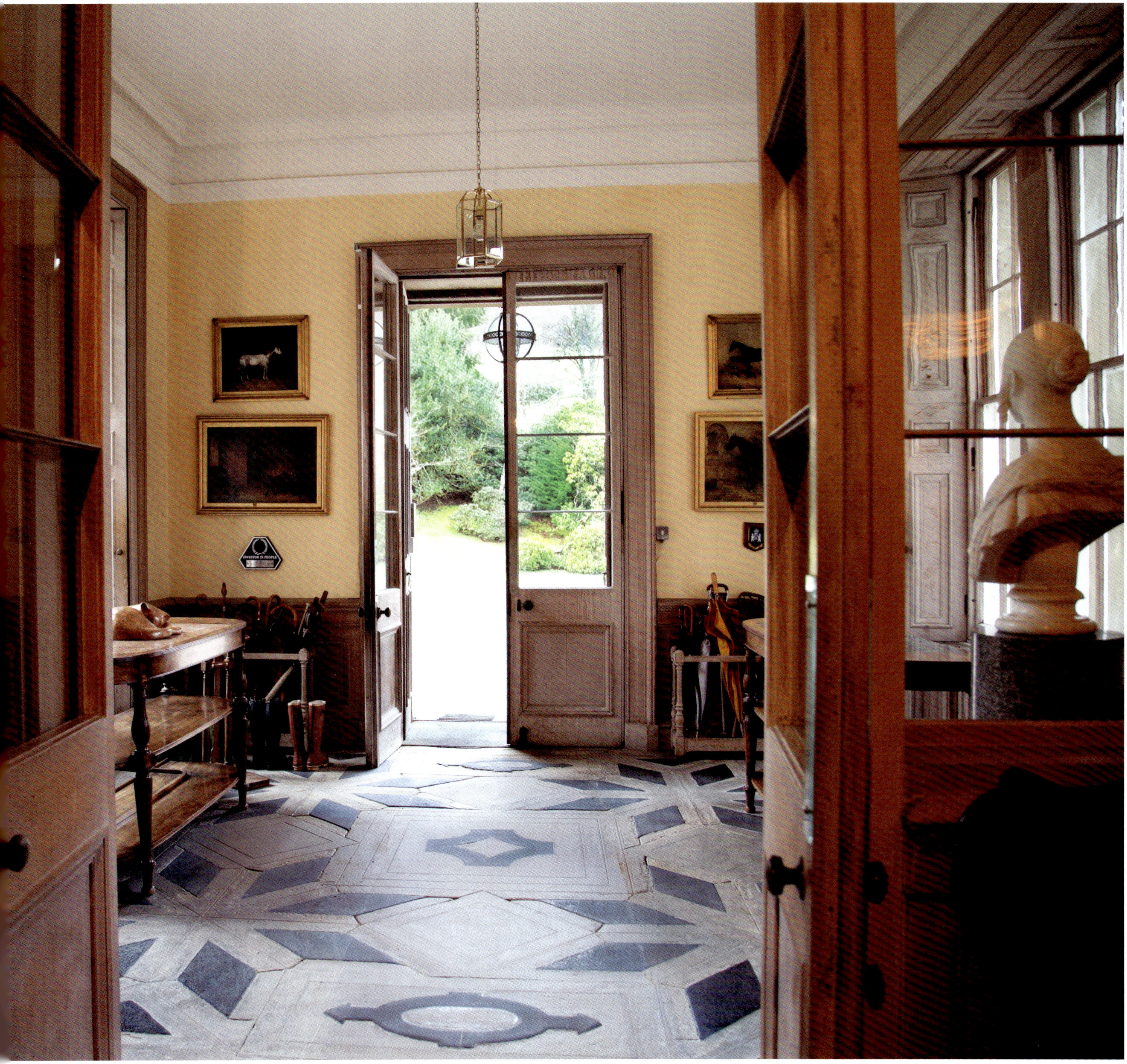

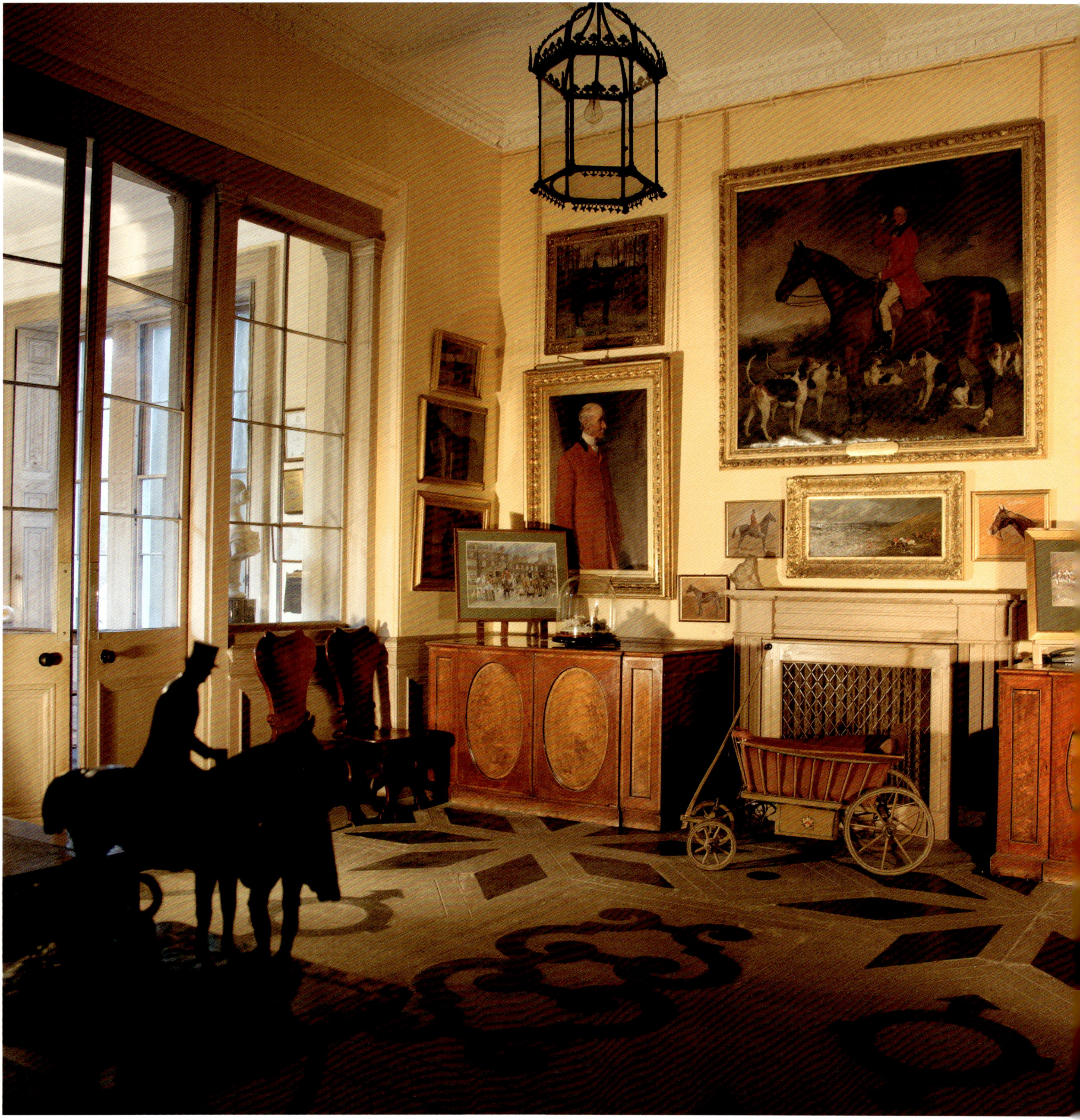

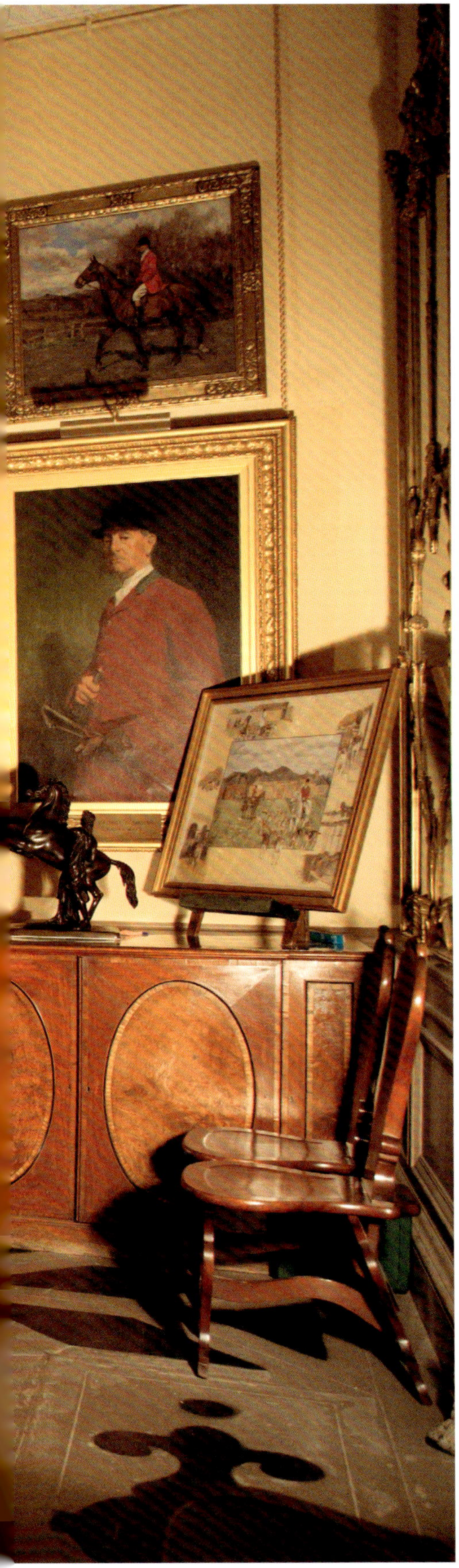

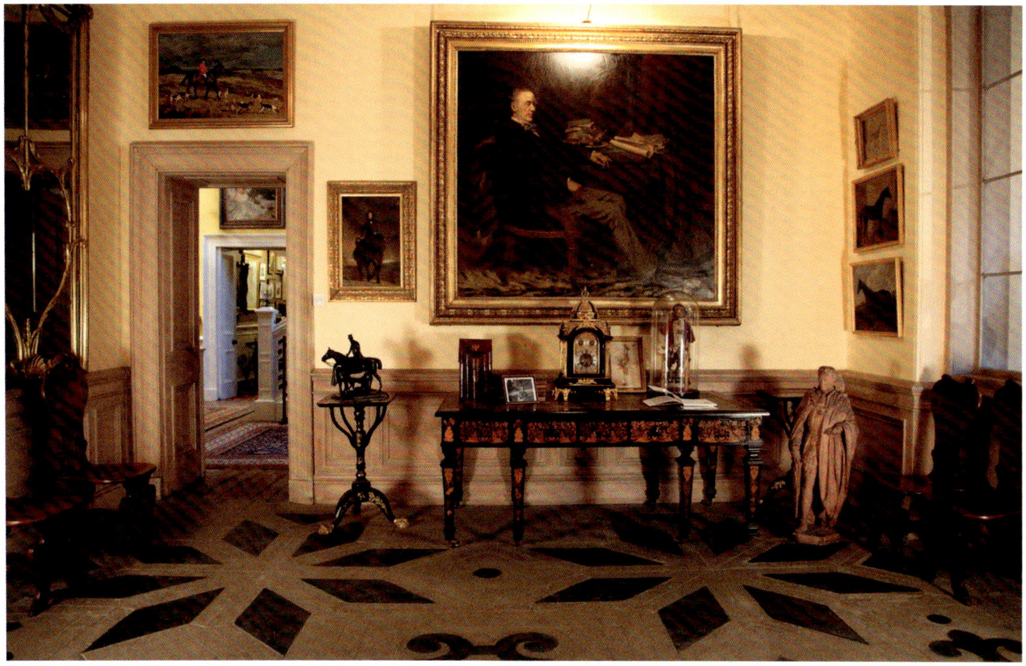

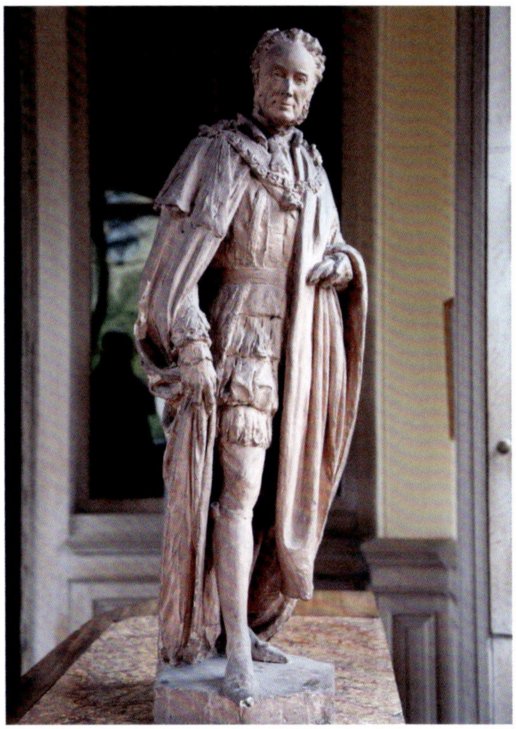

FAR LEFT *The Inner Hall has portraits of Buccleuch huntsmen and an early-19th-century oak child's carriage. By a trick of Victorian ingenuity, the doors have a mechanism that opens them simultaneously. Sir John Steell's bronze group on the right is a scaled-down version of his Edinburgh statue 'Alexander Training Bucephalus', his first work to attract international attention*

LEFT *Sir Joseph Boehm's plaster maquette for his full-size bronze memorial to the 5th Duke in front of St Giles' Cathedral in Edinburgh. It was paid for by public subscription*

ABOVE *The last portrait of the 5th Duke, painted by Knighton Warren at Montagu House in 1884, hangs above an 1830s ebony and marquetry writing table. The bronze group next to the door, again by Boehm, shows Queen Victoria's Highland servant, John Brown, offering the 5th Duke a stirrup cup. Above the door is a view of the Eildon Hills with Tom Smith, huntsman from 1947 to 1977, painted by Leesa Sandys-Lumsdaine*

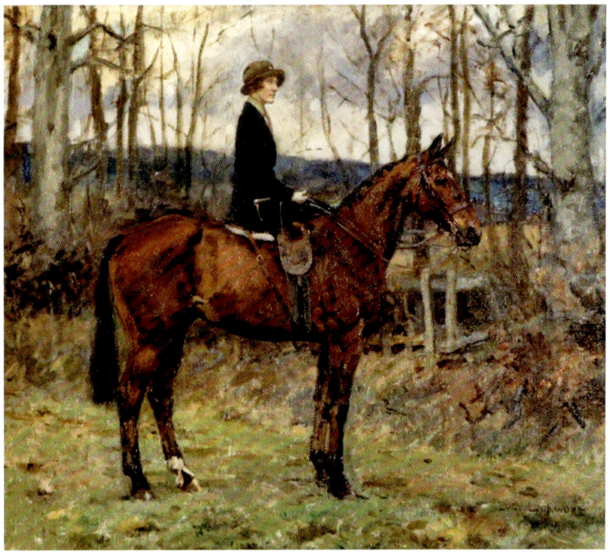

ABOVE *Mary, Duchess of Buccleuch (1900–93), known affectionately as Molly, the present Duke's grandmother, by Lucy Lockwood. She admitted to a grandson that she had never ridden side-saddle before marrying into the family in 1921*

RIGHT *George III giltwood pier glasses and handsome mahogany chairs flank the door from the Inner Hall into the Saloon. Like the satinwood, oak and laburnum folio cabinets and the Regency lantern, they were later introductions from Dalkeith, the main Buccleuch home until the First World War*

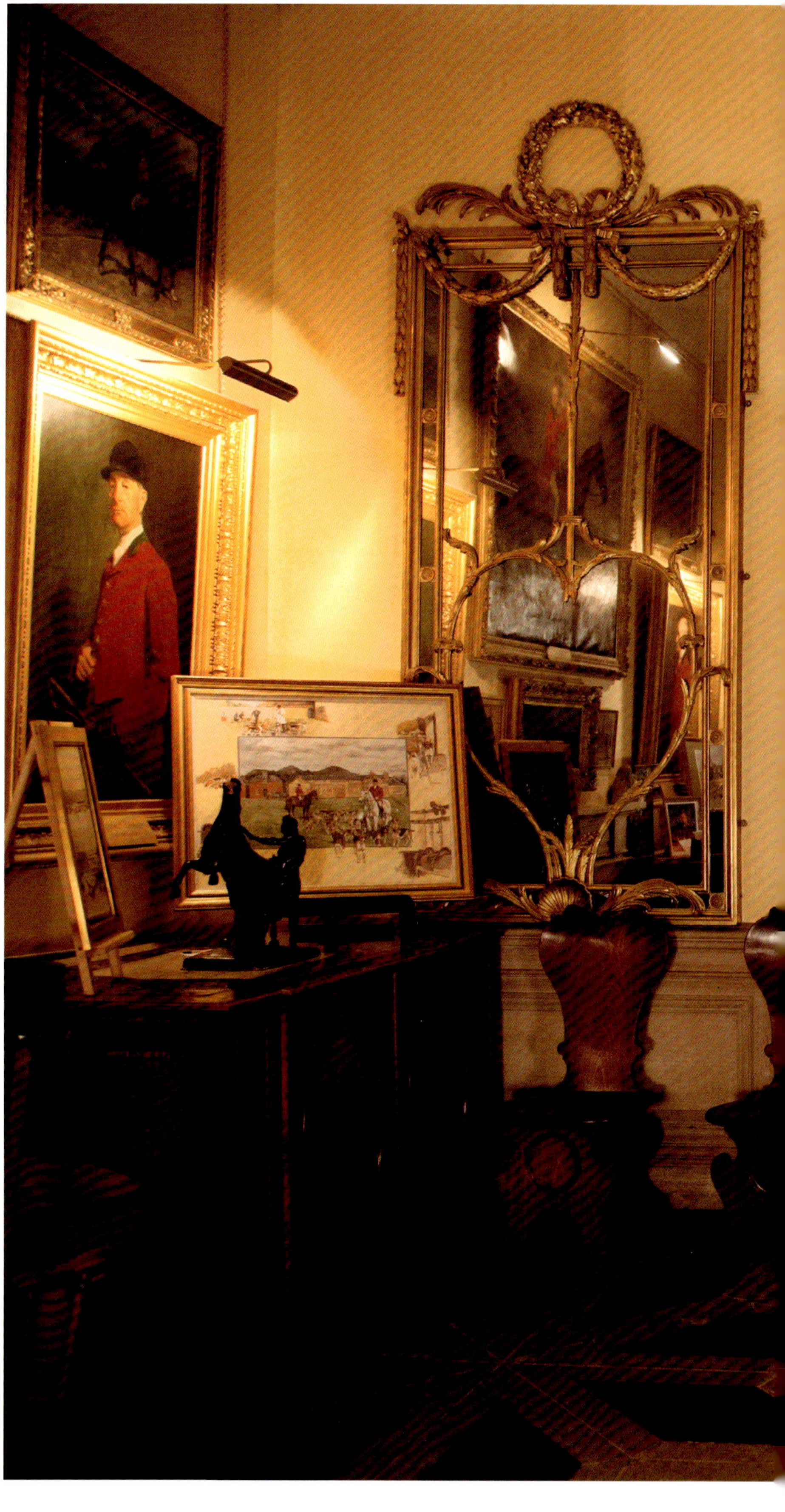

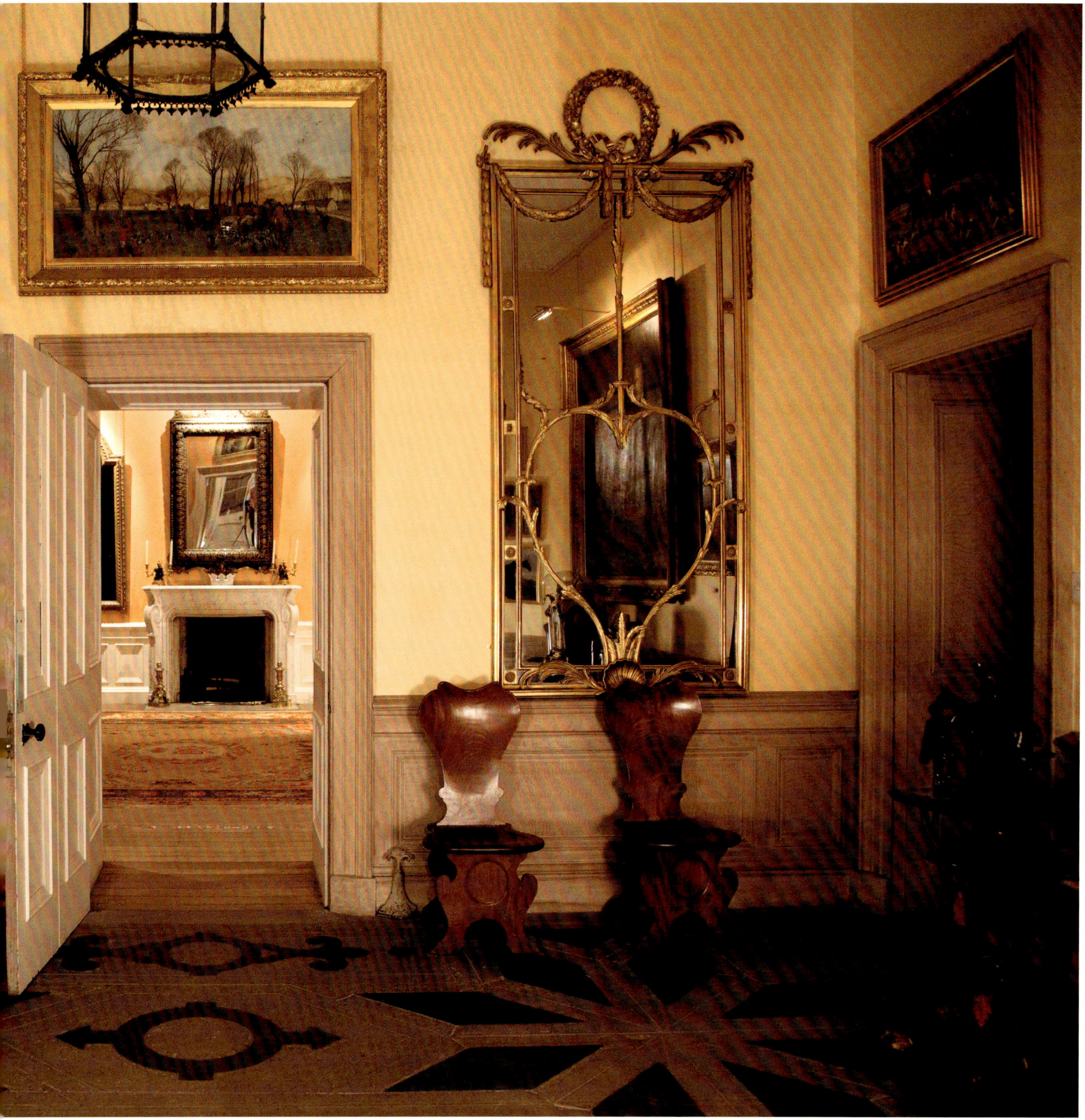

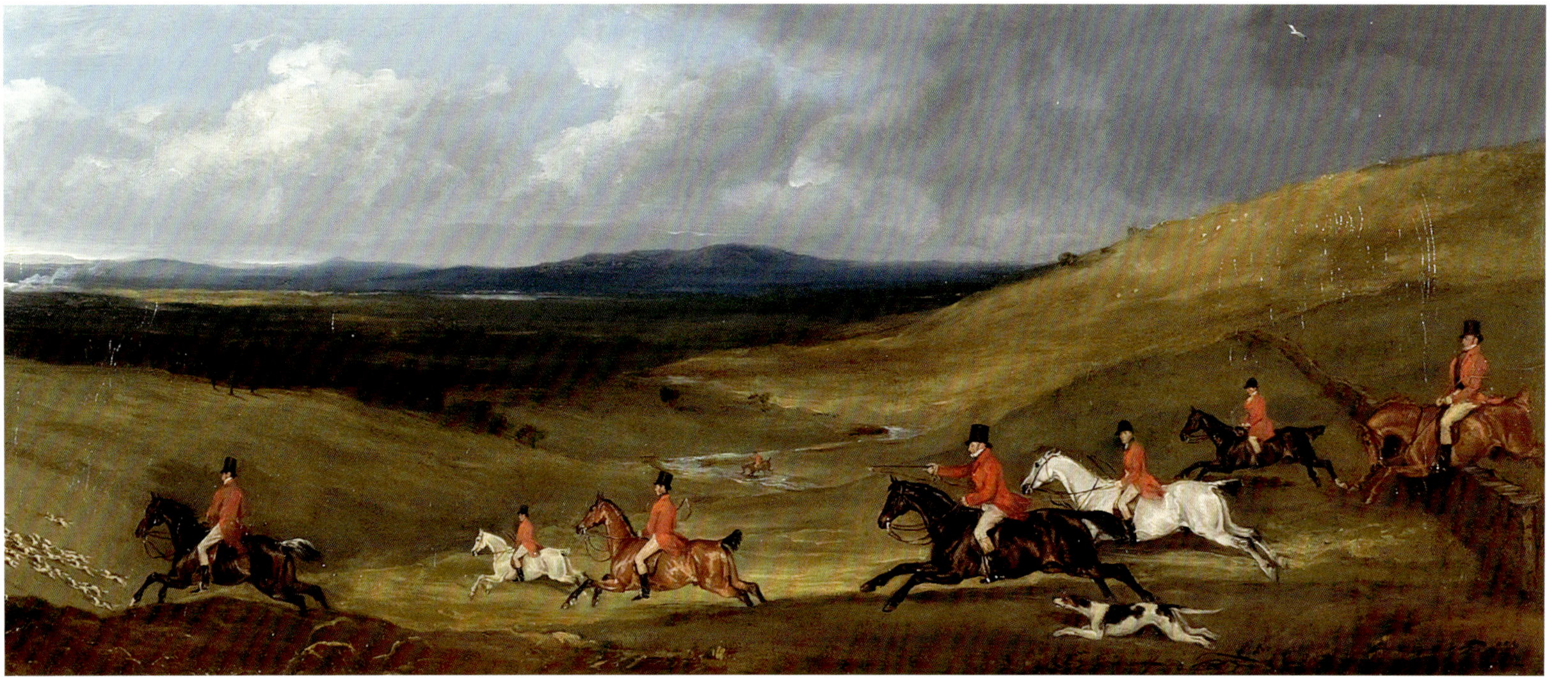

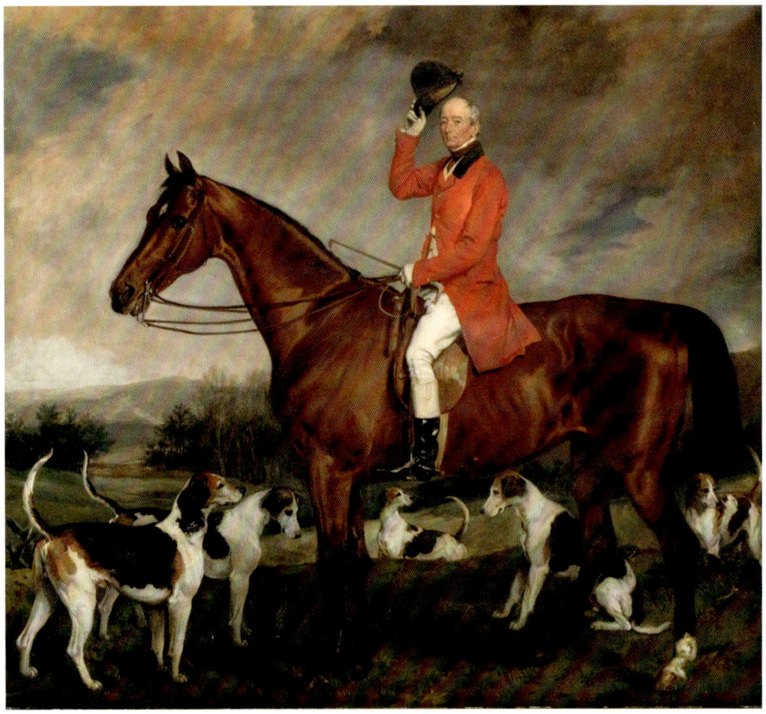

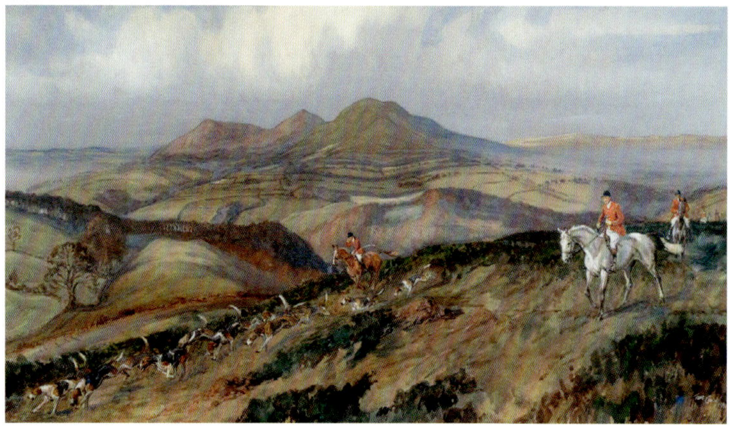

Top *'The Duke of Buccleuch's Hounds', by Sir Francis Grant (1803–78)*
Left *His portrait of the huntsman Will Williamson in Buccleuch Hunt colours. The hounds are Marquis, Hannibal, Hector, Trimmer and Dainty*
Above *'The Hunt in Full Cry', by Tom Carr, 1954 – the late 9th Duke, then Lord Dalkeith, is on the grey mare*
Top right *'Run to Ground', by Tom Scott, 1890.* Right *George Summers, by G Fiddes Watt, 1927*
Far right *In Judith Stowell's 'The Meet at Bowhill', 2005, the late Duke, in the wheelchair, greets the present huntsman, Trevor Adams*

## The Buccleuch Hunt

The kennels built in St Boswells in 1831 were at the heart of Borders hunting country. A succession of paintings of huntsmen, horses and hunting scenes recall this sporting passion. To this day some of the hunt's key figures, in particular its long-serving huntsmen, are still recorded in portraits that hang in the Inner Hall. Just three of them, Will Williamson, George Summers and Tom Smith, spanned more than a century. The hunt has now moved a short distance from St Boswells to kennels on the slopes of the Eildon Hills, where the present huntsman, Trevor Adams, continues in the footsteps of his predecessors, despite the changes to hunting legislation made in the Scottish Parliament in 2002.

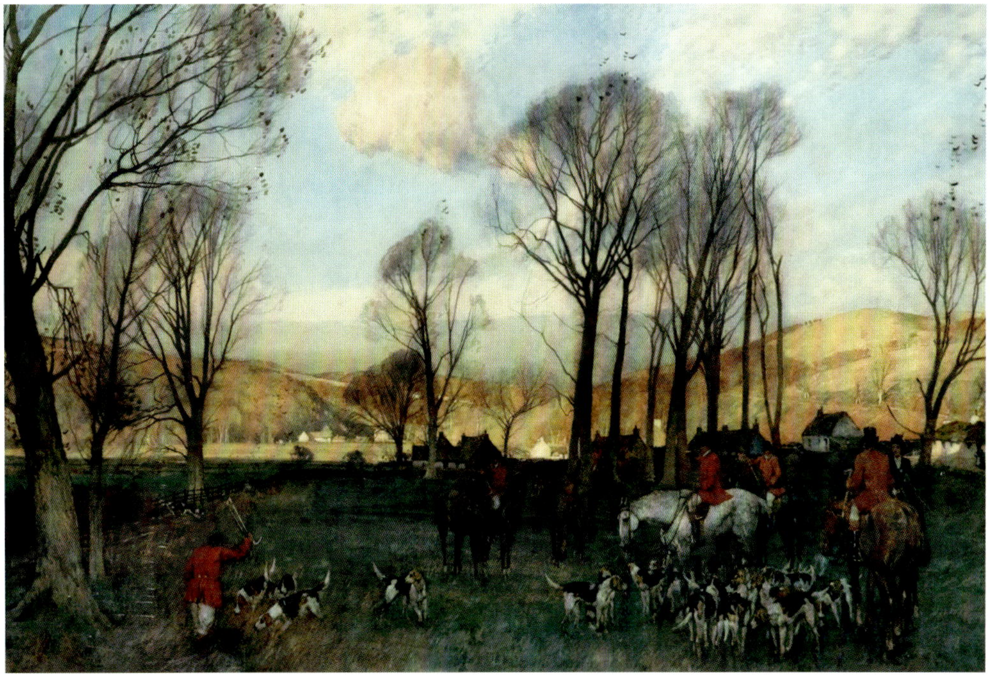

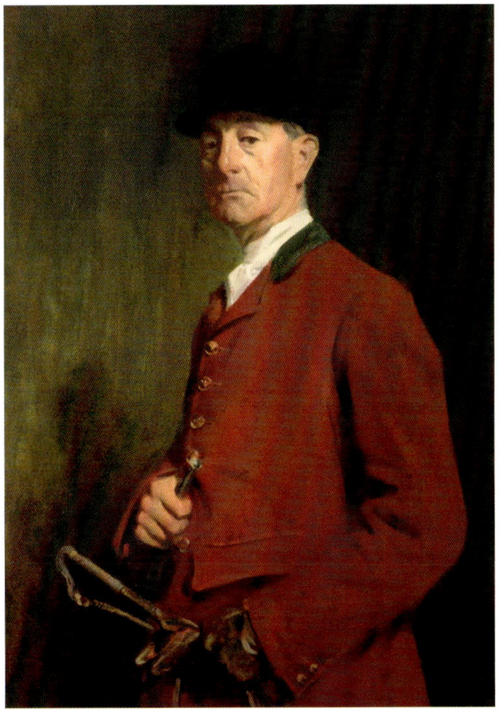

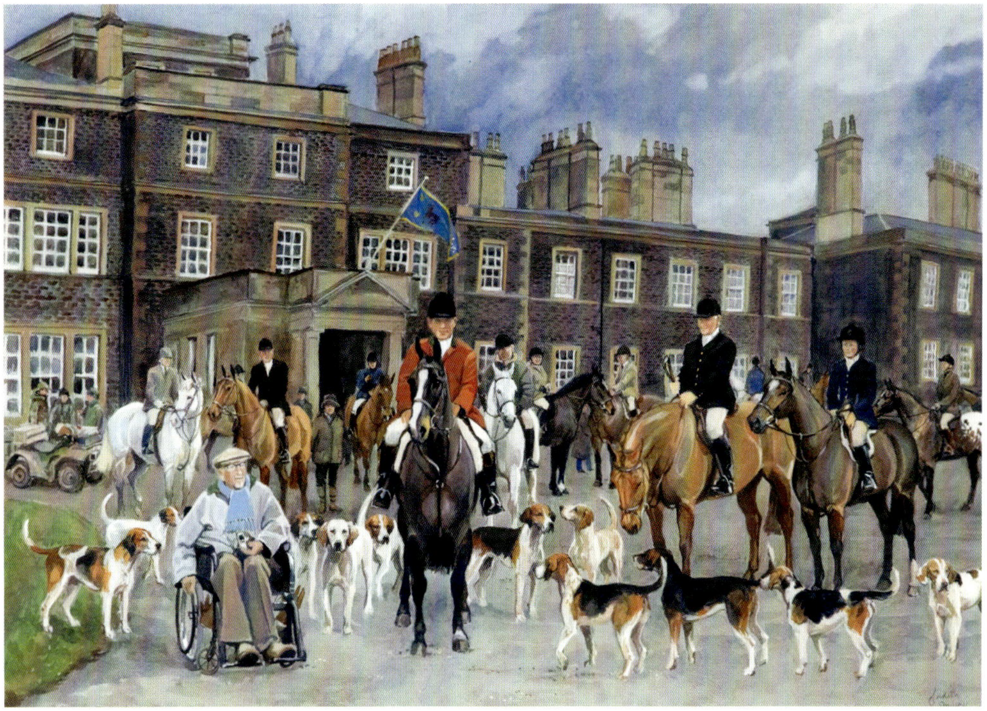

# The Saloon

*At the heart of Bowhill, rising to the full height of the house, the Saloon creates a gallery at each level for paintings and magnificent tapestries*

At the centre of the house, a sort of crossroads, lies the Saloon. Part of Atkinson's early building, the Saloon was greatly expanded by Burn, sideways by incorporating an earlier corridor, and vertically into a tower-like space that reaches up to become the highest part of the building. It is at once impressive – a splendid gallery for the magnificent Mortlake tapestries of Mantegna's *Triumphs of Julius Caesar* – yet impractical, siphoning off skywards any heat that might briefly hang around the occupants at ground level.

After the First World War the complex woodwork balustrade was greatly simplified and painted. The present Duke's father remembered helping to saw off what he described as the 'stalactites' that hung down. Although this would be frowned on nowadays, it must have lightened the impression and created a happier setting for the French furnishings, a 19th-century carpet in the Savonnerie style, with the Buccleuch and Queensberry monogram, an exceptional Boulle mirror and a Louis XV writing desk. From the same period are chairs and a large sofa, known as a 'canapé à confidante', which provided a wildly unsuitable home base for rough childhood games such as 'rescue'.

Full-length portraits of James, Duke of Monmouth and Buccleuch, by Sir Peter Lely,

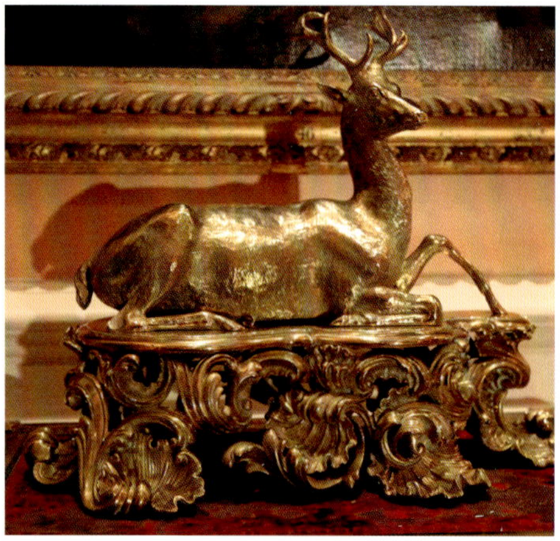

and his wife, Anna, and their two children, by Sir Godfrey Kneller, hang on either side of the central doorway (overleaf). Both boys, James, Earl of Dalkeith, and Henry, later Earl of Deloraine, predeceased their mother.

Some 15 years after her husband's execution in 1685, Anna moved back to Scotland and set about enlarging and improving the family seat in Dalkeith in a picturesque setting created on the edge of the market town between two branches of the River Esk that meet in a deer park. Paths ran along the river banks to rustic summerhouses and through grottoes. These were wonderfully captured in huge landscapes by the Irish painter George Barret, who was working for the family from 1768 to 1771.

RIGHT *The Saloon, with the important Mortlake tapestries in the gallery above. The Louis XIV mirror is attributed to André-Charles Boulle. The dolphins on the cresting suggest it may have been made for the Grand Dauphin's apartments at Versailles. Portraits from the studio of Van Dyck show Robert Rich, Earl of Warwick, and Mary, Charles II's sister, with William II of Orange. Like the marble ducal coronet on the mantelpiece, the arched frames are early 18th century*

LEFT *One of a pair of ormolu stags, dating from the second quarter of the 19th century, which stand on Regency side tables*

BELOW *The Buccleuch and Queensberry monogram in the Savonnerie-style carpet*

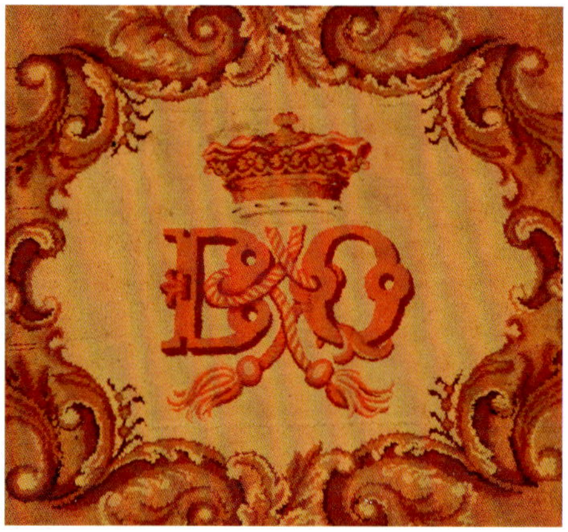

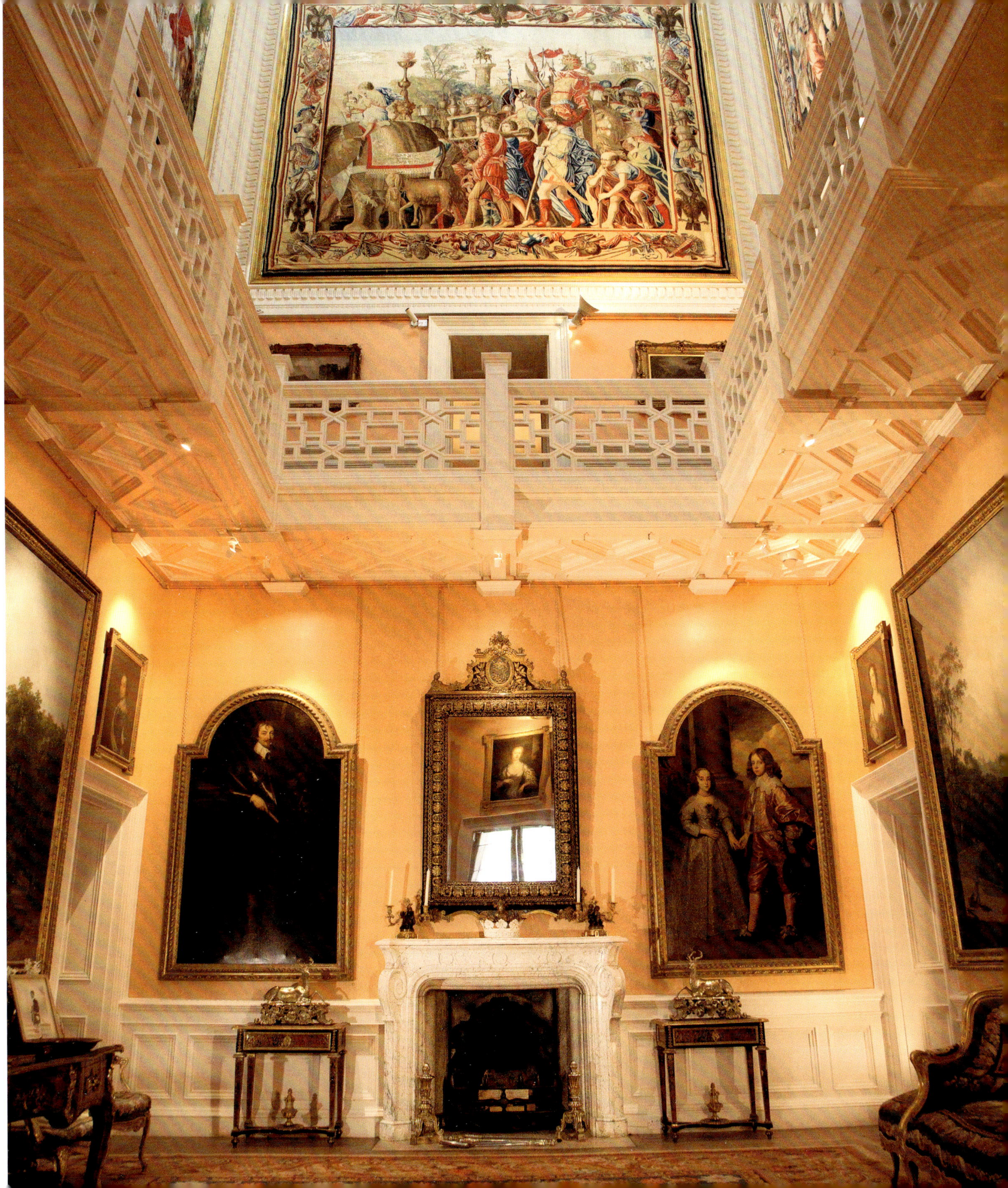

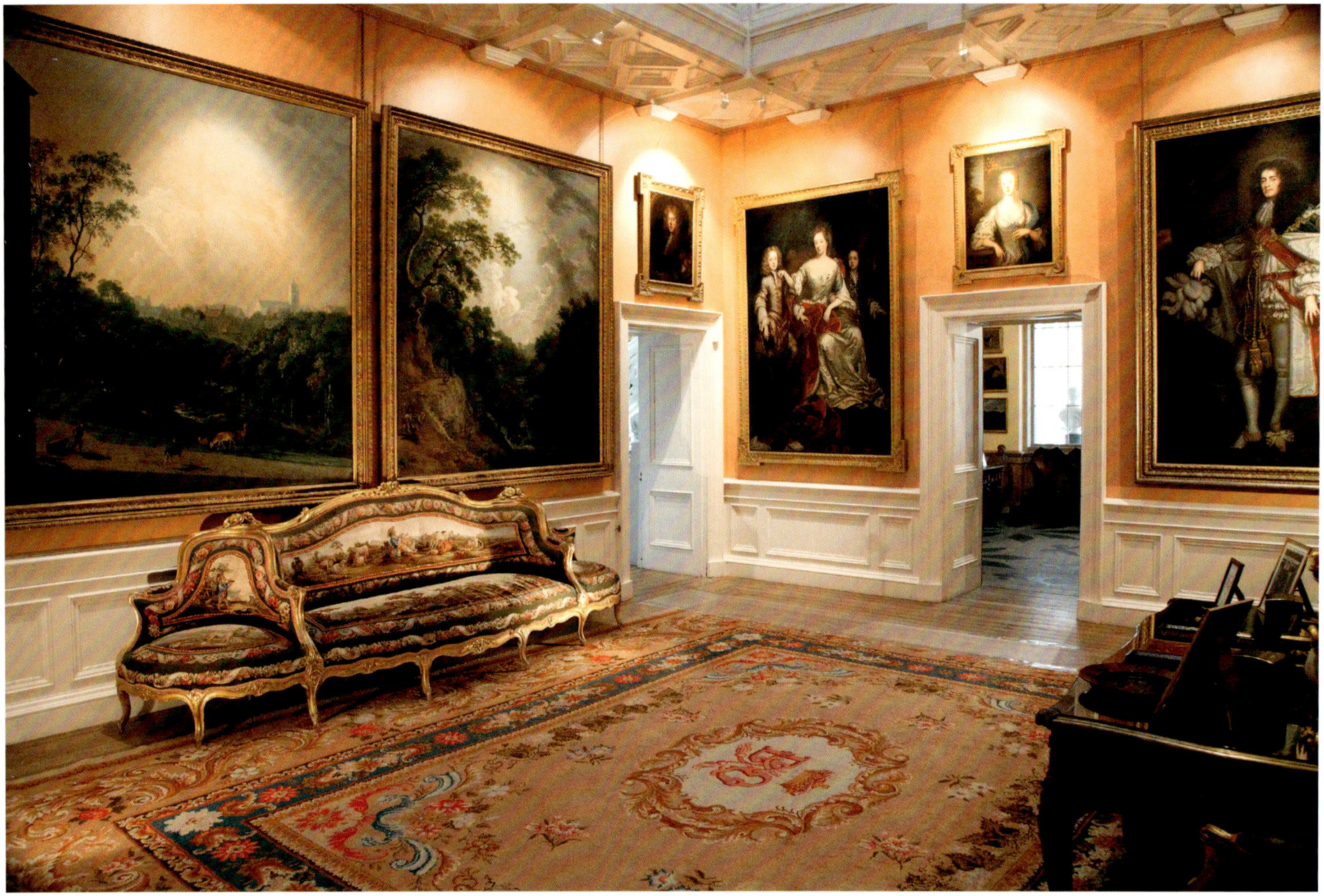

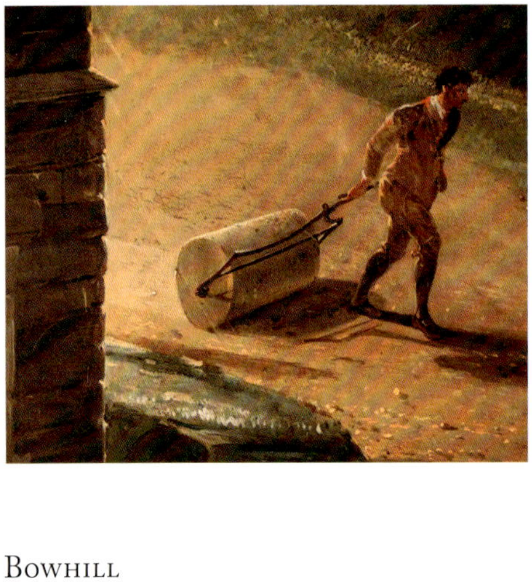

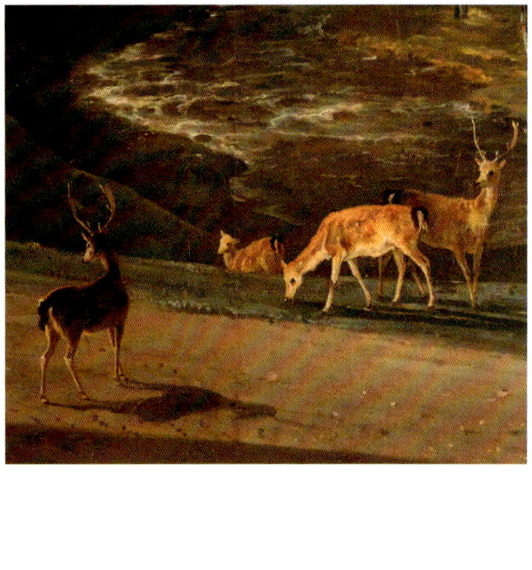

ABOVE *The French furniture in the Saloon sets the tone for the reception rooms throughout Bowhill. The large Louis XV giltwood 'canapé à confidante', attributed to Nicolas Heurtaut, is upholstered in 18th-century Aubusson tapestry. The Staircase and Entrance Halls can be spied through the doors*

BOTTOM ROW *Details of 'Dalkeith Park', George Barret's set of four views in the Saloon: from left, gravel-rolling; deer grazing above the Esk; paths being laid; a party touring the grounds, presumably led by the 3rd Duke*

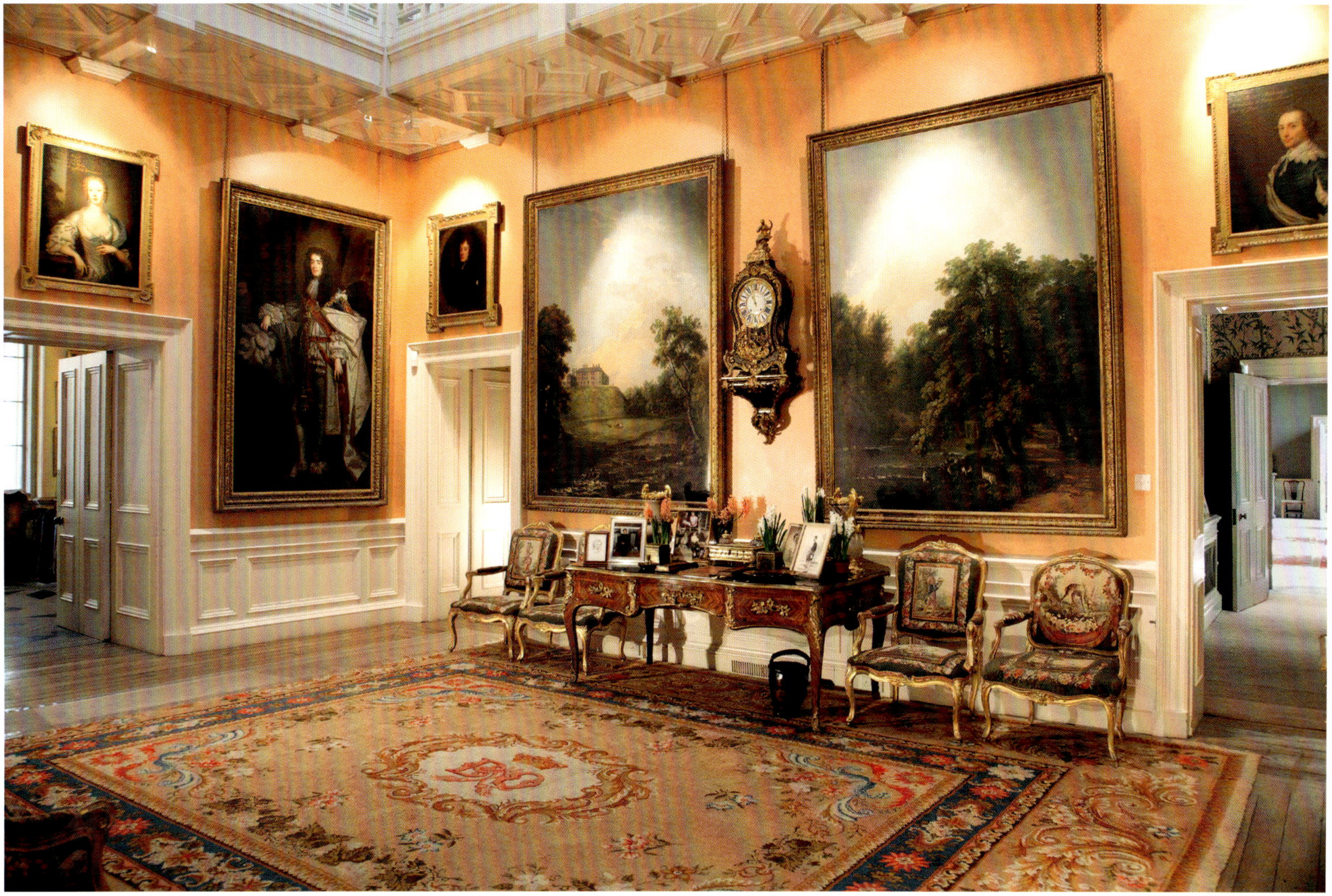

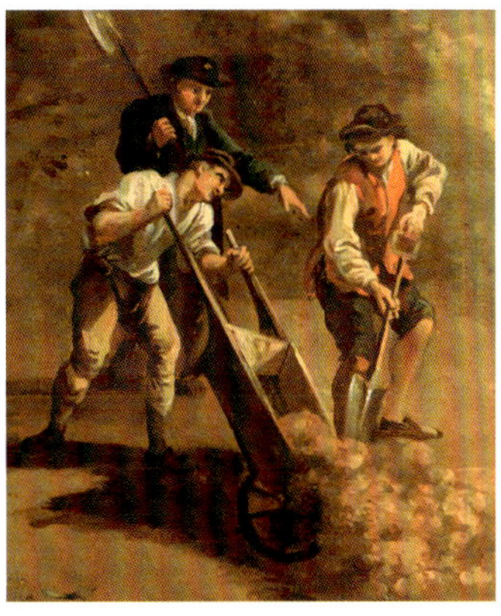

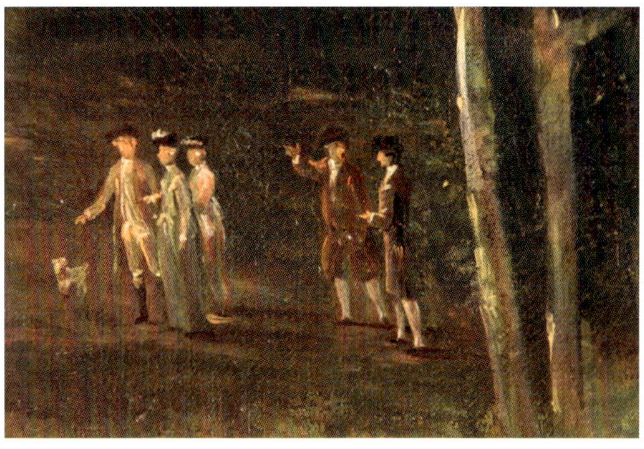

ABOVE *The Saloon's French theme continues in the bureau-plat by Jacques Dubois. The handsome bracket clock inlaid with brass and tortoiseshell has a movement by 'Melot à Paris'. The four Louis XV fauteuils, with their Aubusson tapestry, are stamped 'L. Mayeaux'. The grille beneath the desk – next to the Georgian fire bucket – provided a badly needed early form of central heating. The door on the right leads to the Morning Room and Dining Room. The middle door leads to the East Passage*

# The Mortlake Tapestries

*The 17th-century Mortlake tapestries in the Saloon's upper gallery are based on Mantegna's celebrated cycle of paintings 'The Triumphs of Caesar'*

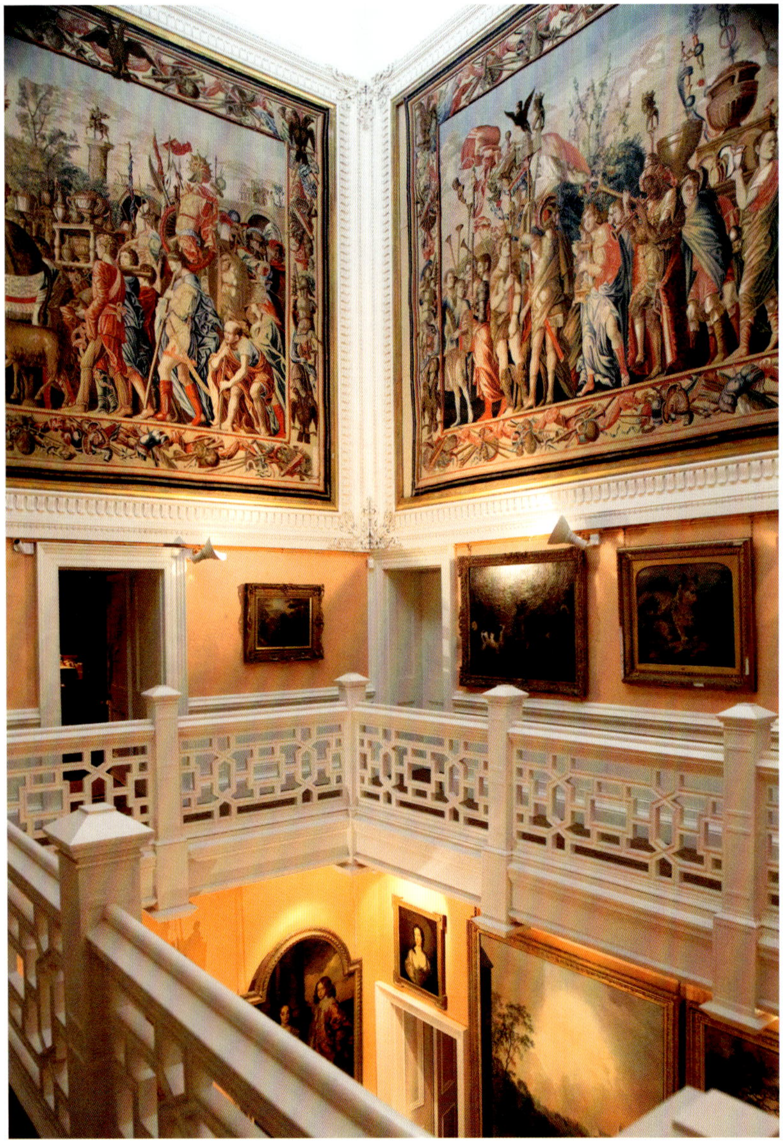

The four martial tapestries hanging in the upper gallery of the Saloon were moved here from England when Burn created this top-lit gallery in the 1830s. One, woven in Brussels, shows a procession with Bellona, the goddess of war, and is signed 'V. Leyniers'. The other three were woven at Mortlake, on the Thames, and are based on Andrea Mantegna's *Triumphs of Caesar*, painted between 1485 and 1505 for the Gonzaga Ducal Palace in Mantua. Charles I bought the cycle of paintings in 1629, when the Gonzaga collection was dispersed. Cromwell had much of Charles's great collection sold, but the Mantegnas remained, as they do to this day, at Hampton Court.

The cycle of nine paintings was compressed into three tapestries, so the weavers, while accurately reproducing individual figures, reordered the sequence. Woven around 1670 for Ralph, 1st Duke of Montagu, whose family owned the Mortlake factory, they appear to be the only tapestries from this series to survive.

Mortlake tapestries after Mantegna
**The Triumphs of Caesar, c.1670**
Left *The Saloon's gallery, with two of Bowhill's three Mortlake tapestries. They draw on Mantegna's cycle of paintings of Roman triumphs celebrating Julius Caesar's defeat of the Gauls and conquest of the kingdom of Pontus in Asia Minor*

Right *Caesar's triumphal procession with elephants is a conflation of two of Mantegna's paintings. Men bear gold vessels and gold coin, and corselet bearers carry the armour of Perseus*

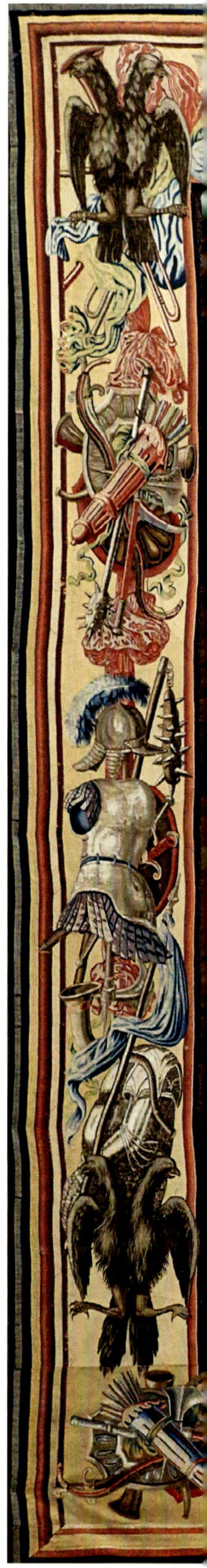

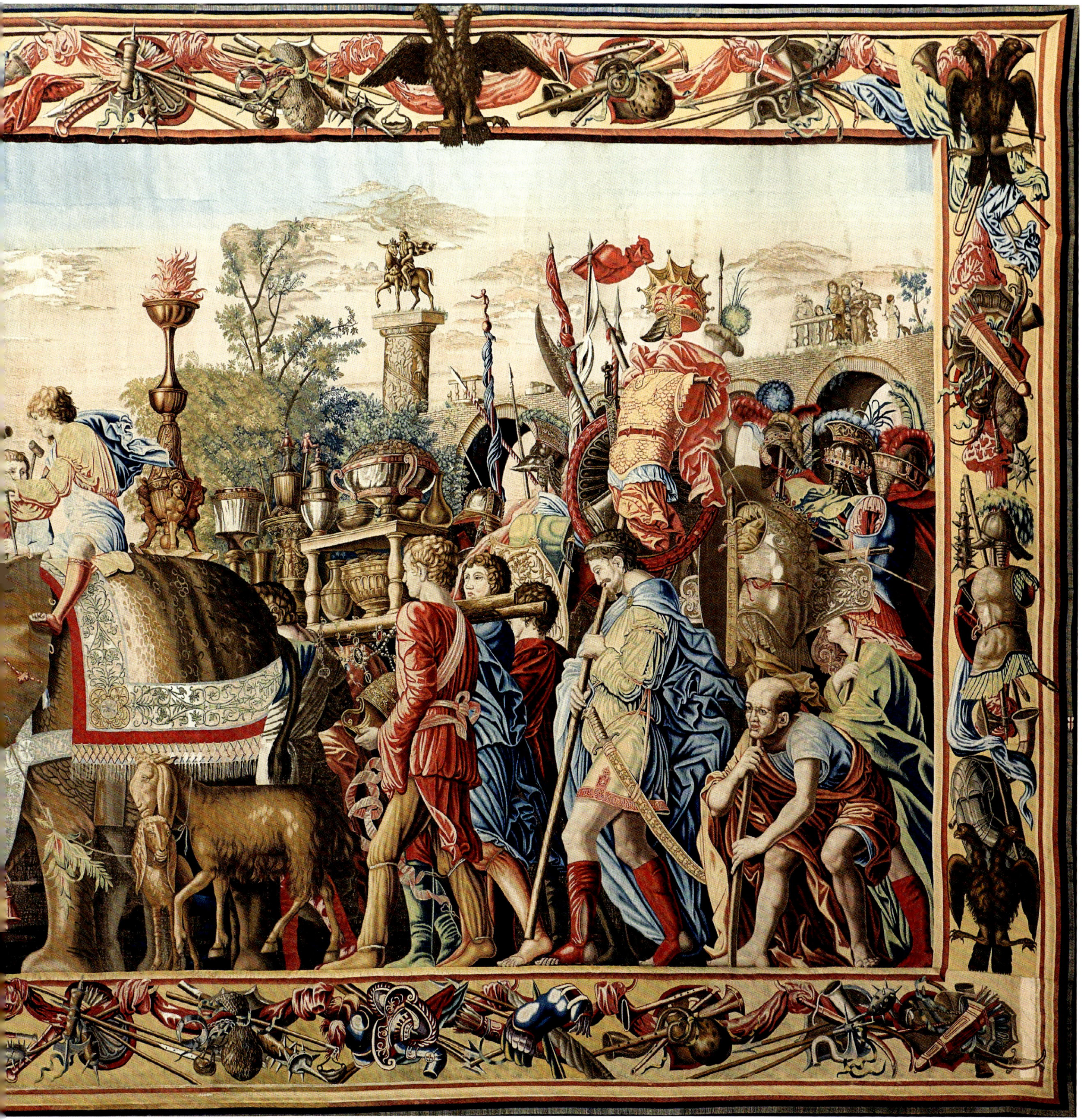

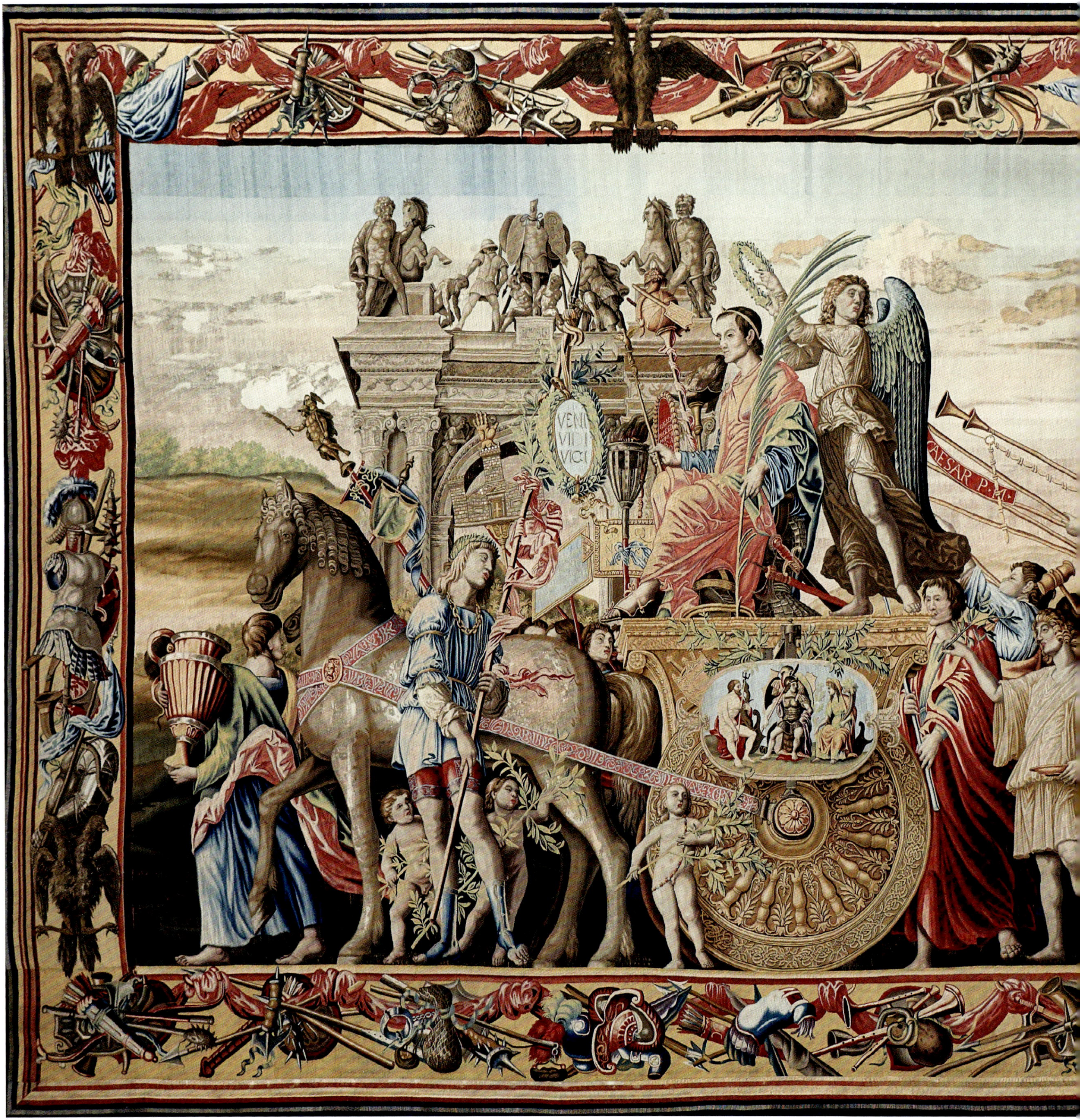
VENI
VICI
CAESAR P.

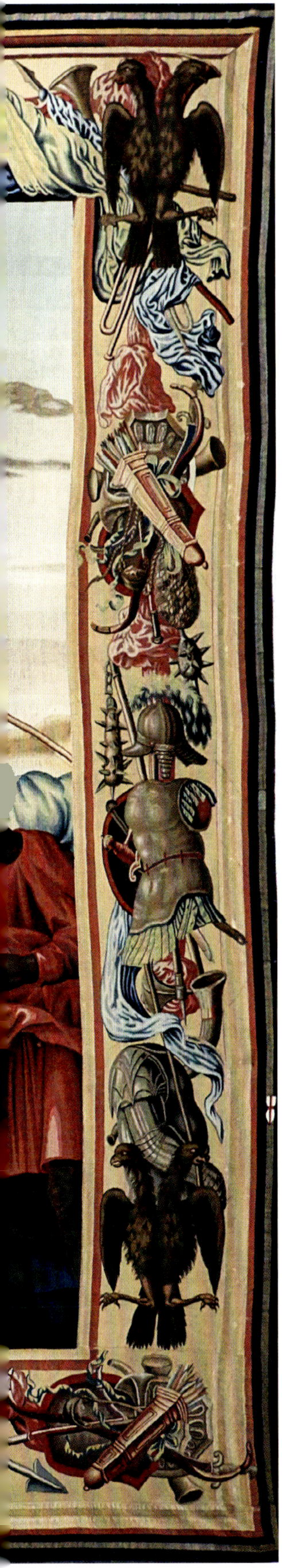

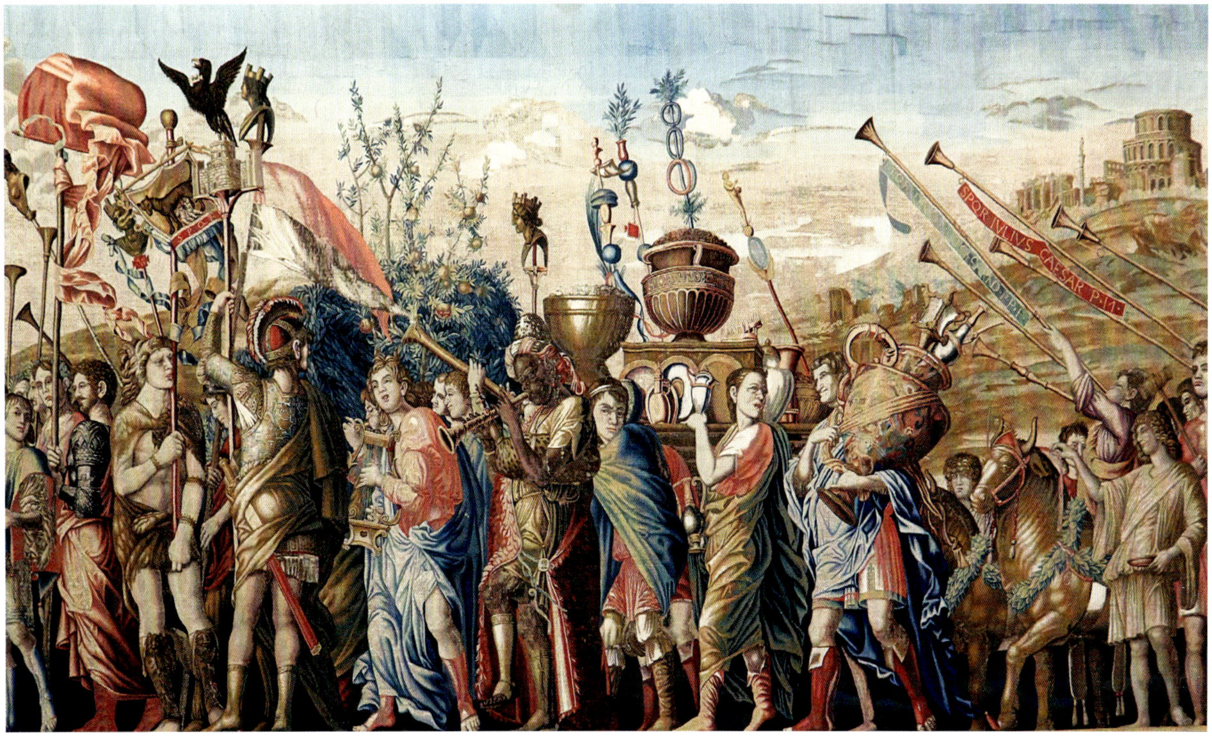

Left and above
Mortlake tapestries after Mantegna
**The Triumphs of Caesar, c.1670**
*Julius Caesar on his triumphal chariot (left), based on the ninth and final canvas of the Mantegna series at Hampton Court. Musicians followed by trophy bearers carry Caesar's spoils of war (above). The cycle was originally painted in tempera on canvas but much reworked. The tapestries retain certain details that were later lost in the paintings*

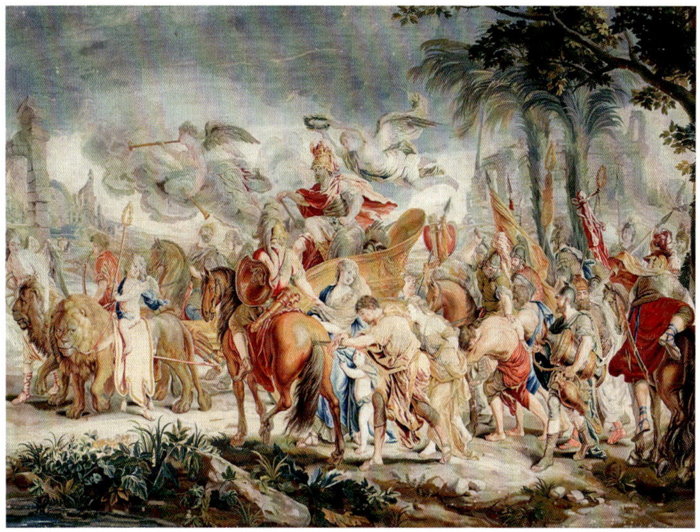

Right Brussels tapestry from the Leyniers workshop
**Triumph of Bellona, c.1670**
*In this Baroque triumph designed by Jan van Orley, the goddess of war's chariot is drawn by lions. The landscape is by Augustin Coppens*

# The Staircase Hall

*Portraits of Duchesses dominate the Staircase Hall. Having moved to the front of the house as part of William Burn's grand plan in the 1830s, it is flooded with light from two storeys of windows*

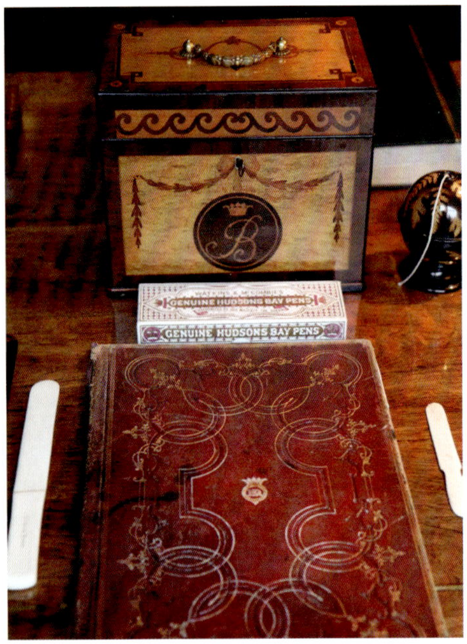


RIGHT *In pride of place on the staircase is Sir Francis Grant's portrait of Charlotte Anne, wife of the 5th Duke, with two of their sons, the future 6th Duke, and the future 1st Lord Montagu of Beaulieu (see page 126). The Duke in evening dress, by George Richmond, is next to them*

ABOVE *A crested leather blotter, a Victorian marquetry casket and an inlaid string dispenser*

In moving the front entrance in the 1830s, Burn had to sacrifice the central location of the main staircase, but it still provides a wide route to the Gallery and the main bedroom floor. Accessible from the Inner Hall and the Saloon, the Staircase Hall also serves as the entrance to the west wing of the house – the 'family wing'. Like the Saloon, it was redecorated to great effect by the late Duke and his wife, Jane, to whom Bowhill owes much of its sense of colour and style. Dominating the ascent are large portraits of Charlotte Anne, Louisa Jane and Margaret, wives of the 5th, 6th and 7th Dukes.

Henry, the 3rd Duke, figures prominently at the foot of the stairs (overleaf). His portrait as a young man in a dashing green suit is by Reynolds. Either side of him are his parents, Francis, Earl of Dalkeith, and Caroline Campbell, the eldest daughter and heiress of John, Duke of Argyll. She was to be given the title of Baroness Greenwich in her own right in 1767 and inherited wonderful mirrors and silver, now at Bowhill, as well as Caroline Park, a house near Edinburgh.

The Louis XIV-style ebony and *pietra dura* cabinets were bought in the mid-19th century. From time immemorial a gong has stood here to announce meals and provide an opportunity for amusement and mischief to small children.

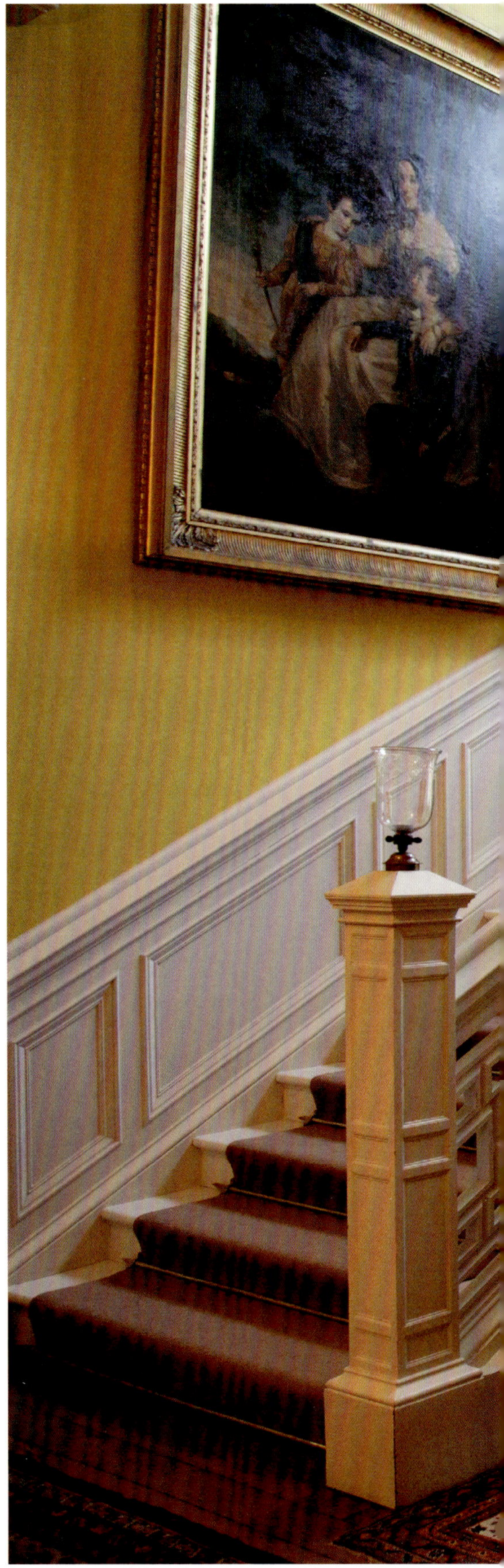

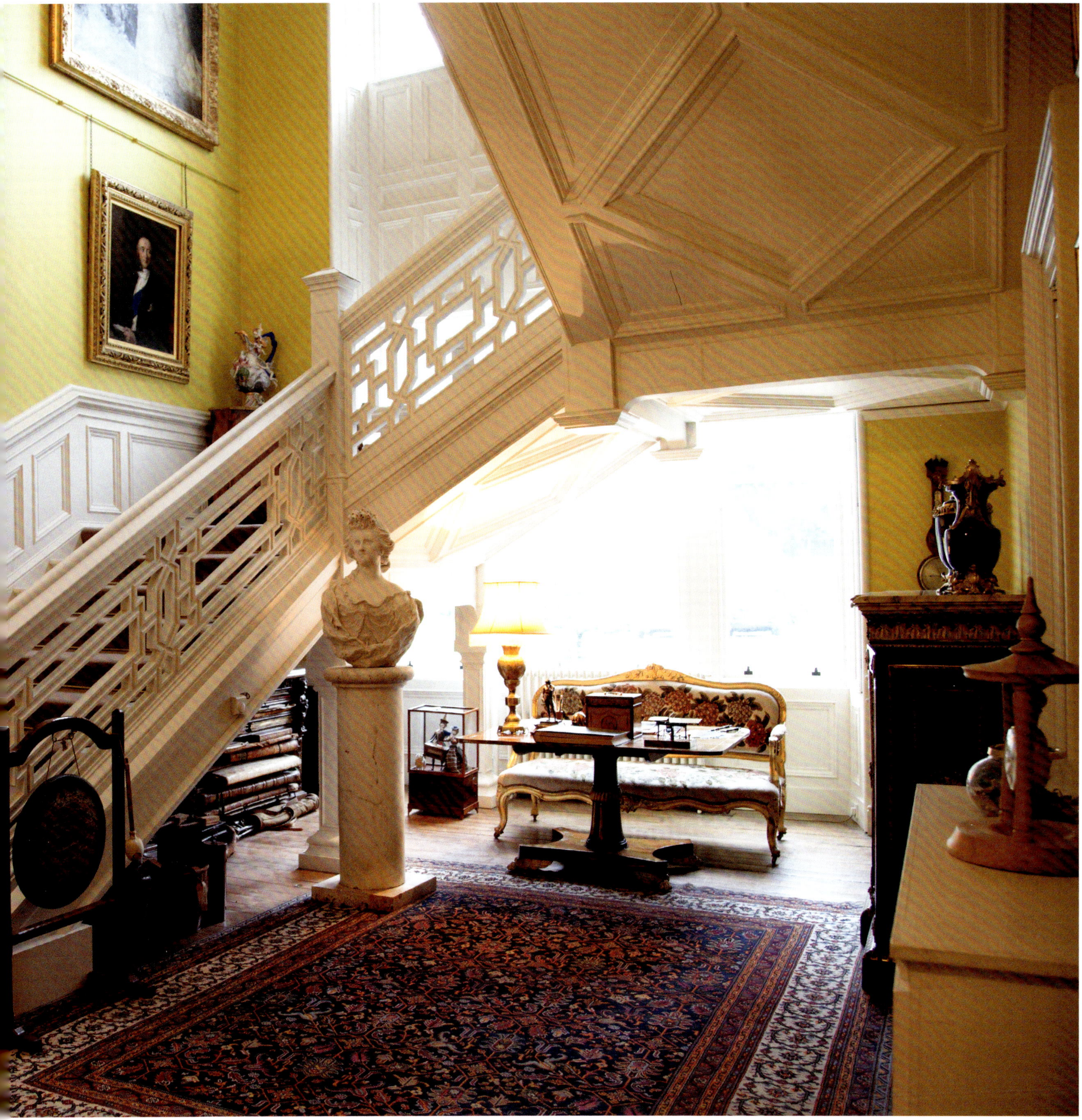

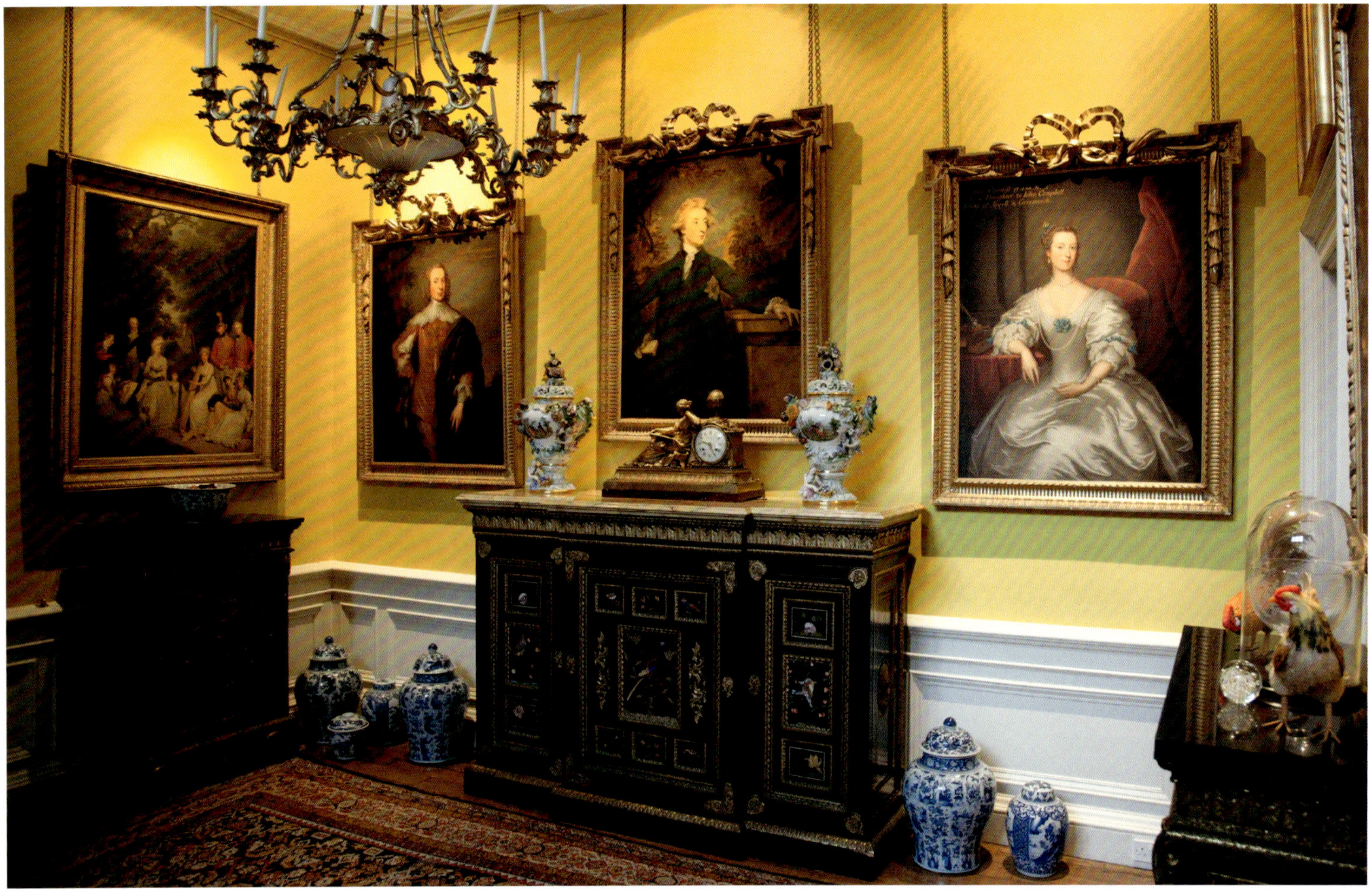

ABOVE *At the foot of the stairs, Kangxi jars bring a dash of blue. Danloux's portrait of the 3rd Duke and family is on the left; in the centre, Reynolds' likeness of him hangs between Thomas Bardwell's portraits of his parents, Francis, Earl of Dalkeith (1721–50), and the Duke of Argyll's daughter Caroline Campbell (1717–94)*

RIGHT *An 18th-century Meissen dinner service fills the George III breakfront bookcase on the landing. The attic stairs can be glimpsed beyond*

OPPOSITE *Charles Edmund Brock's portrait of the late 9th Duke as a boy, when he was Lord Eskdaill (also overleaf), hangs at the entrance to the Library*

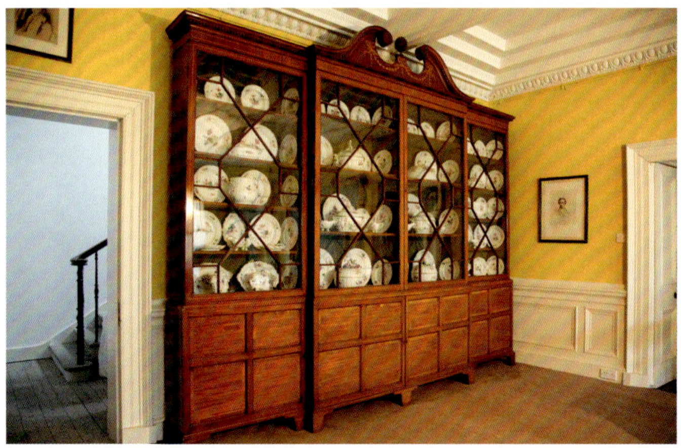

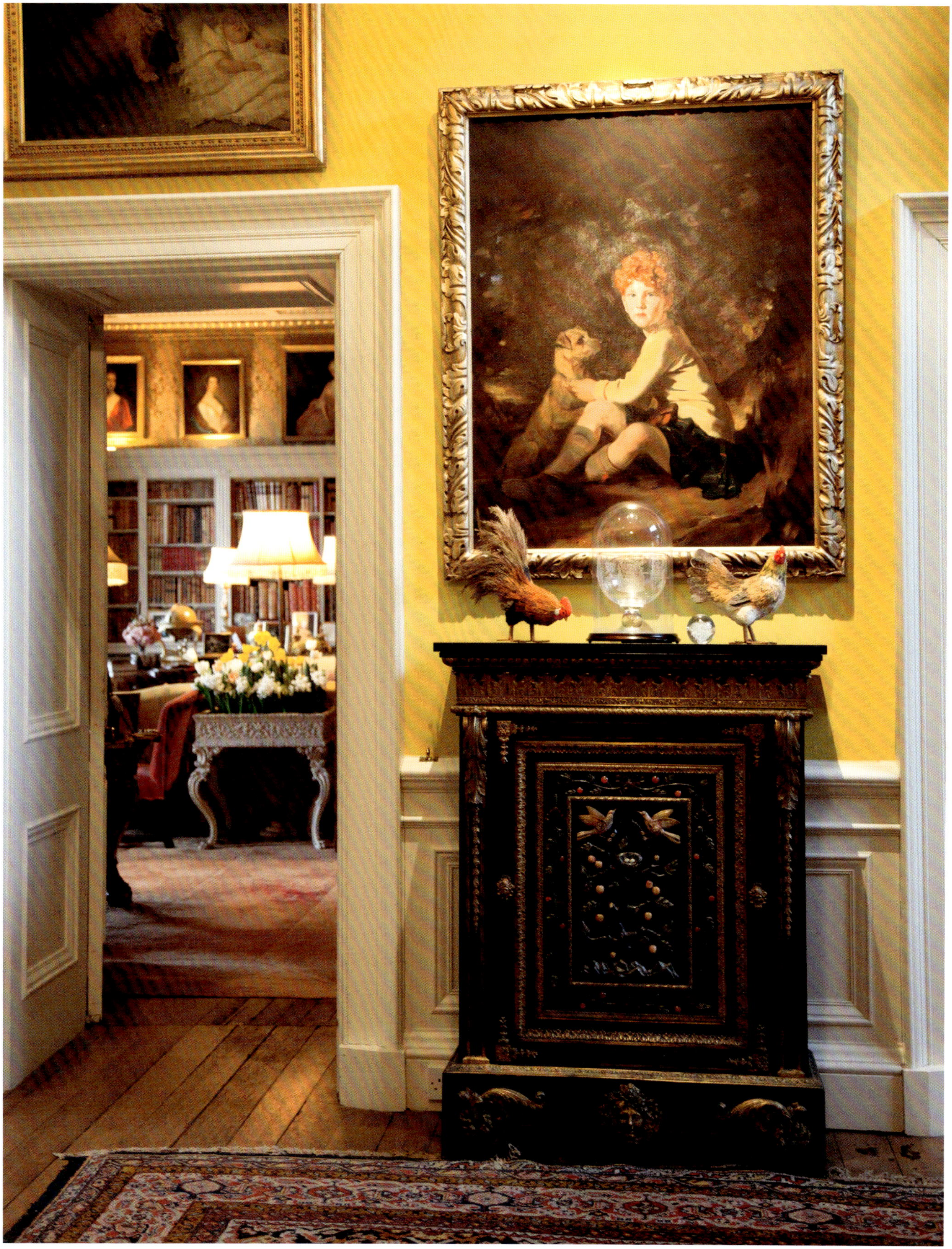

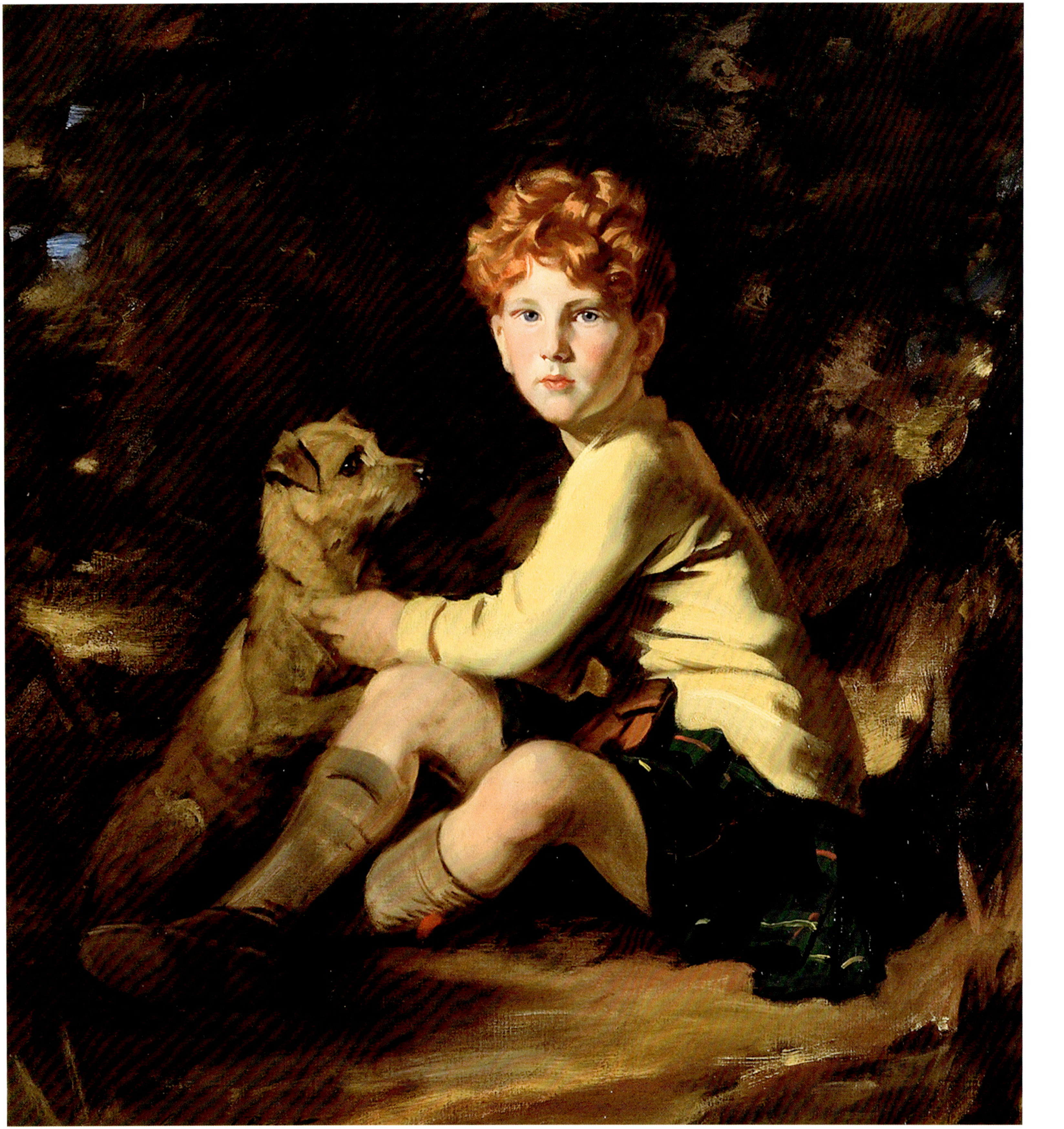

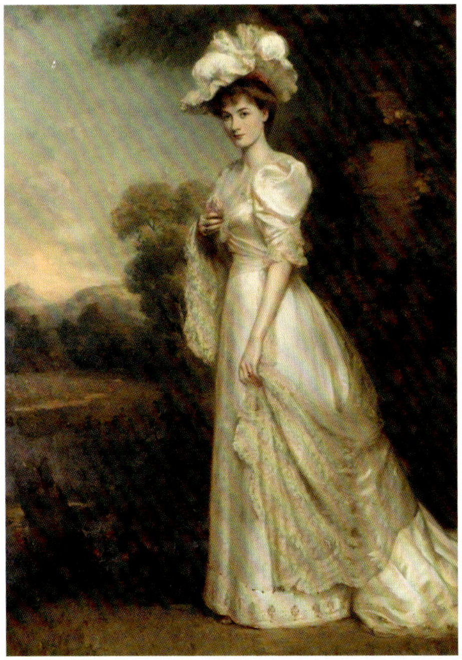

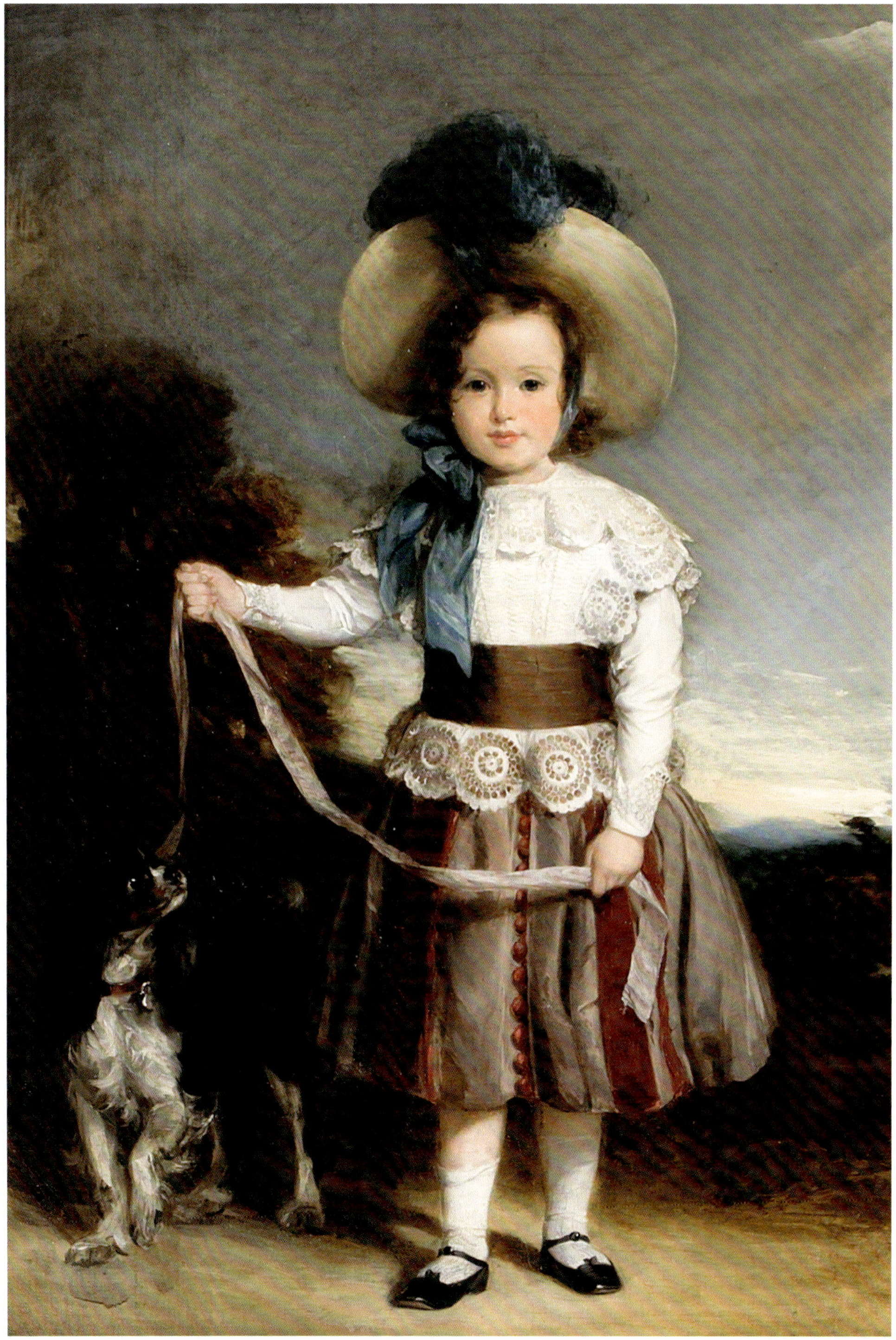

ABOVE ELLIS ROBERTS (1860–1930)
**Margaret, Duchess of Buccleuch (1872–1954)**
*A fashionable portrait of the wife of the 7th Duke, daughter of the Earl of Bradford, in a plumed hat*

RIGHT SIR FRANCIS GRANT (1803–78)
**Lord Charles Scott (1839–1943)**
*Charles, son of the 5th Duke, holding a spaniel, wears the fetching children's clothes of the day – lace shirt, silk skirt and plumed straw hat. He went on to become an admiral and married the Australian butterfly- and flower-painter Ellis Rowan. His longevity was matched by that of his son, Sir David Scott, a great collector of Victorian paintings, who created a legendary garden at Boughton, the seat in Northamptonshire inherited from the Montagus. He died aged 99, in 1986*

LEFT CHARLES EDMUND BROCK (1870–1938)
**Lord Eskdaill, 1929**
*The future 9th Duke of Buccleuch, father of the present Duke, with his shock of Scott red hair, is seen here in a Hunting Stuart kilt and yellow jersey, with his border terrier, Prunella*

# The Library

*A close friend of Walter Scott and a passionate countryman, the 4th Duke put his heart and soul into the Library, with its views of the Ettrick Valley. His enjoyment of it was brief*

Charles, the 4th Duke, died shortly after finishing his Library, before he could commission a portrait of his great friend Sir Walter Scott. As he had explained to the author, he wished to place him, 'the Guardian of Literature', at the heart of his new Library. In 1814 he had asked William Atkinson to add wings to the original 1812 house, the Dining Room to the east, the Library to the west. The latter was to be Duke Charles's sanctum; at the far end a door disguised as shelves of books led to a study, then to his bedroom and dressing room, where he could keep his guns and fishing tackle.

The book collection spreads over four centuries and many generations. Not surprisingly, works by Scott and his contemporary James Hogg, 'the Ettrick Shepherd', are well represented. But it is a reminder, too, of the period's curiosity and hunger for knowledge – many volumes are on scientific subjects, exploration and discovery.

Anna, 1st Duchess of Buccleuch, wife of the Duke of Monmouth, hangs where Sir Walter Scott would have been, above the chimneypiece bearing her monogram, which was brought in the 1920s from Dalkeith. Scott is present, albeit in a small oil, painted as an old man by Sir Edwin Landseer; he stands on an easel opposite Charles's wife, Harriet, who was herself his friend and muse.

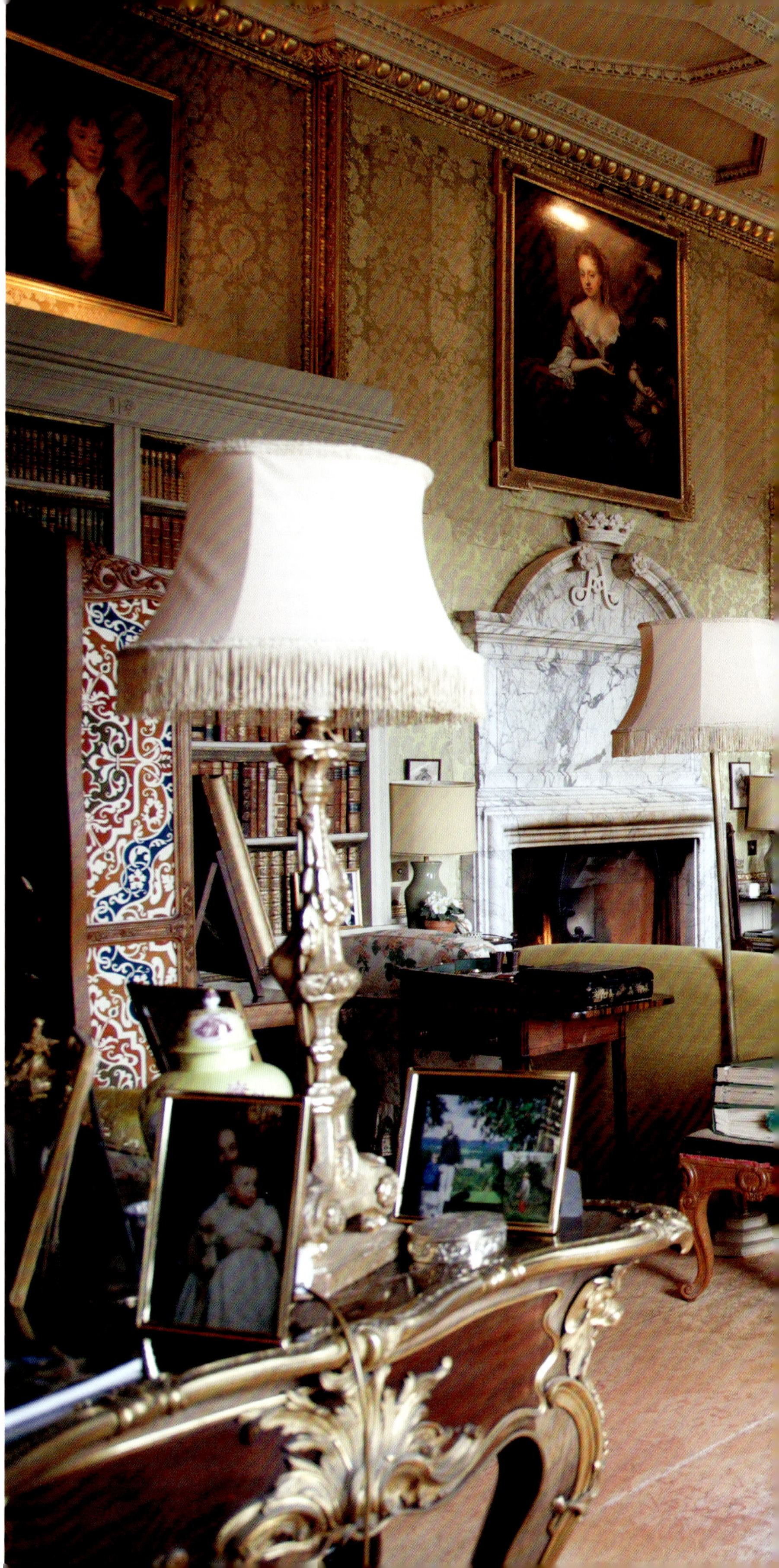

THE LIBRARY, LOOKING EAST
*Dresden desks at either end give a certain formality to the comfortably furnished room. Duchess Anna hangs above the fireplace*

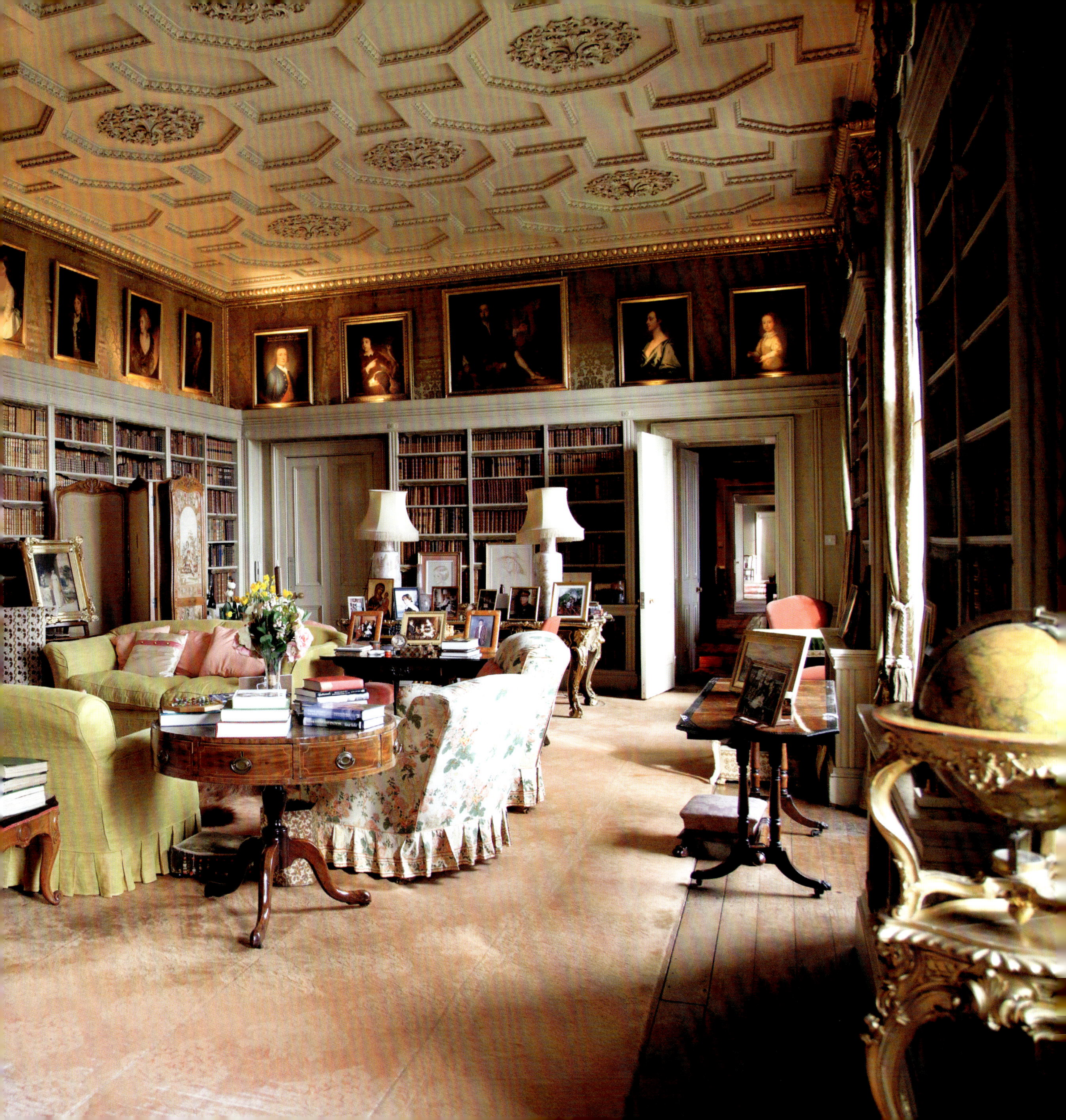

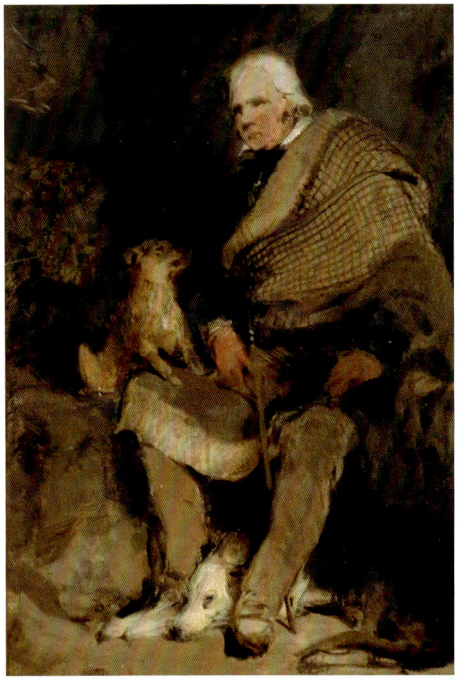

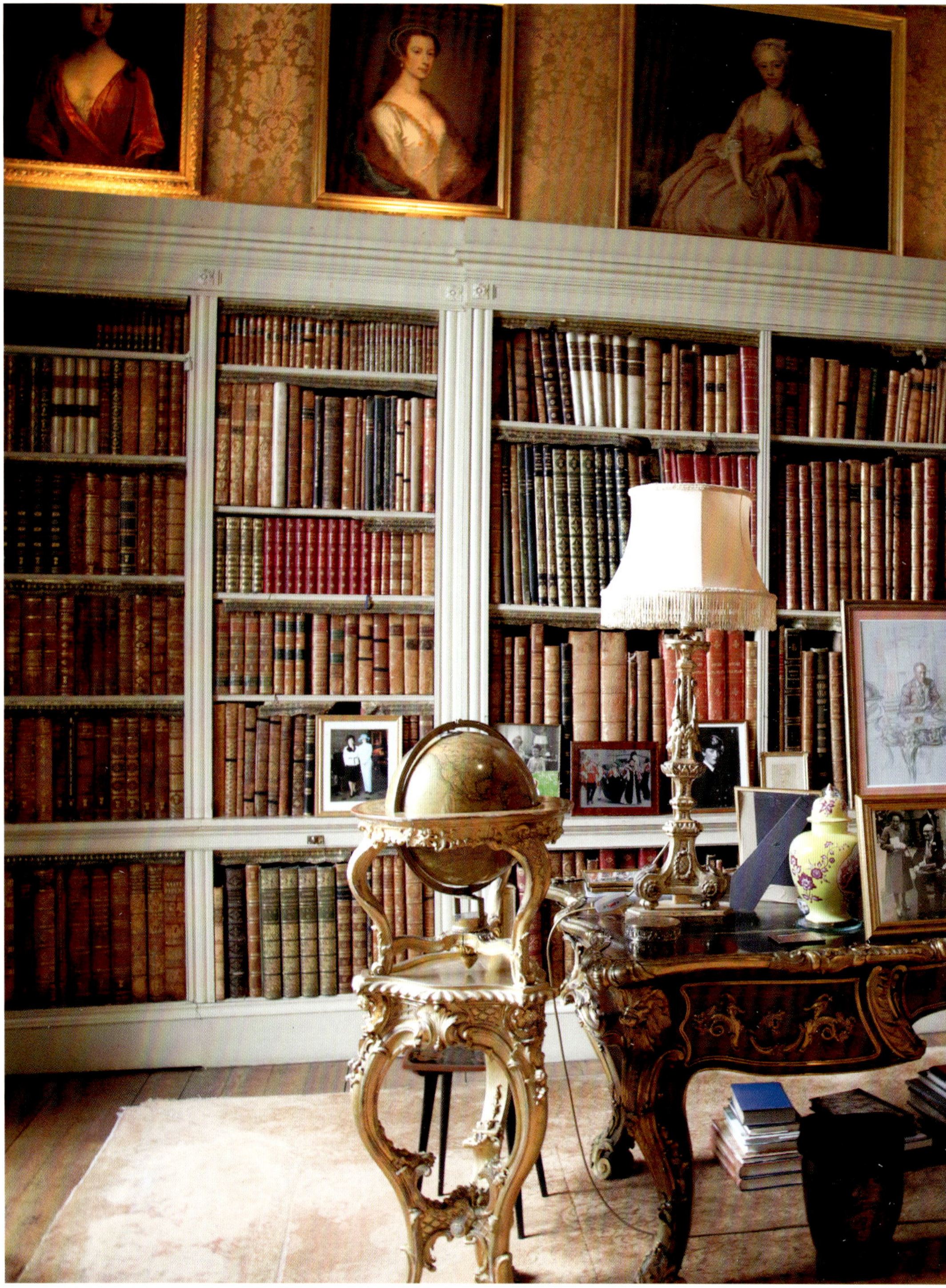

ABOVE SIR EDWIN LANDSEER (1802–73)
**Sir Walter Scott (1771–1832)**
*A small oil study of the elderly writer with his dogs, bought by the 5th Duke in 1882, stands on an easel next to the fireplace. Charles, 4th Duke, who built this room, shared Scott's literary interests*

RIGHT *The globes either side of this Dresden desk, one terrestrial, the other celestial, are inscribed 'Made & Sold by J. & W. Cary Strand London, Jan. 11 1816' and were supplied by Baldock in 1831. The shelves on the left conceal a secret door to Duke Charles's Study*

OPPOSITE *Above the bookcases are charming portraits, many by Sir William Beechey (top). A first edition of Adam Smith's 'Wealth of Nations' (centre), published in 1776, is inscribed in the author's own hand to his pupil, Henry, 3rd Duke. Behind the desk (bottom) is a drawing of Walter, 8th Duke, by his sister-in-law Molly Bishop, next to a photograph of his daughter Elizabeth (future Duchess of Northumberland) as a Wren*

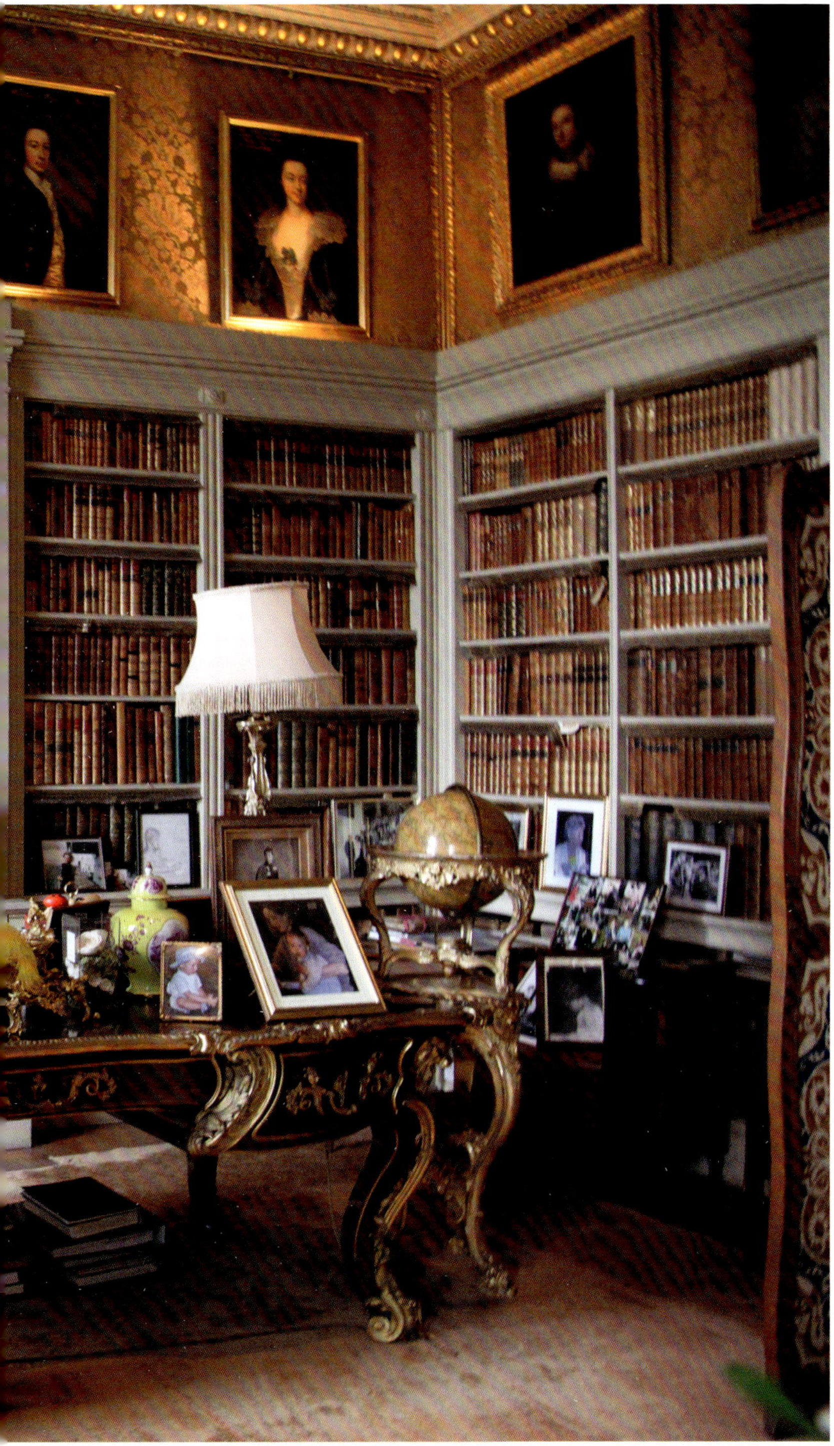

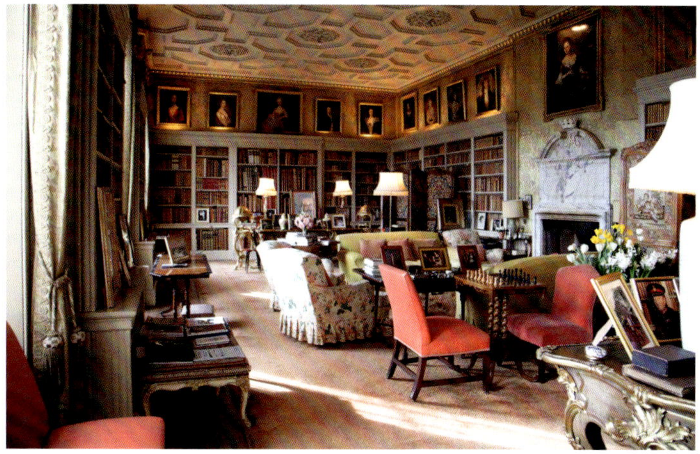

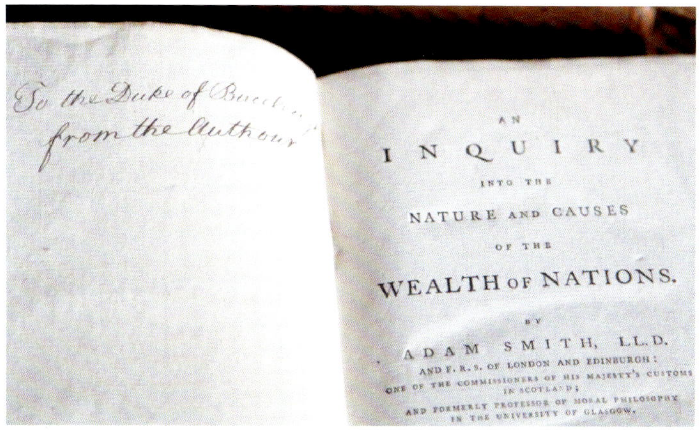
AN
INQUIRY
INTO THE
NATURE AND CAUSES
OF THE
WEALTH OF NATIONS.
BY
ADAM SMITH, LL.D.
AND F.R.S. OF LONDON AND EDINBURGH:
ONE OF THE COMMISSIONERS OF HIS MAJESTY'S CUSTOMS
IN SCOTLAND;
AND FORMERLY PROFESSOR OF MORAL PHILOSOPHY
IN THE UNIVERSITY OF GLASGOW.

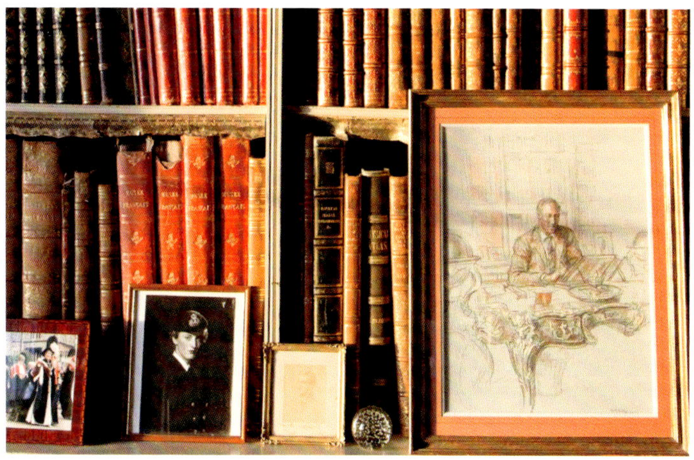

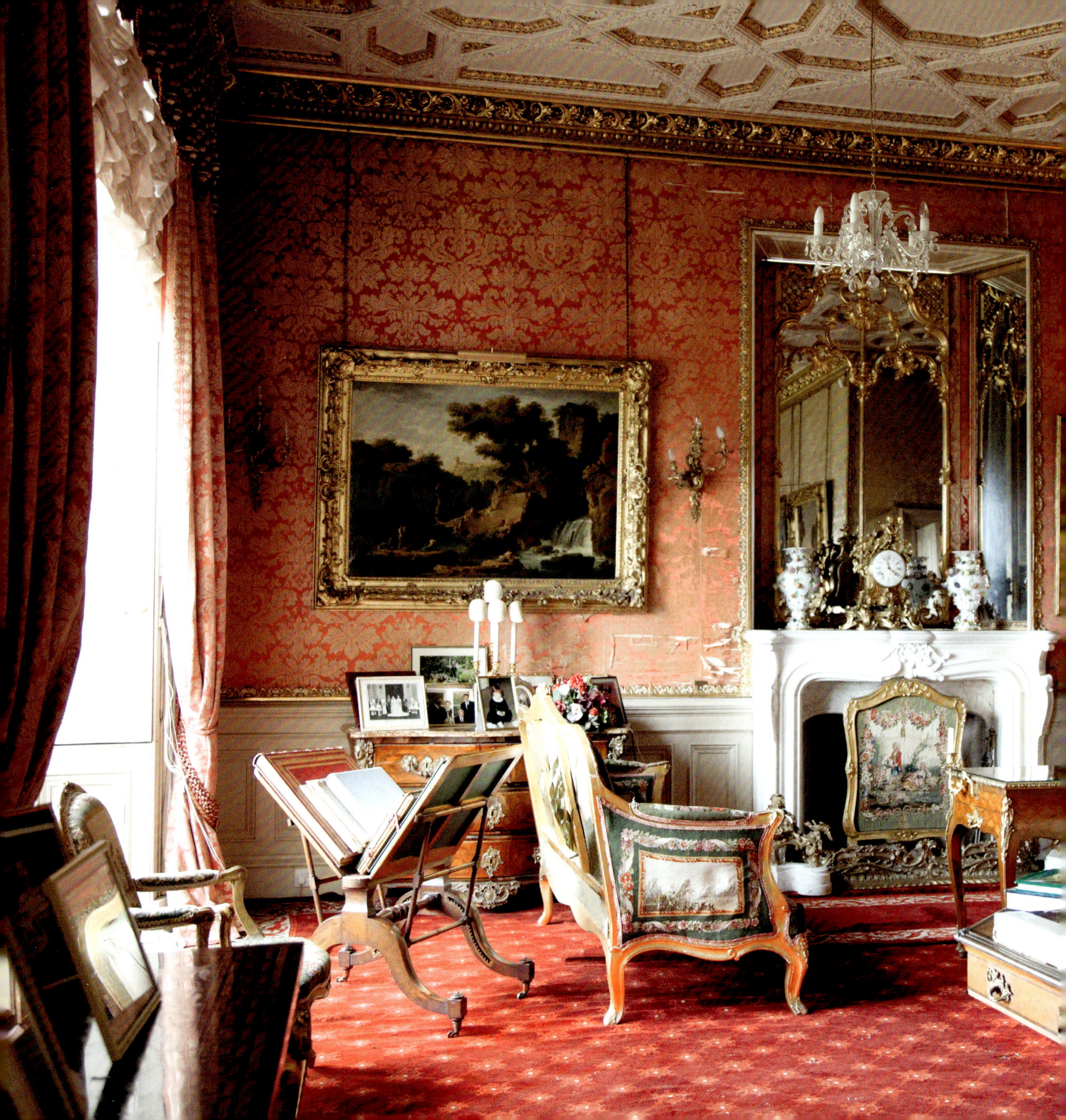

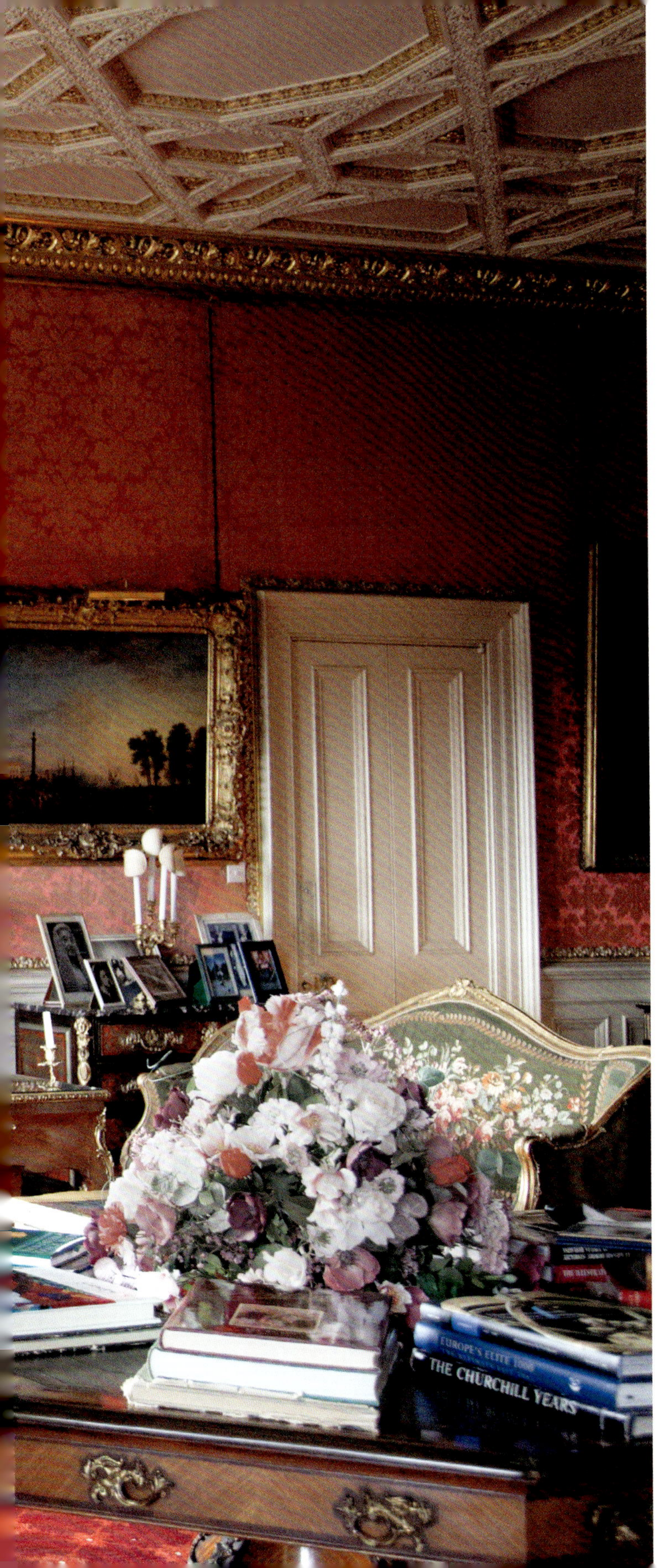

# The Drawing Room

*This is Bowhill at its most opulent: walls of crimson damask, an elaborate gilded ceiling and magnificent mirrors that reflect fine views and masterpieces of landscape painting*

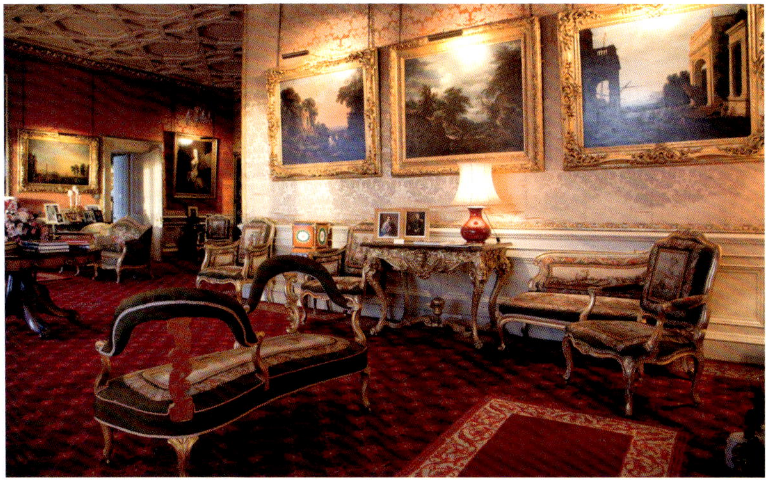

The opulent Drawing Room, with its damask walls and elaborate gilded ceilings, is a curious shape that reflects the evolution of Bowhill. By turning the house back to front, as Burn did in 1832, it was possible for all the major living rooms to face south, with fine views. An alcove with French windows replaced the front door in the new Drawing Room. Burn persuaded the 5th Duke that the room's 'irregular shape' would make it 'exceedingly beautiful and most comfortable'.

The furniture is predominantly French. In front of the fireplace is a Louis XV games table by JF Oeben that opens to reveal chess and backgammon boards. Either side of the fireplace overleaf (but barely visible) are Boulle side tables from the Duchesse de Bourgogne's apartments in the Menagerie at Versailles.

LEFT *Crimson damask walls, bleached gold by the sun, and furniture disposed informally rather than stiffly against the walls. The fireplace here is ingeniously designed: the mirror above it is hinged and opens to reveal a window; the flue divides in two and now runs behind the Vernet landscapes on either side*
ABOVE *A stormy Ruisdael is flanked by a pair of serene views by Claude*
OVERLEAF *The piano stands where the front door once was. The Dining Room lies beyond the Saloon and Morning Room*

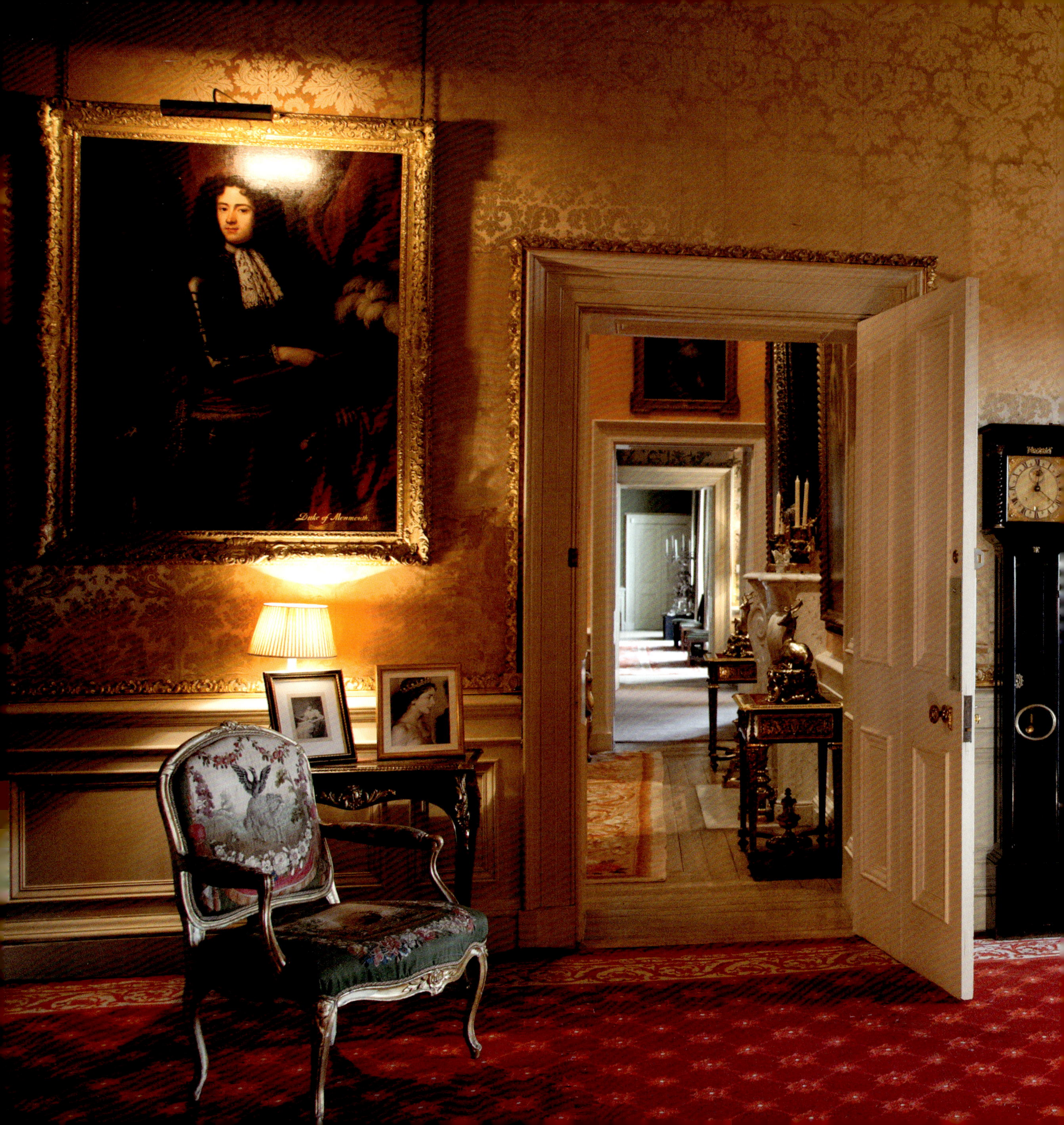
Duke of Monmouth

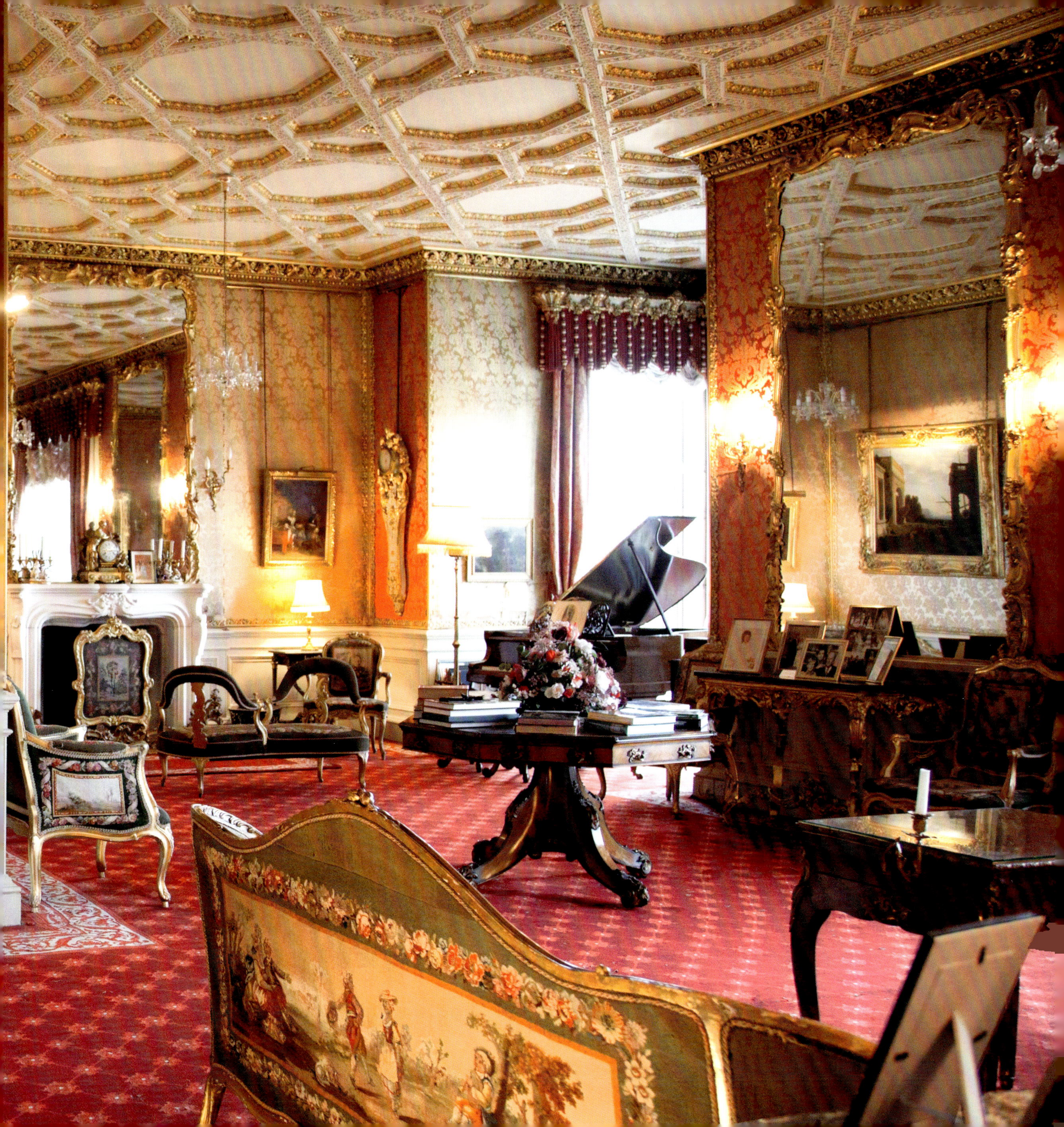

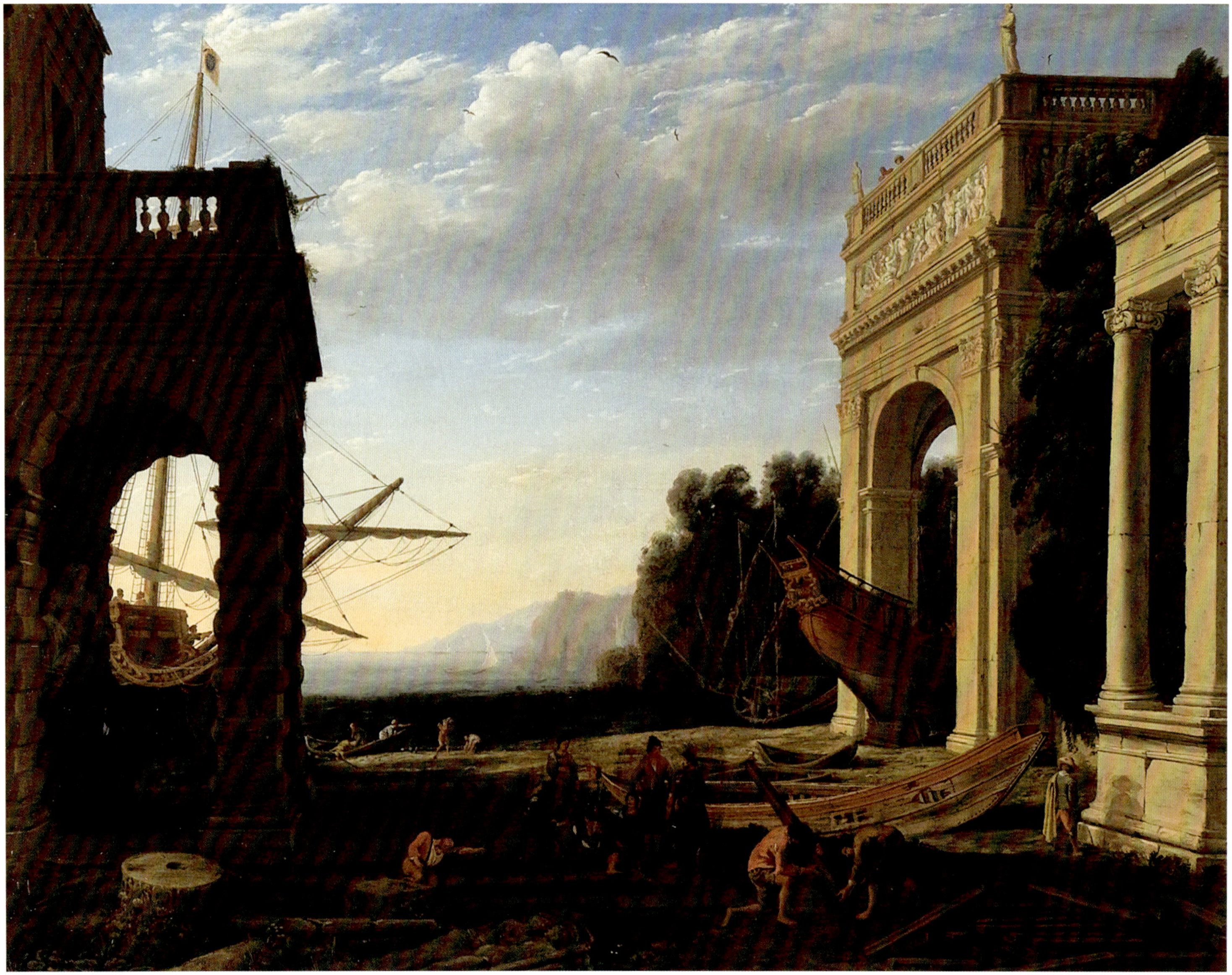

## Paintings in pairs

Two pairs of pictures – in both cases a contrasting seascape and landscape – are the jewels of the Drawing Room. They were inherited by Duchess Elizabeth, wife of the 3rd Duke of Buccleuch, from her parents, the Duke and Duchess of Montagu, who had bought them in Paris in the 1760s.

On the wall facing the huge windows hangs two works by the French 17th-century master of poetic landscape painting, Claude Gellée, better known as Claude Lorrain or simply Claude. *The Mediterranean Harbour* and *The Judgement of Paris* are the first examples of the paired paintings for which he became famous.

Either side of the fireplace is another fine pair of paintings, by Claude-Joseph Vernet, an admirer of Claude working a century later (following pages). Vernet often painted canvases intended to hang alongside works by Claude himself.

Claude, an exceptional draughtsman and engraver who spent most of his life in

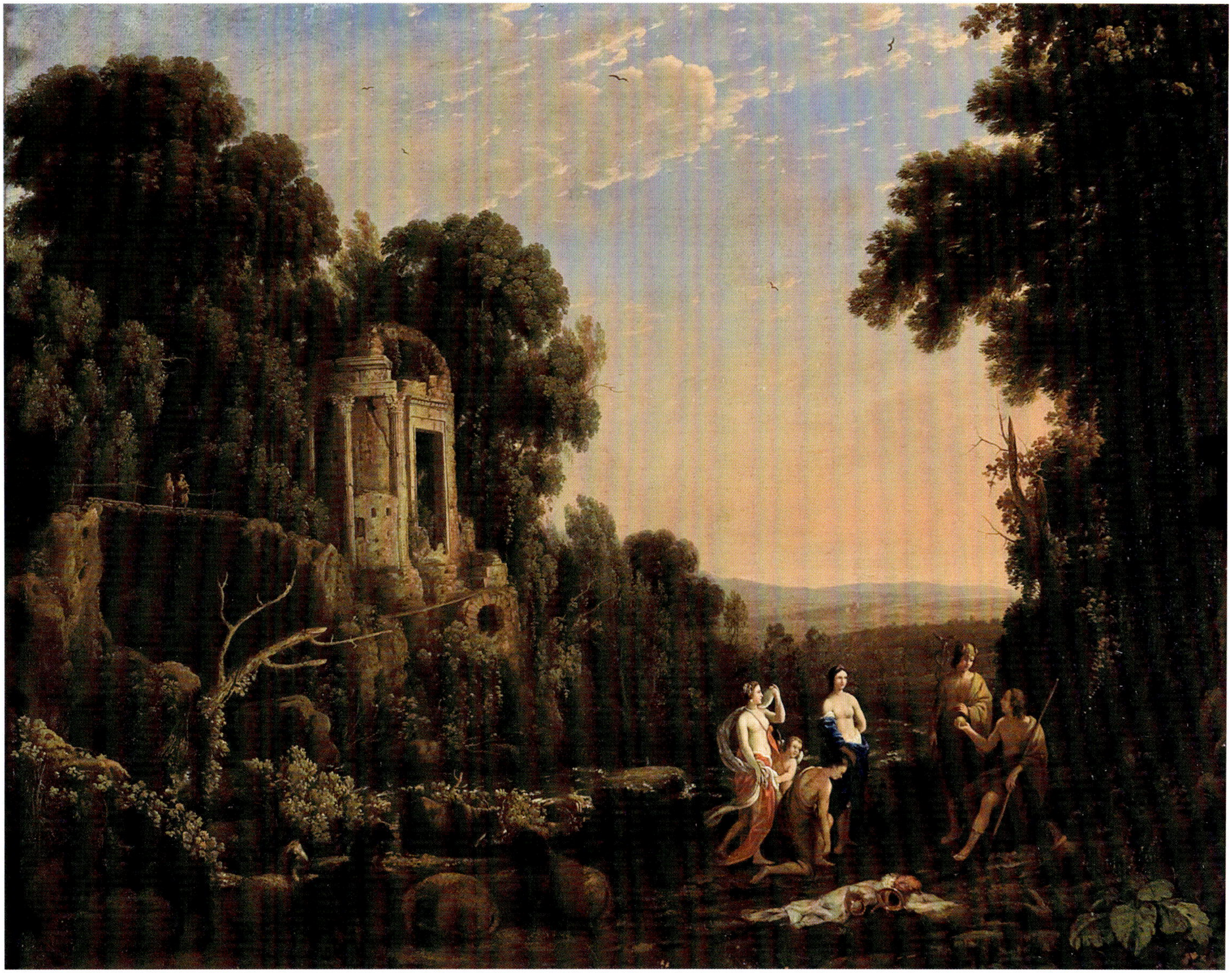

Italy, was hugely influential and popular with his original, predominantly Italian and German, patrons and with later generations of British art collectors. His mastery of light was acknowledged by subsequent painters, including Turner. The Bowhill Claudes are allegorical works that make dramatic use of contrast: the golden dawn in one of the pair is contrasted with melancholy dusk in the other, new public buildings with crumbling ruins, progress with disaster.

Between the pair by Claude hangs another masterpiece, an atmospheric landscape painted in the 1650s by Jacob van Ruisdael (overleaf). Inherited by Caroline Campbell, it once hung in the Duke of Argyll's house in Oxfordshire.

Claude Gellée, Le Lorrain (c.1600–82)
**A Mediterranean Seaport (opposite) and The Judgement of Paris (above), both 1633**
*The earliest of Claude's famous paired paintings hang in the Drawing Room. The melancholy crumbling ruins in 'The Judgement of Paris' foretell the ruin of Troy*

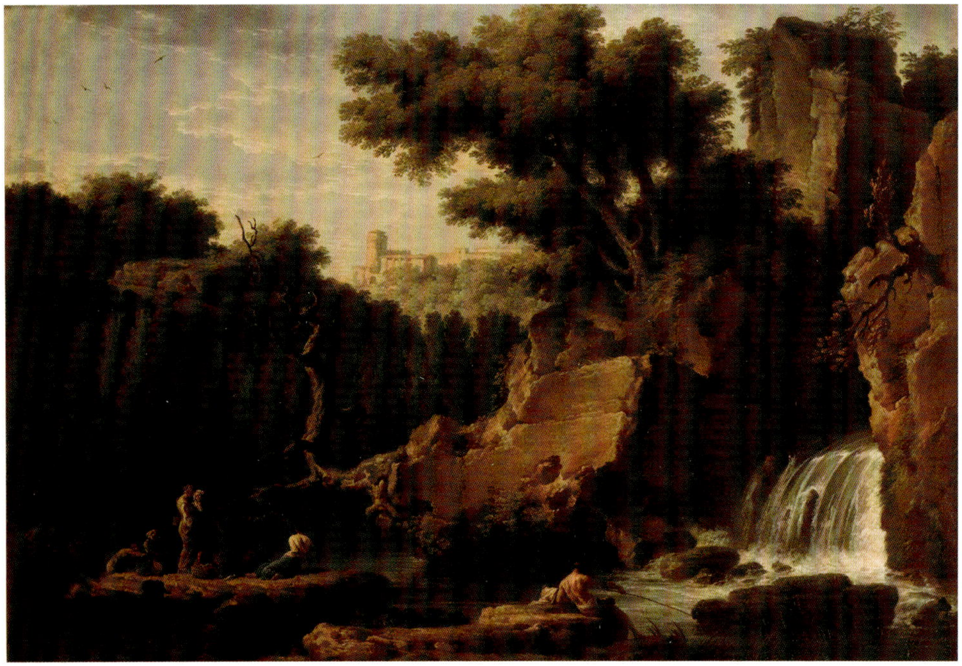

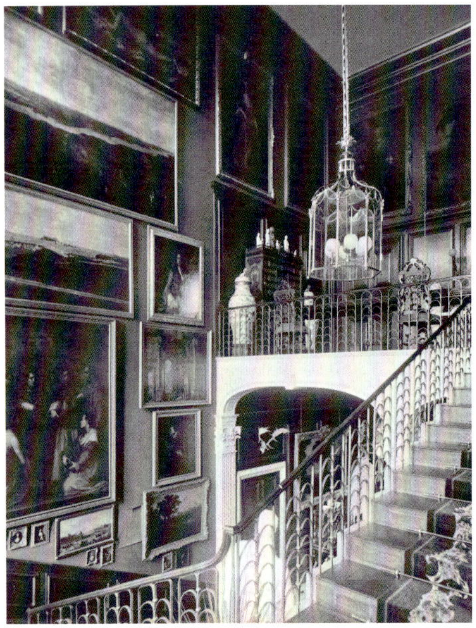

Above and overleaf
Claude-Joseph Vernet (1714–89)
**View of Tivoli, 1746, and A Mediterranean Seaport, 1750**
*These were acquired in Paris in the 1760s by the Duke and Duchess of Montagu, who also bought the Leonardo. The 'View of Tivoli' was a wedding gift to their daughter Elizabeth. Like his hero Claude, Vernet was a favourite of British collectors*

Right Jacob van Ruisdael (c.1628–1682)
**Hilly Wooded Landscape, early 1650s**
*Rich ochres and vivid green foliage are typical of the Dutch artist in his 20s, when he first used the device of high ground framing a distant view. His three-dimensional monogram is on the left*

Left *Many of Bowhill's paintings were once hung in tiers at Dalkeith, as in this 1902 photograph*

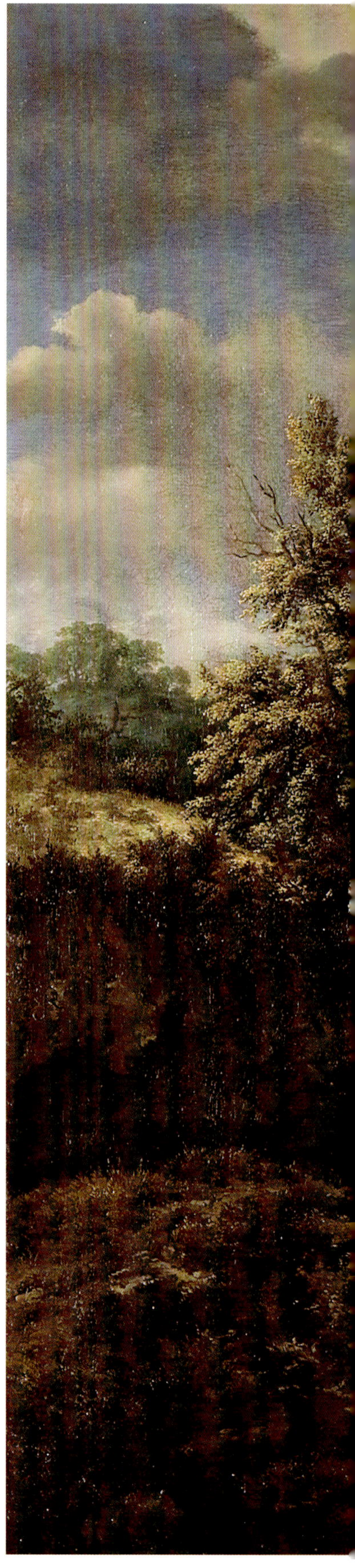

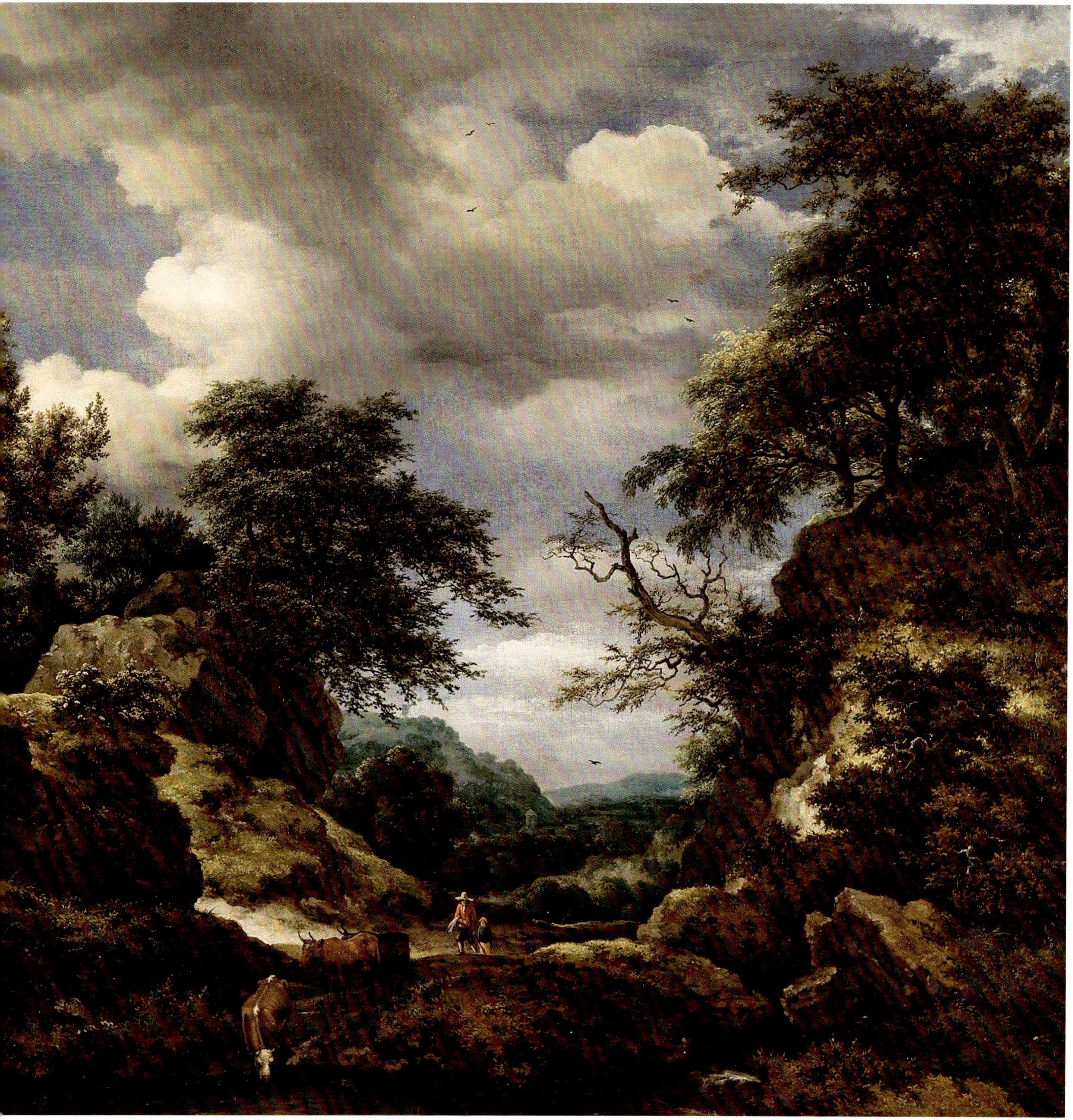

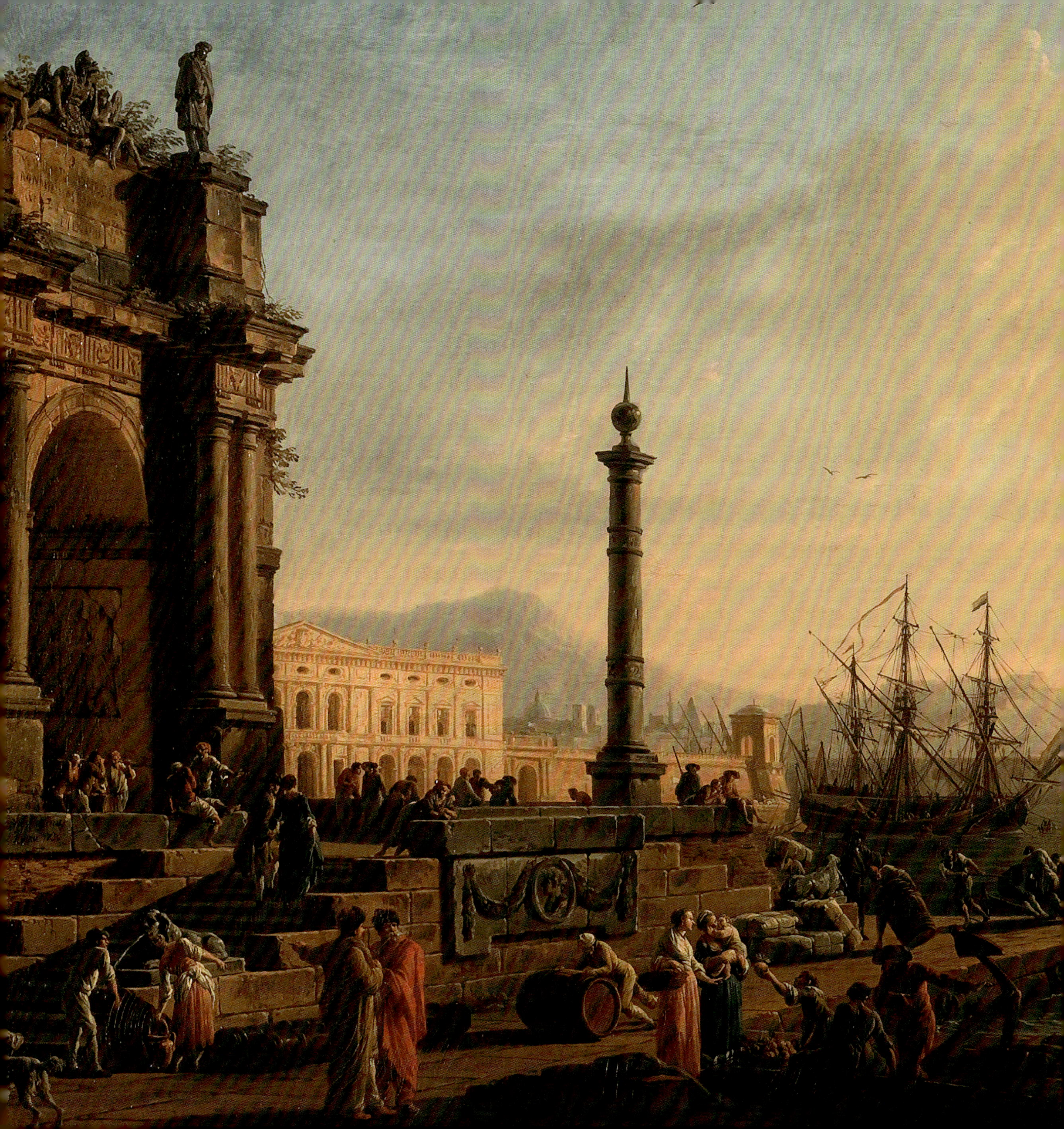

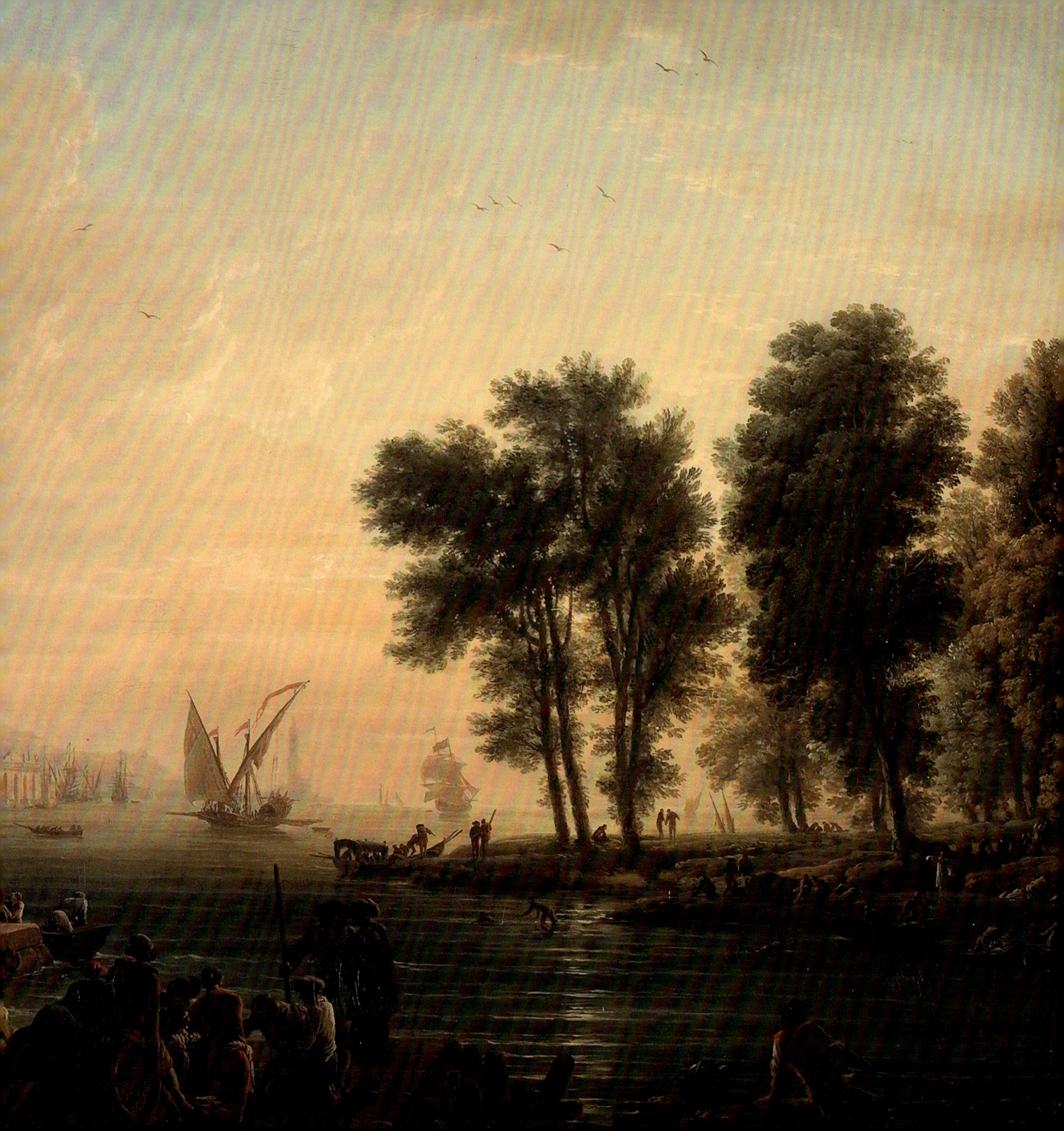

# The Morning Room

*The Morning Room brings a touch of light relief to the centre of the house with its pale colours, comfortable furniture and beautifully fanciful Chinese wallpaper*

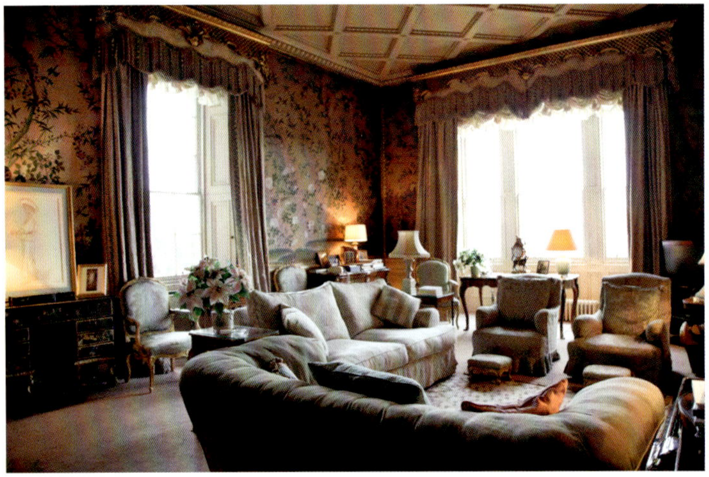

Subtle pastel shades make this a relaxed family sitting room, with sofas and chairs designed for comfort. As its name suggests, the room catches the morning light, and was a place to read the papers, meet for a drink before lunch in the Dining Room next door – and perhaps enjoy a quiet snooze afterwards. The room evokes the spirit of the present Duke's grandmother Molly Buccleuch, who was a close friend of the artist Edward Seago. His watercolour of the room, painted in October 1953, picks up the lovely Chinese wallpaper and captures the mood, as does a pastel of the Duke's sister, Charlotte Anne.

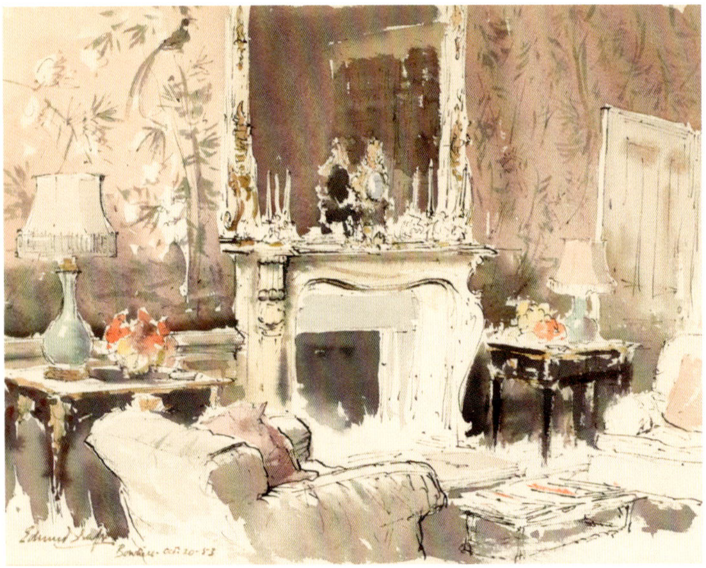

CAPTURING THE LIGHT

RIGHT *The tone of this light and airy room is set by the pale-pink Chinese wallpaper and the celadon and ivory damasks that hang at the windows and cover the armchairs and Louis XV fauteuils. 'Sea-green' Meissen soup tureens on the mantelpiece add dashes of colour*

TOP LEFT *The portrait of Charlotte Anne de Castellane, the present Duke's sister, is by their great-aunt, the portrait painter Molly Bishop. It sits on the far left on a coromandel lacquer and gilt desk attributed to Gerrit Jensen, c.1685*

LEFT EDWARD SEAGO (1910–74)
**The Morning Room, Bowhill, 1953**
*This is one of numerous works by Seago acquired by the present Duke's grandparents*

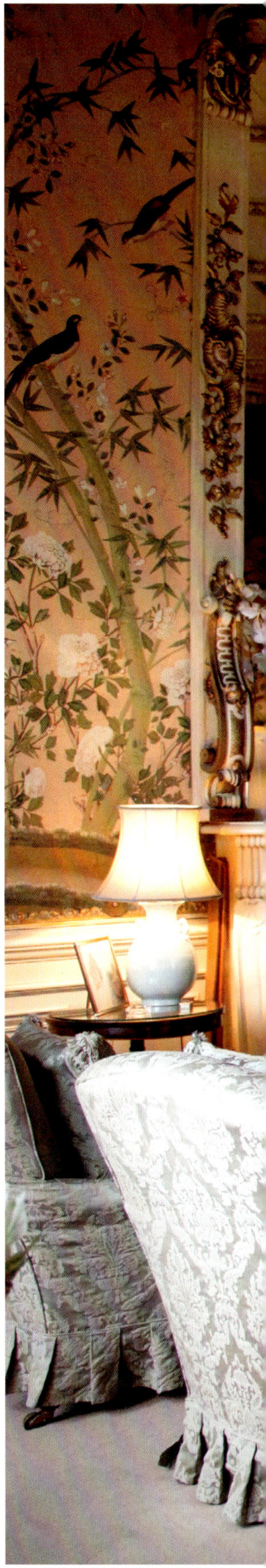

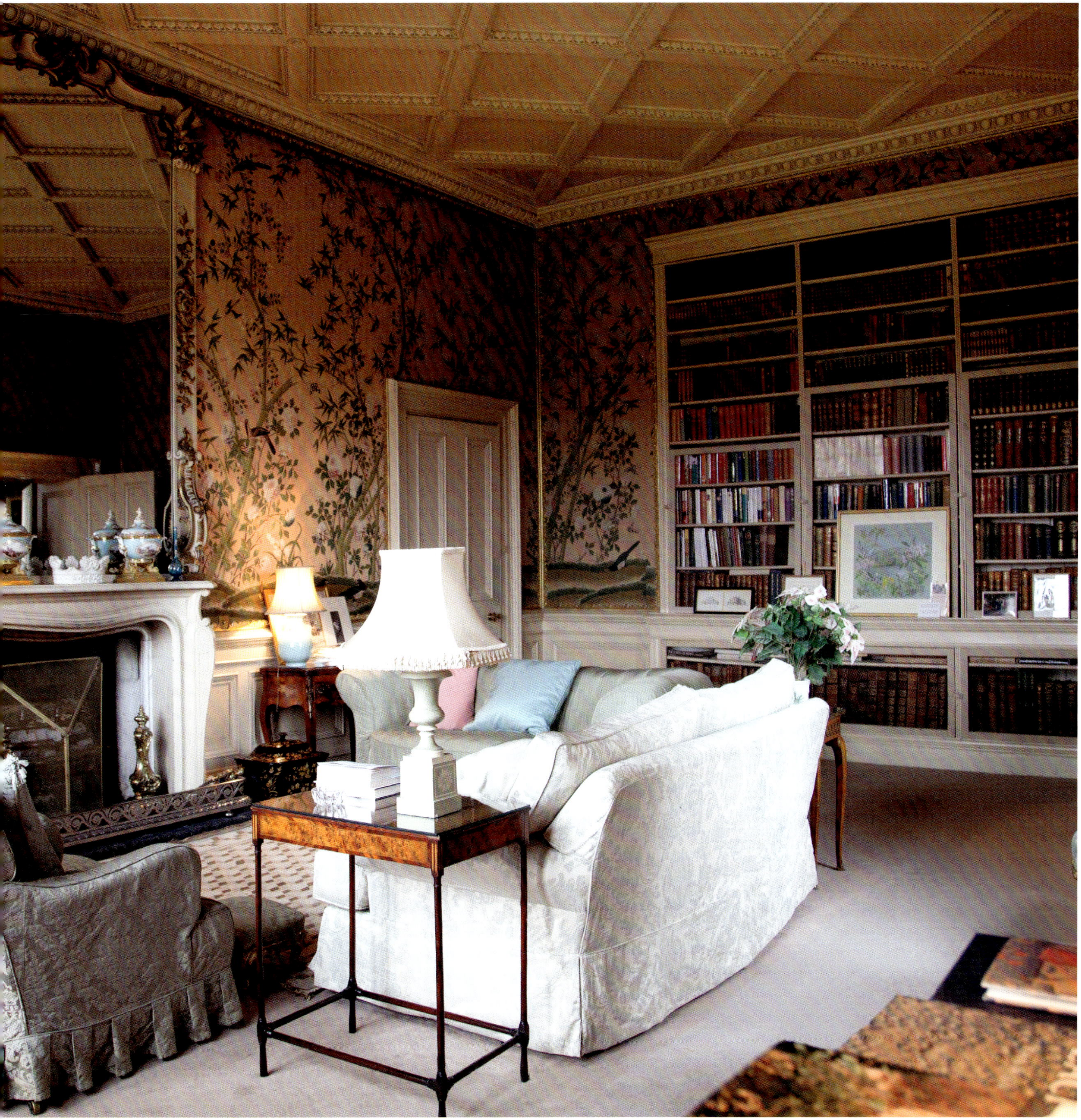

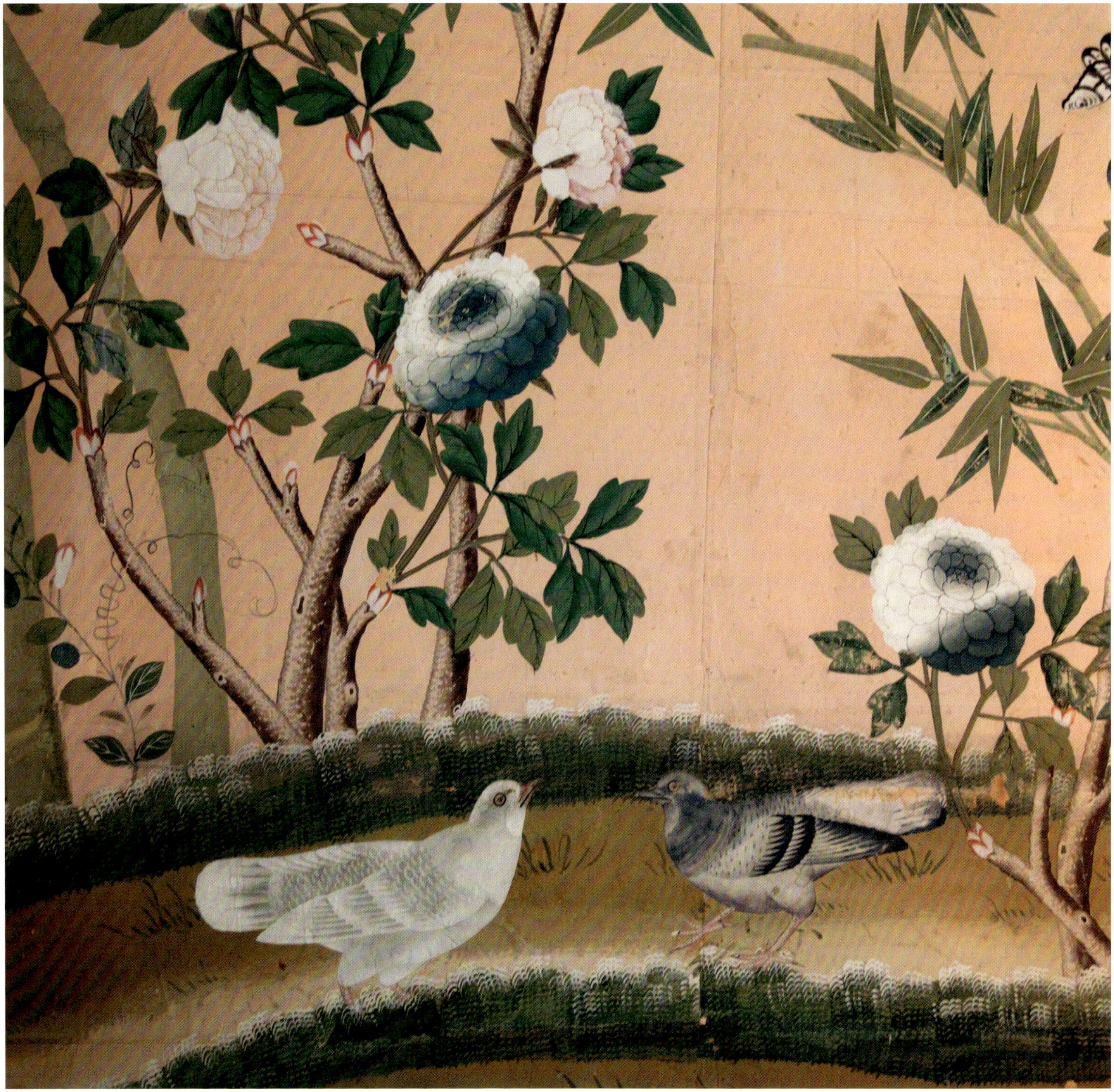

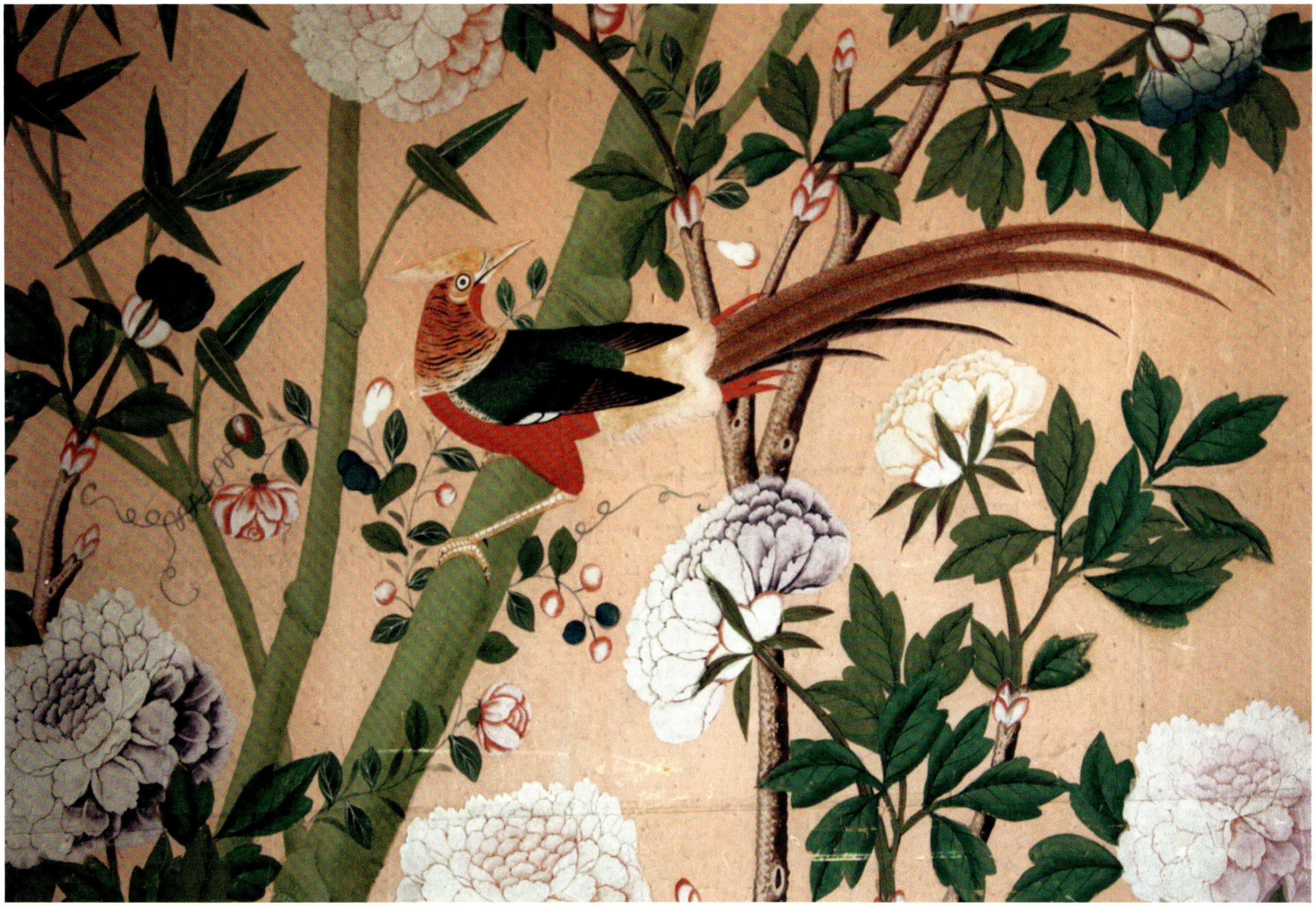

## The Chinese wallpaper

The family were particularly fond of hand-painted Chinese wallpaper. At Bowhill it appears in the Morning Room (on these pages) and in the Duchess's Boudoir, at the far end of the house (pages 112–117), where the design is even paler and more delicate.

Another example, with a dark green ground, is to be found in the dining room at Eildon Hall, a family home a few miles away where generations of Montagu Douglas Scotts have been brought up.

According to family tradition, the rolls of wallpaper, exquisitely hand-painted with no obvious repeating patterns, were given to Duchess Harriet, wife of the 4th Duke, by Lord Macartney, who led the British embassy to the Emperor of China in the late 18th century. Sadly, this is belied by correspondence indicating that at least one set was provided by the London firm of Cowtan, in December 1834.

ABOVE *An exotic bird with bright plumage perches among peonies on a giant bamboo*

OPPOSITE *A dove and pigeon on the forest floor. It is a wonder that these wallpapers survived two world wars in which the house served as a military hospital and barracks. Although there is no evidence, rumour has it that soldiers used the birds for target practice*

# The Dining Room

*Added in an era of expansion, as a counterpart to the Library, this is where family and friends have always gathered for feasting and reeling. It is also a gallery for Bowhill's finest 18th-century paintings*

Built by the 4th Duke in 1817, and enlarged by his son in the 1830s, the Dining Room provides space for a great gallery of paintings – as well as serving as a ballroom for Christmas reel parties. Dominating either end are Jan Griffier's view of the Thames at Westminster and Canaletto's panorama of Whitehall, showing the back of Montagu House, both painted in the middle of the 18th century.

Between them is a series of exceptional portraits by Gainsborough and Reynolds of Henry, 3rd Duke of Buccleuch, Elizabeth Montagu, his wife, two of their children and his Montagu parents-in-law.

Standing at the end of the room is a massive silver candelabra by Garrard, with an animated stag and figures, which tells the story of the origins of the Buccleuch name. Similar in scale is the gigantic silver wine cooler made in 1702 for the 2nd Duke of Argyll's appointment as ambassador to Spain.

Three of the early Meissen vases below the Griffier were acquired in the 19th century. A sharp-eyed Christie's expert spotted the matching two in a sale in 2008; they were bought to reunite the full original set of five.

The fireplace came from Montagu House in London, replacing an austere black one now stored in the basement. On the mantelpiece are a pair of double-magnum decanters by William Bielby, made circa 1770 and inscribed with the word 'claret'.

THE DINING ROOM, LOOKING WEST

*The white marble caryatids of a Neoclassical fireplace brought from Montagu House watch over a table set for 20. The Turkey-pattern carpet appears in early inventories. Jan Griffier the Younger's 1748 view of the Thames hangs at the far end of the room. In the corner is a double portrait of Elizabeth Montagu (1743–1827), future wife of the 3rd Duke, and her sister Henrietta. Two of Elizabeth's children are the subjects of Reynolds portraits next to the fireplace: 'Winter' shows Caroline Scott, later Marchioness of Queensberry. 'The Pink Boy' is her brother Charles, future 4th Duke, in Van Dyck costume*

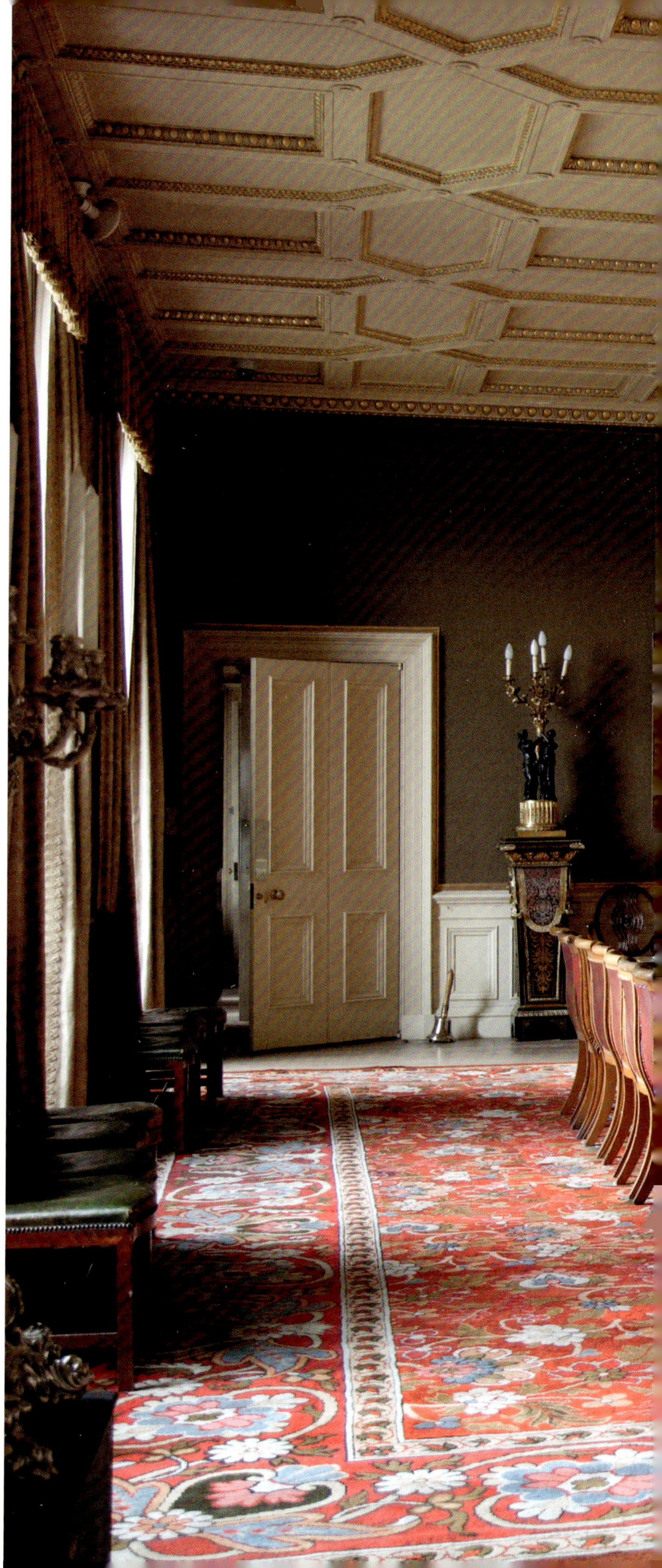

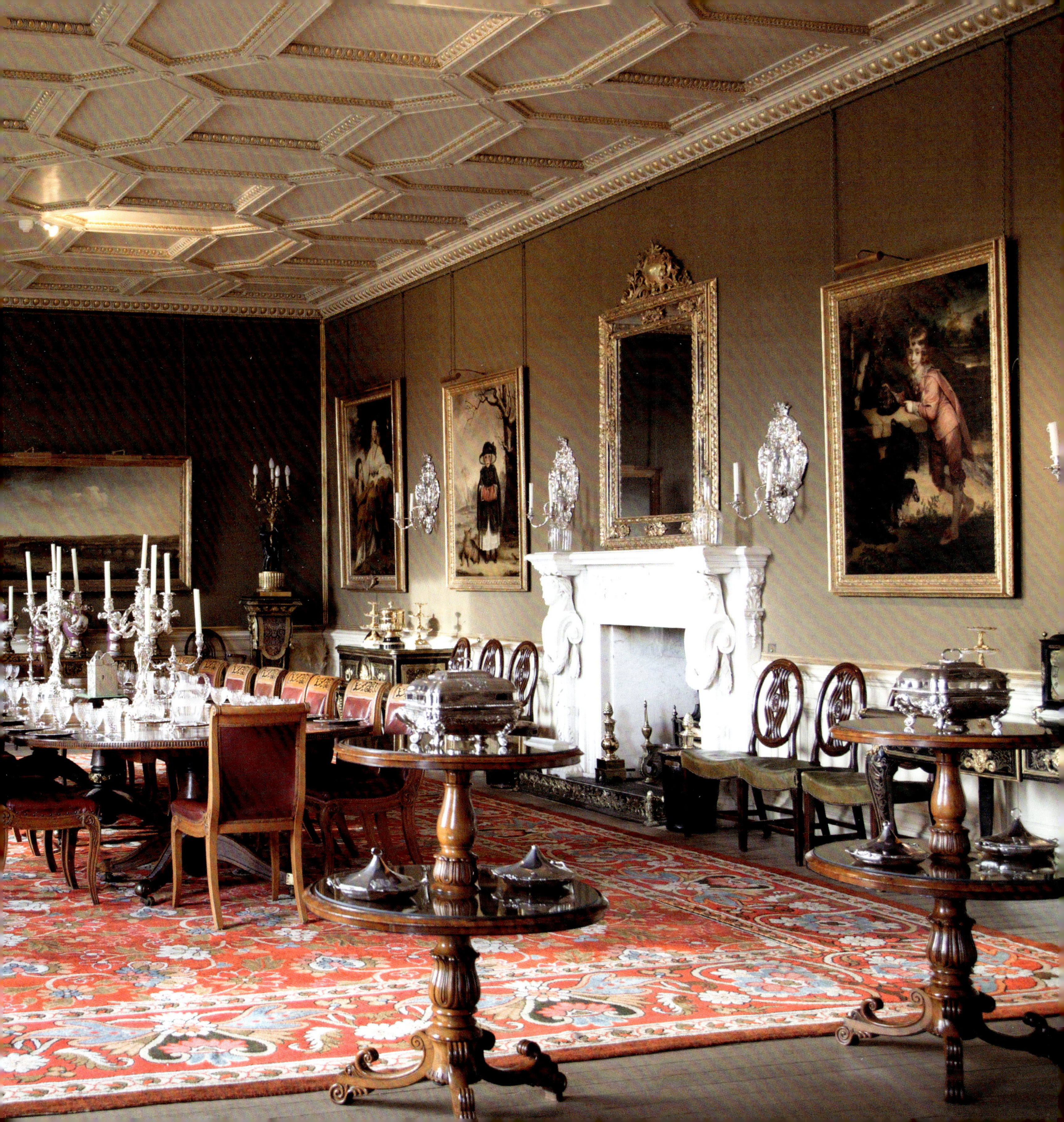

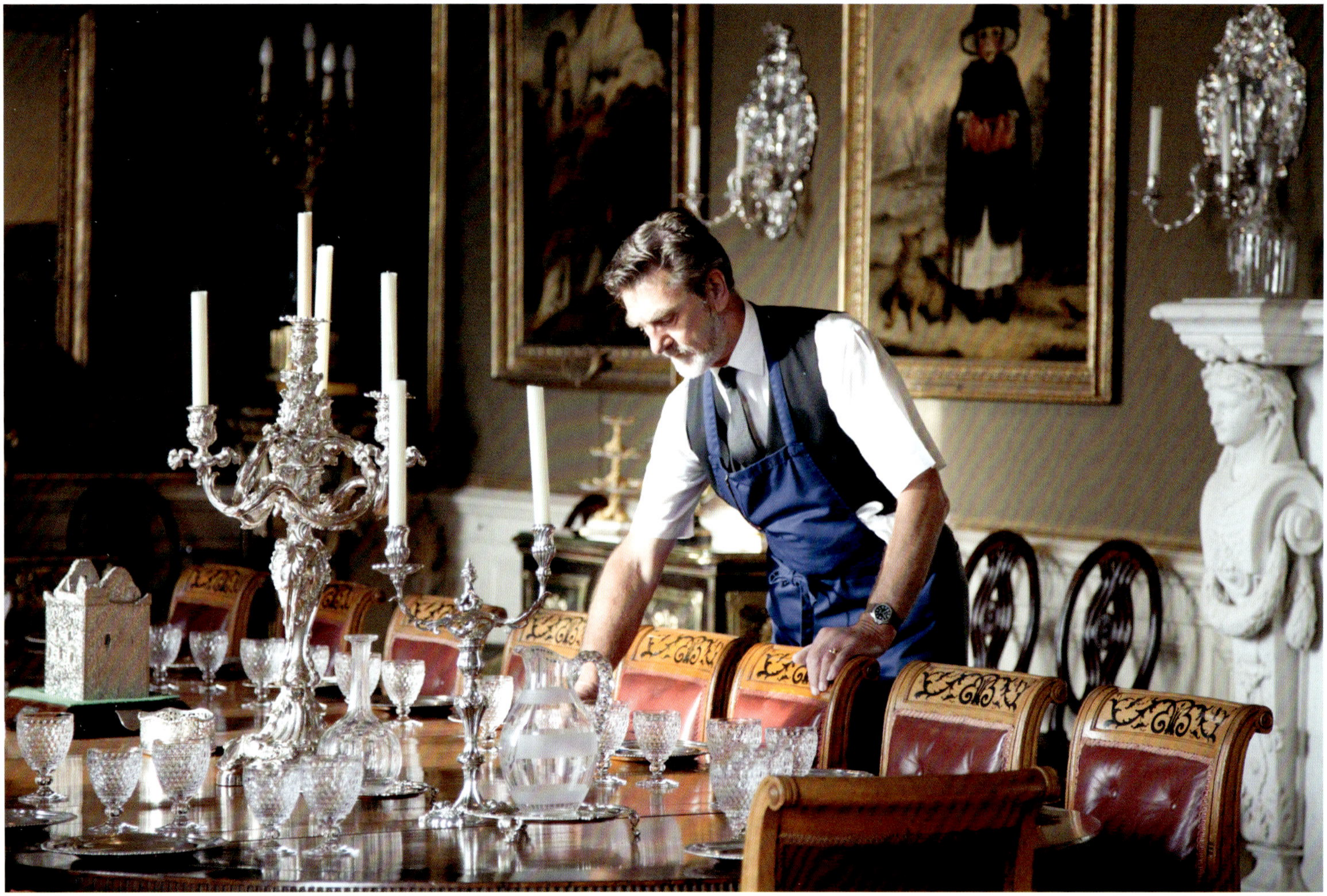

SETTING THE TABLE
*Colin MacIntosh, the family butler seen in these photographs, is tireless in cleaning and caring for the silver. On the right he is carrying a George IV three-light candelabra, one of a pair delivered in 1828 by Robert Garrard. The silver sconces in the photograph above are German, circa 1735, with branches added by Garrard in 1829. The cabinet-maker George Bullock, who had a short but spectacular career, made the George IV dining table, with the matching 'Grecian' dining chairs, as well as the two-tier dumb waiters on the previous page*

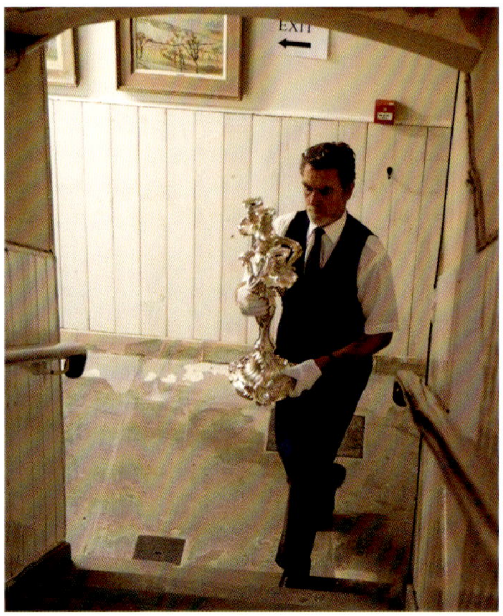


RIGHT SIR JOSHUA REYNOLDS (1723–92)
**Lady Caroline Scott, 1777**
*Reynolds was enchanted when the three-year-old Caroline rushed in from the snow while he was painting her brother Charles as 'The Pink Boy' at Dalkeith. This appealing portrait of her with her red silk muff was painted at his request*

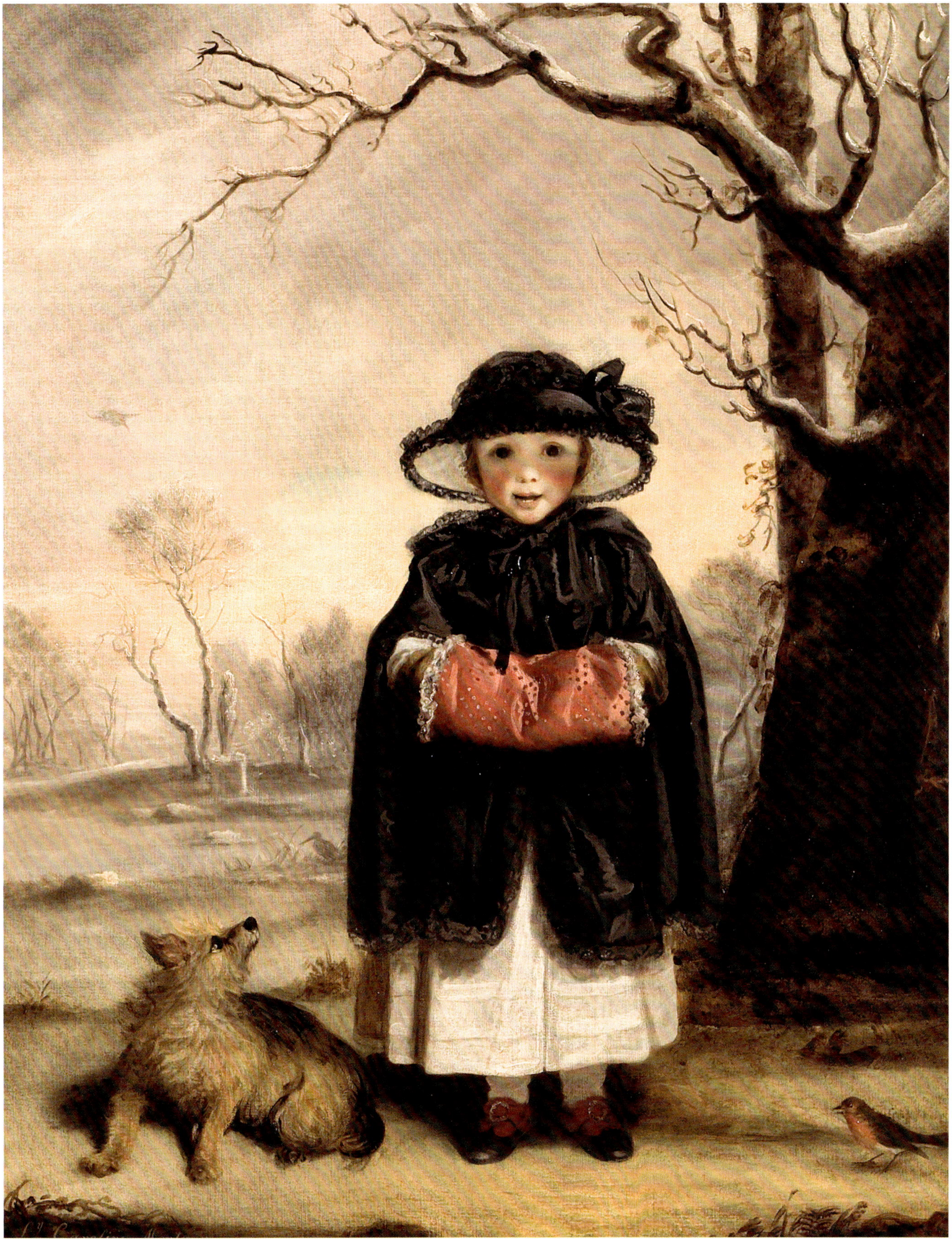

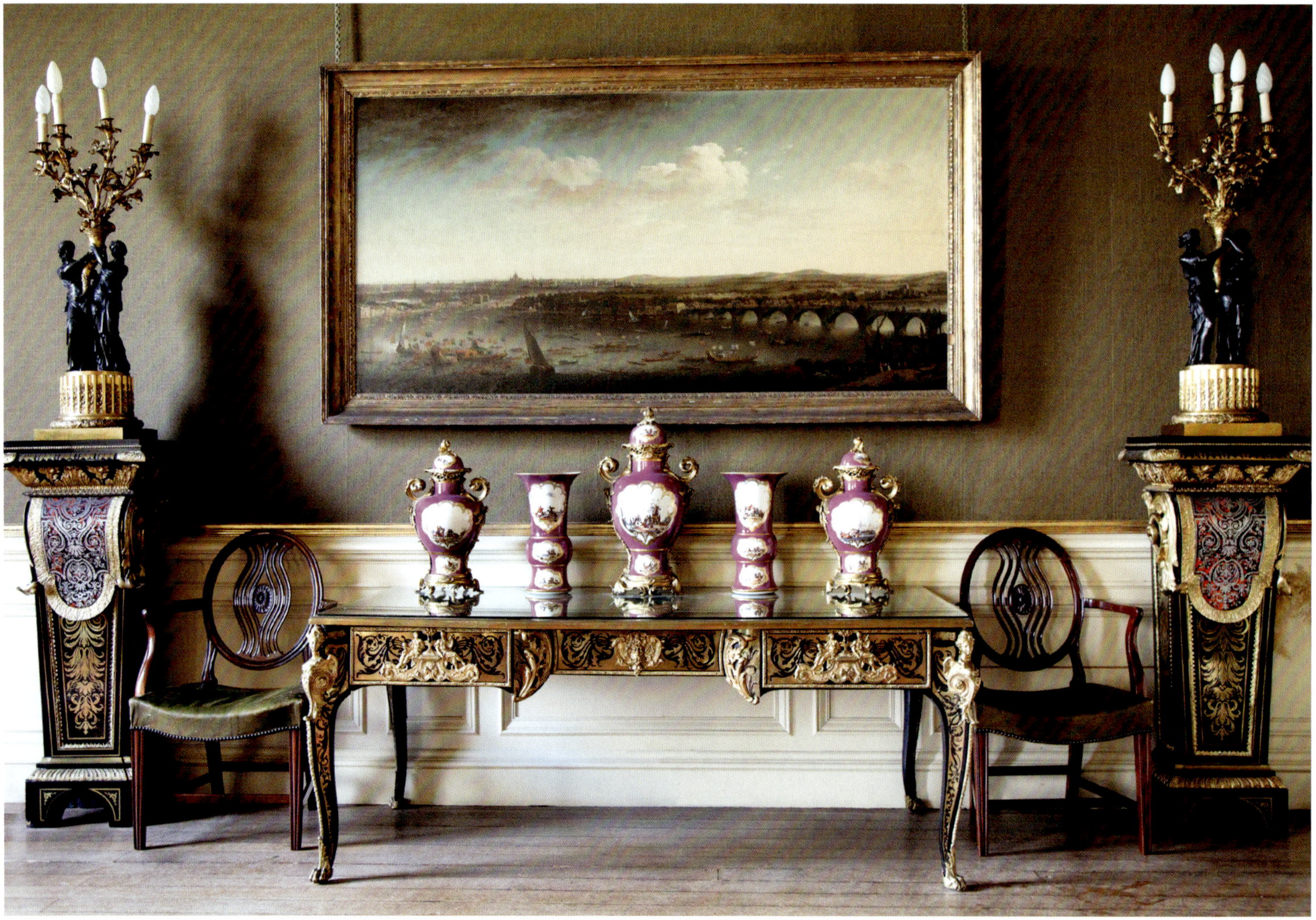

THE DINING ROOM, WESTERN END
*Jan Griffier the Younger's panorama of London was painted only three years before Canaletto's masterpiece (opposite) but is in an obviously earlier style. 'The River Thames with the Royal Barge' depicts a broad stretch of the Thames from Lambeth Palace – visible in the countryside on the right of the picture – downstream all the way to St Paul's, and is signed and dated 1748, the year it was commissioned by John, 2nd Duke of Montagu, who died the following year. His executors paid the artist £36.15s in 1749. The 'Boulle' bureau-plat and pair of pedestals inlaid with tortoiseshell were all supplied by Baldock and are apparently 19th century. The 'garniture', or set, of powdered lilac early Meissen vases is finely painted by CF Herold with camp and battle scenes. The narrow vases were acquired in 2008, reuniting the set*

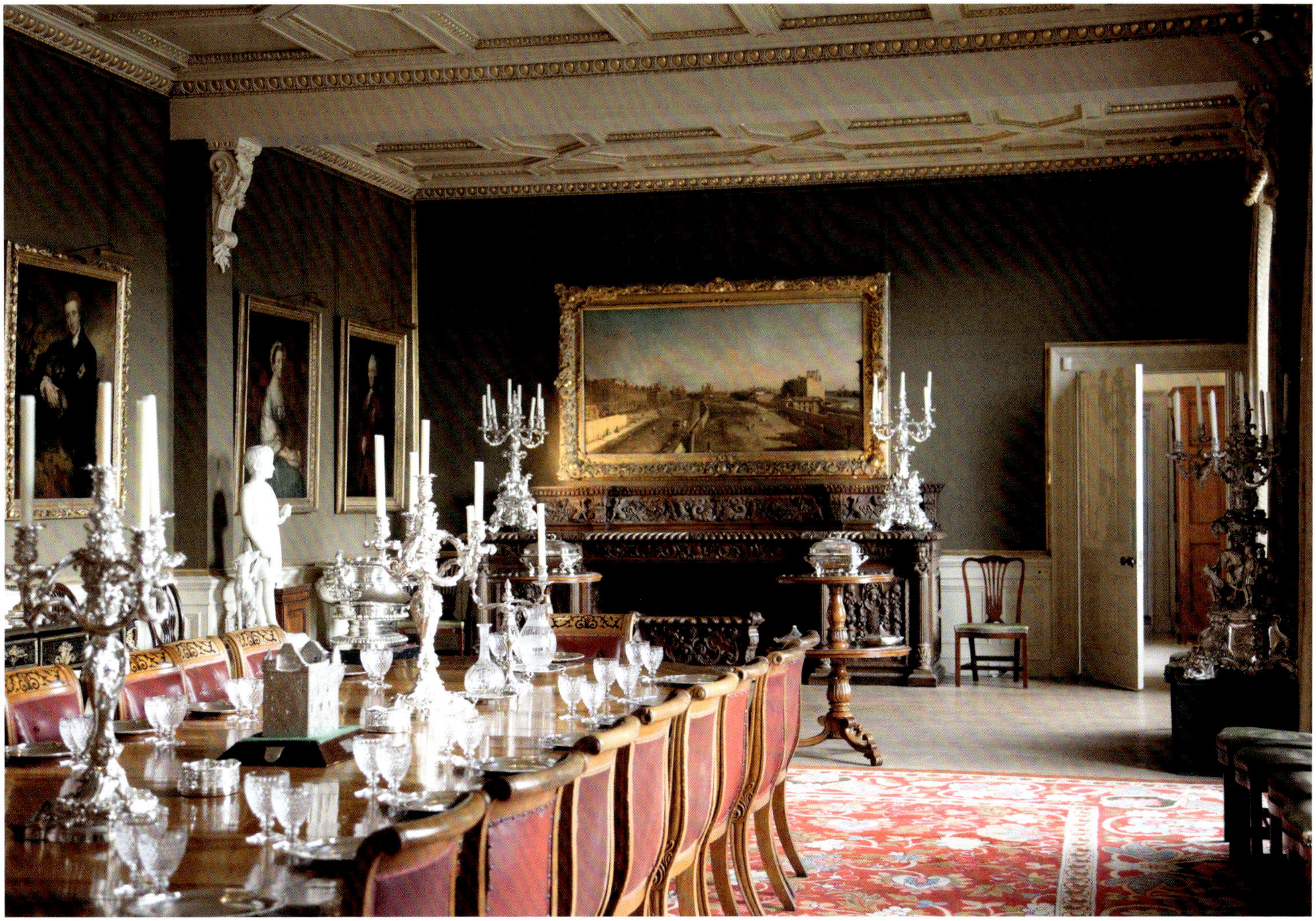

The Dining Room, looking east
*The massive Victorian oak sideboard and wine cooler below the Canaletto may seem surprising in view of the finesse of so many of the 5th Duke's choices. They were made up from antique carvings in 1833 by the Scottish cabinet-maker James Morison. The three Gainsborough portraits show the 3rd Duke and his parents-in-law, Mary, Duchess of Montagu, and George, 3rd Duke of Montagu. The candelabra on the far right depicts the origin of the Buccleuch name (see the Exhibition Room, page 128)*

Overleaf
Antonio Canaletto (1697–1768)
**View of Whitehall, 1751 or 1752**
*Painted on Canaletto's second visit to London, this is a most unusual panorama in terms of subject matter. Almost eight feet wide, it was bought by the 5th Duke for its depiction of Montagu House, his residence on the Thames (page 23), seen on the right with its tall chimneys and view of St Paul's. In the distance stand the Palace of Westminster and the Banqueting House, The Duke paid £400 for the painting in 1839*

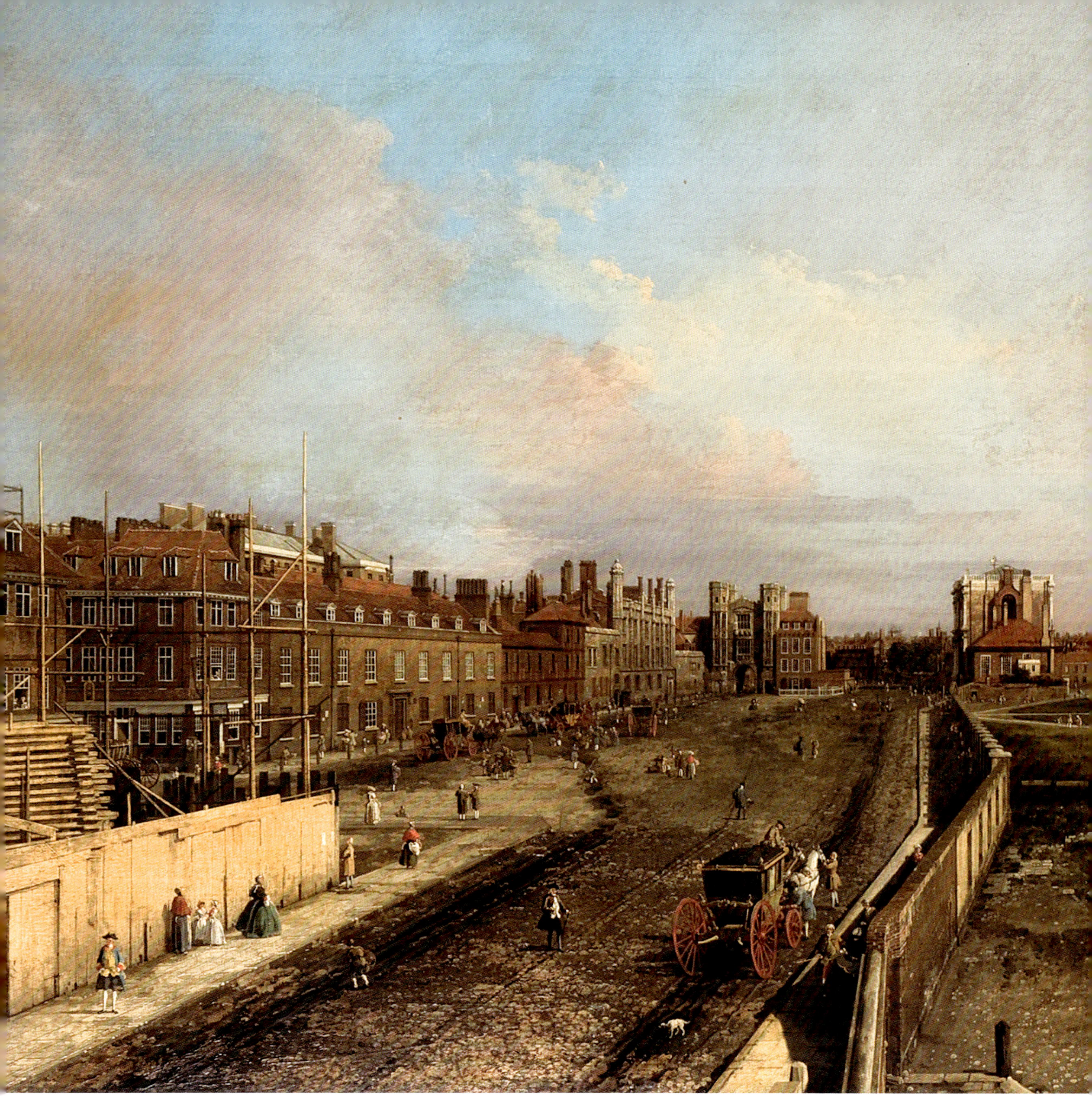

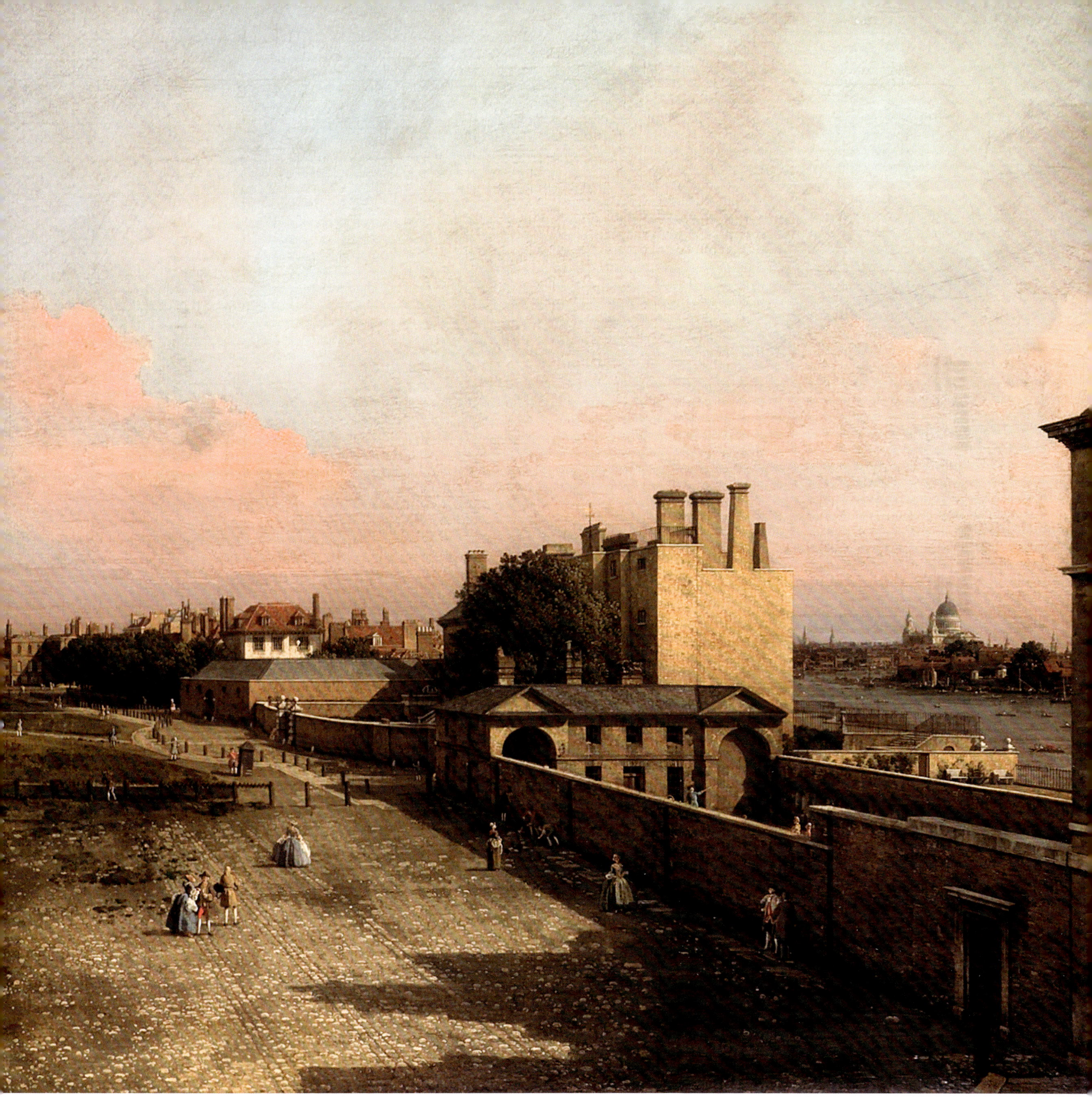

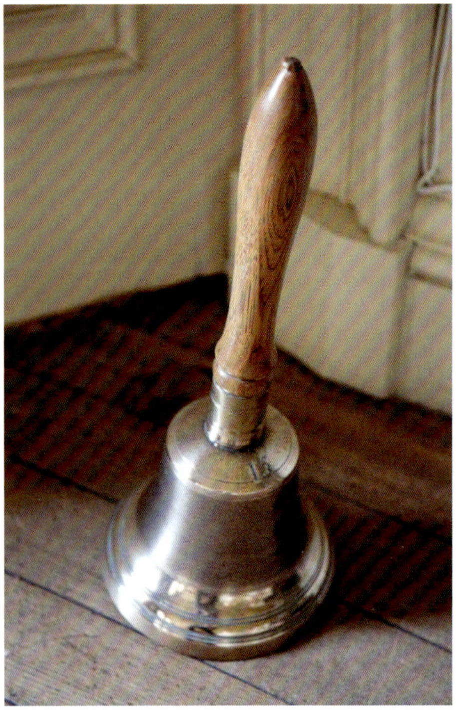

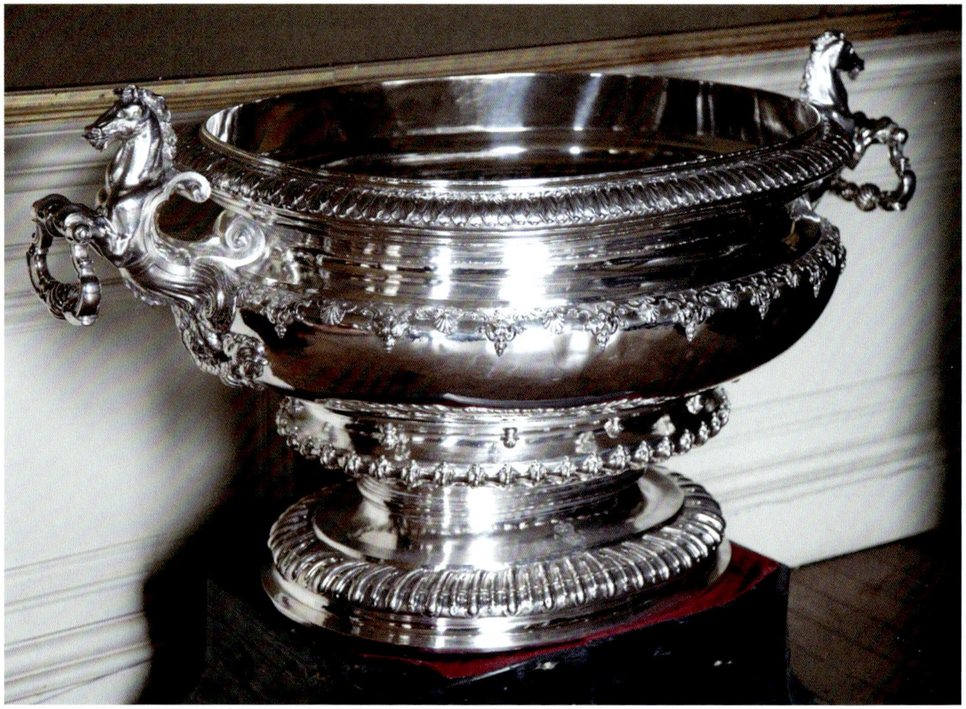

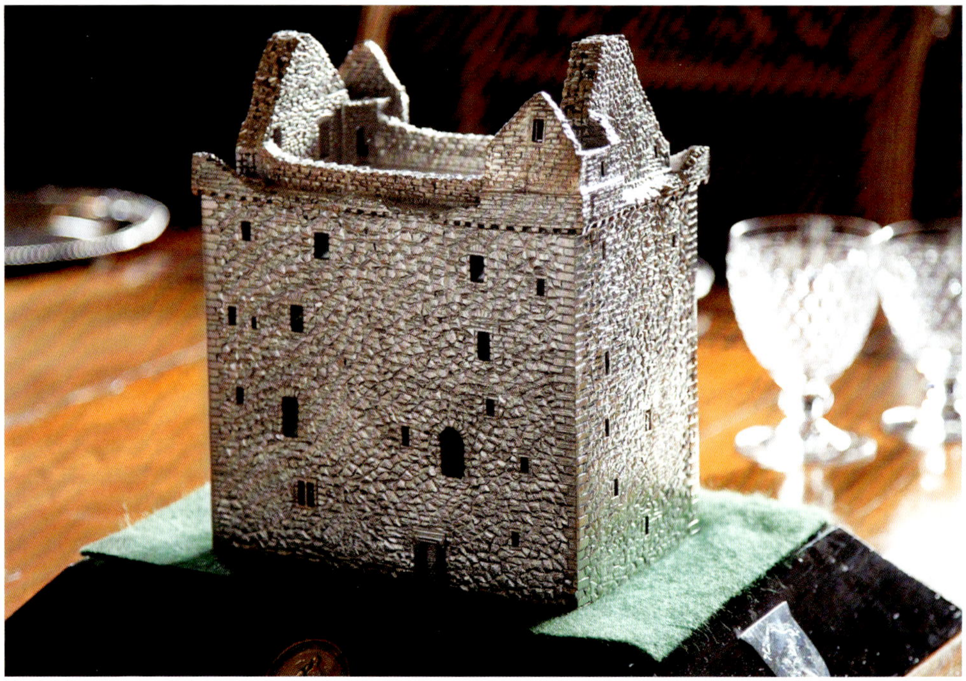

ABOVE *A large brass 'table bell' engraved with the number 15 – the significance of which is unclear – stands on the floor*

ABOVE RIGHT *This huge Queen Anne oval wine cistern, made by Benjamin Pyne in 1711, weighs more than 9 stone and, unusually, stands on a plinth of solid coal. It was made for John, 2nd Duke of Argyll, on his appointment as ambassador to Charles II of Spain*

RIGHT *This silver model of Newark Castle in its ruined state was a wedding gift to the Earl of Dalkeith, the future 7th Duke, from the Royal Burgh of Selkirk in 1893. It was cast by Messrs Elkington of Birmingham under the direction of the Edinburgh silversmith William Sturrock. Newark Castle is where the Last Minstrel told his tale in Scott's famous poem*

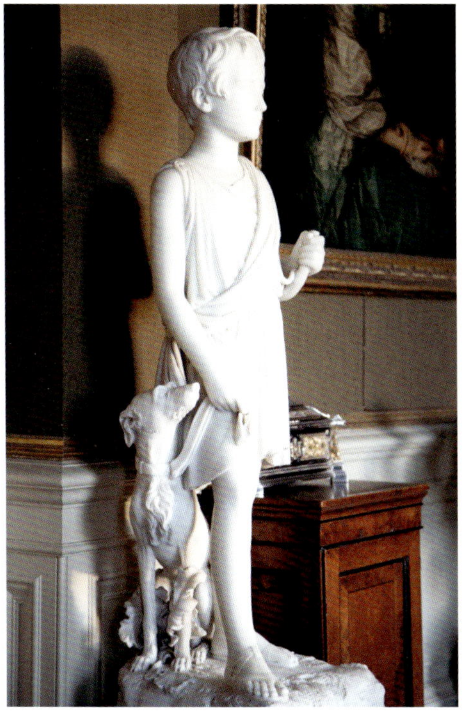

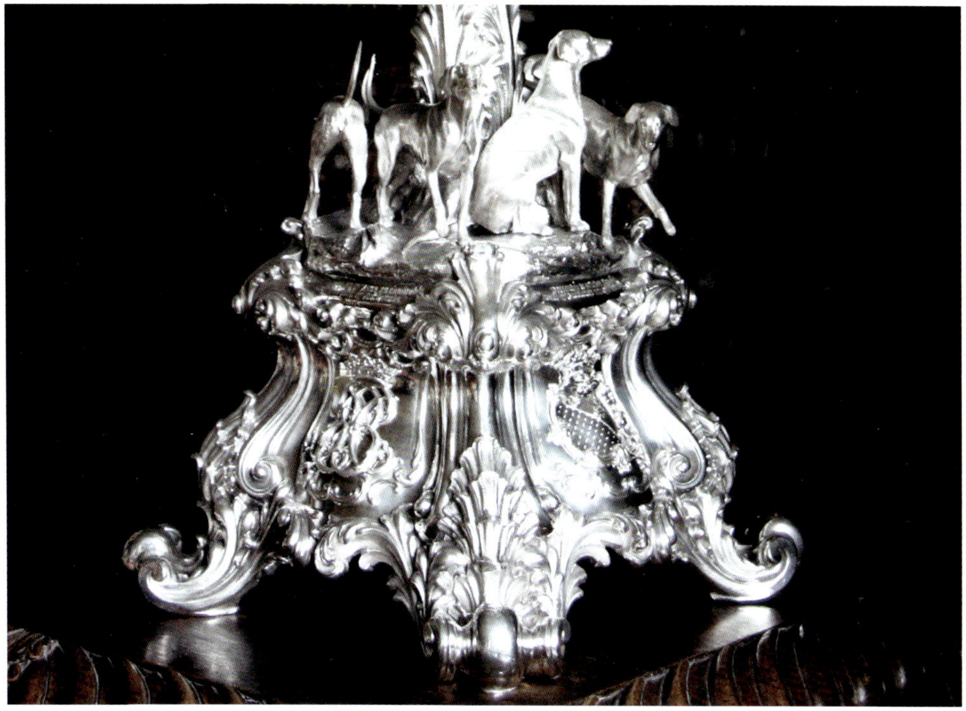

ABOVE *The Earl of Dalkeith, later the 6th Duke, sculpted as a boy by Thomas Campbell in 1840, in Roman dress with a hound at his side. Campbell was paid £1200. He told the Duke in 1845 that it was 'a small group but a very elaborate one', with a price a little over half that of full-sized figures*

ABOVE RIGHT *Hounds decorate a pair of silver candelabra by Garrard, a gift in 1872 from followers of the Buccleuch Hunt. Male hounds appear on one, female on the other*

RIGHT *A double-magnum claret decanter with vines and butterflies on the neck. It is one of a pair, made c.1770, by the pioneering enameller and glassmaker William Bielby of Newcastle-upon-Tyne*

FAR RIGHT *Part of a set of 26 elegant 19th-century wine glasses, enamelled in white with scrolling foliage*

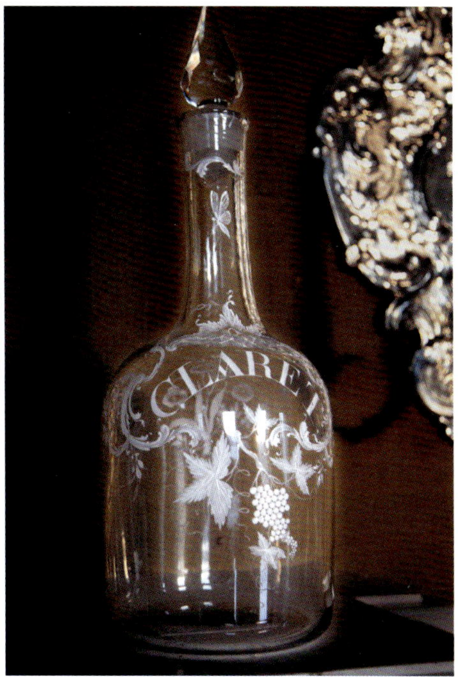


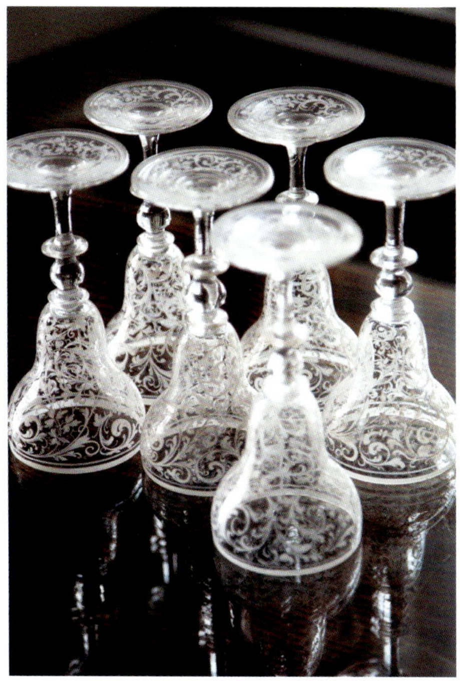

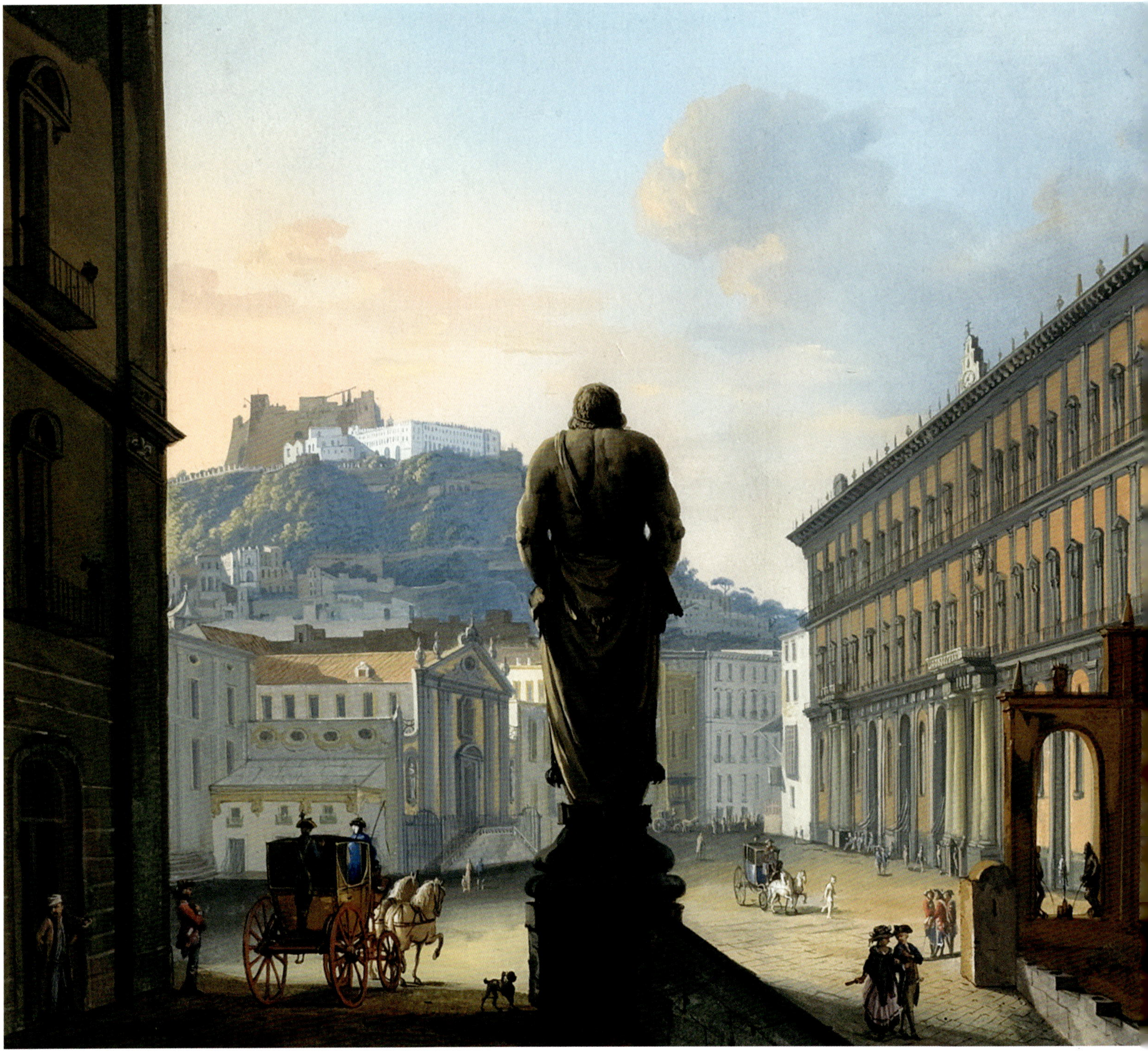

# The Billiard Room

*Beyond the Dining Room, as far as possible from the Duchess's realm, is the male domain – the Billiard Room and Smoking Room. These have now been given over to books and to paintings from the Grand Tour*

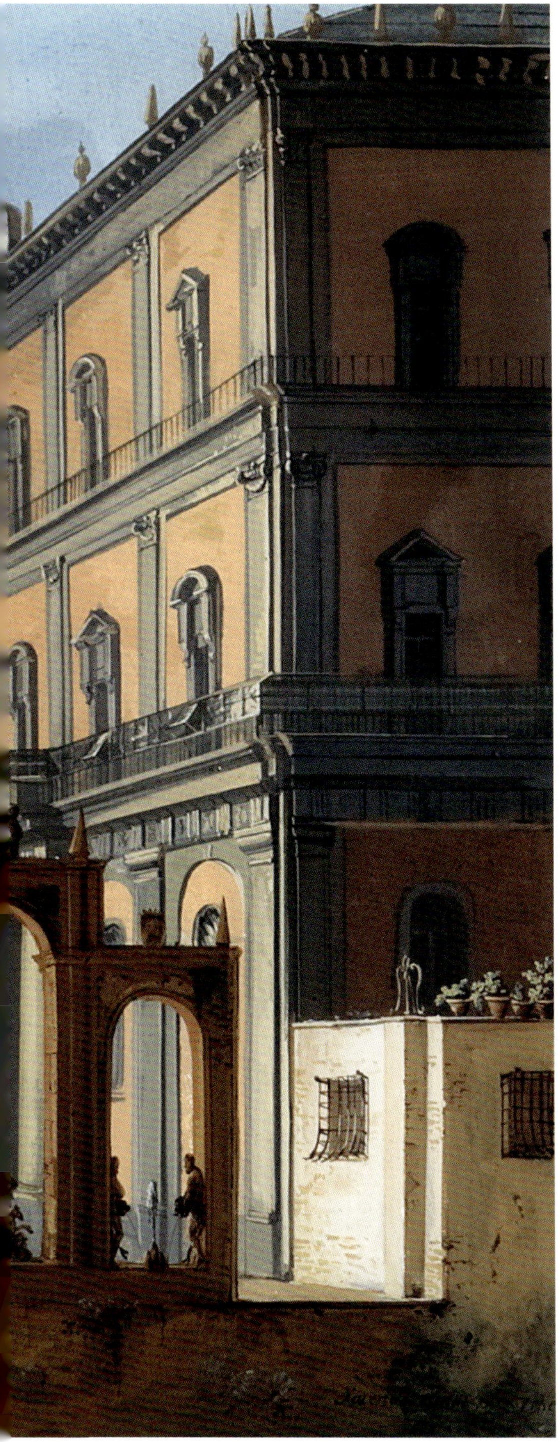

Two rooms of male retreat, the Billiard Room and the Smoking Room, were added in the 1870s, at the farthest possible remove from the Duchess's Boudoir. This 'zoning' was typical of William Burn. He objected when the Duke suggested having the gun room in the western 'female' or 'family' wing. The Billiard Room houses the Italian views collected on his Grand Tour by John, Marquis of Monthermer. His sister Elizabeth Montagu, wife of the 3rd Duke of Buccleuch, would inherit them. The billiard table was moved to a place where robust games of billiard fives and Freda could not damage the art.

Monthermer (1735–70), son and heir to the 3rd Duke of Montagu, set out on his Grand Tour at the age of 17, with his tutor, Henry Lyte. After two years in France, he arrived in Italy in 1754, where he spent six years and some £2,000 on works of art. In Rome he was painted by Pompeo Batoni holding a Corelli sonata (the portrait is now at Boughton) and by the German artist Anton Raphael Mengs. Views of Venice include works by Francesco Guardi and Marieschi. In Naples Monthermer bought paintings of the city by Antonio Joli, in one of which Vesuvius, highly active at this time, is smoking in the background.

Monthermer started the collection of Italian views, but his sister Elizabeth, who travelled widely with the 3rd Duke, added to it and probably bought the dramatic Della Gatta of the Royal Palace in Naples seen here.

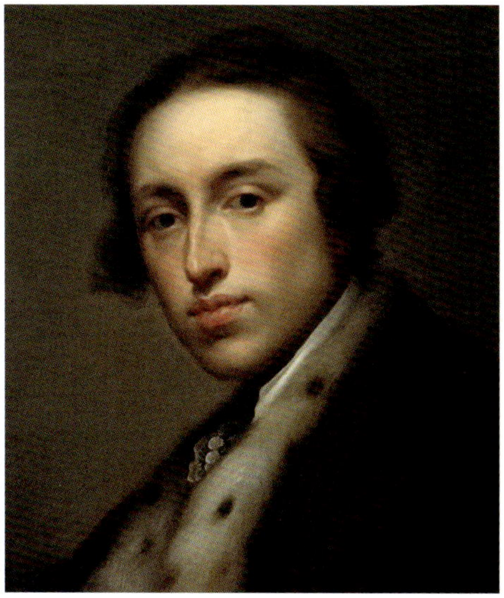

ABOVE ANTON RAPHAEL MENGS (1728–1779)
**John, Marquis of Monthermer (1735–70)**
*The consumptive heir apparent of the 3rd Duke of Montagu died at 35, before he could inherit the dukedom. Known as Lord Brudenell in the 1750s, Lord Montagu after 1762 and Marquis of Monthermer after his father became Duke, he was the archetypal Grand Tourist*

LEFT XAVIER DELLA GATTA (1758–1828)
**The Royal Palace at Naples, 1787**
*The Neapolitan Della Gatta is best known for his views of Vesuvius erupting. Duchess Elizabeth bought several Della Gatta views when she was in Naples with Henry, 3rd Duke, in 1786–87, praising them in her diary as 'most exact and highly finished'*

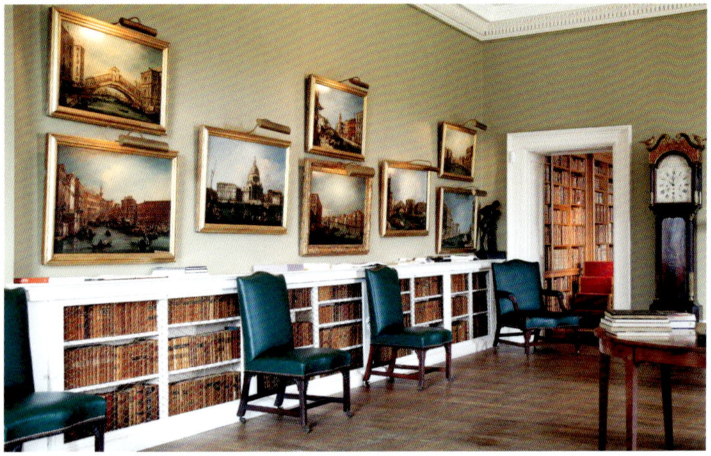

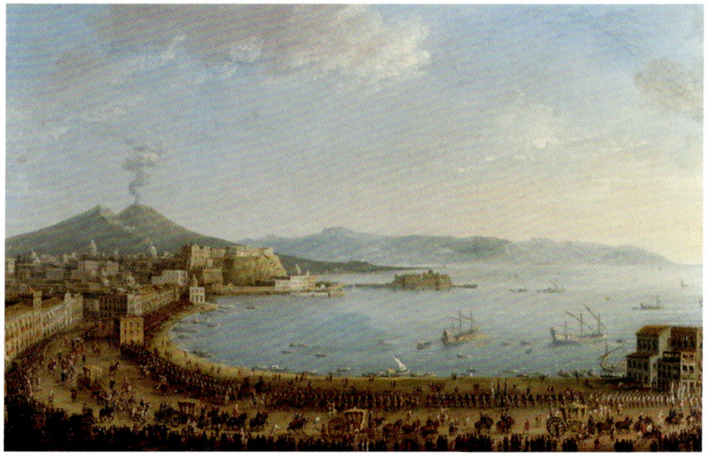

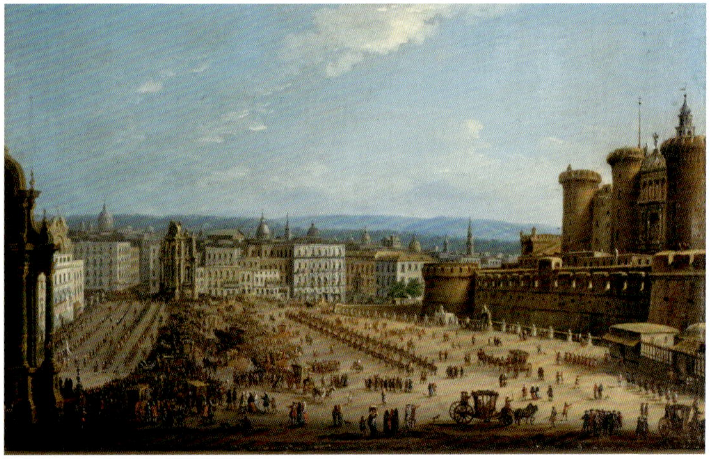

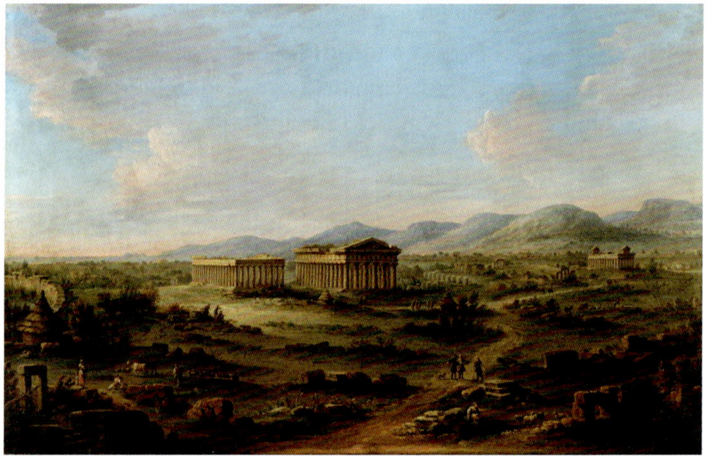

## Views of the Grand Tour

The Grand Tour spawned a whole school of Italian artists, the *vedutisti*, or painters of views. Bowhill's collection is in the old Billiard Room (top left), also known as the Italian Room. The views on these pages – of Naples and Paestum by Antonio Joli, and of Venice by Francesco Guardi and Michele Marieschi – were bought by Monthermer in the 1750s. Much ink has been spilt on attributions of the Venetians painters, but the latest thinking is that of the six paintings opposite, three are by Guardi and three by Marieschi and his associates.

TOP LEFT *The Billiard Room's views of Venice, with a glimpse of the Smoking Room beyond*

ABOVE ANTONIO JOLI (1700–77)
*Monthermer ordered 41 views of France and Italy by the Modena-born Joli. Nine are at Bowhill. Starting out as a stage designer, Joli was skilled at capturing ceremonial life in the streets of Naples, as in 'The Procession to Piedigrotta from Ponente' (top right) and 'The Largo San Fernando during the Carnival' (above left). His work was sought after by Grand Tourists, who are shown admiring the temples of Paestum (above right). Monthermer was only the third Englishman to see them*

OPPOSITE VIEWS OF VENICE
FRANCESCO GUARDI (1712–93)
*Monthermer was in Venice from 1758 to 1760 and bought the four Guardis in the Billiard Room. They include 'The Rialto' (top left), 'The Grand Canal and Rialto' (bottom left) and 'The Grand Canal and Palazzo Corner' (bottom right)*

MICHELE MARIESCHI (1710–1743)
*'The Canareggio' (centre row, left) is by Marieschi, who, like Joli, started as scene painter. For a time Guardi worked in his studio. 'Santa Maria della Salute' (top right) and 'SS Giovanni e Paolo' (centre row, right) are attributed to his associates*

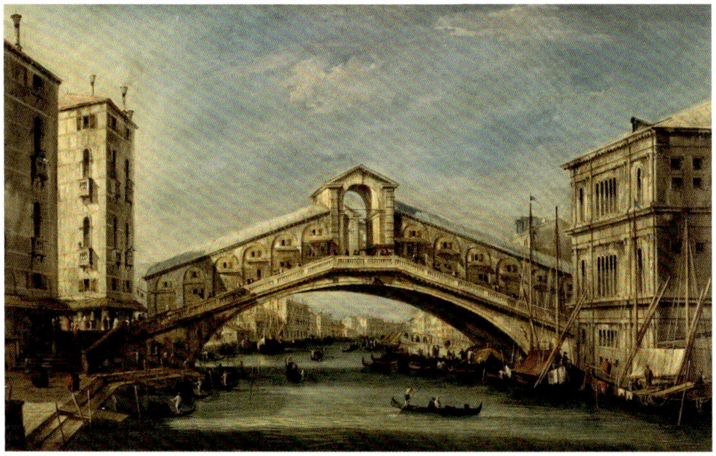
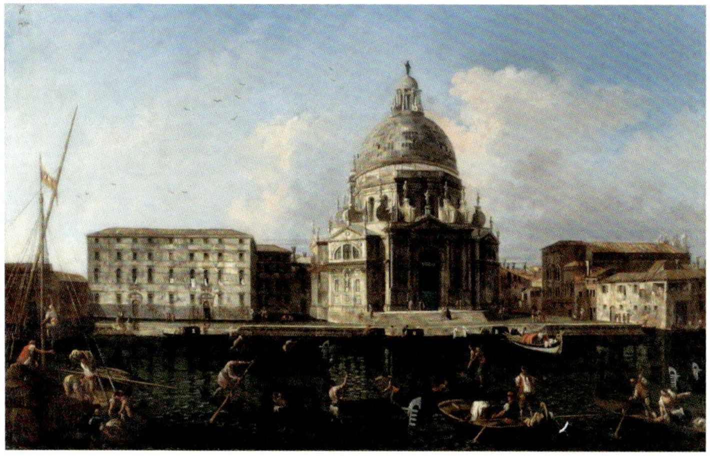
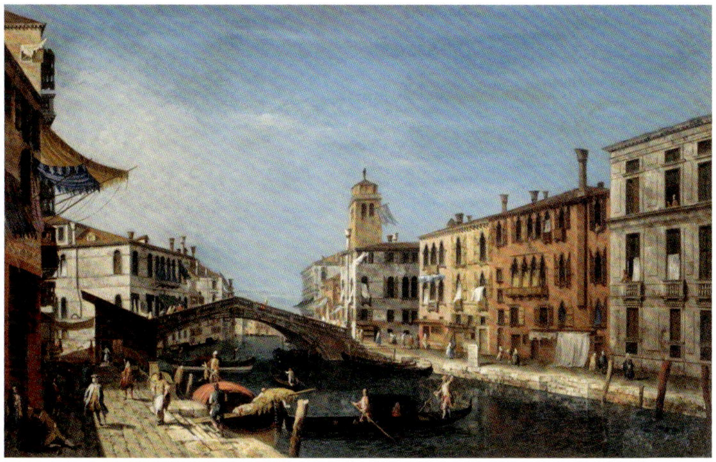
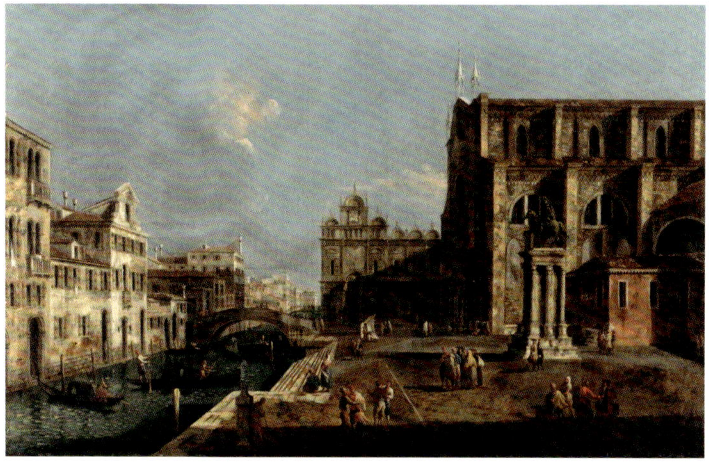
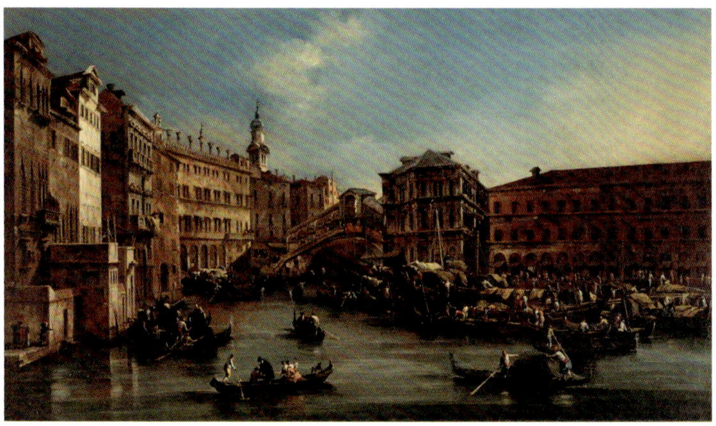
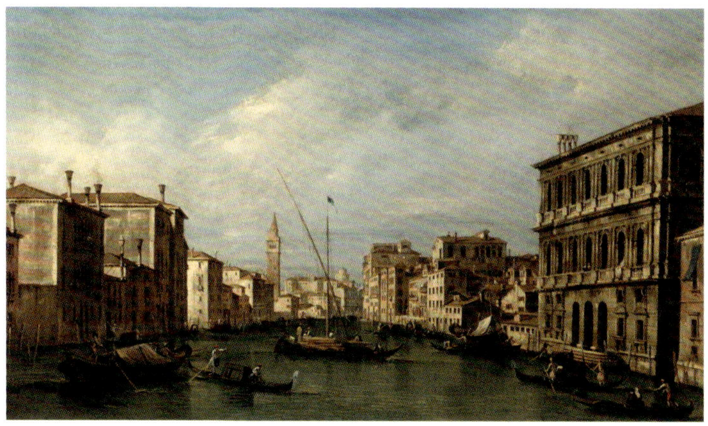

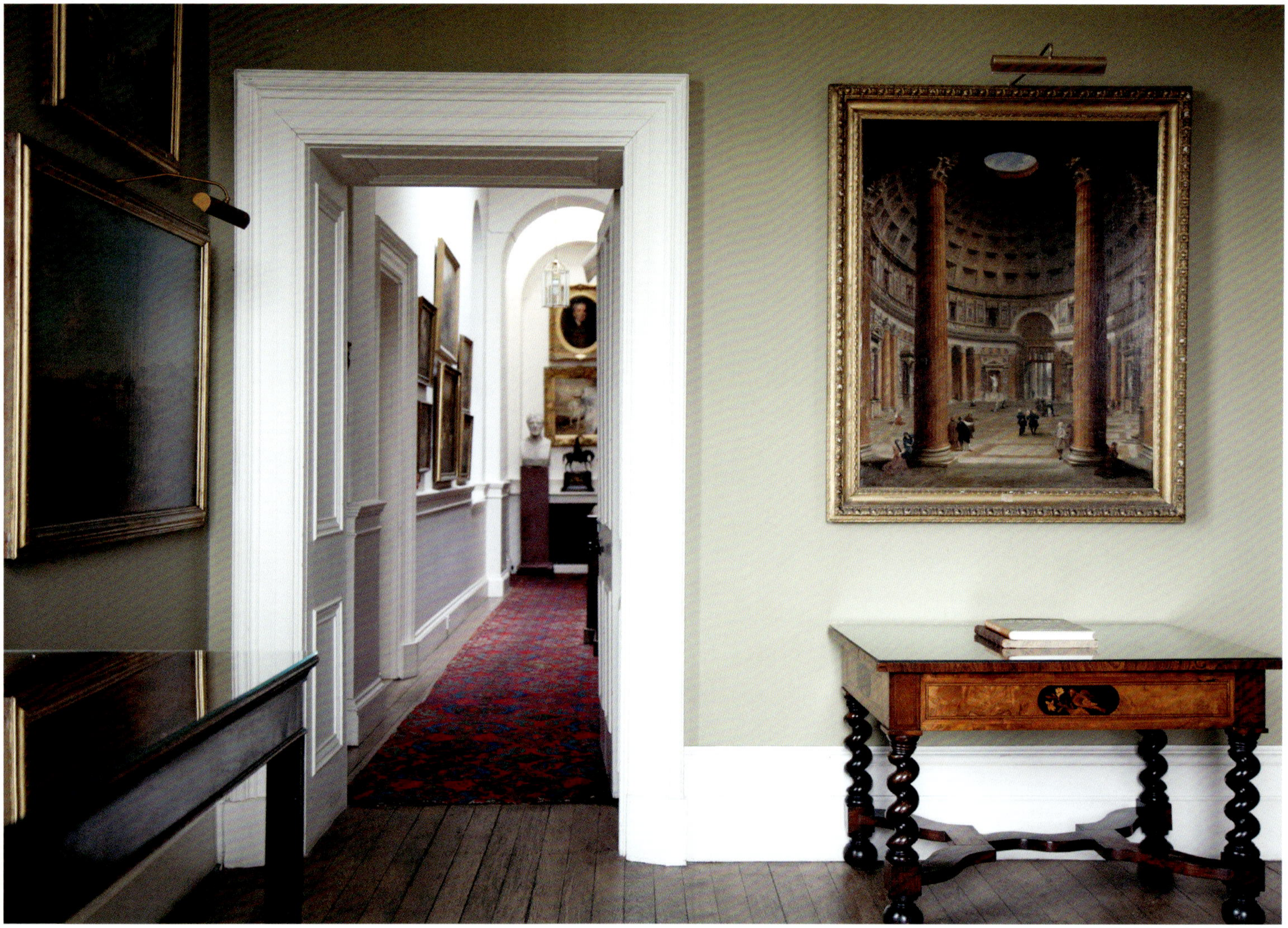

ABOVE THE BILLIARD ROOM AND THE EAST PASSAGE
*'The Pantheon' by Pannini hangs above an early-19th-century table with 17th-century marquetry panels. At the end of the passage, which leads to the Old Chapel, now an exhibition space, is a corner of Wellingtonia: an 1854 marble bust of the Iron Duke by George G Adams, who had made his death mask, an unfinished oil possibly by Lawrence, a watercolour by Thomas Heaphy, and an 1837 equestrian bronze by Garrard*

OPPOSITE
GIOVANNI PAOLO PANNINI (1691–1765)
**The Pantheon (detail),** 1730
*A detail of Pannini's painting of the Pantheon in the Billiard Room as seen above. Interestingly, the painting was only acquired in 1840 by Walter Francis, the 5th Duke, an indication of the influence that the Grand Tourist's taste continued to have on later generations*

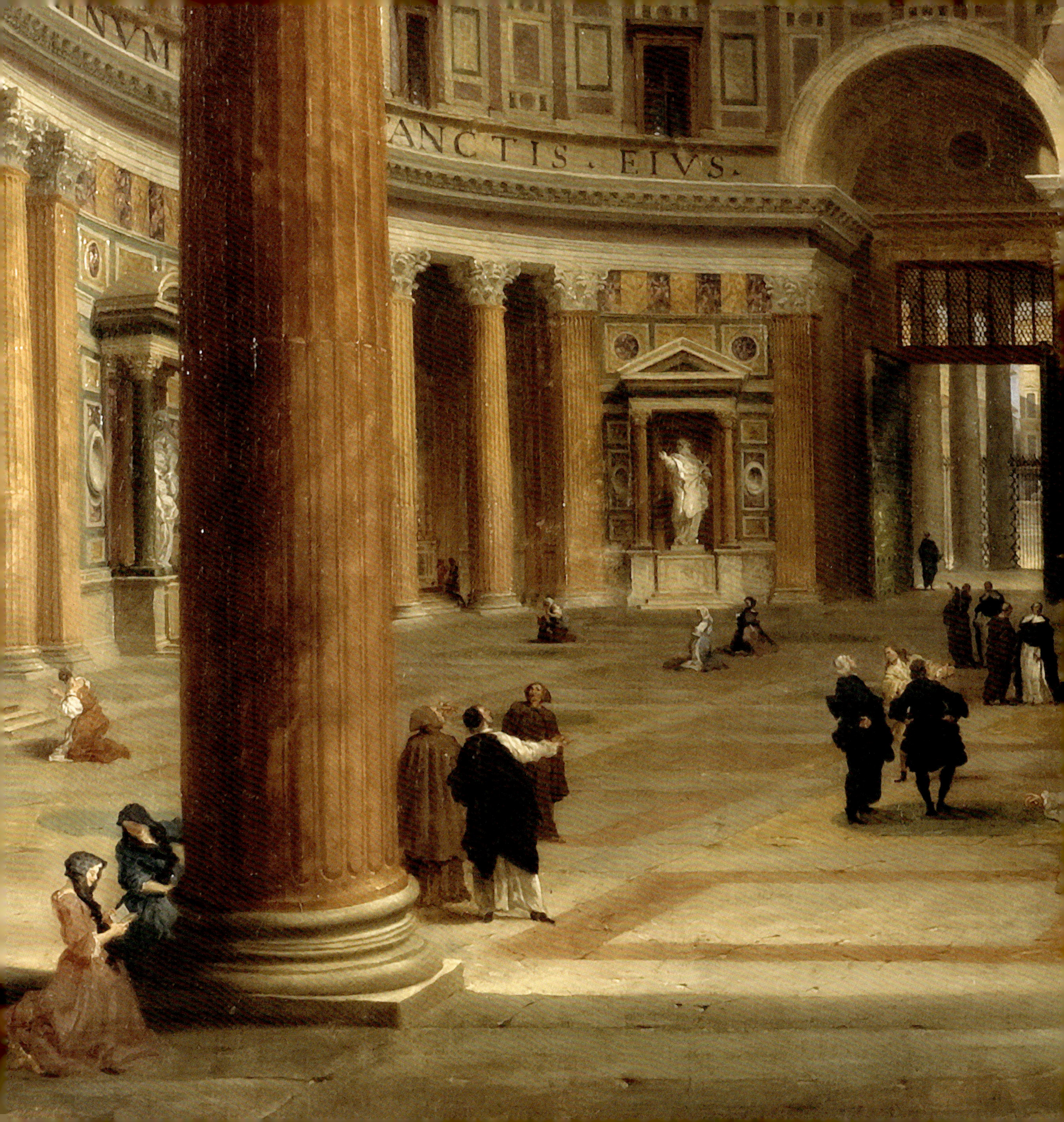
NVM
ANCTIS . EIVS

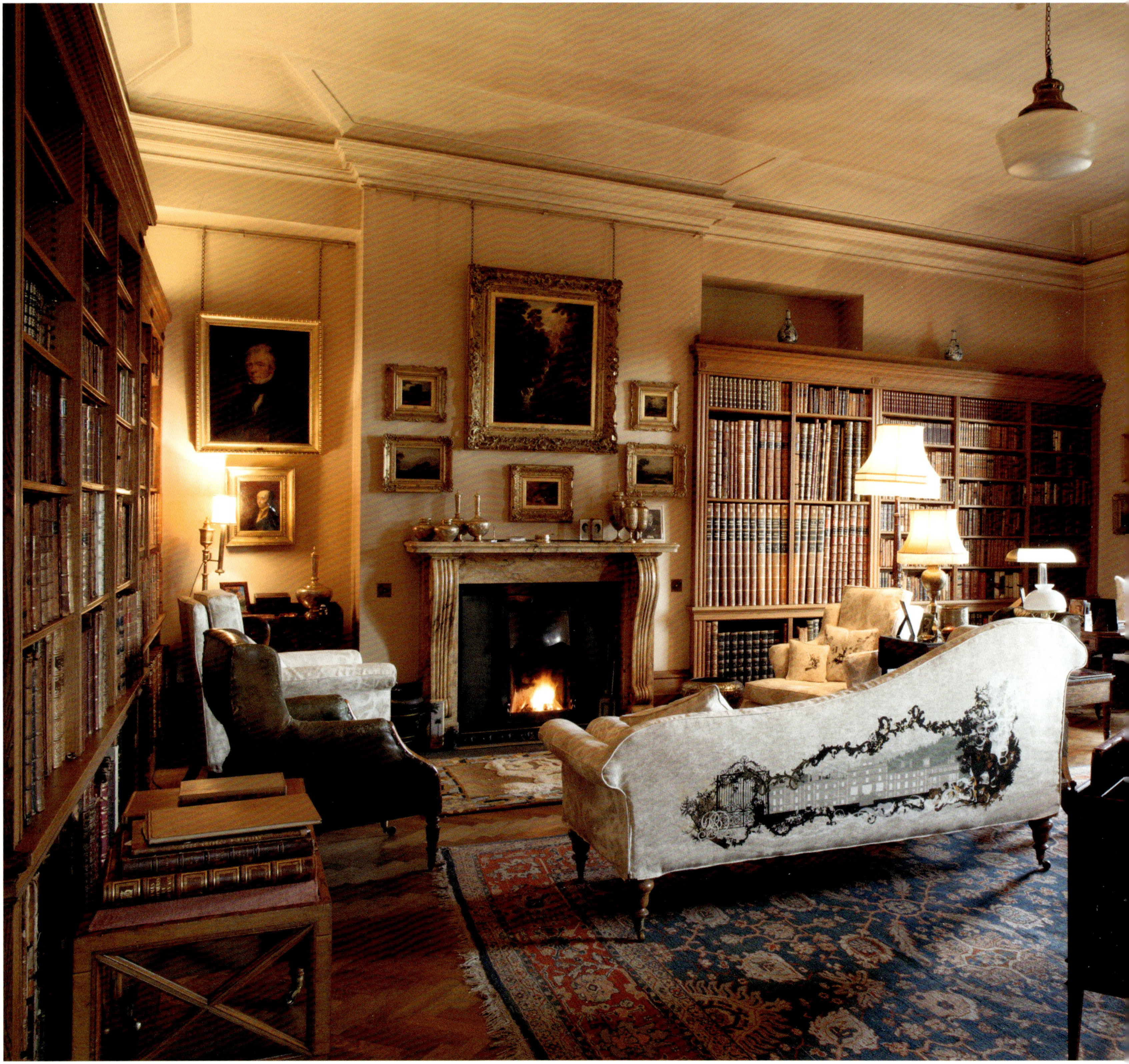

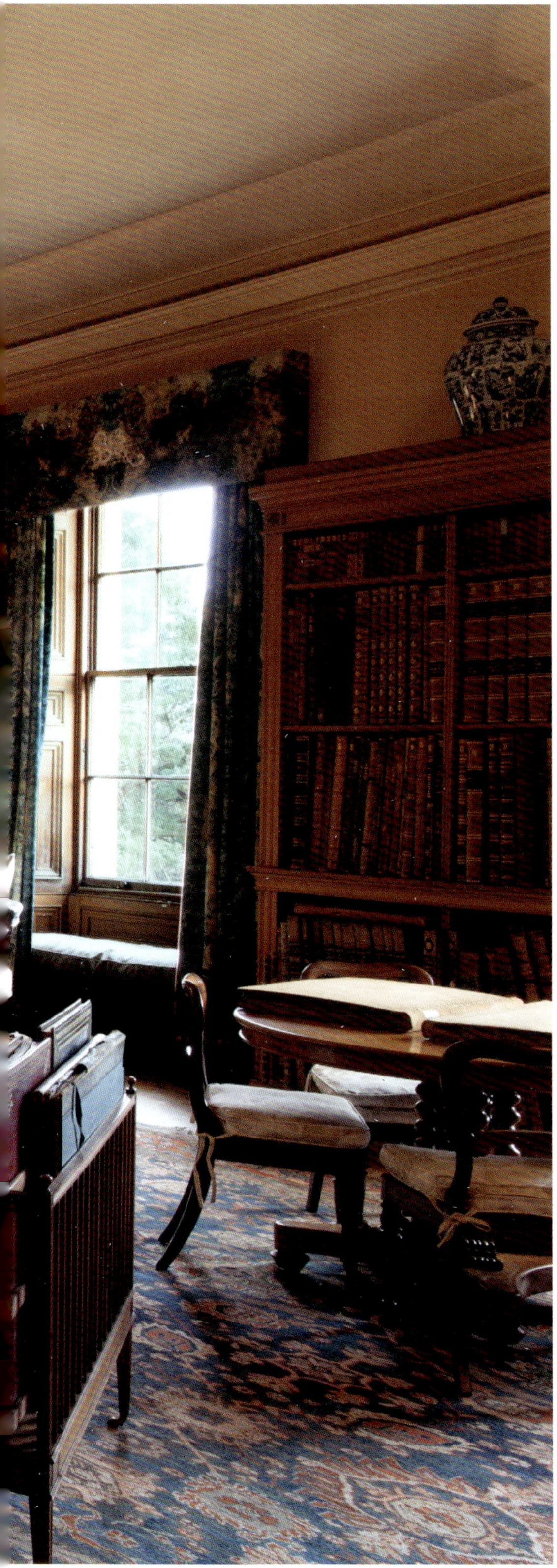

# The Smoking Room

*Beyond the Billiard Room is the gentlemen's inner sanctum, the newly restored Smoking Room. This is the perfect place to leaf through huge leather-bound volumes in seclusion*

The Smoking Room was one of the last additions to Bowhill, completed around 1878 along with the adjacent Billiard Room and the Chapel, and linking the principal façades of the house to the Stables. It lay barely used for over 70 years, a dumping ground for miscellaneous items including a billiard table – the books provided safe cushioning for the balls that flew from the table during energetic games of Billiard Fives.

Its recent restoration was made possible by a study undertaken at Glasgow University by Dr Ben Divall and imaginatively carried out over a three-year period. The catalyst was the realisation that most of the items recorded as being in the room either originally or in an inventory in 1915 were still in the family collection, albeit spread around its historic homes. The striking blue rug, leather-covered chairs, David Wilkie sketch for *Distraining for Rent* and ornate Indian Benares brass pieces from were just a few objects to be reunited.

Smoking rooms reached the height of their popularity in the second half of the 19th century. The first such dedicated room is at Osborne House, Queen Victoria and Prince Albert's seaside retreat on the Isle of Wight. It is the only room there that does not include an intertwined 'V&A' above the door – a simple 'A' denotes it as a space reserved for men.

The smoking room became part of a suite of rooms gentlemen retreated to, particularly

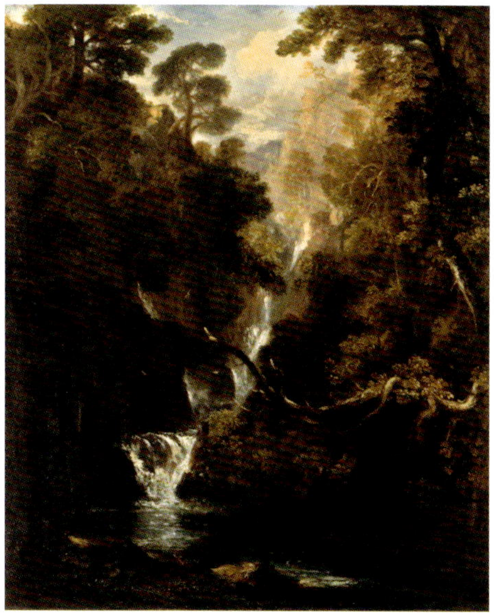

ABOVE THE REV. JOHN THOMPSON OF DUDDINGSTON (1778–1840)
**Glen Altnarie, Moray**
*The highland waterfall over the fireplace is one of 22 Thomson landscapes still at Bowhill. A 1907 inventory records two in the Smoking Room*

LEFT *The room is close to how it looked when it was added in 1878, but with innovative touches, such as digitally printed fabrics and Dovecot Studios' 3D rug by the fireplace. Francis Grant's portrait of Walter Scott (left of fireplace) and the small portrait of his great friend Charles, 4th Duke, beneath it, were both in the room in 1907*

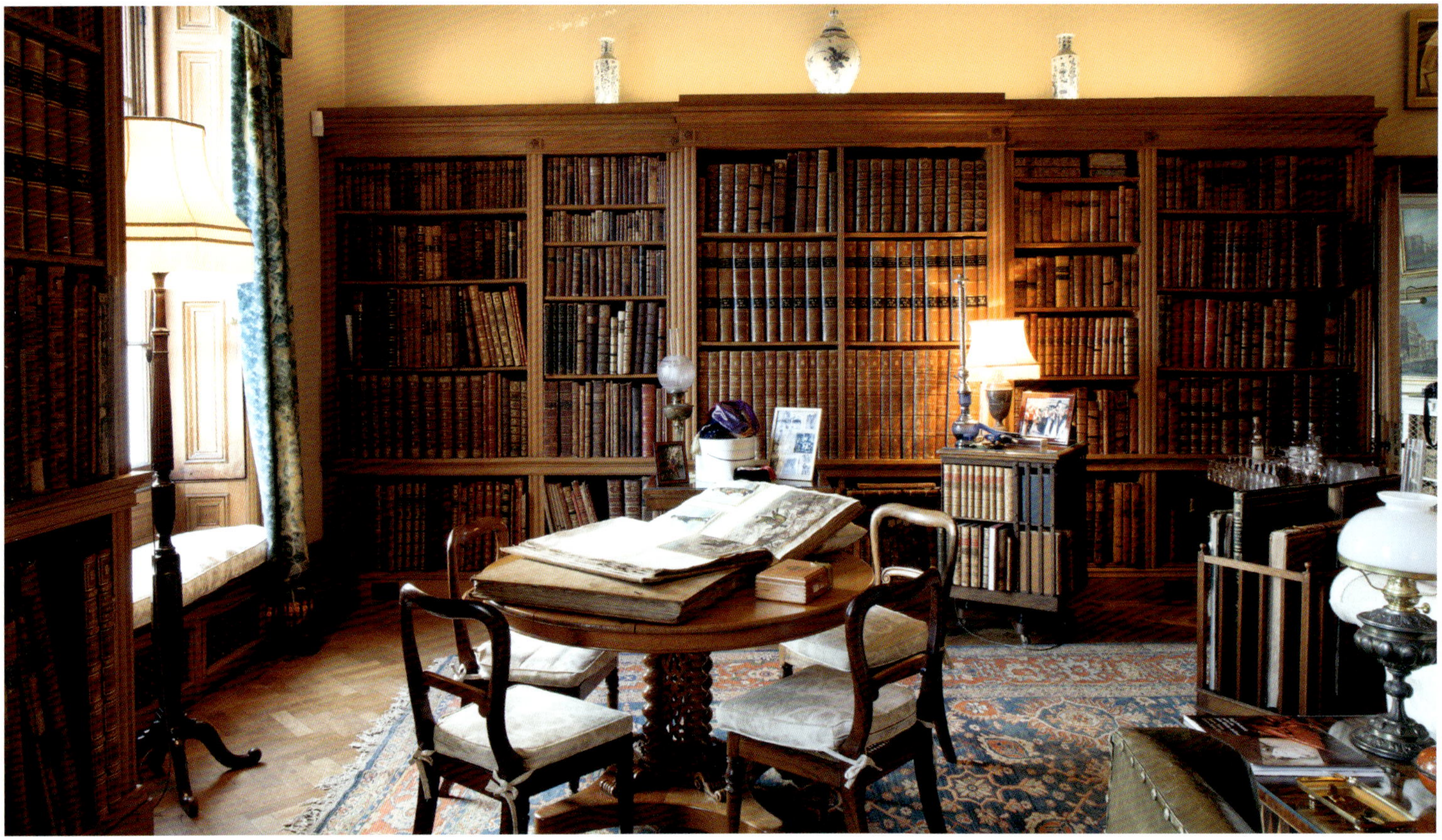

after dinner. Often, however, as at Bowhill, it would be a place for quiet daytime study and contemplation, fuelled by a remarkable collection of books. Here they range from the two- and three-volume novels beloved by Victorians, to Buffon's nine-volume *Natural History of Birds*, and great tomes of engravings, among them James Granger's 1769 *Biographical History of England*. A clergyman and print collector, Granger left blank pages and huge margins so that readers could buy prints of the figures mentioned in the text, then glue them onto the page, a popular pastime known as 'Grangerising' or 'extra-illustration'.

Equally popular was the habit of collecting volumes of contemporary cartoons. Those of Hogarth and Gillray, the best known, make

ABOVE *Designed by Paul Simmons of Timorous Beasties of Glasgow, the new curtains, with their pattern of smoke, take their colour from the original carpet; glowing cigars appear near the floor. A book of caricatures is open on the table. John Stewart, Duchess Elizabeth's librarian at Montagu House, and the 5th Duke both collected caricatures*
RIGHT *An Australian friend with proud Scottish ancestry, Primrose Potter, donated these Victorian smoking hats, worn to keep the hair free from the smell of tobacco, considered offensive to ladies*
FAR RIGHT *Scabrous satire by James Gillray*

TOP RIGHT SIR DAVID WILKIE (1785–1841)
**Distraining for Rent, 1815**
*The signed oil sketch for Wilkie's masterpiece in the Scottish National Gallery is original to the room*

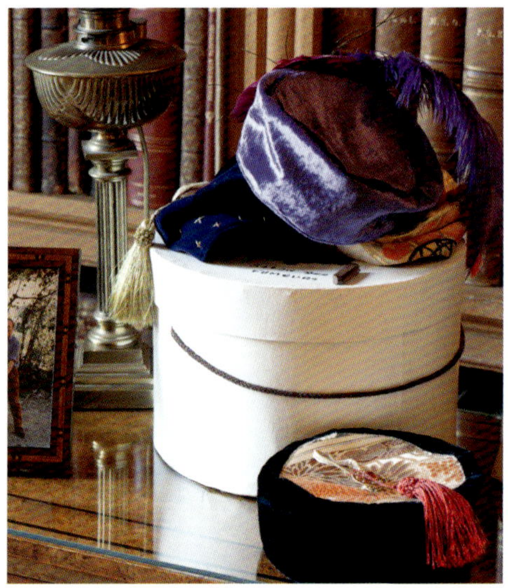

today's press look tame, with their vicious caricatures of the Royal Family and politicians.

Care has been taken to preserve the original paint and woodwork in Bowhill's Smoking Room with minimal change, evoking its spirit with pictures, ornaments and furniture from the original inventory. Rather than reconstruct the fabrics and risk historical pastiche, it was decided to commission new designs from the Glasgow firm Timorous Beasties.

Digital printing has meant that bespoke textiles can be created relatively quickly and at moderate cost. The curtains are made from digitally printed velvet, the blue based on colours from the carpet, still in the room. The aim was to create a contemporary but historically grounded take on a smoking-room theme. The family's BQ monogram appears on the foils round the glowing cigars near the floor, and in smoke rising up the curtains to meet in the centre of the pelmets. The sofa, chair covers and cushions bear similar designs, as does the fireplace rug. Created with Kirsti Vana from Dovecot Studios, Edinburgh, the rug was made using a gun-tufting technique: the pile is pushed through a backing cloth with compressed air, with different lengths adding three-dimensionality to the smoke. The rug features a BQ monogram, and the lightest areas use wool from the Bowhill estate.

It is still a room for smoking in. This is not to romanticise the practice but to respect both its origins as part of the heritage of the house and the fact that smoking remains a matter of personal choice. The 10th Duke, a non-smoker, will not be tempted, but the image of skulking, shivering figures and glowing cigarette butts banished to the front doorstep is unworthy of a great house.

More importantly, though, it will once again be a room of mellow beauty for reflection and study. The hundreds of volumes lining the walls can be explored in peace in front of a glowing fire, the hustle and bustle along distant corridors quietly ignored.

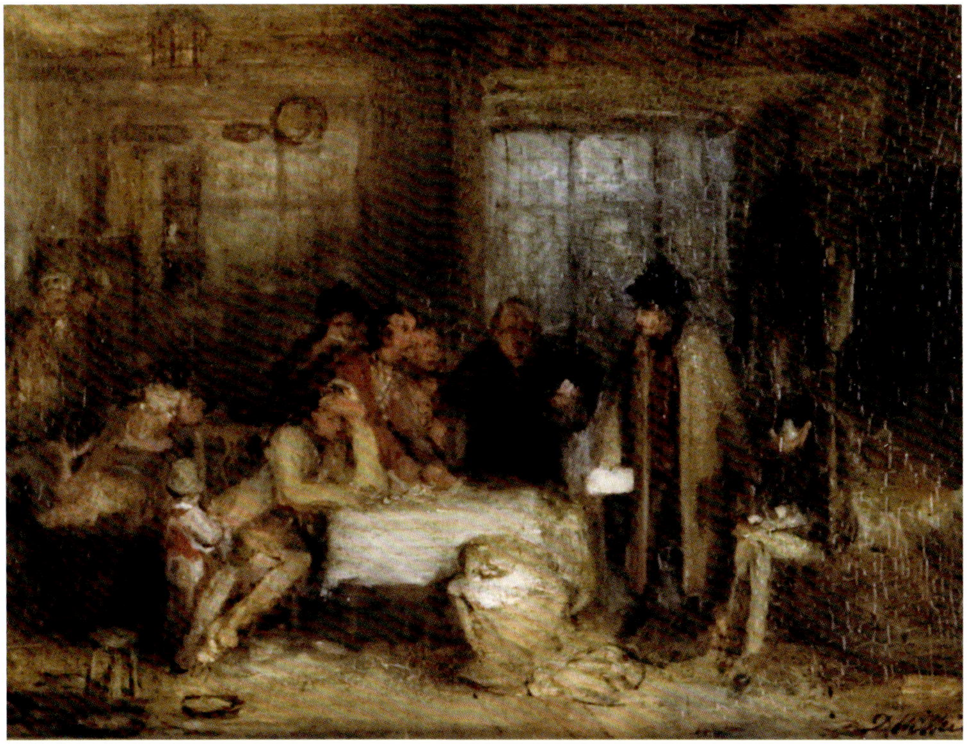

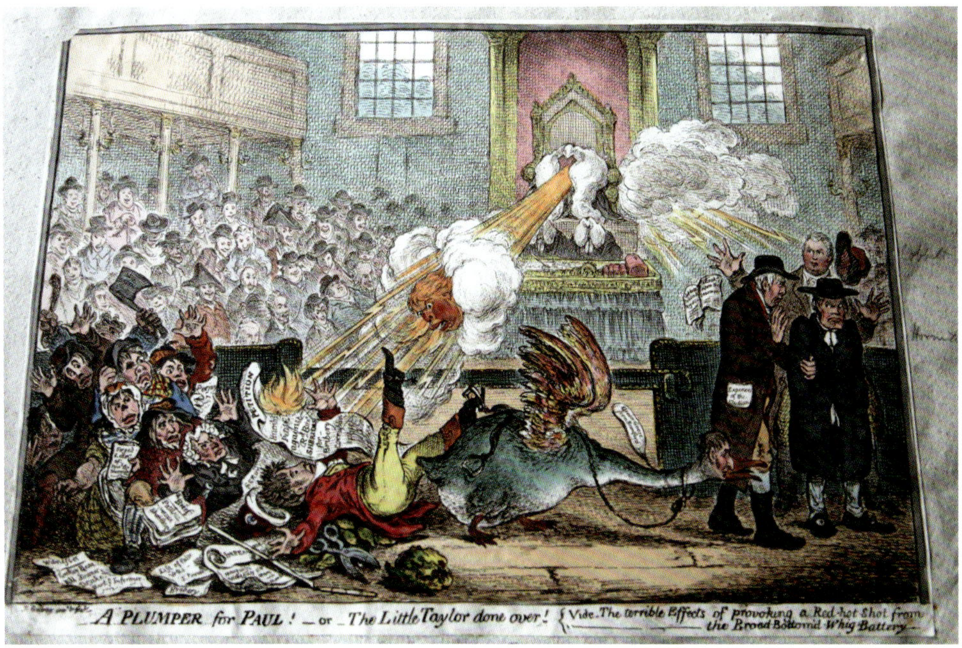

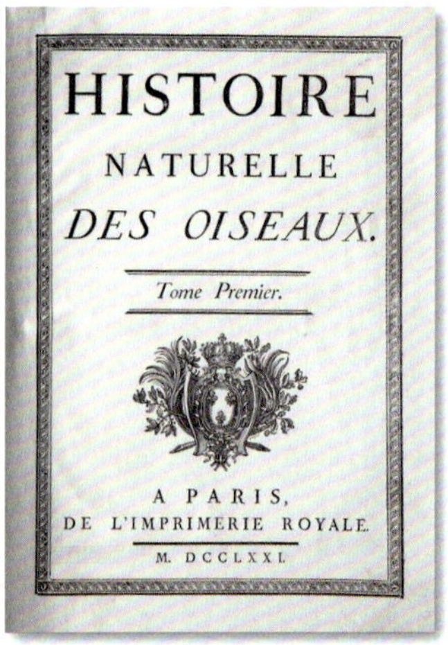
HISTOIRE
NATURELLE
DES OISEAUX.
Tome Premier.
A PARIS,
DE L'IMPRIMERIE ROYALE.
M. DCCLXXI.

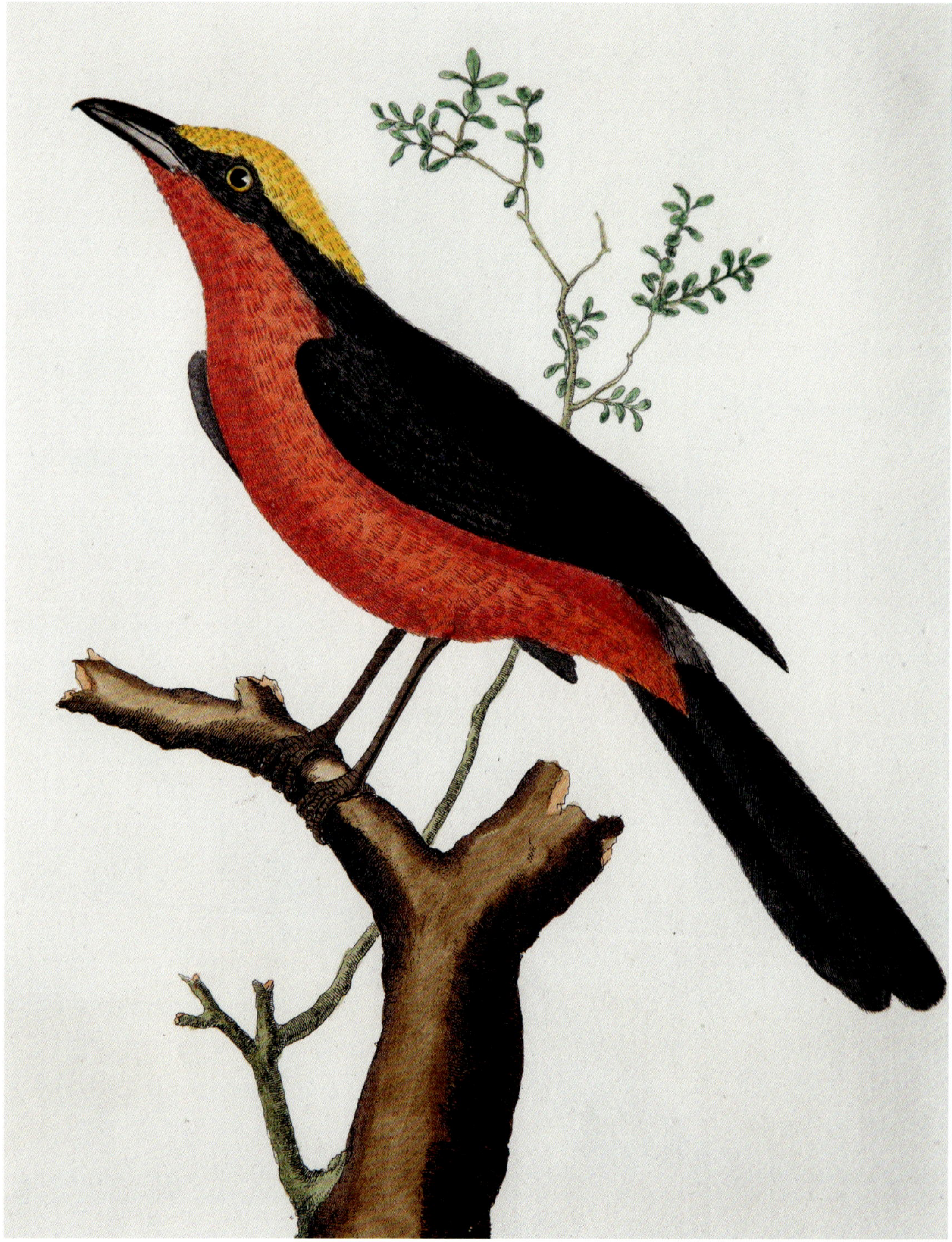

THIS PAGE AND OPPOSITE
*Pages from the nine-volume ornithological work by George Louis Leclerc, Comte de Buffon, published 1771–86. Drawn by François-Nicolas Martinet, the birds include an eagle-owl and kites (top row), an urubu (with orange neck), a buzzard (bottom left) and a Senegal magpie with astonishing red plumage*

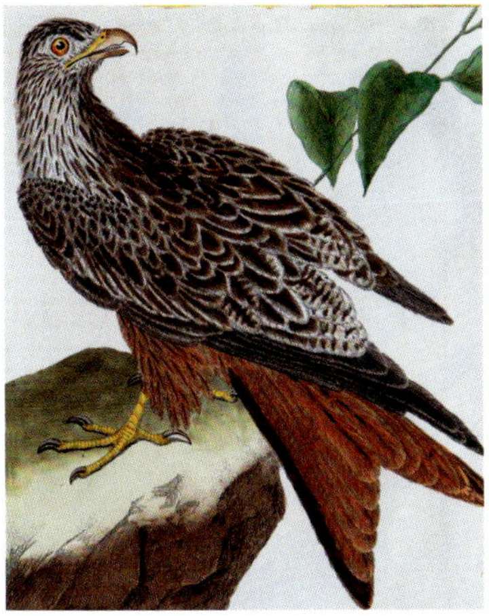
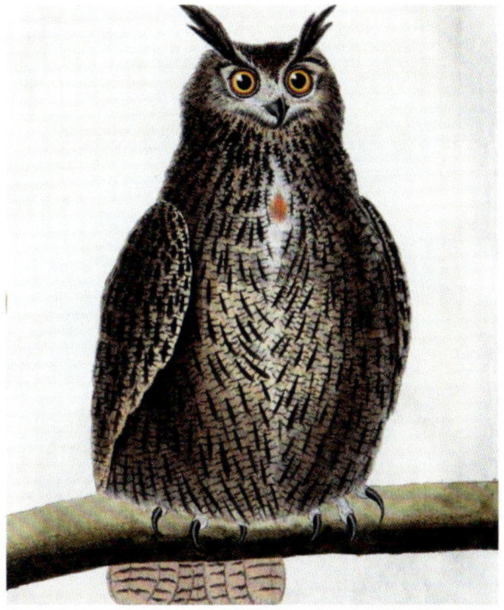
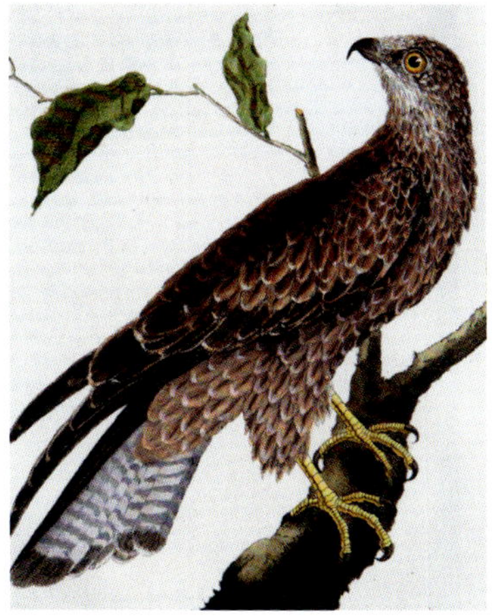
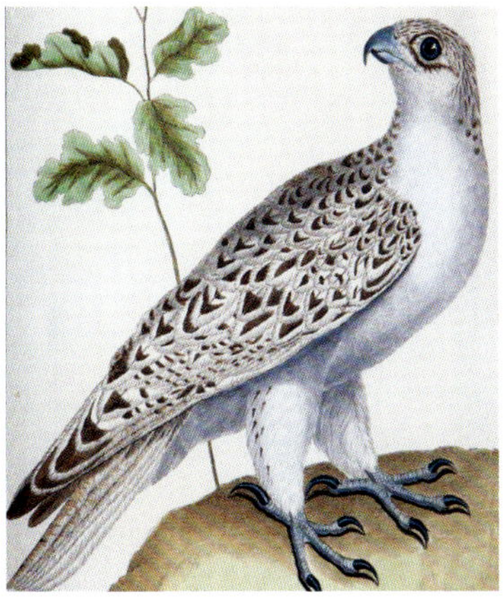
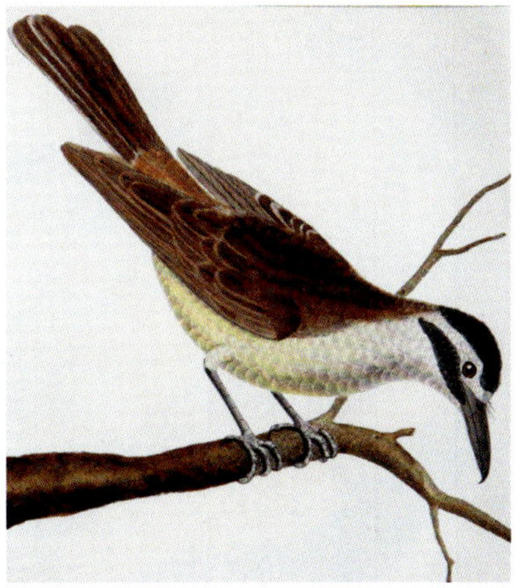
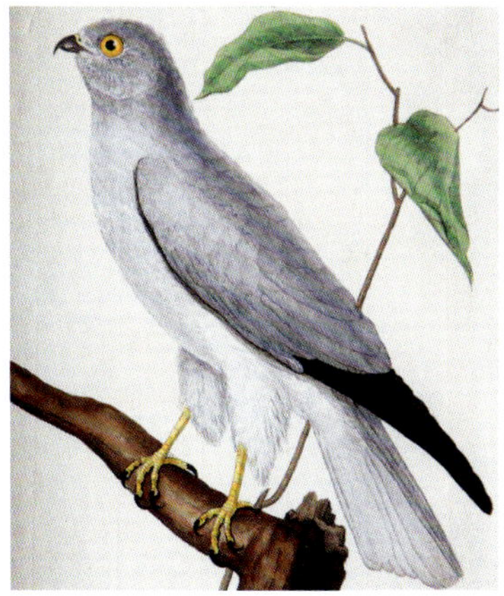
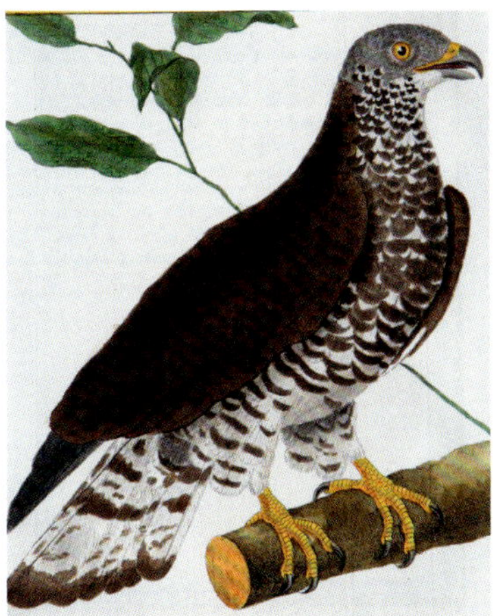
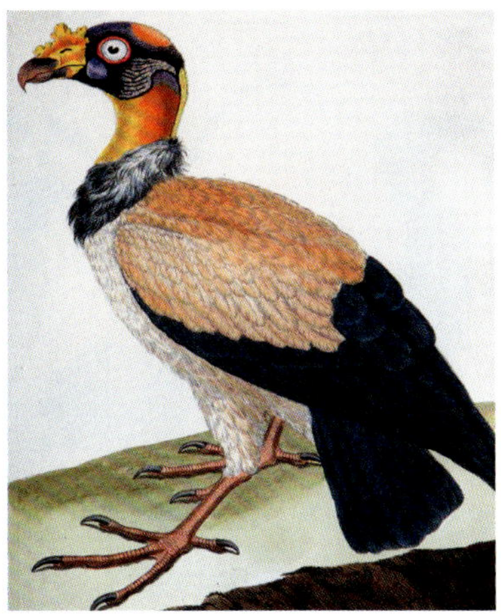
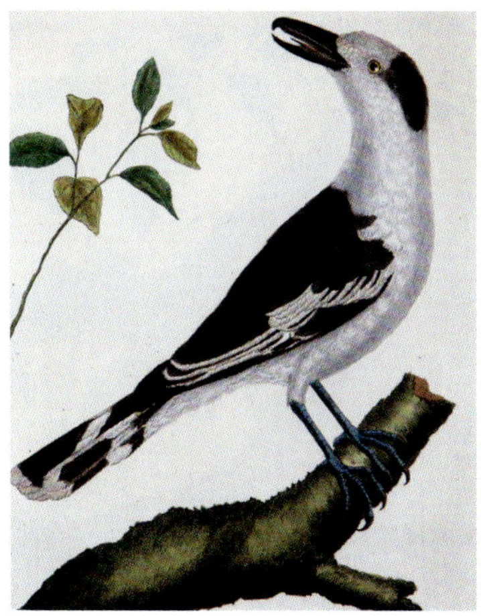

# The East Passage

*The long corridors running from one end of Bowhill to the other are hung with portraits and landscapes, interspersed with cabinets of porcelain and Victorian memorabilia*

The East and West Passages at Bowhill run the full length of the house and are repeated on the first floor and in the basement. They are the backbone of Bowhill, providing easy, discreet access to all parts of the house, and ensured the smooth running of a Victorian household which, with family, guests and staff, might number several score.

They continue to serve this function today while also offering a series of varied gallery spaces. Family portraits from the late 16th century right up to the present day are dominant. Both the late Duke and his father were painted by Derek Hill, the latter in the robes of a Knight of the Thistle.

Generations of the family have played their parts at court and in official roles. Both Charlotte Anne and Louisa Jane held the position of Mistress of the Robes to Queen Victoria, and a display case shows a number of her letters and gifts, including a charming small sketch of children, drawn by the Queen herself.

Fine pieces of Sèvres, Meissen and Dresden porcelain are displayed in the showcases.

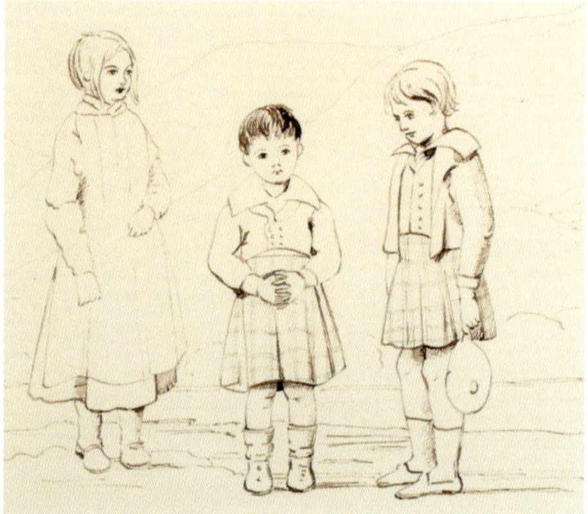

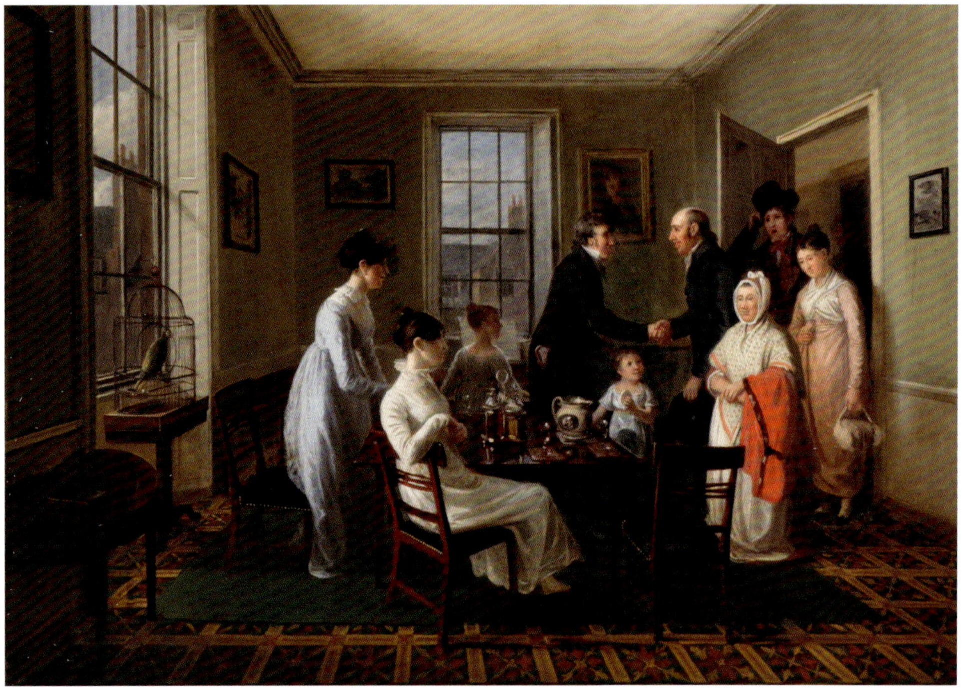

ABOVE HM QUEEN VICTORIA (1819–1901)
**Three Scottish Children, 1847**
*Victoria drew this charming group at Ardverikie during her first Highland holiday with Prince Albert. One boy is later said to have turned round and lifted his kilt. He was never forgiven*

LEFT ALEXANDER CARSE (1770–1843)
**The Arrival of Country Cousins, c.1812**
*Admired by David Wilkie and patronised by Duchess Elizabeth and her son the 4th Duke, the Scottish painter Carse originally worked as a wigmaker. This delightful painting appears on the Penguin cover of Jane Austen's 'Persuasion'*

RIGHT *Glyn Philpot (1884–1937) painted Molly, Duchess of Buccleuch, in 1921, the year she married. Winston Churchill, one of her many admirers, said that when she entered a room it was as though a light was turned on. At the 1937 coronation, she was one of the four duchesses to bear the canopy of Queen Elizabeth, the present Queen's mother*

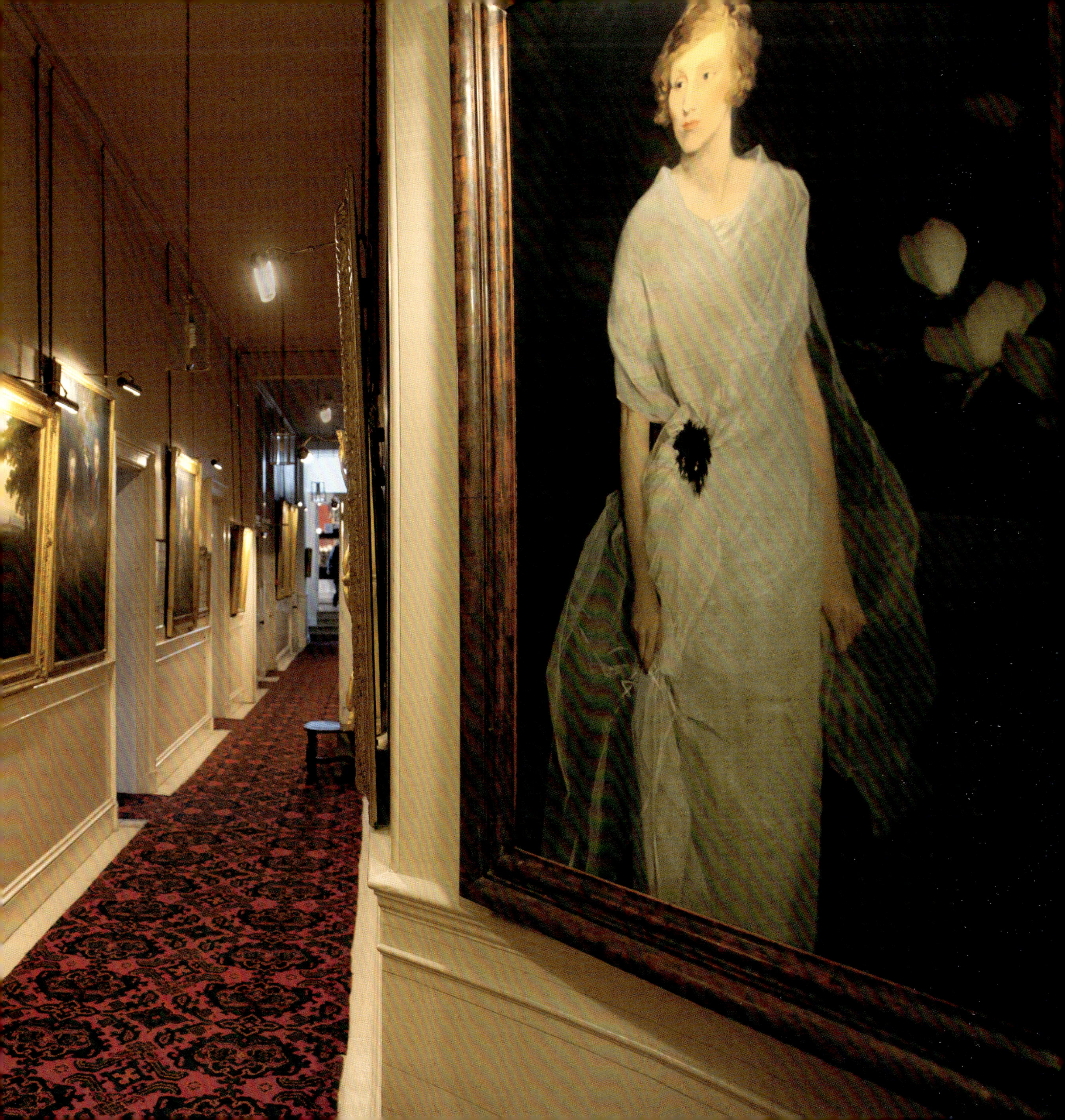

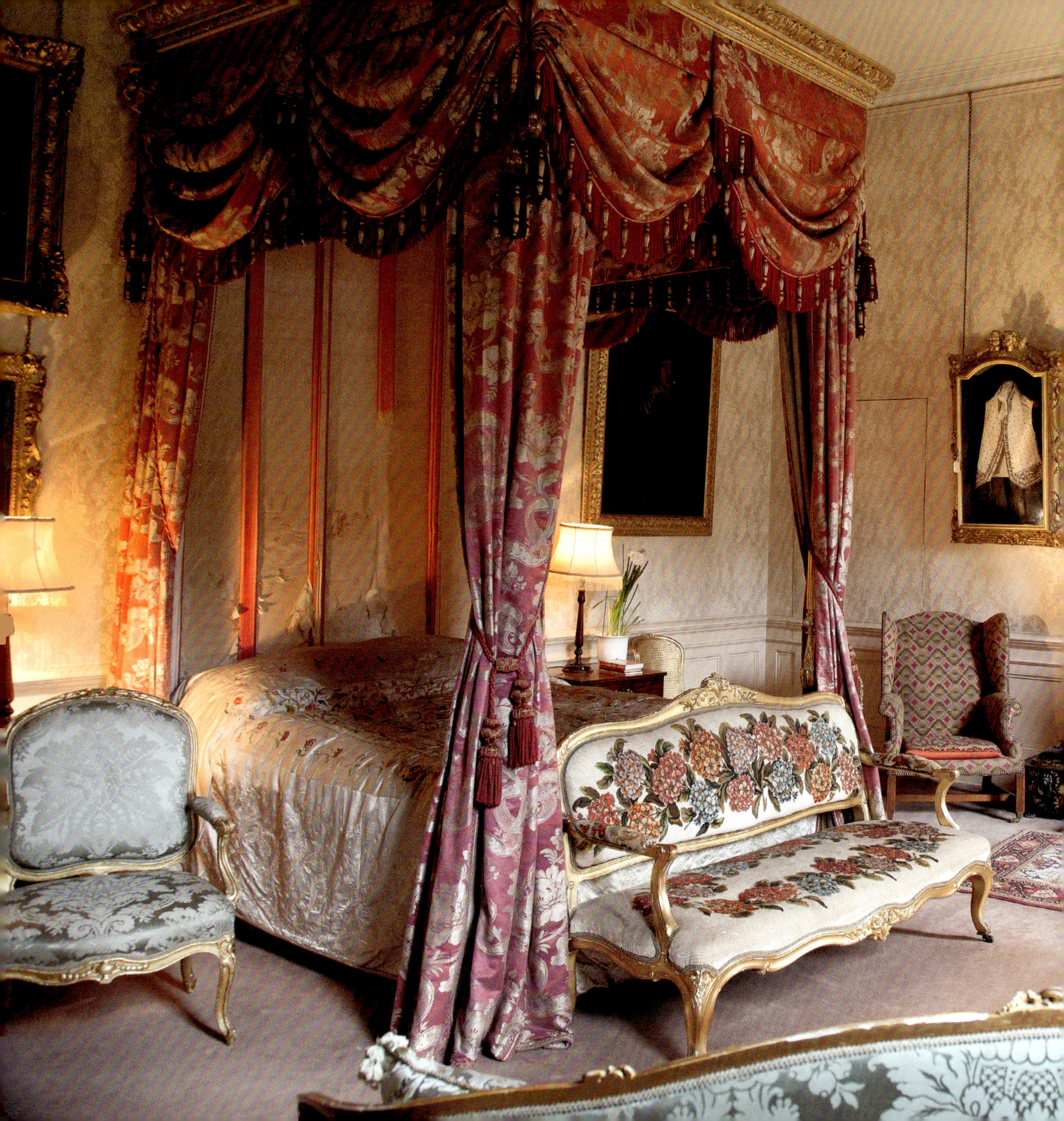

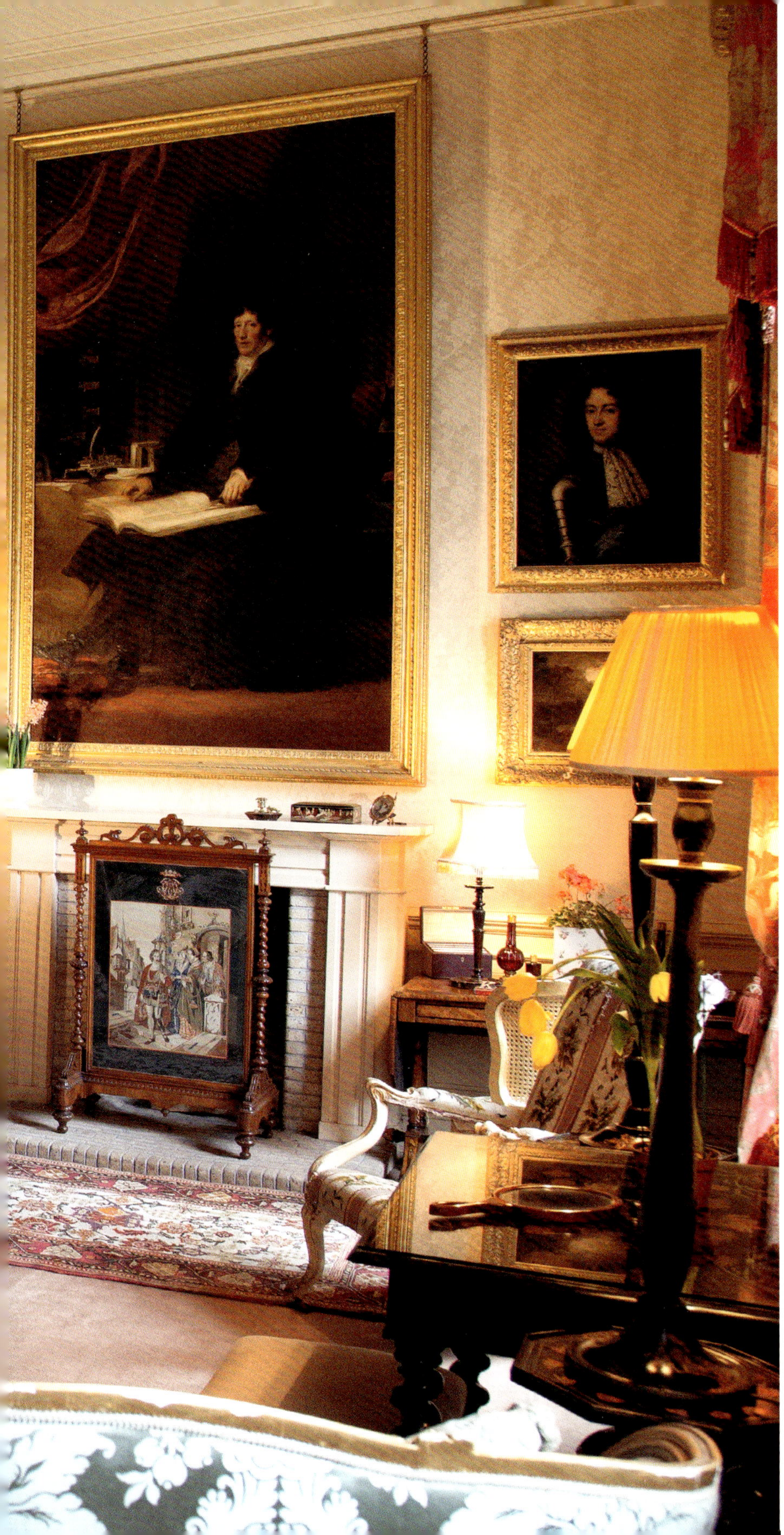

# The Dalkeith Bedroom

*An easy combination of styles gains a dash of magnificence with a sumptuous bed brought from the palace at Dalkeith*

The room takes its name from the huge William IV canopy bedstead which came, along with matching window pelmets and cornices, from Dalkeith Palace. Above the fireplace is Sir David Wilkie's portrait of the bibliophile Henry, Lord Montagu, brother of Duke Charles and a lively correspondent of Sir Walter Scott's. He lived at Ditton, the family home at Datchet, where he had an important library.

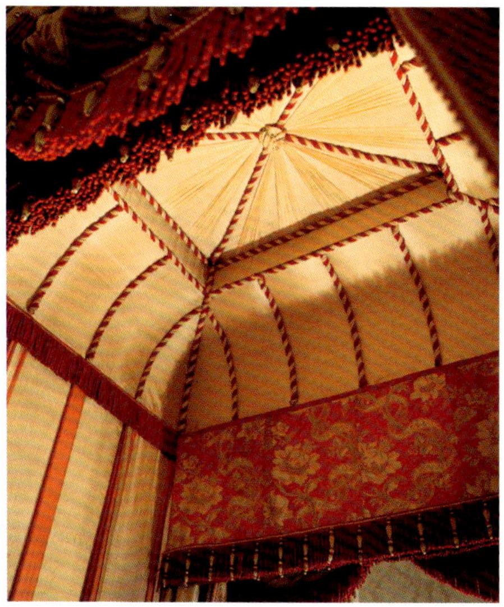

*The William IV bed with its raspberry damask curtains (left) and tent-like canopy (above). The George III armchair by the fireplace is Scottish. At the end of the bed is a 'canapé' of Louis XV design*

# The Walter Scott Room

*Sir Walter's friendship with Charles, the 4th Duke, and his wife and brother played an important role in the shaping of Bowhill – a memory kept alive by the 5th Duke. This room is dedicated to the author*

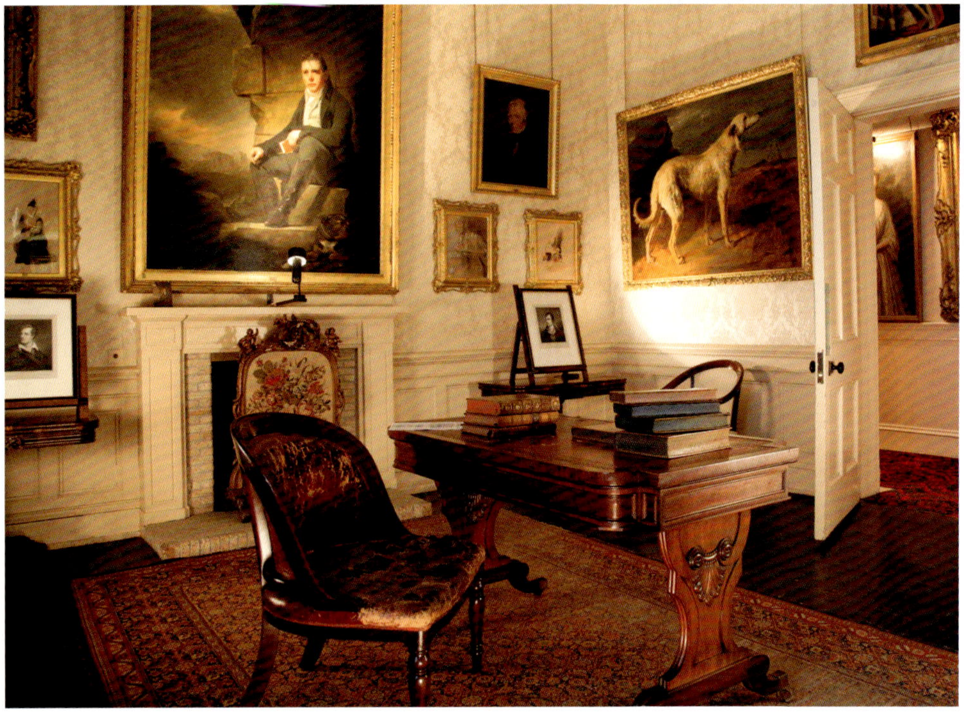

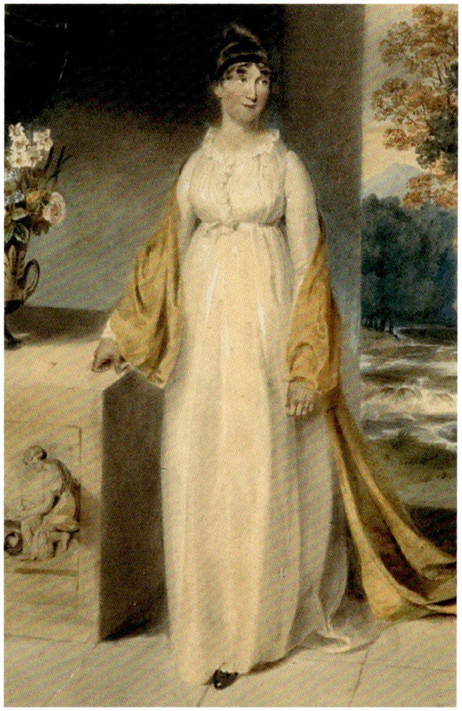

Raeburn painted his portrait of the young Scott in 1808. Its setting, with Hermitage Castle in the background and Camp, his faithful hound, at his side, reflects Scott's vital research forays into the wilder parts of his Scottish Borders homeland. Pen and paper in hand, he was gathering material for his books of Borders minstrelsy and antiquities, as well as character sketches for his extraordinary output of historical fiction, the Waverley novels.

But Scott's achievements extended beyond literature. He was a tireless organiser of unusual events, ranging from the

ABOVE THE WALTER SCOTT ROOM
*Alongside Raeburn's 1808 portrait of the newly famous Scott are watercolours from the 1830s by David Wilkie, a fellow Scot, whose career in London was almost as meteoric. Francis Grant's smaller portrait of Scott (right of fireplace), painted the year he died, has now been moved back to the Smoking Room. The large painting of a deerhound, Braan, on loan from the National Gallery of Scotland, recalls the crucial involvement of the present Duke's mother's McNeill forebears in rescuing the breed, as well as Scott's own fascination with dogs. The desk and chair were used by George IV when he stayed at Dalkeith*

ABOVE THOMAS HEAPHY (1775–1835)
**Harriet, Countess of Dalkeith, 1805**
*Harriet was the wife of the future 4th Duke. The manuscript of 'The Lay of the Last Minstrel', on view in the Walter Scott Room, is inscribed to her*

OPPOSITE SIR HENRY RAEBURN (1756–1823)
**Portrait of Sir Walter Scott, 1808**
*In green suit and Hessian boots, Scott sits with his dog Camp in front of the ruined Hermitage Castle, another family stronghold. The 5th Duke bought the painting from Scott's bankrupt publisher, Constable, in 1826. It had pride of place in the Dining Room, first at Dalkeith, then at Bowhill*

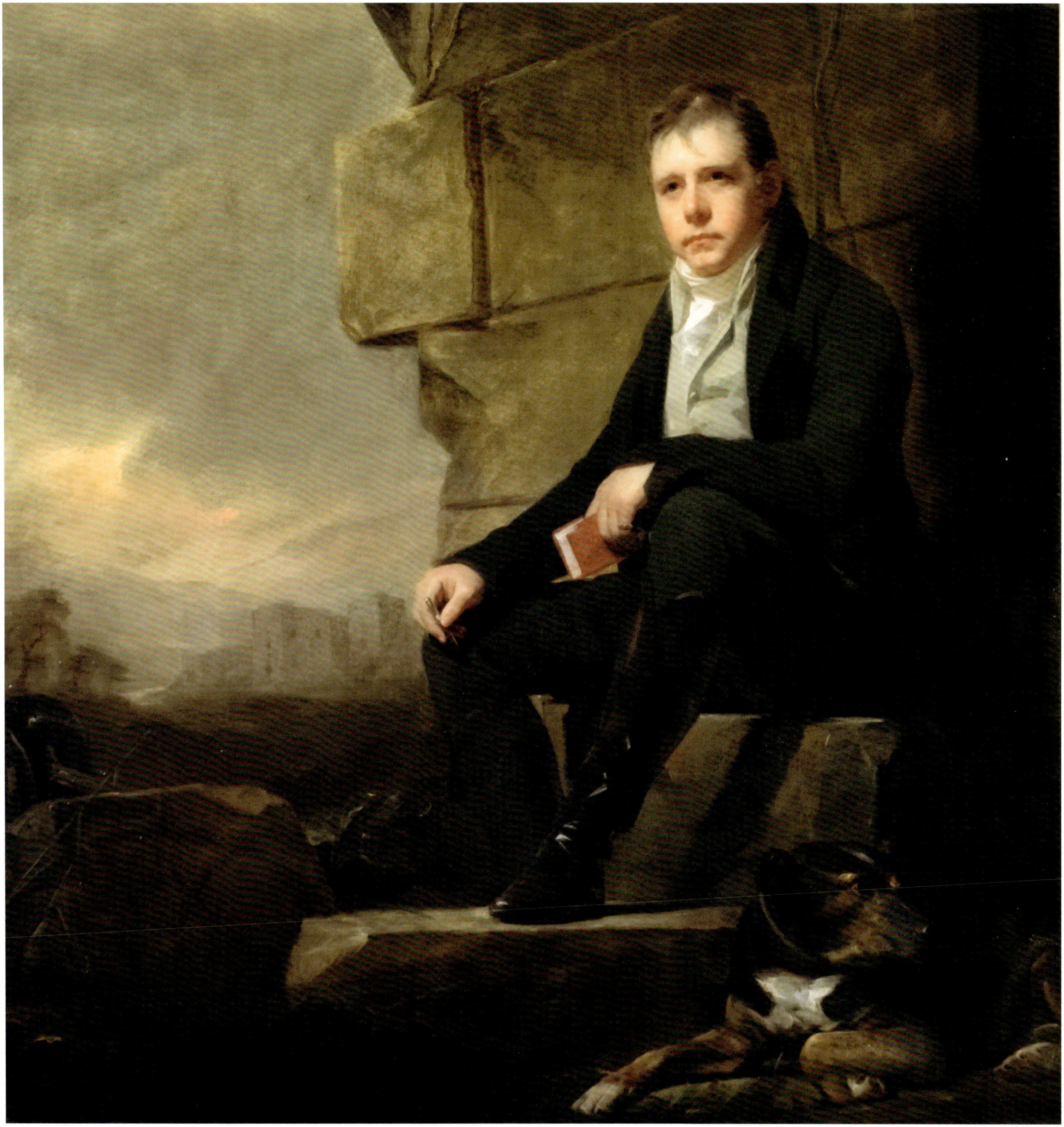

Carterhaugh Ba' Game in 1815 – which involved over a thousand local competitors and was arguably the first game of rugby football – to the spectacular visit of George IV to Edinburgh in 1822. This was hugely significant, the first visit by a sovereign to Scotland for nearly two centuries and the first occasion when the wearing of tartan, which had been banned after the '45 Rebellion, was not only permitted but required.

The Palace of Holyroodhouse in Edinburgh was in such a state of neglect that alternative accommodation was required for the King and court. Scott organised this at Dalkeith, where Walter Francis, the young Duke, then 16, played host. To thank him, the King later gave him the three-quarter-length portrait by Sir David Wilkie, which shows the specially made royal kilt and accoutrements.

As well as other portraits of Scott and drawings by Wilkie, who was a visitor to Bowhill, are landscapes by their contemporary, the Rev. John Thomson. Sadly these are now disfigured by bitumen used in the paint, but at one time in the 19th century works by this prolific artist would have been the pictures most commonly found on the walls at Bowhill.

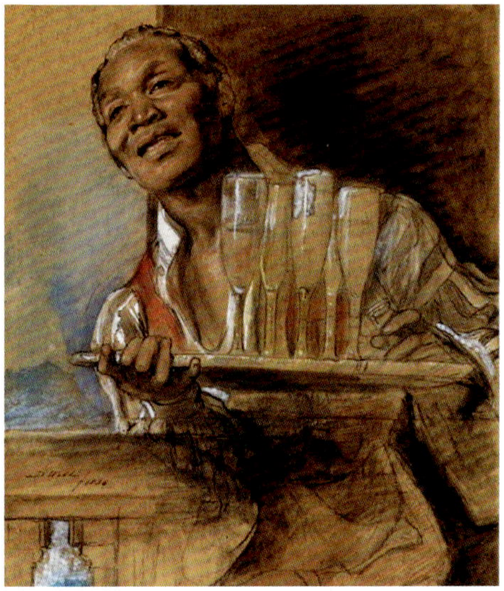

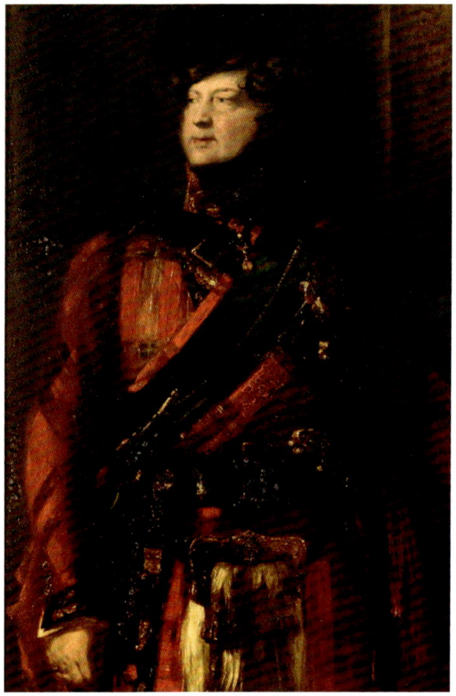

SIR DAVID WILKIE (1785–1841)
ABOVE **King George IV, 1805**
*This version of a full-length portrait of George IV in the Royal Collection was commissioned by the King as a gift for the 5th Duke in 1830 after staying at Dalkeith in 1822. The first visit to Scotland by a reigning monarch since 1633, it was orchestrated with much pageantry by Scott, down to detailed instructions as to what gentlemen of the city should wear. As tartan had been banned after Bonnie Prince Charlie's '45 Rebellion, kilts and plaids were in short supply. Jewelled dirks and belts added immensely to the cost of the King's Royal Stuart outfit, which came to £1,354. 18s. (equivalent to more than £100,000 today)*

LEFT **Study of a Black Page, 1836**
*This late sketch by Wilkie was a study for 'Empress Josephine and the Fortune-Teller', now in the National Gallery of Scotland. The setting is Martinique, as described in Josephine's 'Memoirs of Napoleon', which appeared in 1829*

## Memories of a lifelong family friendship

*The letters and diaries of Walter Scott and his friends reveal his affectionate ties with the Scotts of Buccleuch*

### HARRIET, THE ANGEL

*Walter Scott on Harriet, Countess of Dalkeith, after publishing 'The Lay of the Last Minstrel', 1805*

I don't know if ever you saw my lovely chieftainess – if you have you must be aware that it is impossible for anyone to refuse her request, as she has more of the angel in face and temper than anyone alive so that if she had asked me to write a ballad on a broomstick I must have attempted it.

### ON LUNCHING AT BOWHILL

*Sir David Wilkie, a guest at Abbotsford in 1815, describes a lunch at Bowhill to his sister*

On coming down from Yarrow I met Mr and Mrs Scott at the Duke of Buccleuch's at Bowhill. Mr Scott introduced me to the duke and as it was a day on which there was to be a great cattle show there was a large assemblage of people at the place and an immense number invited to dinner. The dinner was given quite in the ancient style of Border conviviality. Mr Scott presided at a by table in the principal room, at which the Ballantynes, Hogg the poet and some others besides myself were present. This gave occasion to our being toasted the Table of Talents which made some merriment. The company sat till 2 o'clock. There was a great variety of songs and before parting the gentlemen were so enthusiastic with music and claret, that the song of 'Weel may we a be' was sung no less than five times, and 'God save the King' about four times in full cry. I never saw such a flow of conviviality and high spirits and at the same time the greatest good humour.

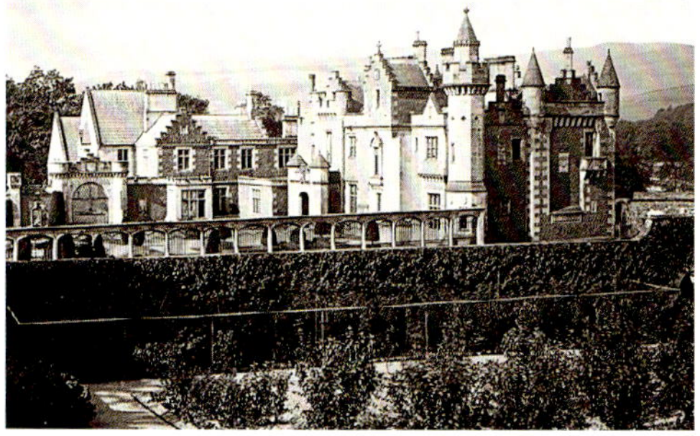

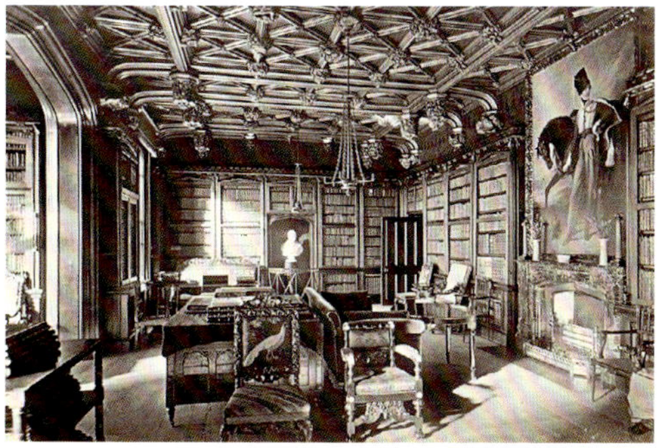

ABBOTSFORD *Scott's influential house on the Tweed, which he had been 'at work to Scottify', created a vogue for Scottish baronial architecture. It was the work of the architect Atkinson, who, surprisingly, also built the 4th Duke's austere Georgian wings at Bowhill*

SCOTT'S FIRST BRUSH WITH BANKRUPTCY
*The 4th Duke rescues Scott after Ballantyne, the author's own publishing company, collapses, offering a guarantee equivalent to £300,000 today.*
*To Walter Scott, August 28, 1813:* I received your letter of the 24th yesterday. I shall with pleasure comply with your request of guaranteeing the £4,000. You must, however, furnish me with the form of a letter to this effect, as I am completely ignorant of transactions of this nature.'

SCOTT ON LOSING VALUED FRIENDS
*In a letter of condolence, August 23, 1819, following the death of Charles, 4th Duke of Buccleuch:* I cannot tell you how severely I felt when the horse from long habit turned its head immediately to go to Bowhill.

*To Lady Abercorn, November 25, 1819:* The Duke of Buccleuch's death was indeed a very severe blow to me. We had many feelings and pursuits in common – and perhaps it is uncommon for two men, so different in rank, to have lived more intimately and familiarly.

*Scott's Journal on the death Elizabeth, wife of the 3rd Duke, November 23, 1823:* She was a woman of unbounded beneficence to, and even beyond, the extent of her princely fortune. She had a masculine courage, and great firmness in enduring affliction, which pressed on her with continued and successive blows in her later years. She was about eighty-four, and nature was exhausted; so life departed like the extinction of a lamp for lack of oil.

SCOTT ON THE YOUNG 5TH DUKE OF BUCCLEUCH
*To Lady Louisa Stuart, June 20, 1824:* I would not have him quite so soft natured as his grand-father [the 3rd Duke], whose kindness sometimes mastered his excellent understanding. His father had a temper that better jumped with my humour. Enough of ill nature to keep your good nature from being abused is no bad ingredient in their disposition who have favours to bestow.

*To Lady Louisa Stuart, February 21, 1825:*
Little Buccleuch turns out to be a goodly youth with fine points of sense and generosity about him. A better selected course of reading and, still more, of conversation will do very much for him.

*Scott's Journal, December 19, 1826:*
Went out to Dalkeith, and dined with the [5th] Duke. It delights me to hear this hopeful young nobleman talk with sense and firmness about his plans for improving his estate, and employing the poor. If God and the world spare him he will be far known as a true Scots lord.

*Scott's Journal, January 8, 1827:* The young Duke of B. came in to bid us good-bye, as he is going off to England. God bless him! He is a hawk of a good nest.

## 'Tis Sixty Years Since

Walter Scott's novel *Waverley* is considered the first historical novel. Set in the time of Bonnie Prince Charlie and the 1745 Rebellion and published anonymously in 1814, its subtitle – *'Tis Sixty Years Since* – provided the inspiration for the Walter Scott Prize, founded in 2010 and sponsored by the Duke and Duchess of Buccleuch. The prize is awarded at the Borders Book Festival in Melrose in June every year. The winner receives £25,000 and five shortlisted authors each receive £1,000.

Books must have been published in the UK, Ireland or the Commonwealth and be set more than 60 years from the present day. Early winners include Hilary Mantel's *Wolf Hall*, set in Tudor times, Andrea Levy's *The Long Song*, set in 1820s Jamaica, and Robert Harris's *An Officer and a Spy*, about the Dreyfus Affair. Sebastian Barry has won the prize twice, for *On Canaan's Side*, set in 20th-century Ireland and Chicago, and *Days Without End*, set in the US Civil War.

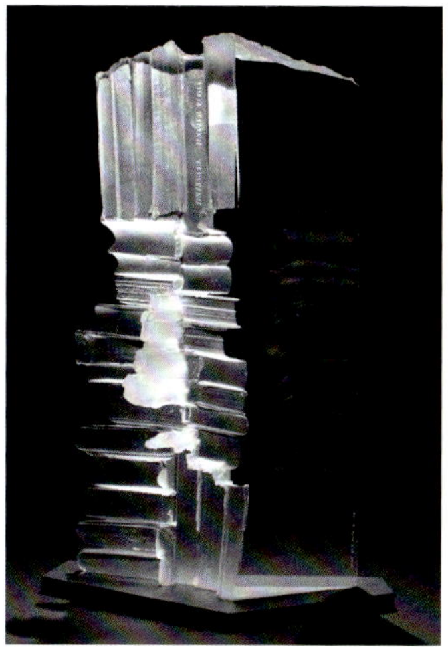

# The family dogs

The large part played by dogs in family life, both as pets and for sporting purposes, is emphasised by the regularity with which they too had their portraits painted. There were 19 in the Billiard Room alone in 1908. Dandie Dinmonts had a particular family association, but terriers and hounds abound, along with a particularly charming Newfoundland, painted by Alexander Nasmyth.

THIS PAGE, CLOCKWISE FROM TOP LEFT
HENRI-PIERRE DANLOUX (1753–1809)
*George Henry Scott (1798–1808/), asleep in his cradle, guarded by Kellach, a Skye terrier belonging to the Countess of Home*
HENRY PICKERSGILL (1782–1875)
*'Hirsel' by the fashionable Victorian portraitist*
ALEXANDER NASMYTH (1758–1840)
*In Nasmyth's group portrait, the 4th Duke's Newfoundland, Grog, poses with other family dogs: top left are Caroline Scott's small black dog, Busy, and Mary's red and white Swedish dog, Minette; on the right is the 3rd Duke's red and white spaniel, Gubbins. Looking up at Grog are Spy, a brown and white dog with sharp ears and curled tail, and Oscar, a white long-haired Scotch terrier belonging to Elizabeth, the 3rd Duke's wife. Nasmyth also painted Grog, paws crossed, on his own*

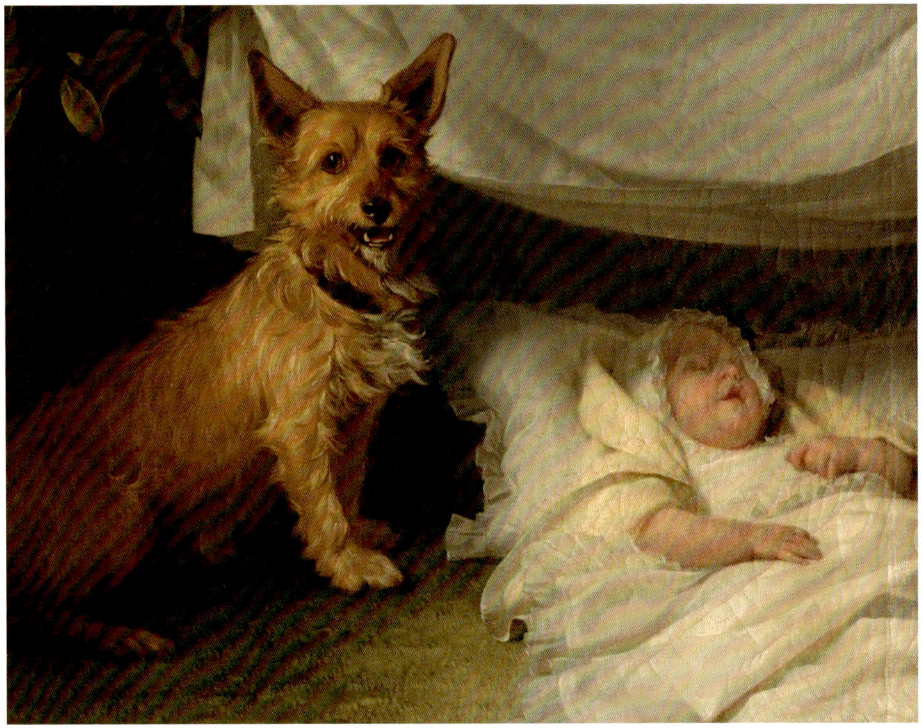

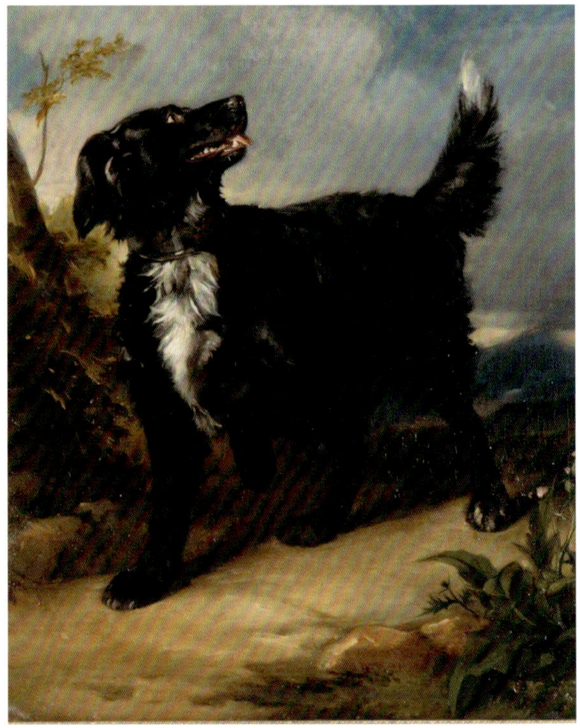

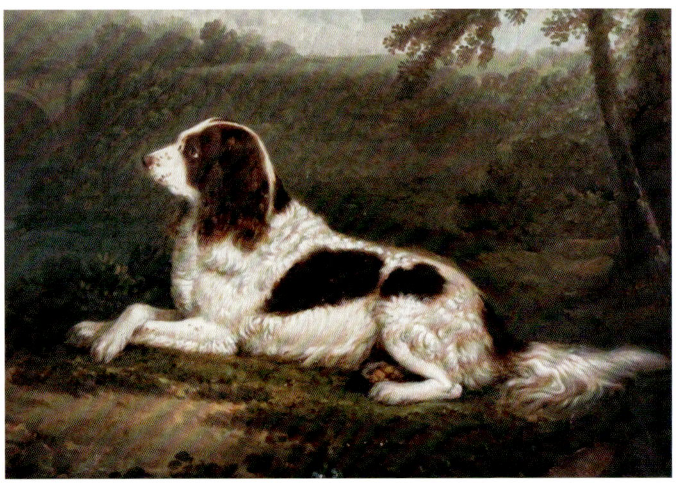

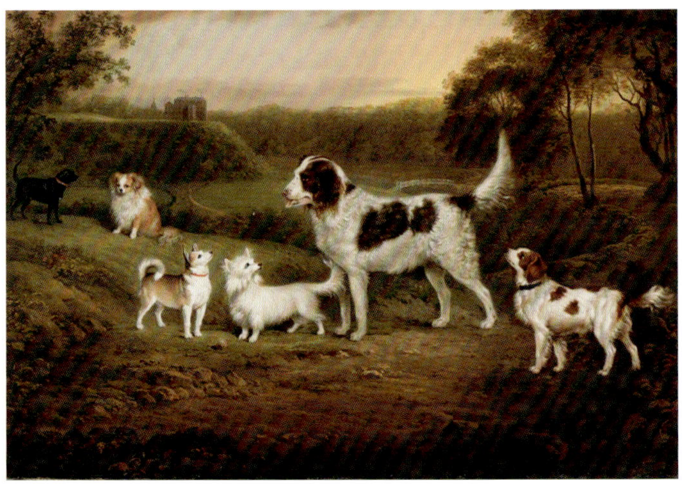

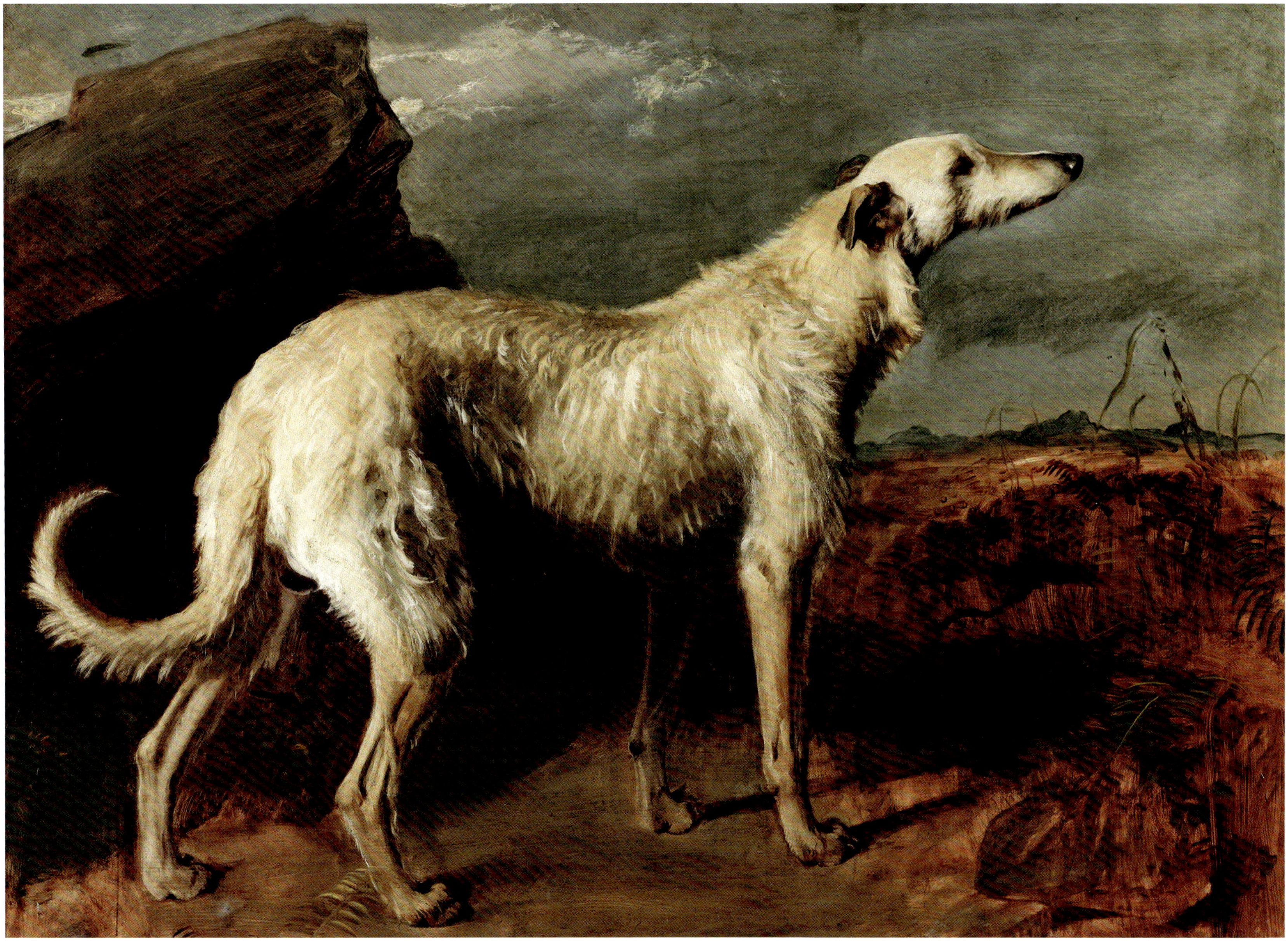

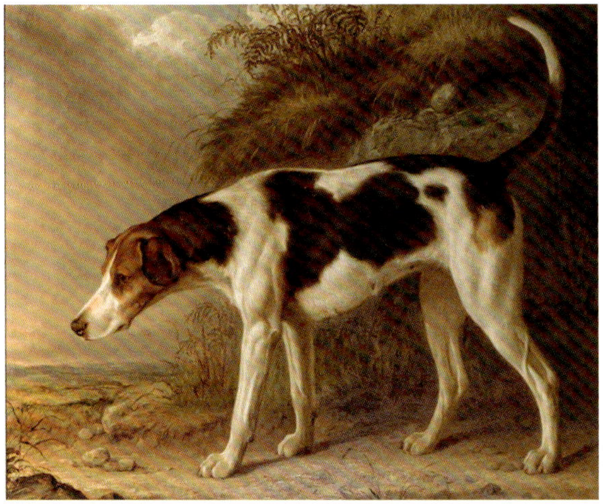

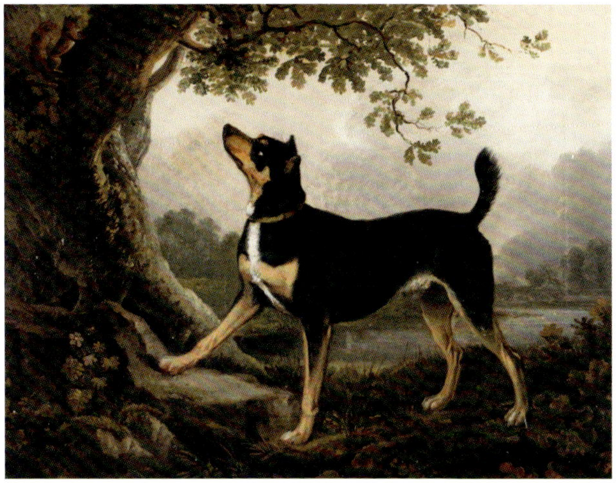

Above Thomas Duncan (1807–45) *'Braan, A Celebrated Deerhound' bequeathed in 1874 to the National Gallery of Scotland by Duncan McNeill of Colonsay. McNeill had saved the Highland deerhound from extinction*
Left *Henry, Lord Montagu's terrier, Pepper, with a squirrel*
Far left Gourlay Steell (1819–94) *Vesta, a foxhound*

# The Old Chapel

*As a final flourish, the great Victorian builder Walter Francis added the luminous Chapel at Bowhill for his Duchess, Charlotte Anne. Unconsecrated, today it is a setting for events, exhibitions and recitals*

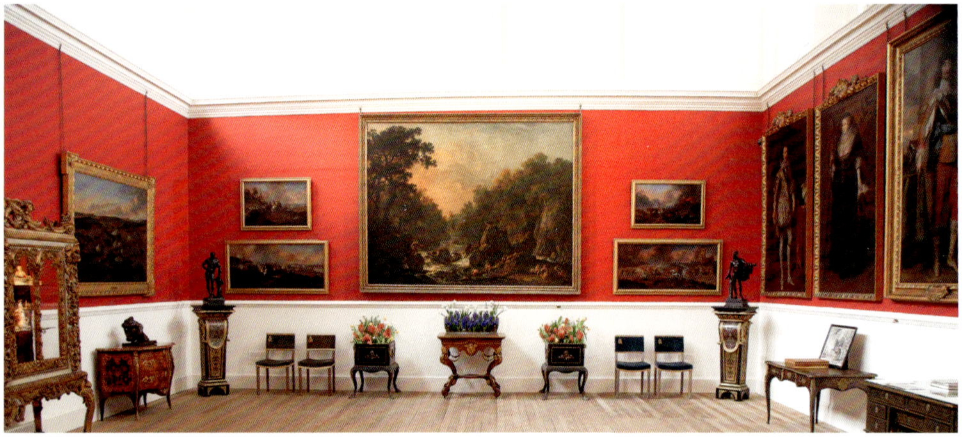

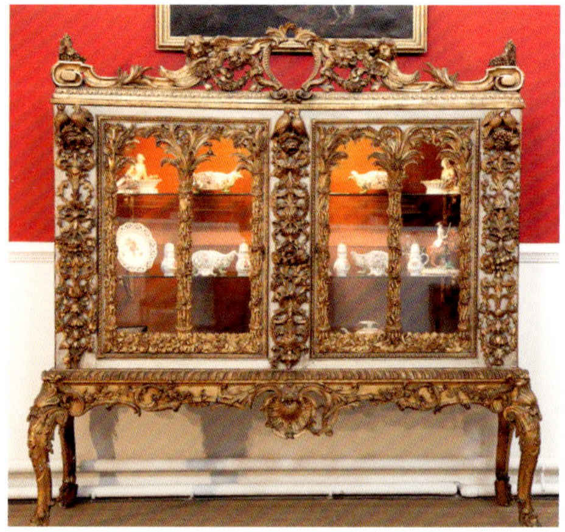

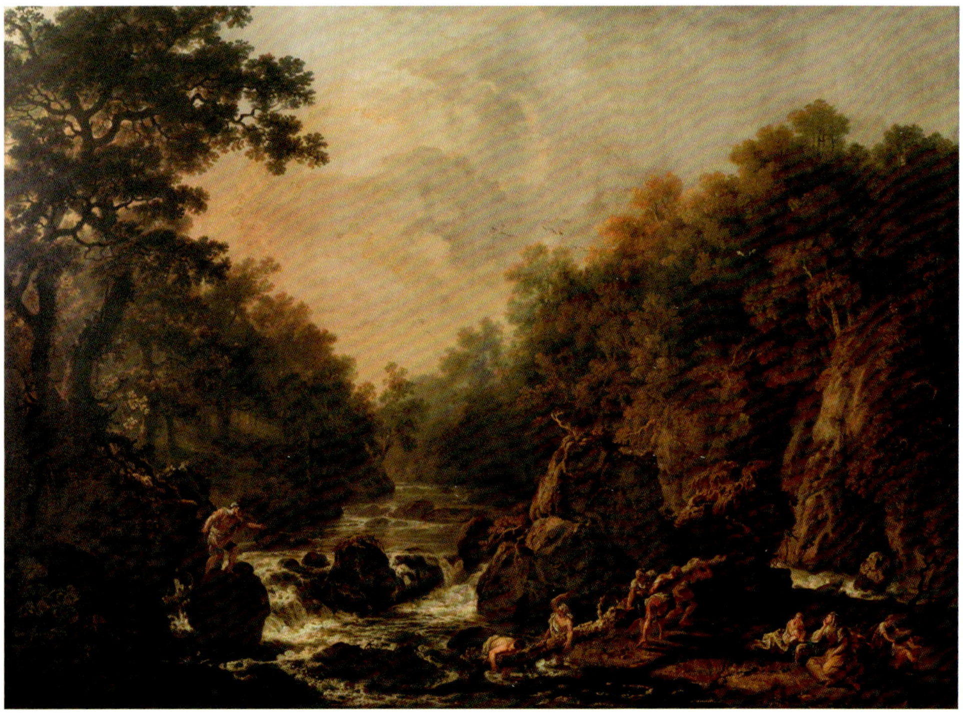

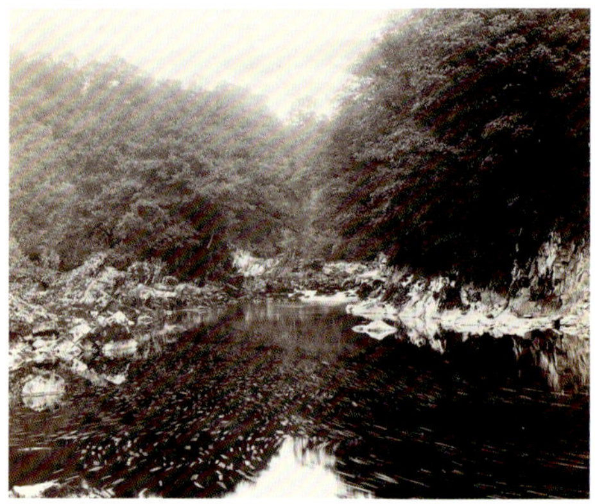

Completed in 1877 by the architect David Bryce, the Chapel was the final element of 19th-century construction work at Bowhill. There is some doubt about whether or not it was ever formally consecrated, although services were undoubtedly held at Bowhill. The family chaplain, the Rev. Severus Majendie, kept a record of them and of those

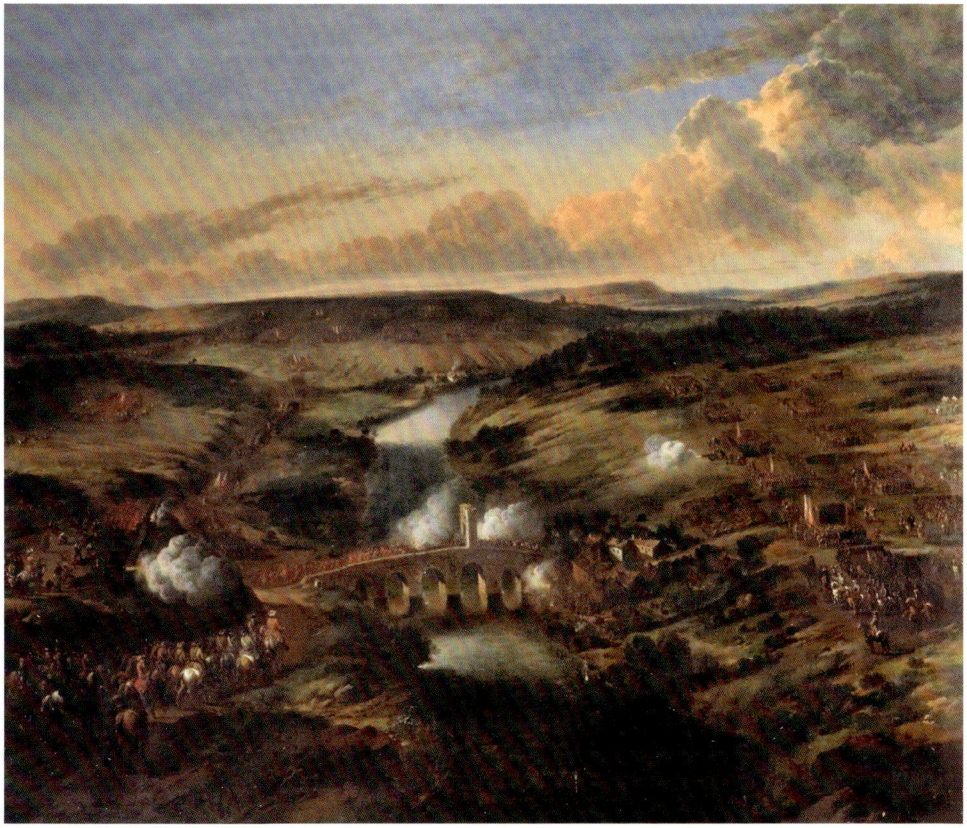

Opposite page
Top left *The Old Chapel now displays 17th-century portraits and battle scenes involving the Duke of Monmouth. The chairs are souvenirs of the coronations of George VI and Elizabeth II*
Top right *The 1833 gilded display case made by WL Bryant and affectionately known as 'Cinderella's Carriage' holds Meissen porcelain*

Bottom left George Barret (1730–84)
**Penton Lynn on the River Liddle**
*This waterfall was painted in the Borders near Langholm by Barret in his 'sublime' manner. It was exhibited at the Royal Academy in 1769*

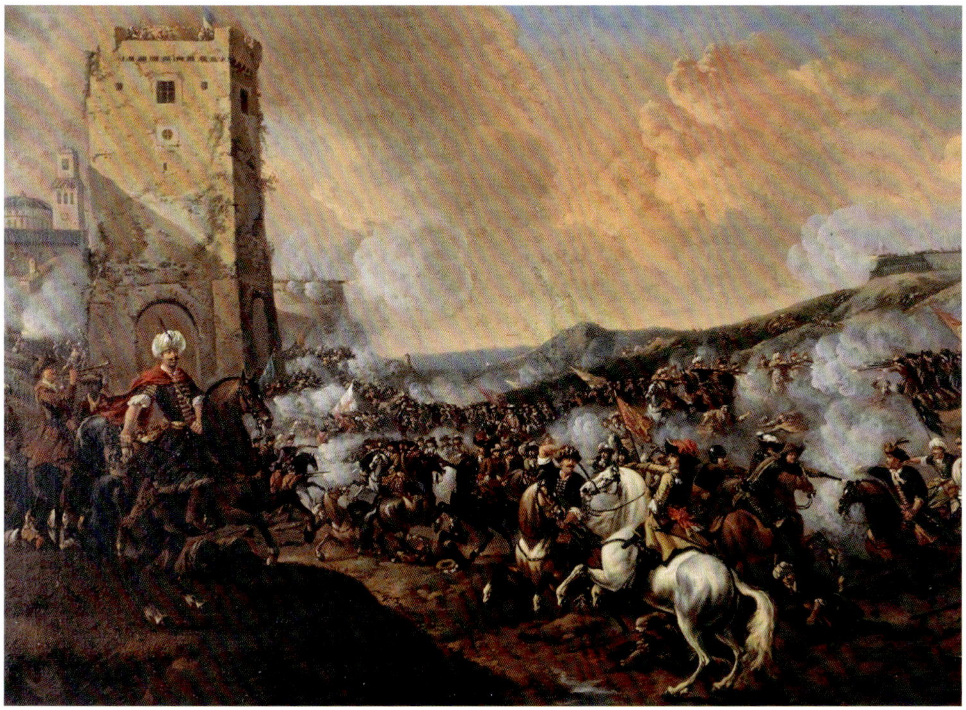

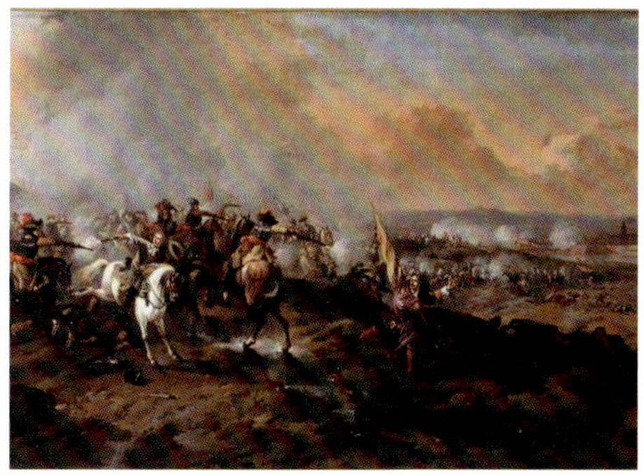

This page Jan Wyck (1652–1702)
**Three battle scenes**
*Monmouth himself commissioned at least four of the 11 battle scenes at Bowhill in 1676, paying the Dutch-born London artist £30. Duchess Anna had them arranged prominently, inset into panelling, at Dalkeith in Monmouth's honour. In 'The Battle of Bothwell Bridge', 1679 (top), he leads the army against the militant Presbyterian Covenantors. The other battles are unidentified*

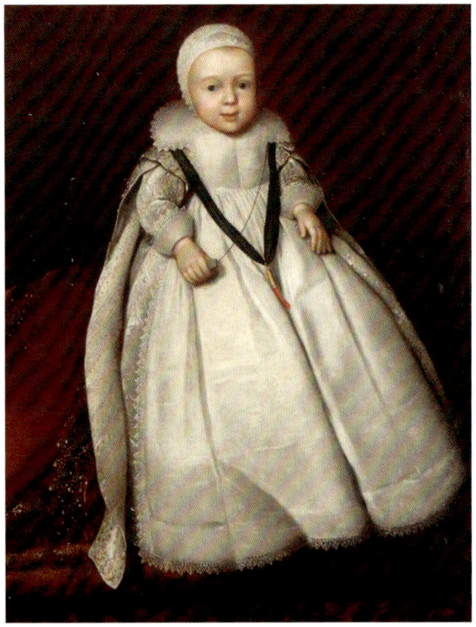

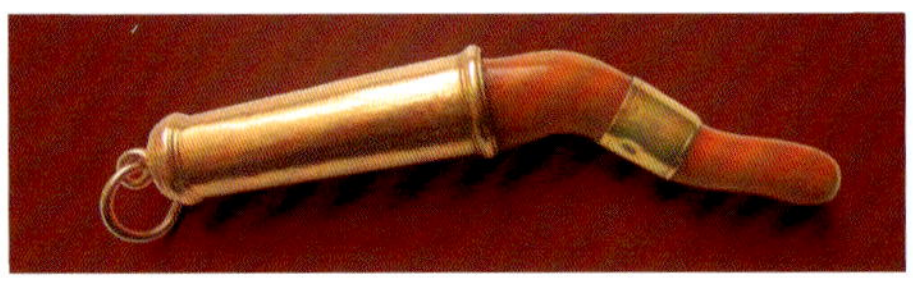

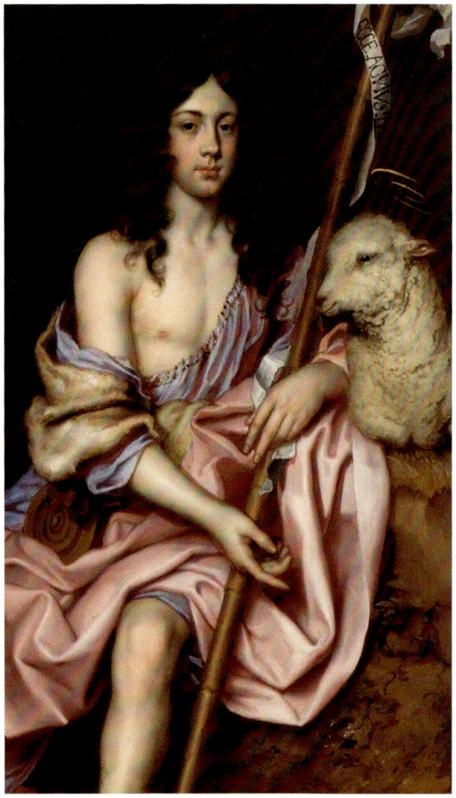

Far left *James, future Duke of Monmouth and Buccleuch, as a baby with a coral teething ring (seen below the portrait). The son of Charles II by Lucy Walter, he was born in Rotterdam during his father's exile. He married Anna Scott, Countess of Buccleuch, in 1663, at the age of 14*

Left Jacob Huysmans (c.1633–96)
**The Duke of Monmouth as John the Baptist**
*Monmouth's widow, Anna, would proudly hang his portraits at Dalkeith, including this prophetic painting. After the Monmouth Rebellion of 1685, her husband, like John the Baptist, lost his head*

Right Caspar Netscher (1639–84) and Jan van Huchtenburg (1647–1733)
**Equestrian portrait of the Duke of Monmouth**
*Regarded as a fine soldier, Monmouth fought many battles as the senior officer of his father's army. In this portrait, bought by the 5th Duke in 1883, he is fighting the Dutch at the Siege of Maastricht of 1673*

Below *Monmouth's saddle, heavily appliquéd with gold, is on display with the magnificent sword seen at the bottom of Kneller's portrait on page 13*

who attended, including poignant details of services held when the 5th Duke lay dying.

Dominant along one wall are a group of full-length 17th-century portraits, most of which hung at Montagu House in London, since demolished, where they were described as Van Dycks. It is an attribution not sustained by modern scholarship, but they do provide a period setting for the various images of the ill-fated Duke of Monmouth, a direct forebear of the present Duke – as a child, as John the Baptist by Huysmans, and as a general on horseback. A display case holds Monmouth's magnificent saddle and other mementos, including the beautiful lace shirt he wore at his execution.

Nowadays the Chapel serves as a gallery for exhibitions, seminars and recitals.

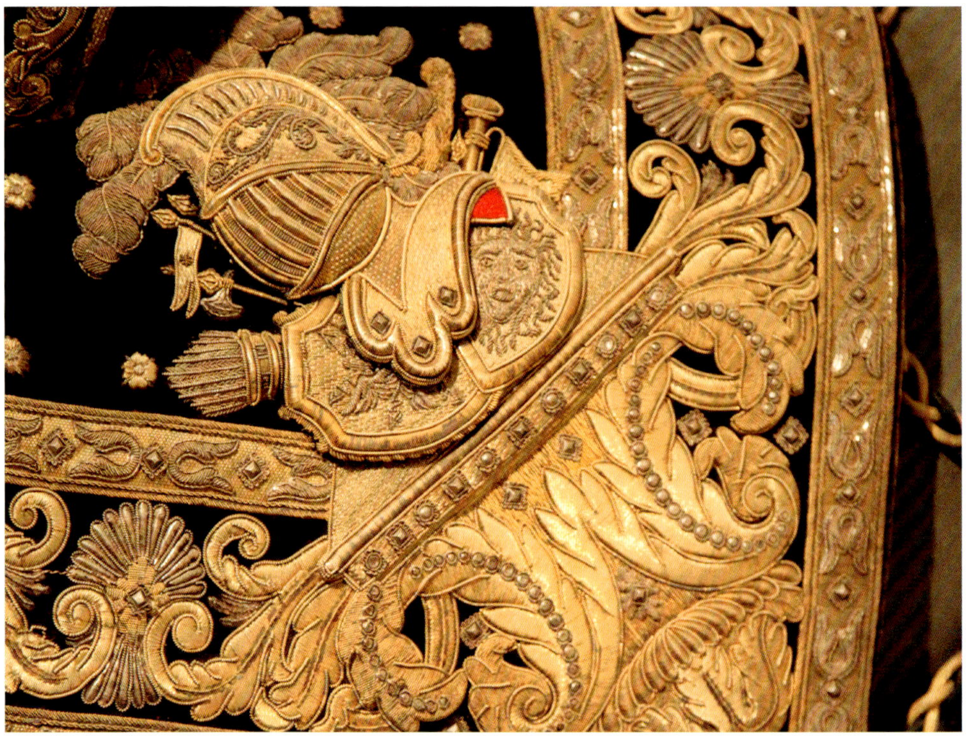

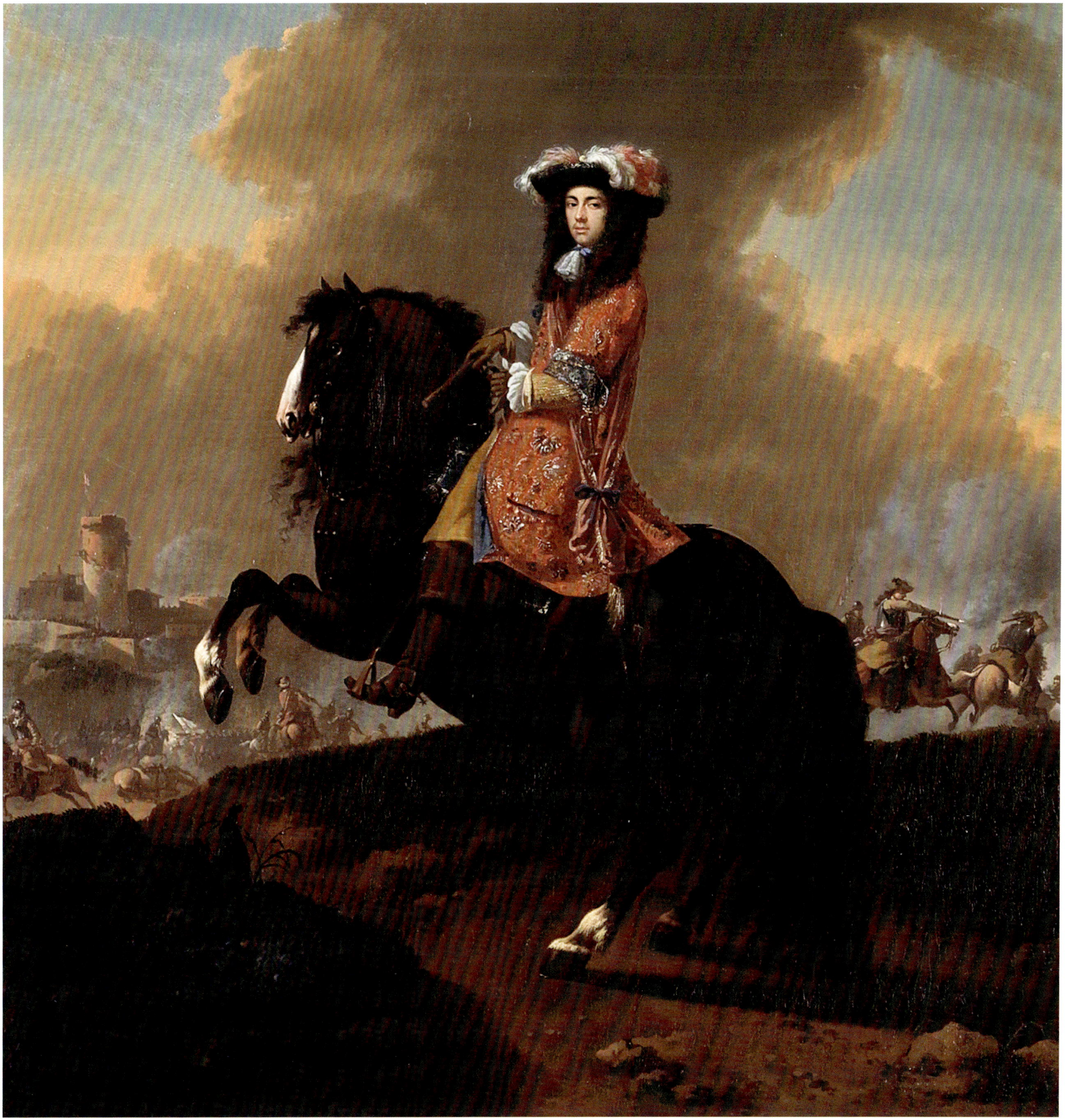

# The Buccleuch Miniatures

*Hilliard and Holbein rub shoulders in Bowhill's outstanding collection of portrait miniatures, now displayed in their own gallery*

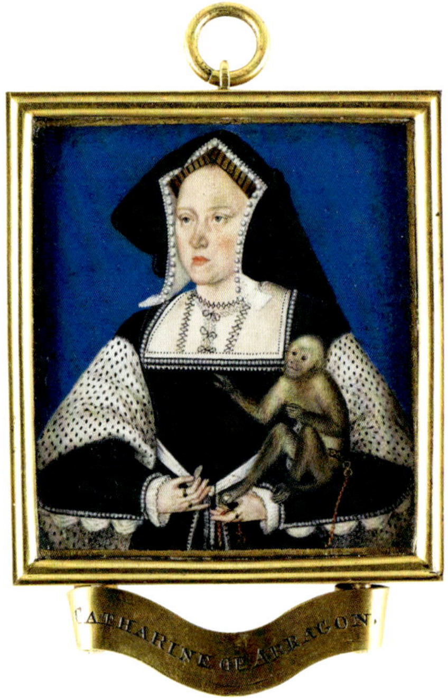

Lucas Horenbout (c.1490–1544)
*Katharine of Aragon, first wife of Henry VIII, with a marmoset*

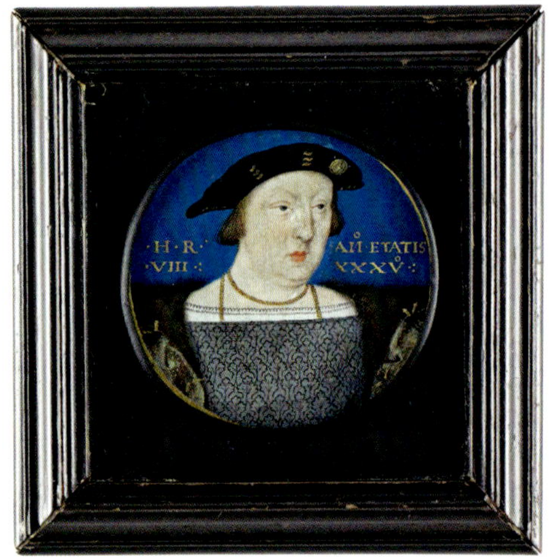

Lucas Horenbout
*Henry VIII as a young man, c.1525, without the familiar beard*

The great majority of the portrait miniatures in the Buccleuch Collection – more than 800 of them despite sales in the 1940s – were bought by the 5th Duke and Duchess. They were helped by Andrew McKay of Colnaghi, who seems to have scoured the salerooms for them. The purchase accounts in the Bowhill archive show that miniatures were sometimes bought 20 or more at a time.

Scholarship has come a long way since the 19th century, when attributions were frequently ambitious, with quite a number described as being by Holbein. The identification of sitters was also haphazard. The collection nevertheless is remarkably comprehensive, reflecting both English and Continental styles, and stretches right back to the origins of the art, which evolved from the illustrations seen in medieval manuscripts. The collection contains several works by Lucas Horenbout (also known as Hornebolte), regarded as the earliest identifiable artist and the tutor of perhaps the greatest miniature painter of all, Hans Holbein. Bowhill has two very rare Holbeins.

Sixteenth-century English painting is particularly strongly represented, with several works by the leading Elizabethan artists, Nicholas Hilliard and Isaac Oliver. From the 17th century there are a substantial

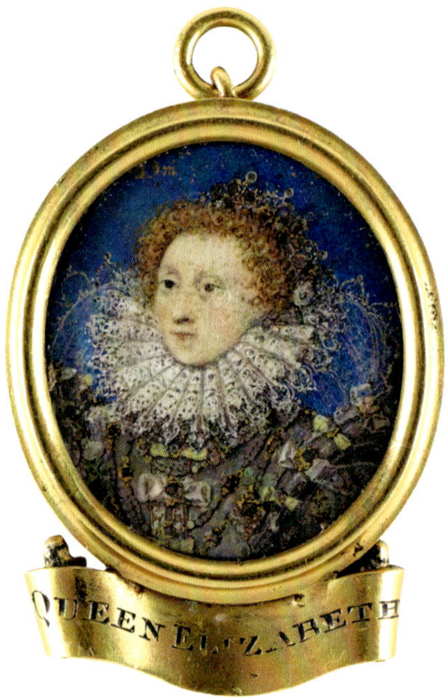

Nicholas Hilliard (c.1547–1619)
*Elizabeth I in a richly jewelled dress and white lace ruff, painted by the master miniaturist*

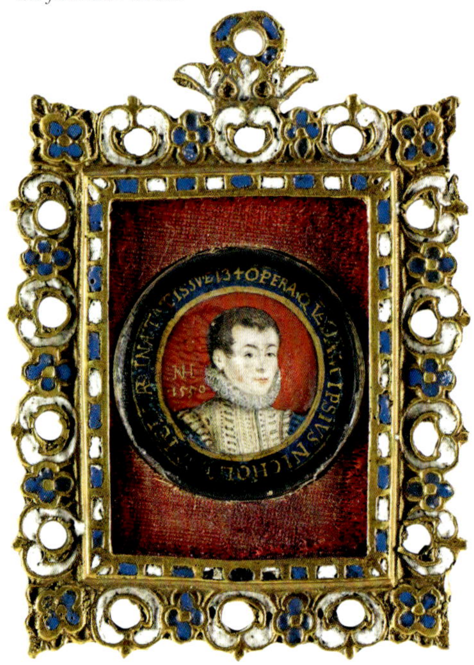

Attributed to Nicholas Hilliard
*Inscribed in Latin 'self-portrait, aged 13, 1560'. The 17th-century enamelled frame is Spanish*

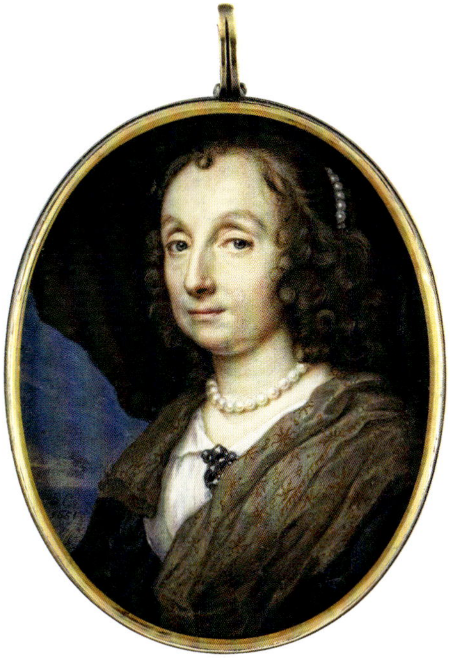

Samuel Cooper (1609–72)
*Mrs Oliver Cromwell, née Elizabeth Bourchier, 1651*

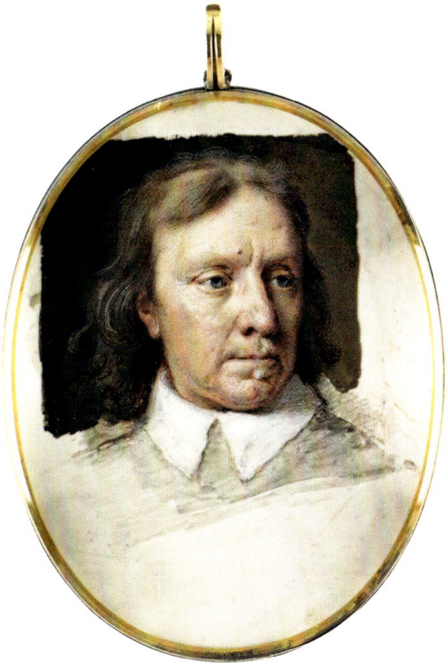

Samuel Cooper *Oliver Cromwell, c.1653. The famous 'warts and all' unfinished portrait of the Lord Protector of England*

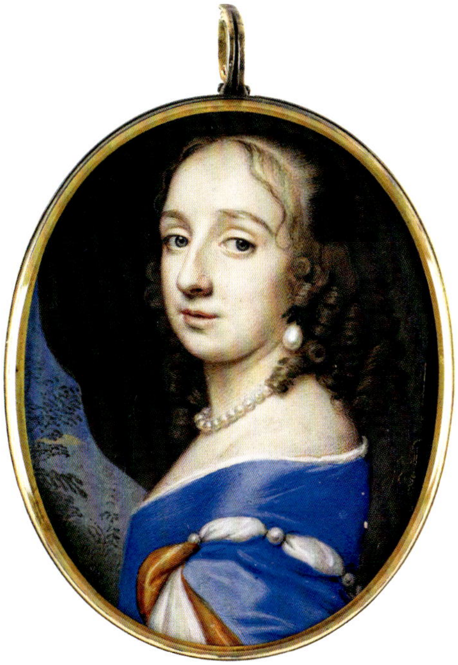

Samuel Cooper *One of Cromwell's daughters, painted in 1653. It is either his favourite, Elizabeth, Mrs Claypole, or his youngest, Frances, Lady Russell*

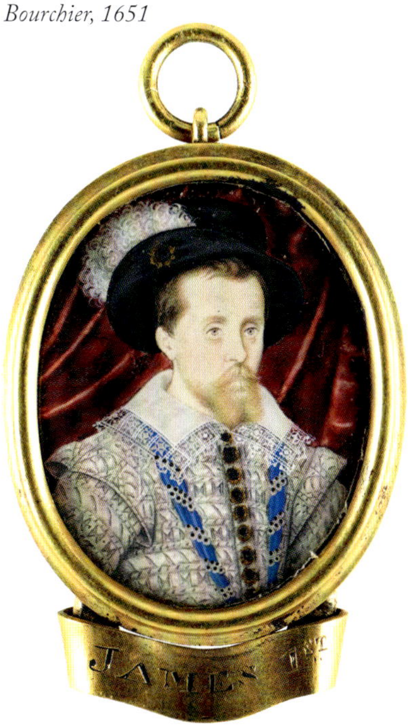


Nicholas Hilliard *King James VI and I, c.1605, wearing a white embroidered doublet and a black feathered hat*

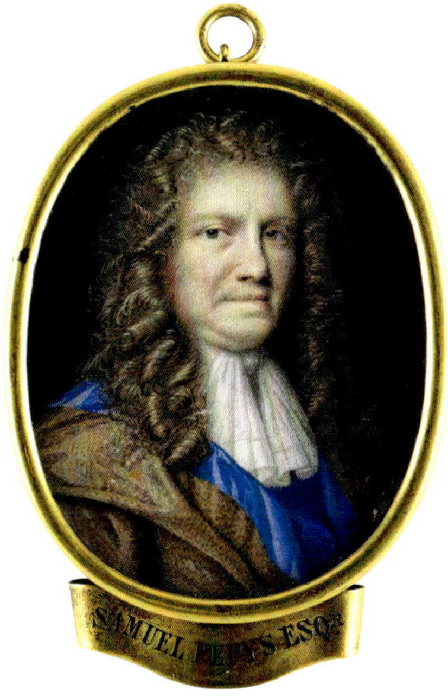


Charles Beale the Younger (1660–c.1726)
*A gentleman, once thought to be Pepys, dated 1688. Both of Beale's parents were established painters*

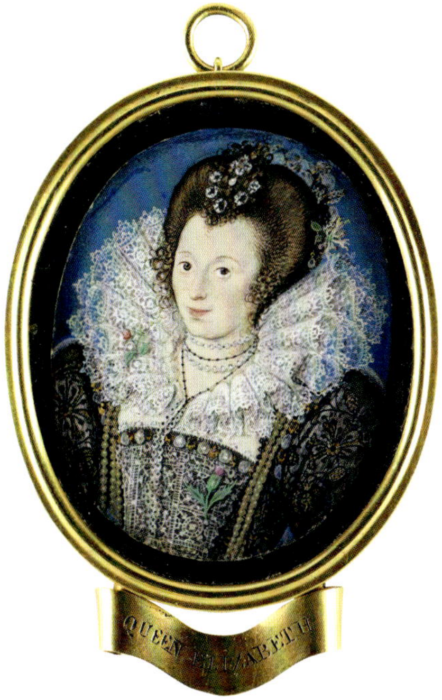


Nicholas Hilliard *Portrait of a lady, wearing a black embroidered dress and a thistle, her hair adorned with jewels, c.1590*

number by Samuel Cooper, including the famous unfinished head of Oliver Cromwell, bought via Colnaghi from a descendant.

Miniatures were painted in a number of mediums, including gouache and oil, and on a variety of surfaces including vellum, playing cards and enamel. The portrait of Queen Mary by Hans Eworth is on gold. Frames were often extremely elaborate and covered with jewels, though sadly those in the collection are mostly 19th-century.

Identified sitters include a roll call of 16th- and 17th-century kings and queens, as well as members of the nobility and others who served at their courts and in public life, alongside famous figures, including Cromwell and his family, who did not.

A similar cast of Europeans appears in the Continental miniatures, while from across the Atlantic come the distinctive features of the American philosopher Benjamin Franklin and General Washington.

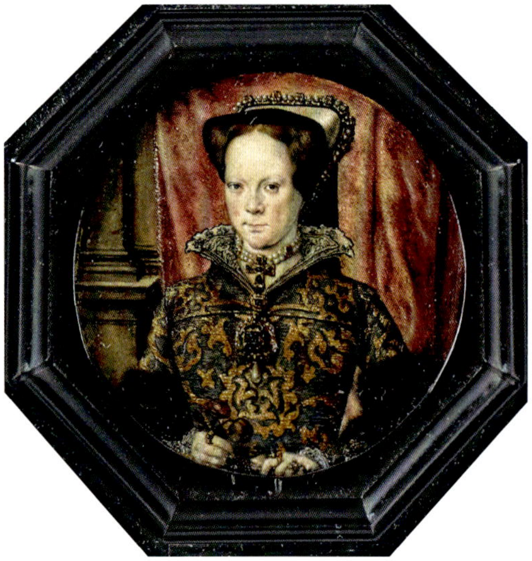

Hans Eworth (c.1520–1574) *Mary Tudor, Queen of England, in a gold damask dress, holds two tulips. Painted in oil on gold, c.1555*

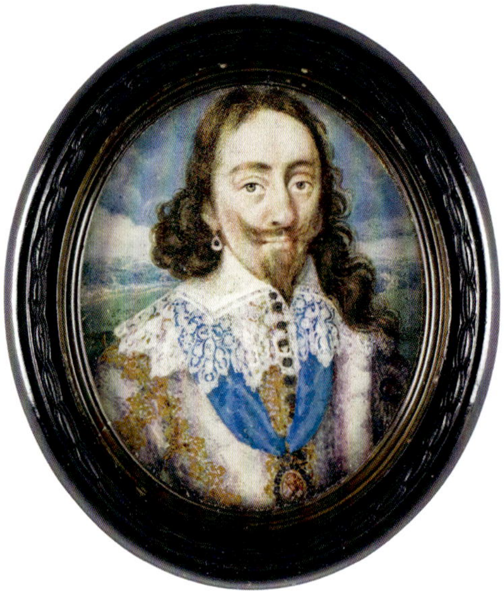

Lawrence Hilliard (1582–1648) *Charles I in a mauve embroidered doublet, by Nicholas Hilliard's son, c.1635*

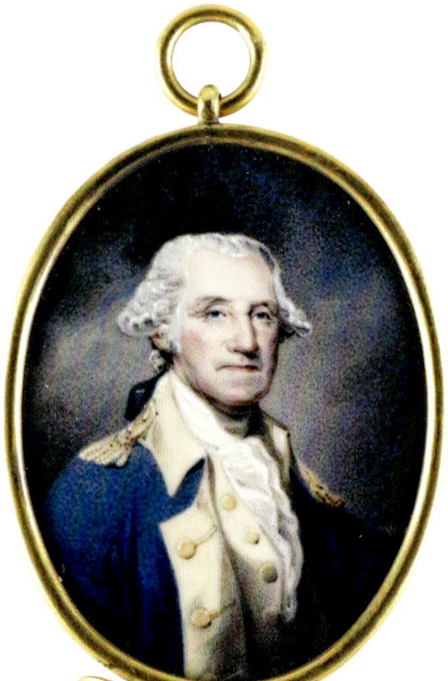


William Russell Birch (1755–1834), after Gilbert Stuart *George Washington, the first American President, painted on enamel*

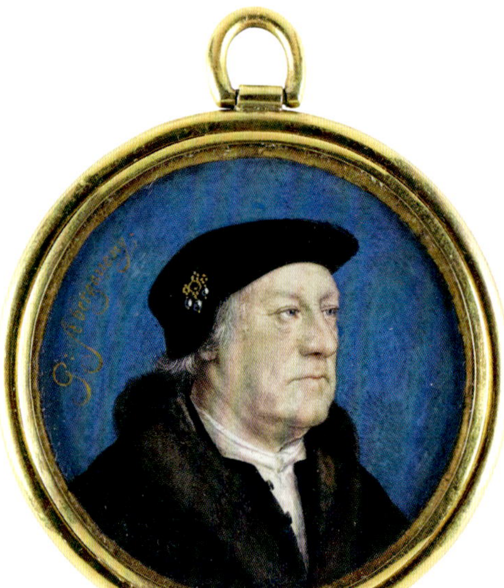

Hans Holbein the Younger (c.1497–1543) *Henry VII's courtier Sir George Neville, 3rd Baron Abergavenny, c.1535, was acquired by the 6th Duke*

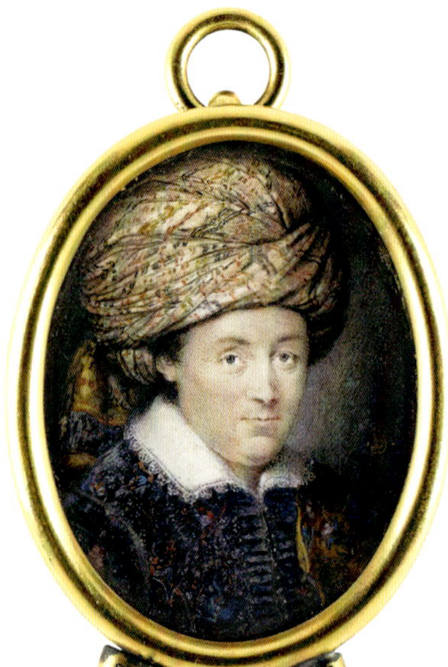

Peter Oliver (1594–1648) *Sir Robert Shirley, the merchant adventurer and envoy to the Shah of Persia, wearing an embroidered turban*

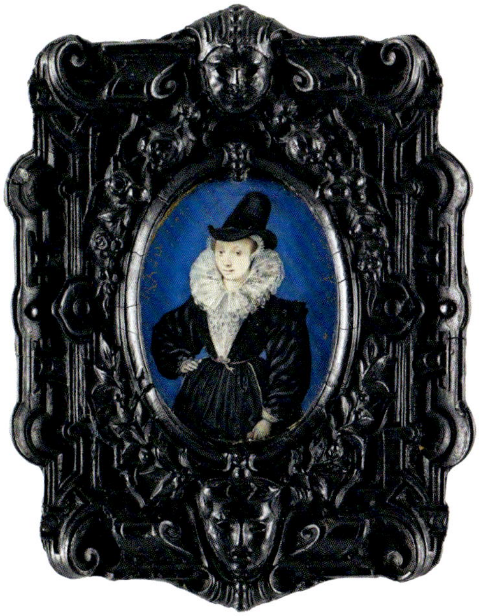

Isaac Oliver (c.1565–1617) *A lady in black hat and dress, inscribed in Latin, '1587, aged 20'. Isaac Oliver was Nicholas Hilliard's pupil*

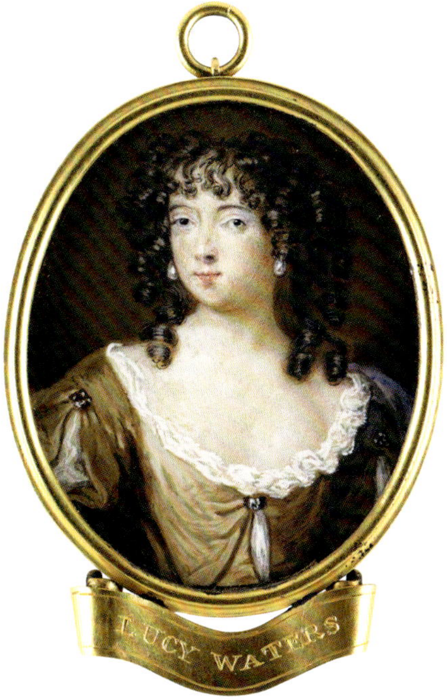


English School, after Sir Peter Lely *Lucy Walter, Charles II's mistress and the mother of the Duke of Monmouth and Buccleuch, c.1655*

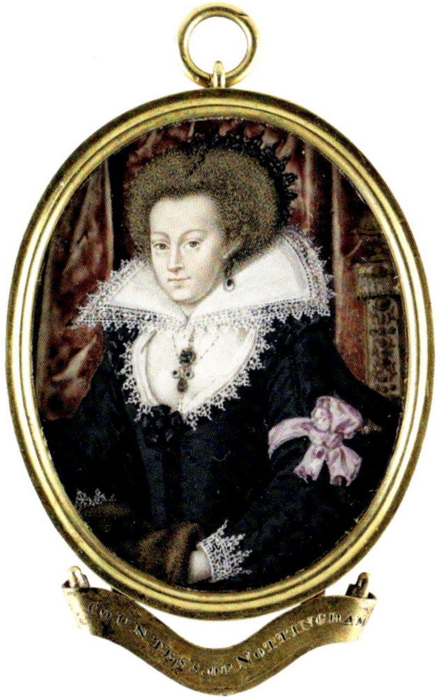

Nicholas Hilliard (c.1547–1619) *Catherine Howard, Countess of Nottingham, for 45 years a close confidante of Elizabeth I, c.1600*

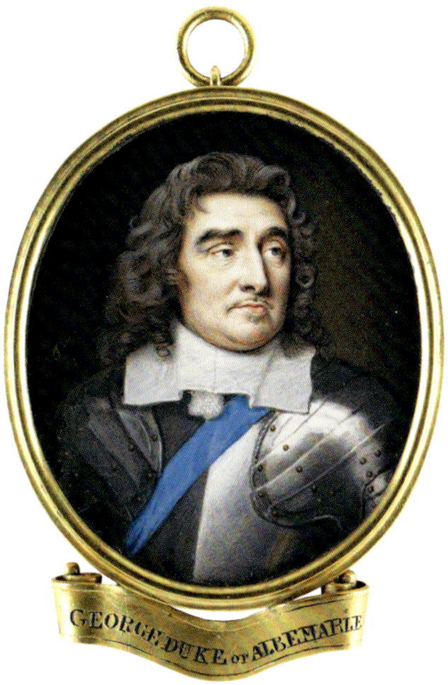


Samuel Cooper *George Monck, 1st Duke of Albemarle, wearing armour, c.1660, the year he played a key role in the Restoration of Charles II*

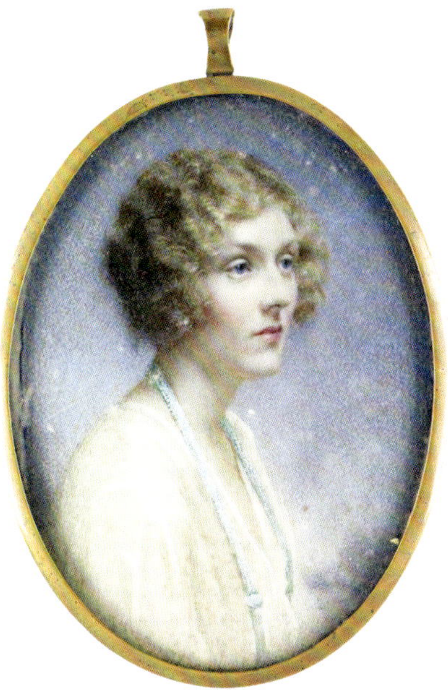

Mabel Lee Hankey (1863–1943) *Watercolour of Mary (Molly), Duchess of Buccleuch, the present Duke's grandmother*

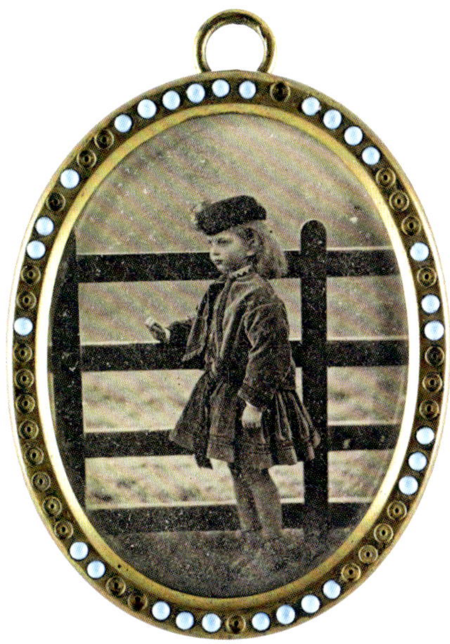

*A Victorian adaptation of the miniature tradition: Lord John Scott, who was to become the 7th Duke*

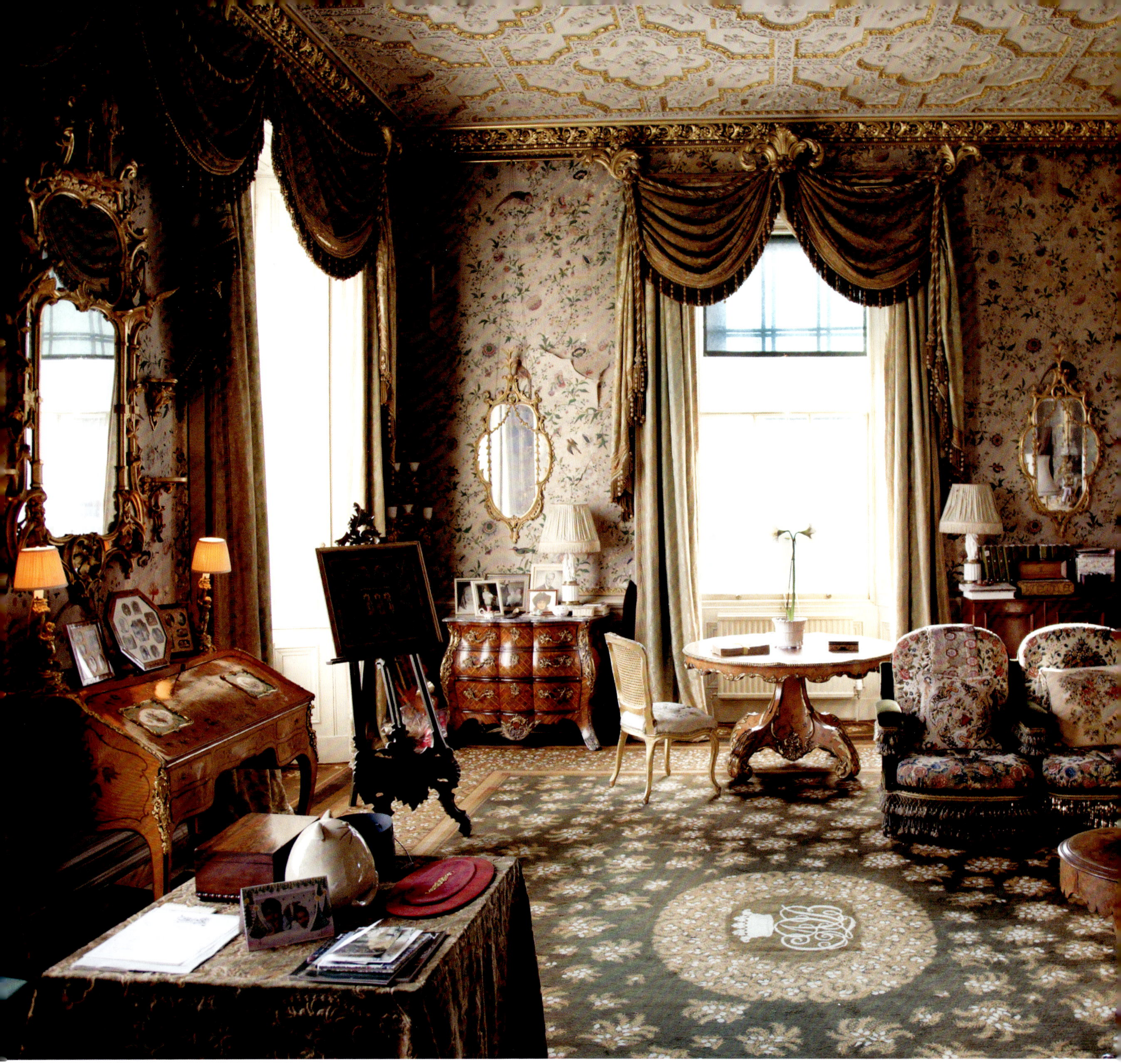

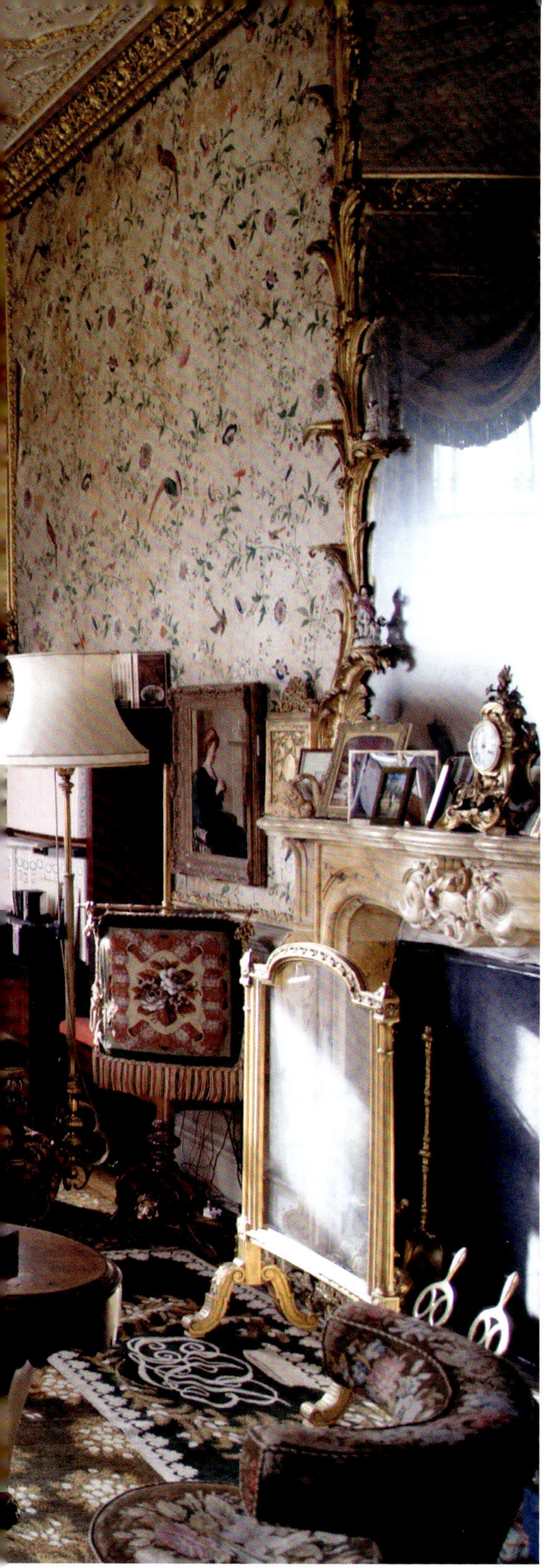

# The Boudoir

*The Duchess's sitting room is the jewel box of early Victorian Bowhill. It was added by Burn soon after the Duke married Lady Charlotte Anne Thynne, daughter of the Marquess of Bath, in 1829*

The relatively dark west corridor, known as the Victorian Passage – a safe home for George Richmond's delicately drawn portraits of the family from the 1850s and '60s and tiers of engravings, striking in their rosewood or giltwood frames – does not prepare you for the effusion of light and colour at the far end.

Easily missed as you as you enter the Duchess's sitting room, usually known as the Boudoir, is a discreet door to a spiral staircase which leads directly to the nursery, the night nursery and the children's bedrooms. This is the domestic, feminine, family end of the house, removed in every sense from the male enclaves of the Smoking and Billiard Rooms.

Today the Boudoir is the most complete surviving interior at Bowhill. In the words of John Cornforth in *Country Life*, it shows the eclecticism of Burn's taste – 'the Louis Revival chimneypiece and Rococo Revival overmantel mirror, the Jacobean ceiling picked out with plenty of gold and the Chinese wallpaper'.

The room's survival is something of a miracle as, along with the whole of this wing of the house, it suffered from dreadful dry rot. During the repair process it was completely gutted.

The curtains and carpet are the originals, and woven into the latter and into the rare hearthrug is the monogram of Charlotte Anne Buccleuch and Queensberry, also to be seen on the Louis XV-style *bureau de dame* with Sèvres plaques supplied by Baldock in 1841.

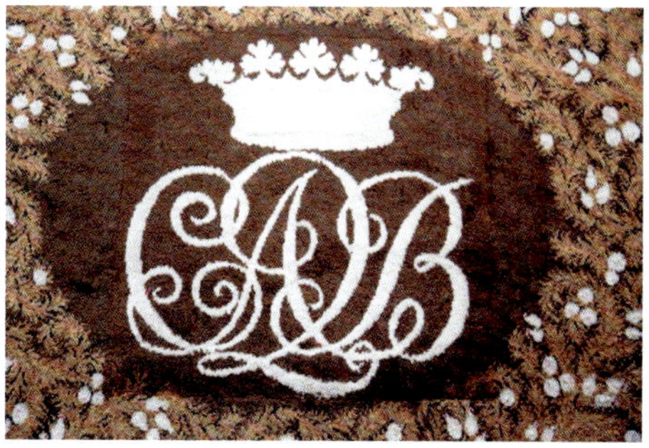

LEFT AND ABOVE *The Boudoir is Bowhill's most completely preserved room, more or less as Charlotte Anne, newly married to the 5th Duke, would have wished it in the early 1830s. Even the original matching Axminster hearthrug, which like the carpet itself bears the Duchess's initials, has survived. This 2010 photograph shows the room before the Chinese wallpaper was conserved*
BELOW *A screen decorated with Simon Jacques Rochard's interior views of Ditton Park, a family house in Buckinghamshire*

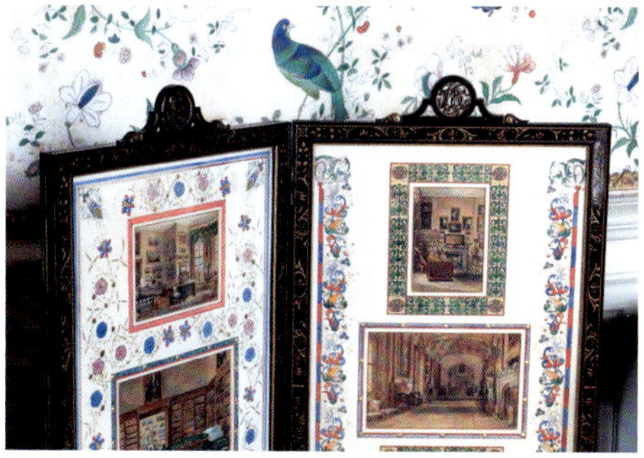

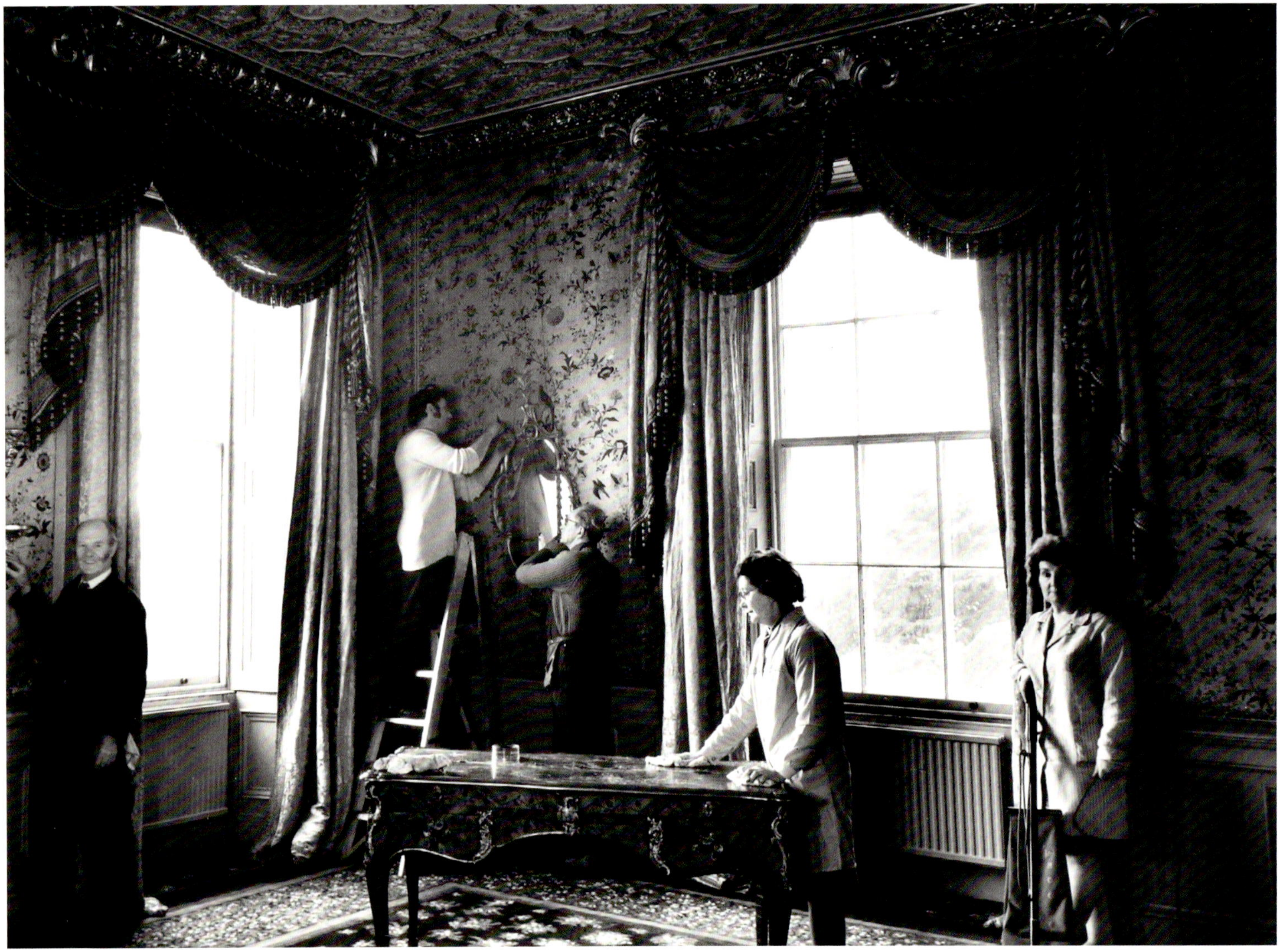

ABOVE RESTORING THE BOUDOIR
*Housekeepers and carpenters return furnishings to the Boudoir after an outbreak of dry rot in the 1970s. From left, David Marshall, the caretaker, stands next to the window; the Laidlaws, a father-and-son team who hung many of the paintings at Bowhill, rehang a George III giltwood mirror with particularly fragile swags; Jenny Snucins dusts a Louis XV bureau-plat by Jacques Dubois; Anna Symons is poised to hoover*

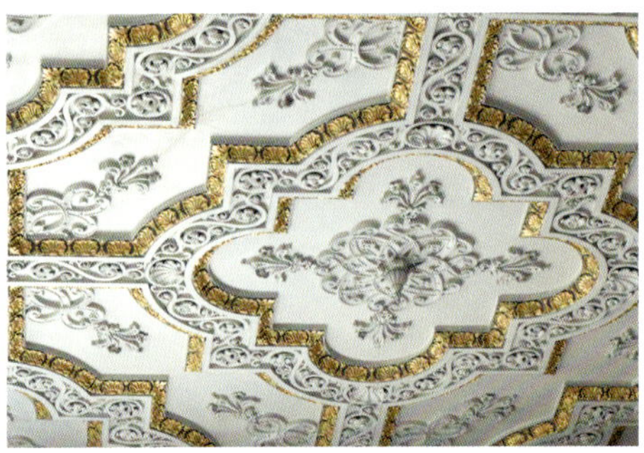

OPPOSITE *A bird flits between peonies and other delicate flowers on the Chinese wallpaper. Below it is the top of an early Victorian giltwood cabinet with gothic tracery doors. Derby porcelain figures adorn the rococo overmantel mirror*
LEFT *Burn's neo-Jacobean trelliswork ceiling. The 5th Duke's architect would eventually lose favour with the Duchess. She so hated his Bowhill clock tower that she asked the Duke to make him pay to take it down. Fortunately, she was not heeded*

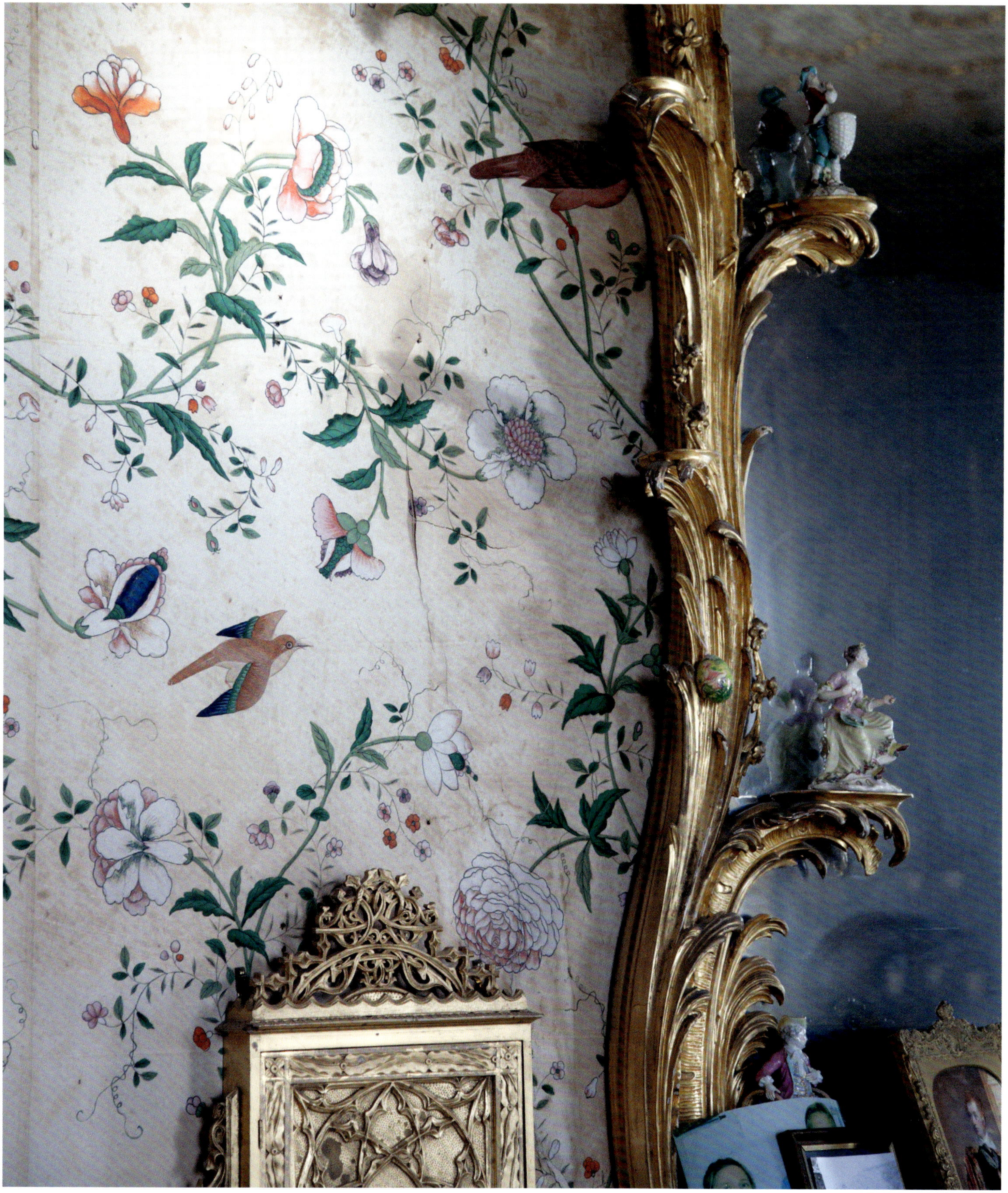

## Restoring the Boudoir's Chinese wallpaper

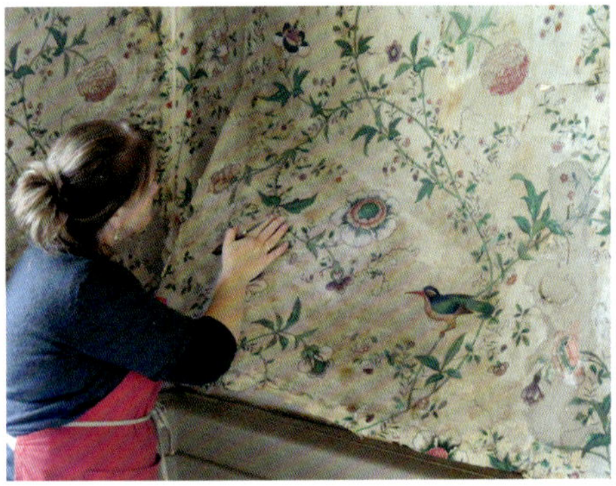

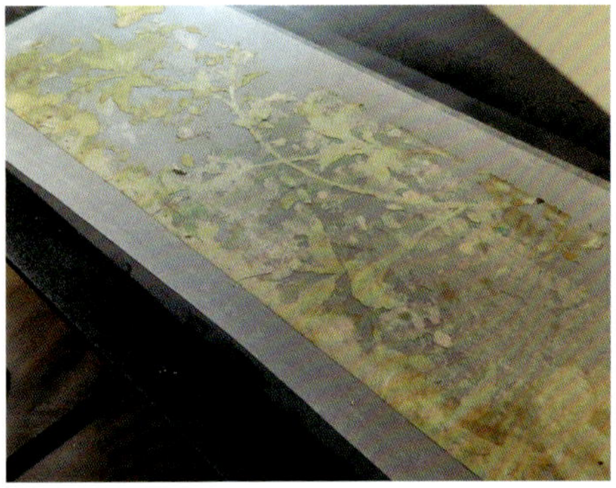

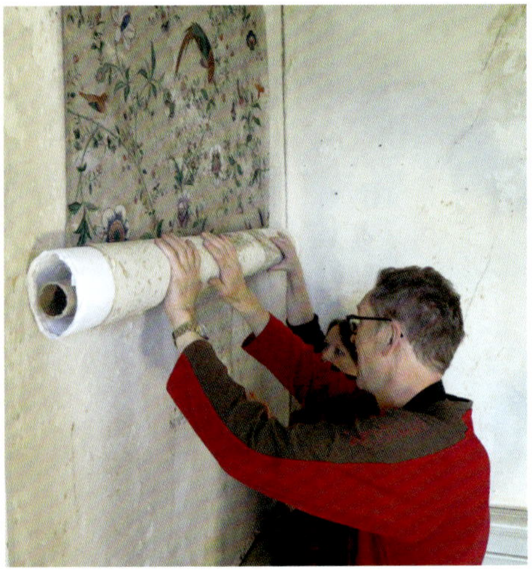

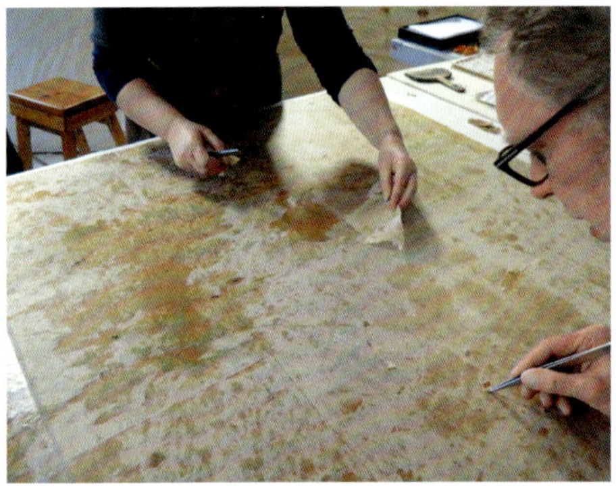

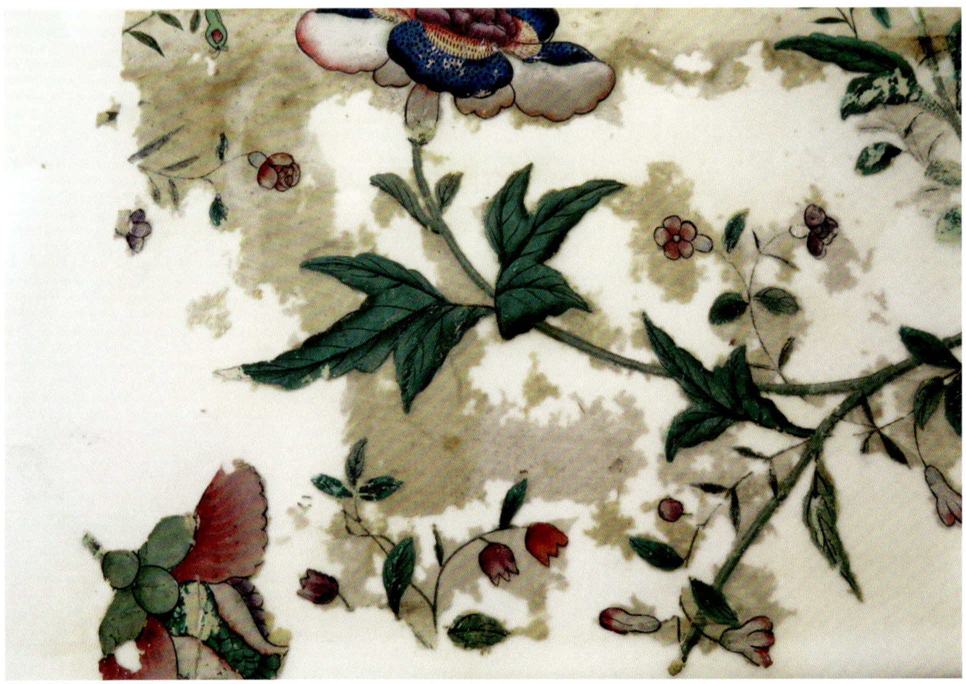

THIS PAGE
TOP LEFT *Louise Drover loosens the paper from the plaster on the west wall of the Boudoir*
BOTTOM LEFT *Mark Sandiford and Louise then roll the paper off the plaster*
LEFT AND BELOW LEFT *Painstakingly dampened fragments are suctioned clean on the suction-table after three layers of delicate lining paper have been removed*
BOTTOM *Silverfish damage is very evident*

OPPOSITE PAGE
CENTRE LEFT *During removal of the lining paper, Louise applies tiny patches to the back of the wallpaper to secure areas of loss or weakness*
TOP LEFT *Particularly bad discoloration requires gentle abrasive treatment*
BOTTOM LEFT *New lining paper is applied*
TOP RIGHT *Sections of wallpaper before and after treatment*
BOTTOM RIGHT *Back on the wall: each of the beautiful birds is depicted in a different pose*

In 2017 a further conservation programme was begun on the Boudoir's wallpaper, which had been supplied in 1834 by the London firm of Cowtans. Hand-painted in China for the European market, it had been seriously damaged by damp and voracious silverfish that had an appetite for particular paints. Similar paper in the Morning Room was unscathed.

Over four months a small team – Louise Drover, Mark Sandiford and Alasdair Peebles – painstakingly removed the wallpaper, teasing off the decayed Chinese rice paper lining, then washing the sheets in a suction bath. When dry, layers of Japanese lining were reapplied and the most damaged areas sensitively retouched.

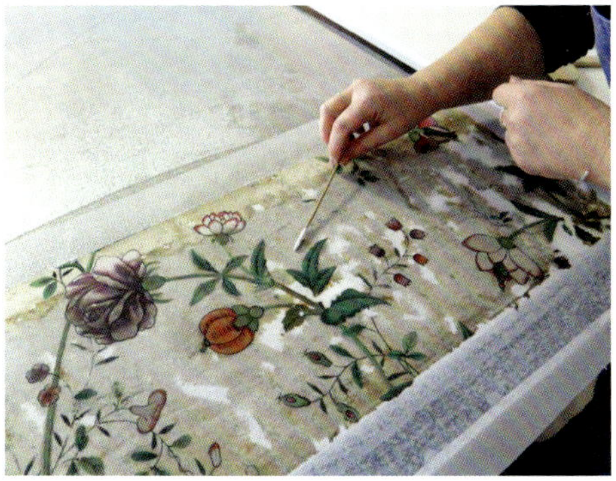

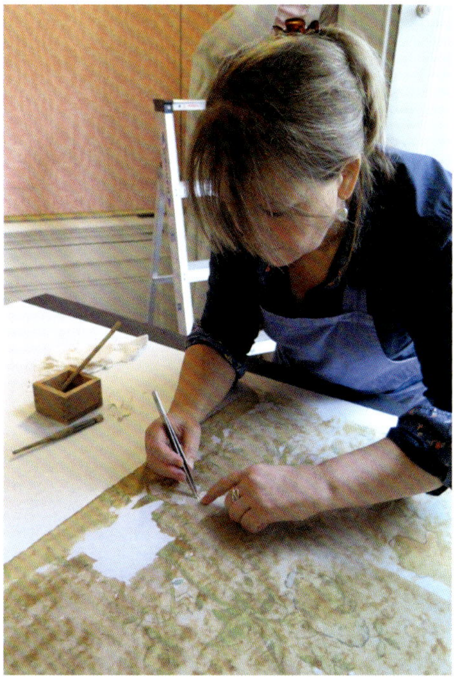

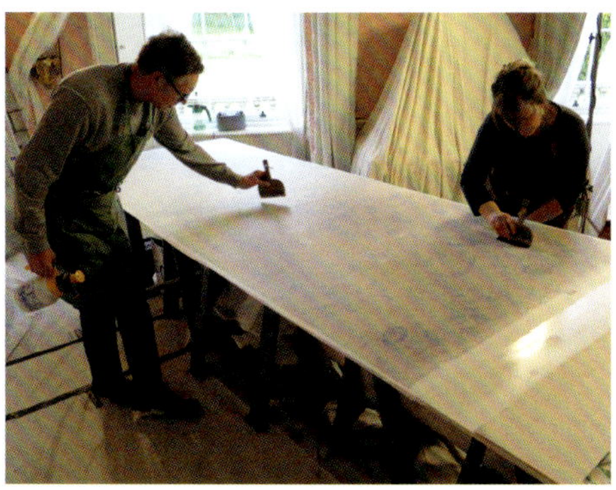

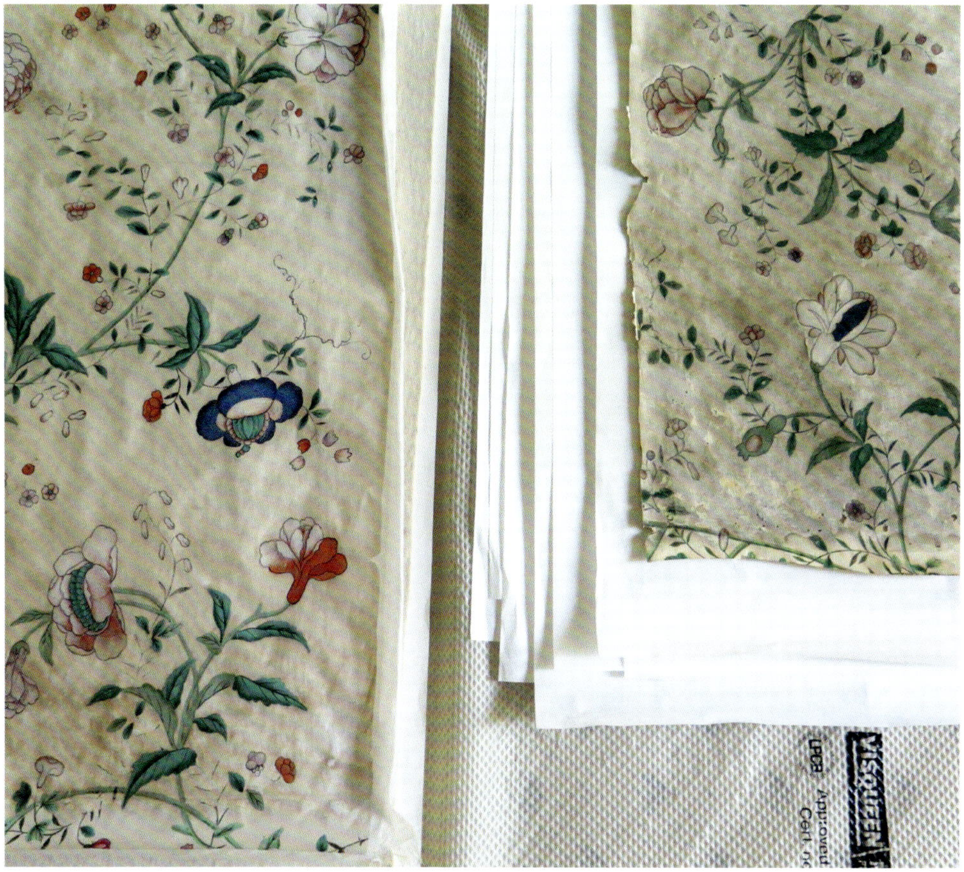

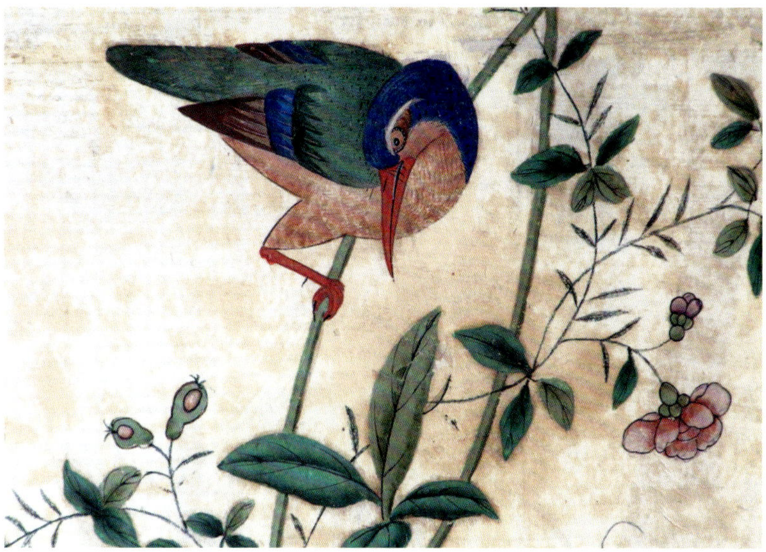

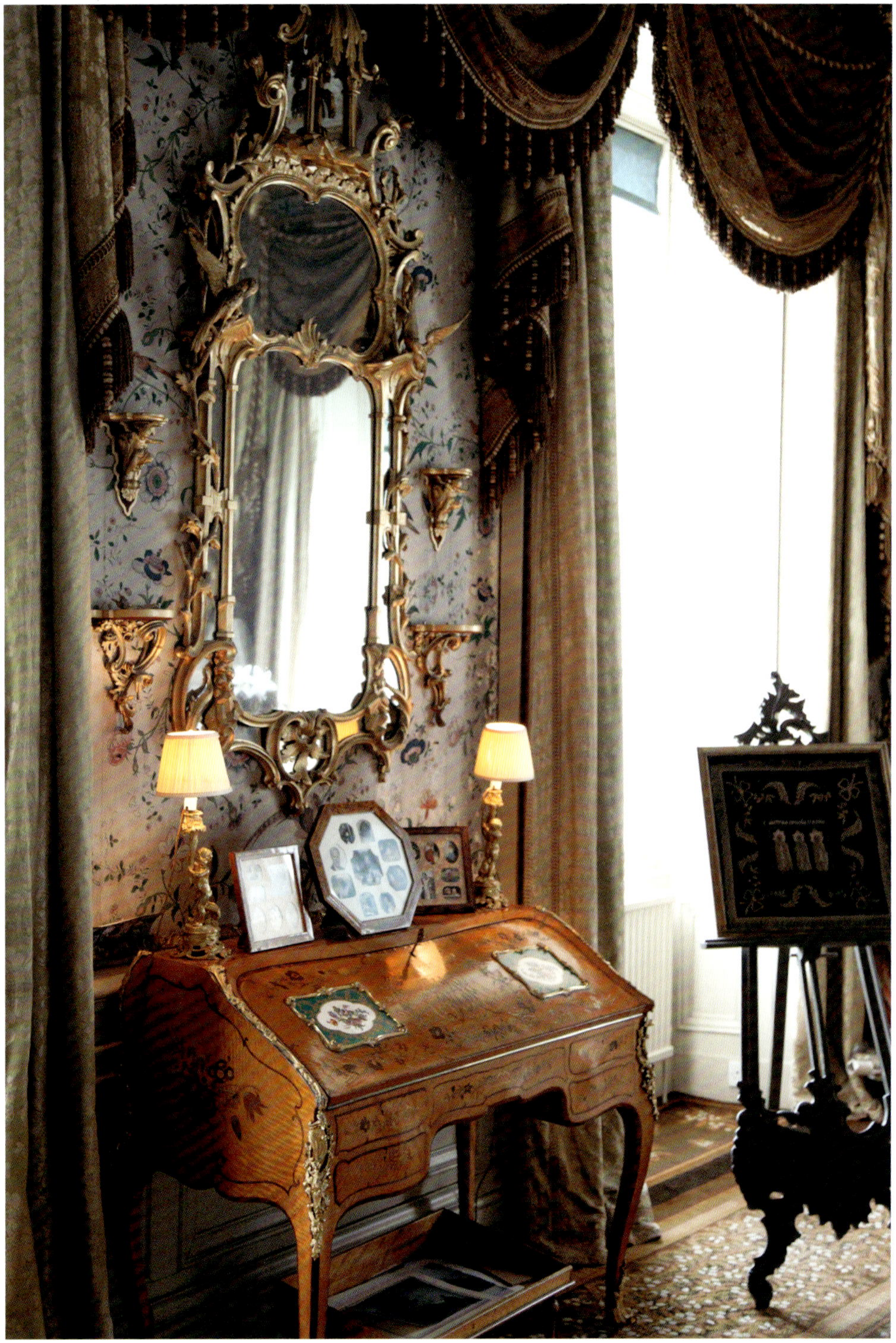

THIS PAGE *A 'Chinese' mirror framed by swags hangs above a satinwood Louis XV-style bureau de dame, c.1830, designed by Baldock and set with Sèvres plaques. Almost certainly an early gift from the 5th Duke, the bureau is inlaid with Duchess Charlotte Anne's coroneted CABQ monogram*

RIGHT *Engravings line the approach to the Boudoir. At the end is 'Blithe October', by William McTaggart (1835–1910), bought by Duchess Jane*

FAR RIGHT, ABOVE *The moiré wallpaper in the Duchess's Bedroom was inspired by early-Victorian examples at Drumlanrig Castle*

FAR RIGHT, BELOW *Sir John McNeill of Colonsay (1795–1883), Duchess Jane's forebear, who served in India and Persia as a diplomat and surgeon to the Shah. His 1853 report on the British debacle in the Crimea led to sweeping reforms in the Army. In later life his energies were focused on the problem of Highland poverty. The deerhound on page 103 belonged to his brother Duncan, Lord Colonsay*

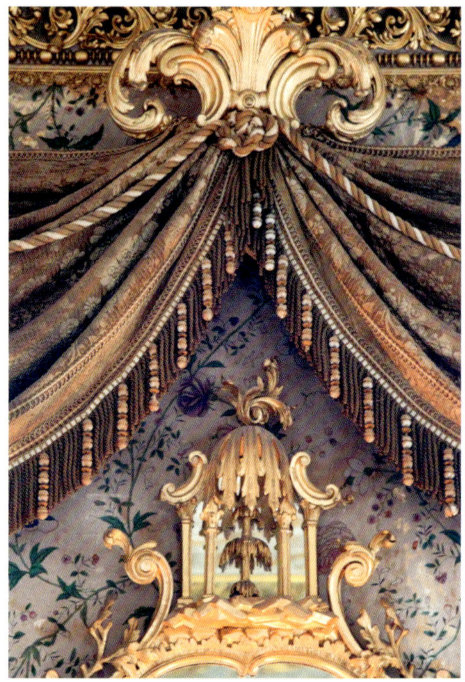

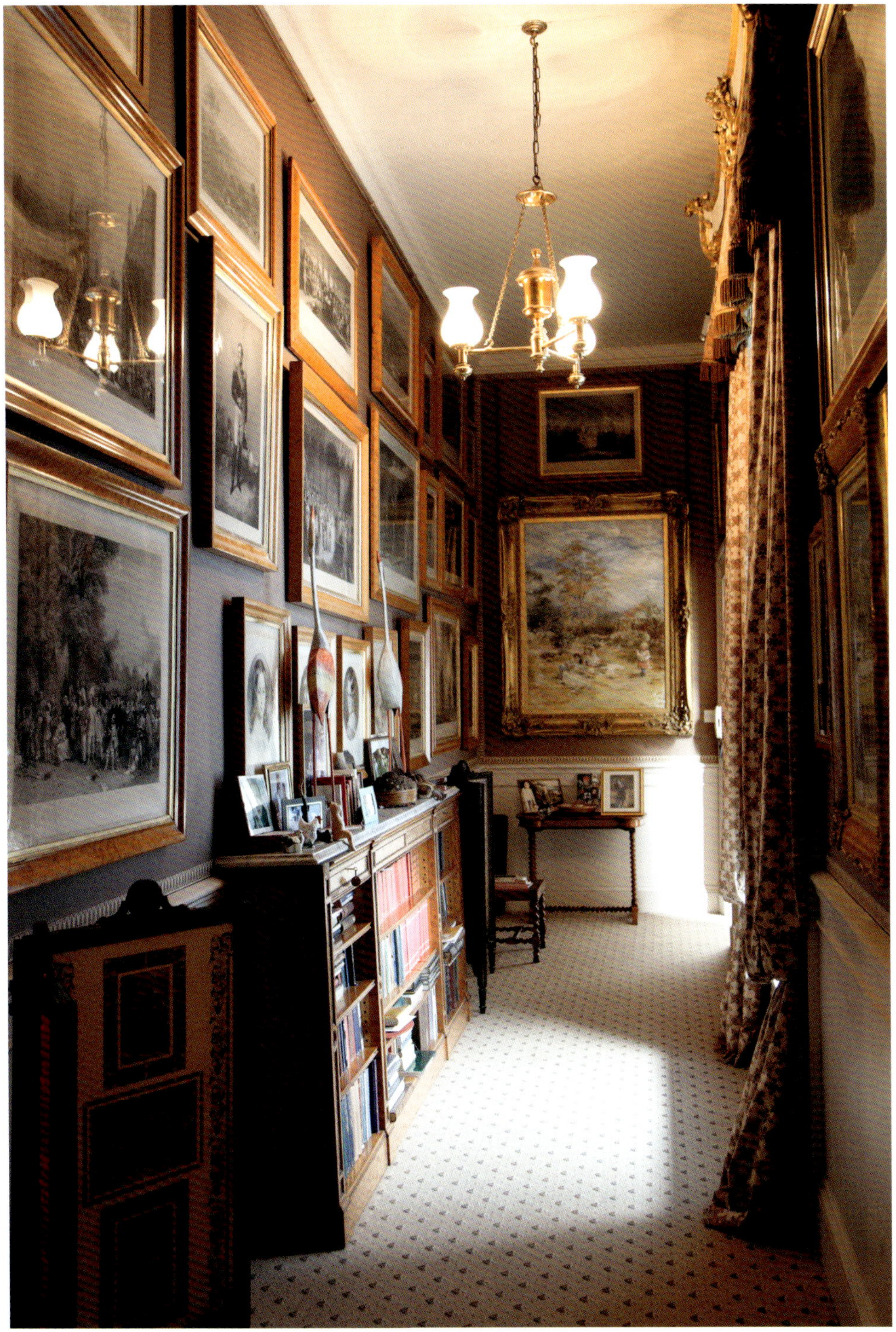

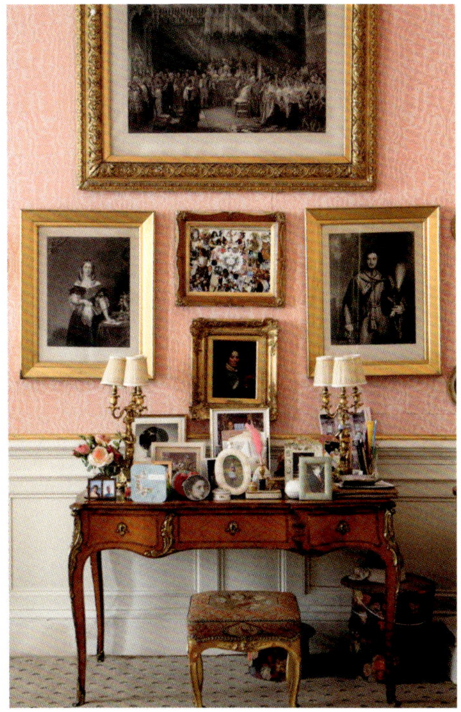

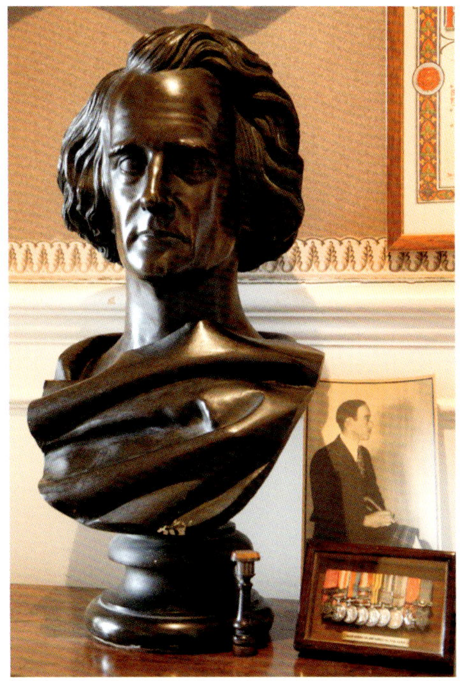

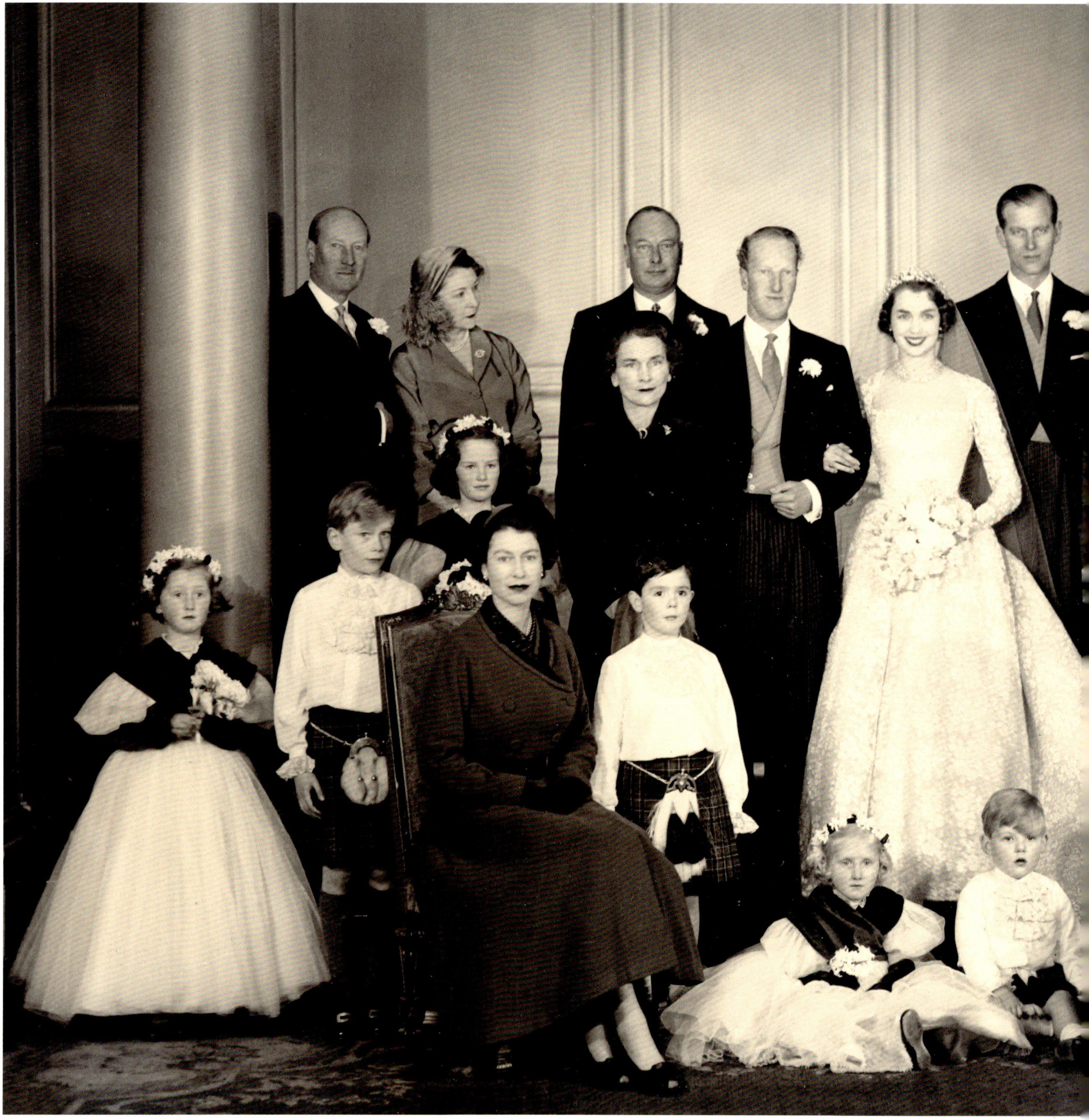

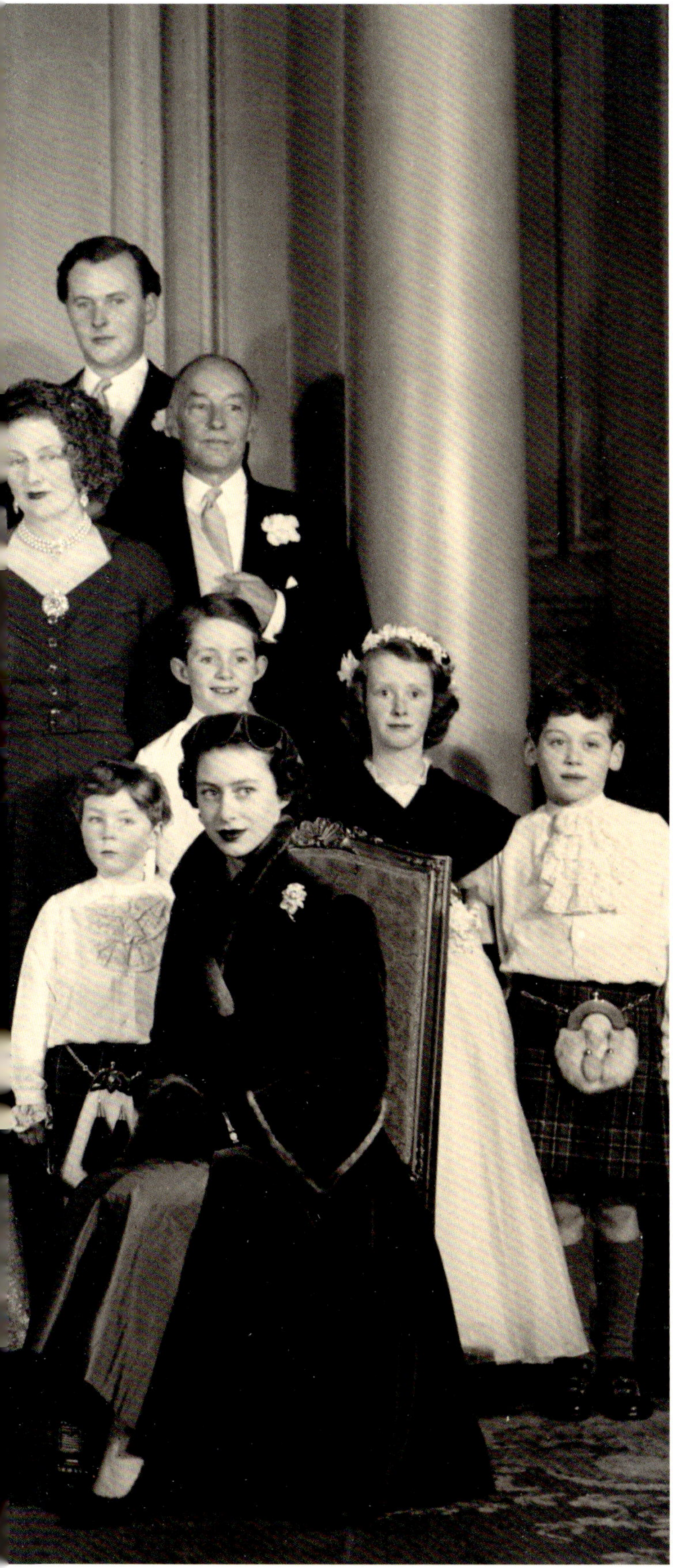

THE DALKEITH WEDDING
*When the Earl of Dalkeith, the future 9th Duke, married Jane McNeill at Edinburgh's St Giles' Cathedral in 1953, 20,000 thronged the streets on a cold January day. The bride wore a Hardy Amies design in white lace woven in a mayflower design picked out in silver (right). Her tulle veil was secured by a diamond tiara in the form of a delicate mayflower wreath* *(page 127)*

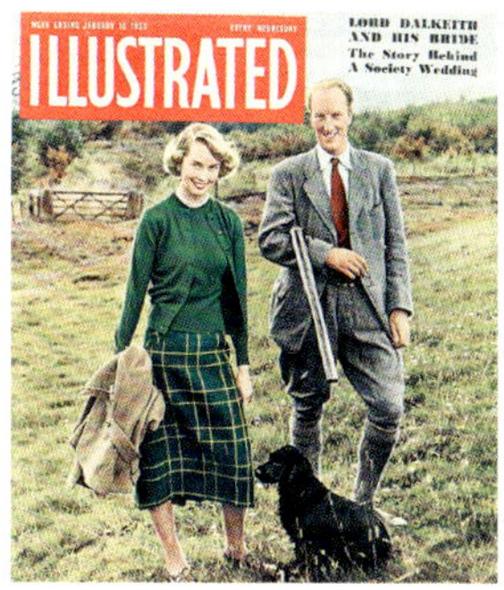


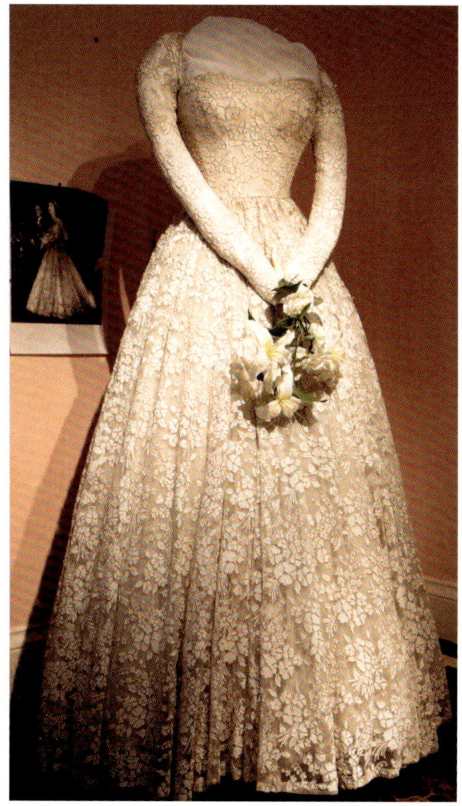

THE WEDDING PHOTOGRAPH
*The Queen and Princess Margaret drove up from Sandringham. To the bride's right are Prince Philip, Molly, Duchess of Buccleuch, John Singe (best man) and the bride's father, John McNeill QC. On the groom's left are his aunt Alice, the Duchess of Gloucester, with the Duke of Gloucester, Mrs McNeill and the 8th Duke. The pages (three in McNeill kilts, three in Stuart) and bridesmaids were, from left: Caroline Percy, Prince Richard of Gloucester, Cherry Cairns, David Ward, Victoria Percy, William Legge, David Scott, Alastair Bruce, Jean Scott and Michael Farquhar*

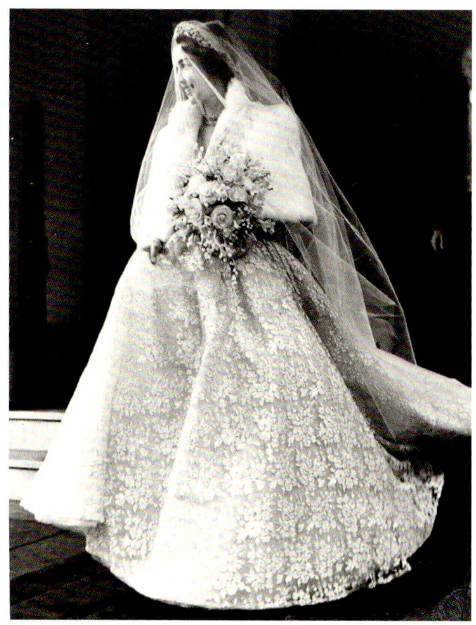

# Family life

*Behind Bowhill's grandeur lay a private and surprisingly modern Victorian family home*

Family was everything at Bowhill and the house is full of visitors' books, albums and portraits, including this delightful sketch of Charlotte Anne, wife of the 5th Duke, with her son William. The architect Burn was a skilled planner of 'the family wing'. Charlotte Anne's apartments were on the main floor at the west end of the house. The nursery was directly above, and the first-floor passages were lined with simple but practical bedrooms. The principal guest rooms opened off the Saloon's gallery.

But in the early 1900s, Bowhill was only used seasonally for hunting and shooting. Before Dalkeith was closed in 1925, spartan interiors were matched by a lack of frills and plumbing: bathrooms only came after the present Duke's grandfather inherited in 1935. According to Molly Buccleuch's *Times* obituary, in their first winter 'the cold was so intense that coats, hats and gloves were worn day and night and dinner was served in the dining room fireplace'. It was her son, the 9th Duke, who, with his wife, Jane, finally turned Bowhill into a welcoming home.

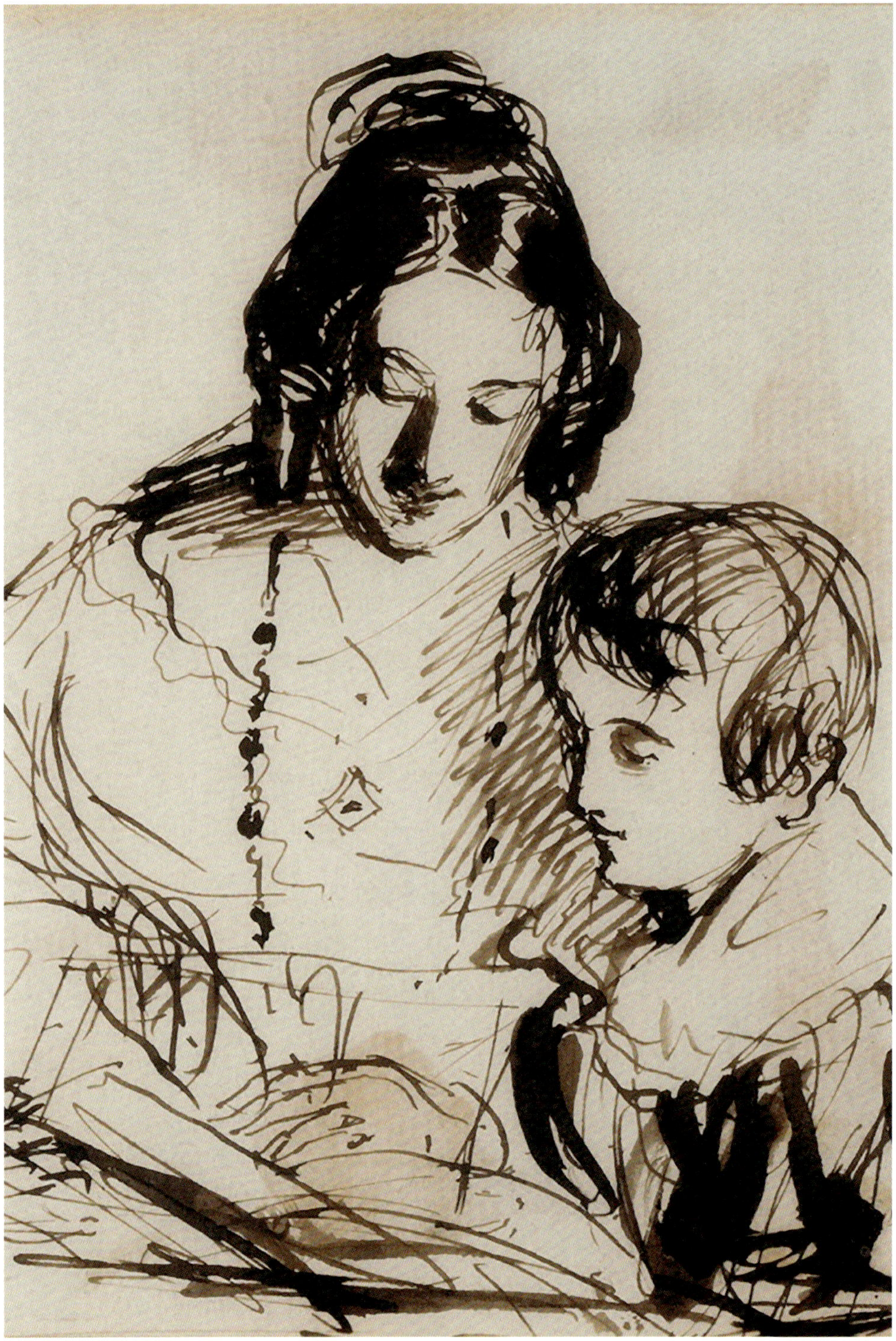

Sir Francis Grant (1803–78)
**Charlotte Anne, Duchess of Buccleuch, and her son, the Earl of Dalkeith**
*A study in pen and ink, dated 28 February, 1838, for a portrait in the Staircase Hall (page 48)*

Opposite *The future 9th Duke with his bride, Jane, after their honeymoon in 1953 (top left). The late Duchess Jane is seen again in photographs by Mme Yevonde, from 1963 (top right), by Fritz von der Schulenburg in 2011, when this book was being prepared (bottom right), and on the Eildon Hills in 1957 with her son Richard (bottom left)*

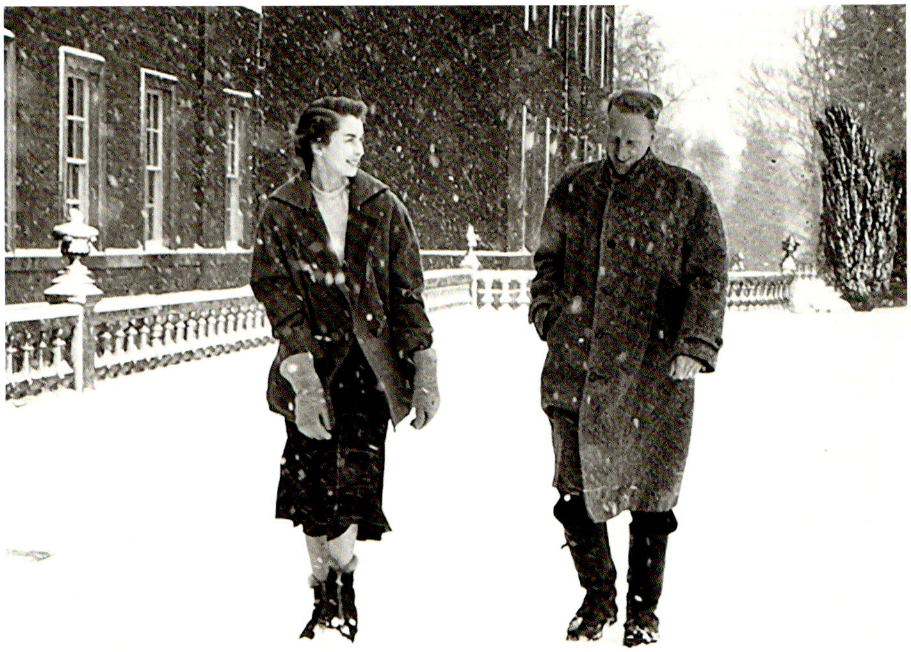

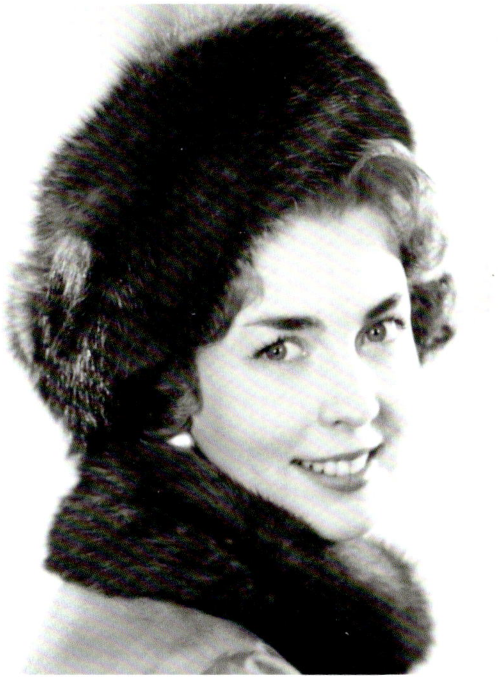

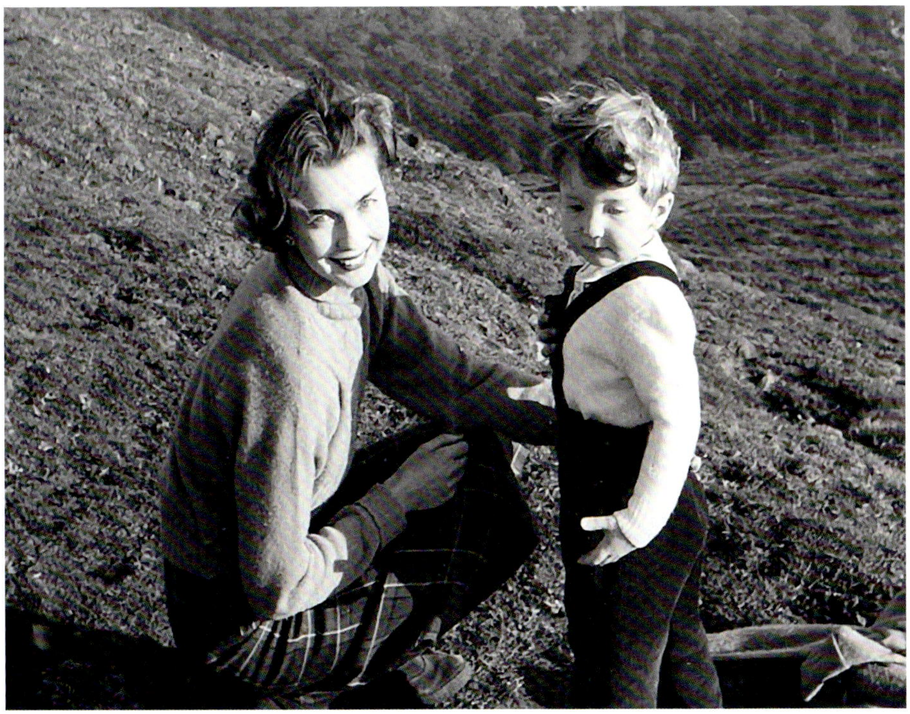

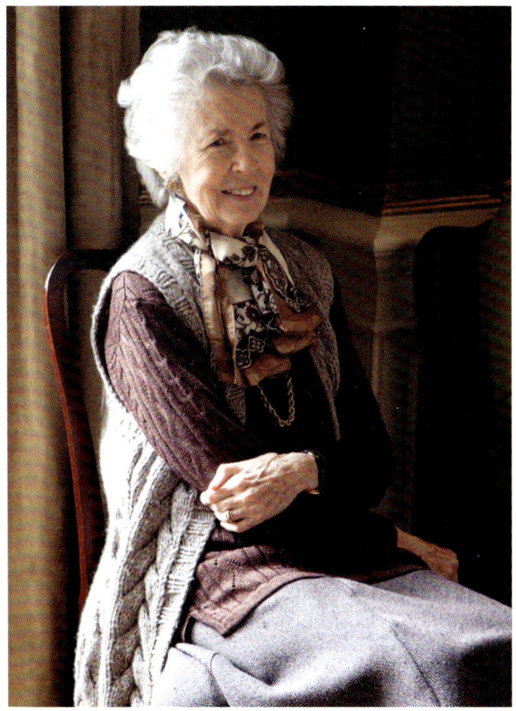

# The Archives

*A small number of the Buccleuch family archives are still housed at Bowhill, enough to make the old Archive Room's floor groan under the weight*

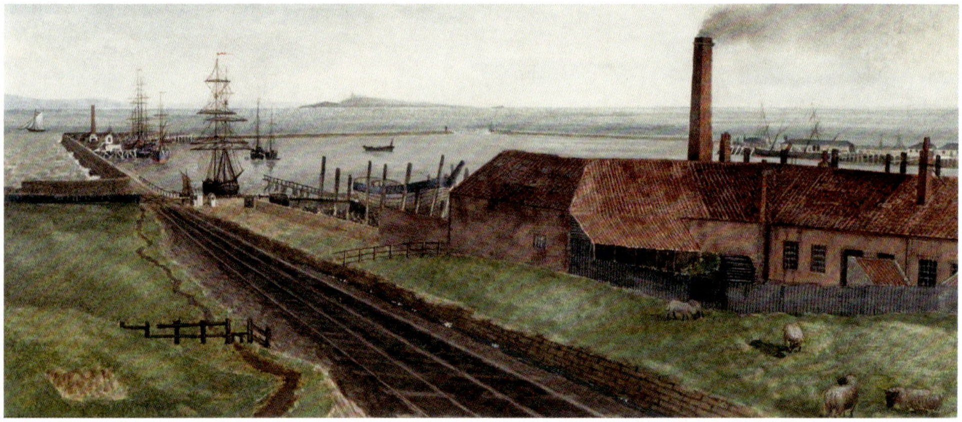

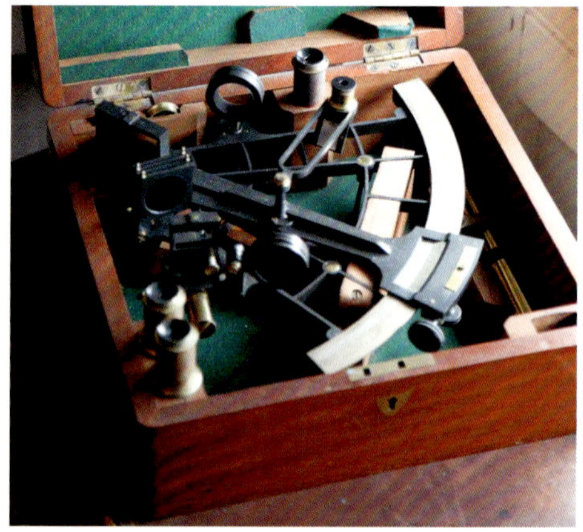

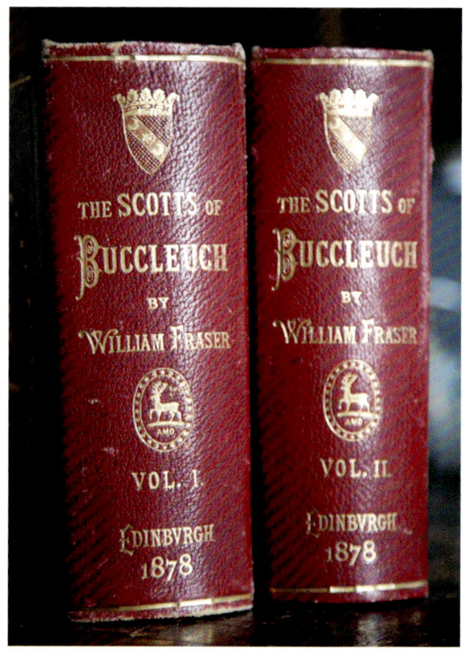


The family archives stretch back to the 12th-century cartulary records of Melrose Abbey, embracing centuries of documents and accounts, as well as correspondence of successive generations. A significant proportion of the archives are on long-term loan to the National Records of Scotland in Edinburgh, where invaluable help is given to ensure their conservation and access provided for scholars. A small quantity of mainly 19th- and 20th-century material is organised in a new archive research room in the basement at Bowhill, where the slow process of recording and transcribing is undertaken.

The development of photography is reflected both in family albums from the 1860s, all of which are being digitalised, and in copies of Maxime du Camp's *Égypte, Nubie, Palestine et Syrie*, of 1849–51, as well as Roger Fenton's photographs of the Crimean War.

ABOVE JOHN BLAIR (1850–1934)
**Granton Harbour, Edinburgh**
*The 5th Duke earned his statue in front of St Giles' in Edinburgh for building Granton Harbour on his land on the Firth of Forth. The idea came in 1834 from the General Steam Navigation Company, which wanted to reduce the city's reliance on tidal wharves. Granton launched the world's first roll-on roll-off train ferry in 1849, linking the Highlands with the south. It was in use until the Forth Bridge opened in 1890. Granton was nationalised in 1968*

ABOVE RIGHT AND RIGHT *A sextant belonging to the 5th Duke's fourth son, Admiral Lord Charles Scott; Sir William Fraser's Herculean two-volume history of the Scotts of Buccleuch*

OPPOSITE *Floor-to-ceiling shelves of books and archive boxes, piles of papers and some of the hundreds of letters between the 5th Duke and his wife still crowd the old Archive Room upstairs*

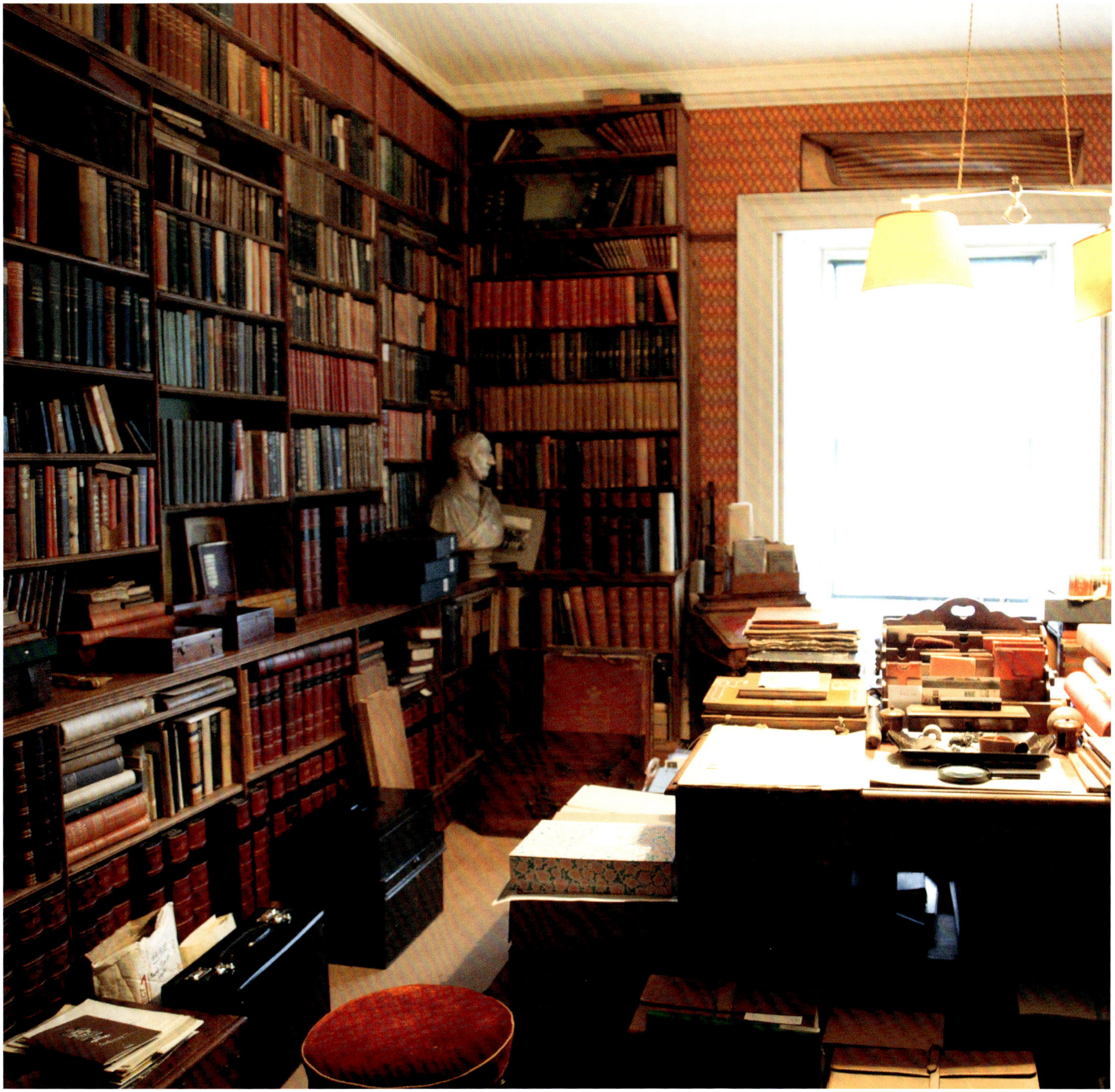

# The Exhibition Room

*The former dining hall for domestic servants has been transformed into an exhibition space for exploring the family collection*

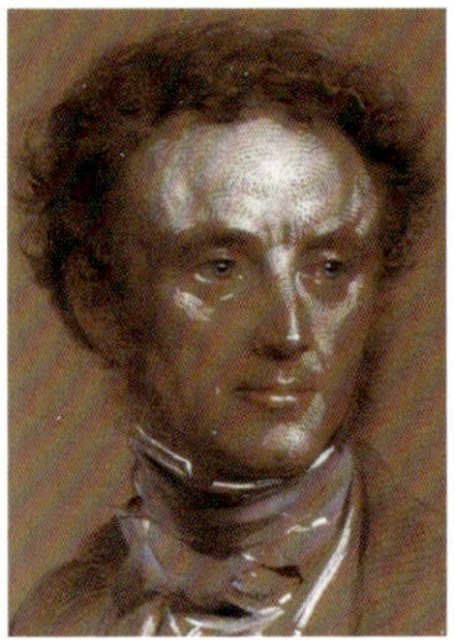

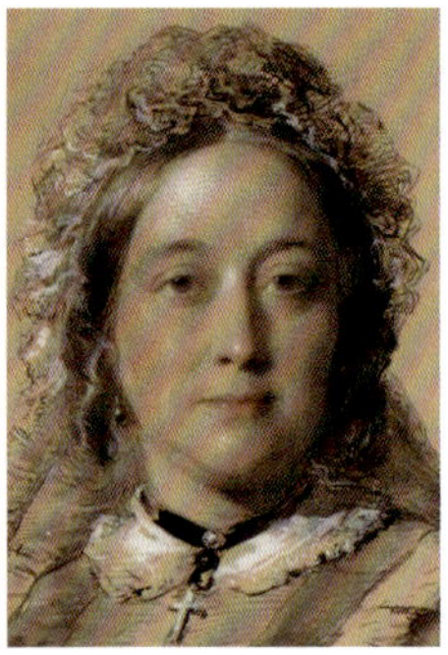

LEFT GEORGE RICHMOND (1809–96)
**Walter Francis, 5th Duke of Buccleuch, 1866, and Charlotte Anne, Duchess of Buccleuch, dated 'Drumlanrig, 1864'**
*'Love and Respect in the Victorian Age', the first exhibition in the Old Servants' Hall, tells the story of the fruitful marriage of the 5th Duke and his wife. Richmond, son of a miniature painter, was a follower of William Blake and a keen cricketer*
RIGHT *Five-foot-high silver candelabra by Robert Garrard, 1830, telling the story of how the Buccleuchs got their name (see front cover flap)*
OPPOSITE *Charlotte Anne portayed in gouache on ivory by Sir William Ross, 1843, next to the 'mayflower' tiara, c.1870, traditionally worn by Buccleuch brides. It divides into nine separate brooches. The diamond earrings are c.1850*
BELOW *Made by Garrard's rivals Abud and Kitching, patronised by Prince Albert, this gold and turquoise bracelet bearing a miniature of Queen Victoria is inscribed on the reverse: 'To the Duchess of Buccleuch, from her sincere friend, VR'*

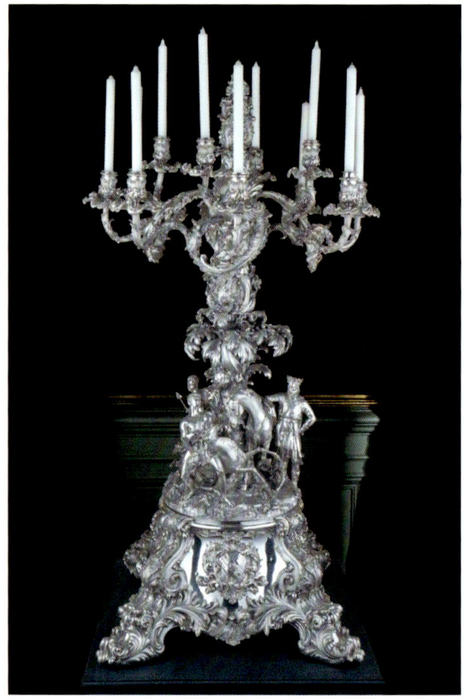

The Old Servants' Hall, which lay between the Kitchen and the main house, has been transformed into a modern exhibition space. In time the exhibitions will be refreshed and replaced, but the focus at the start has appropriately been on the lives of Walter Francis, 5th Duke, and his wife, Charlotte Anne. Theirs was a complex relationship, two devout people who were fellow supporters of the Scottish Episcopal Church in the 1830s and 1840s but grew apart as she pursued the path of many followers of Cardinal Newman to Roman Catholicism.

The exhibition acknowledges their differences, but also celebrates their closeness and creativity in transforming Montagu House and Bowhill, among other houses, and in enriching the collections with miniatures, objets d'art and jewellery, examples of which are on display. Walter Francis's dying words to Charlotte Anne – 'I should never have loved you as I did, had I not respected you more' – are a testament to the couple's ability to surmount their differences.

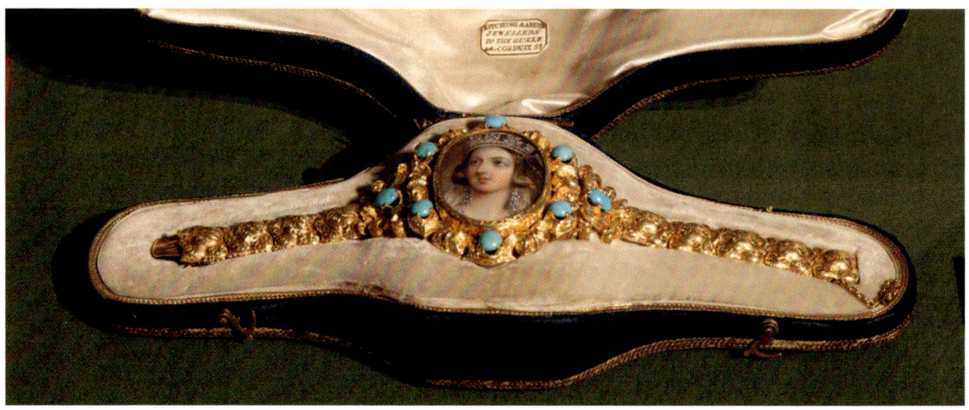

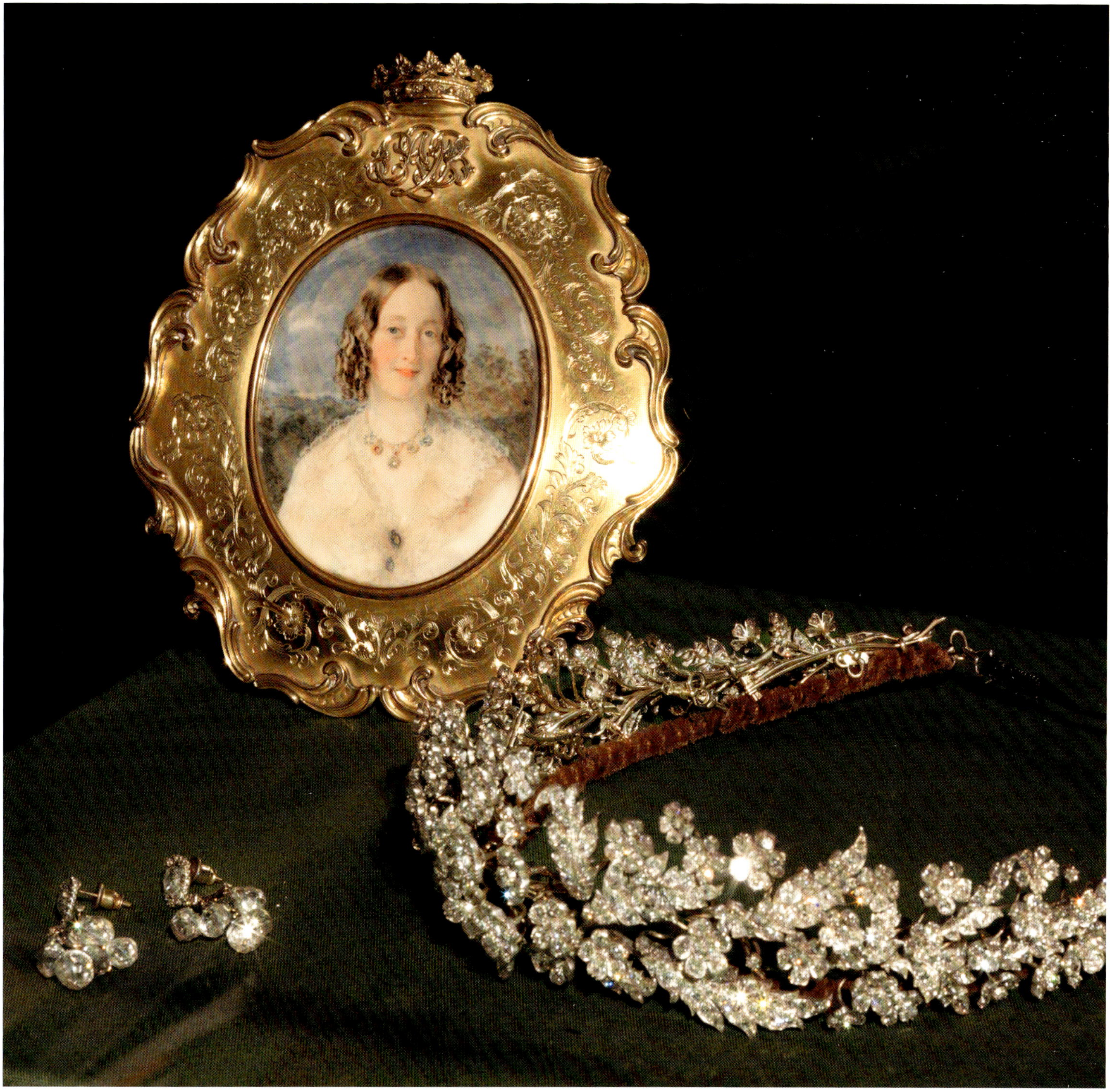

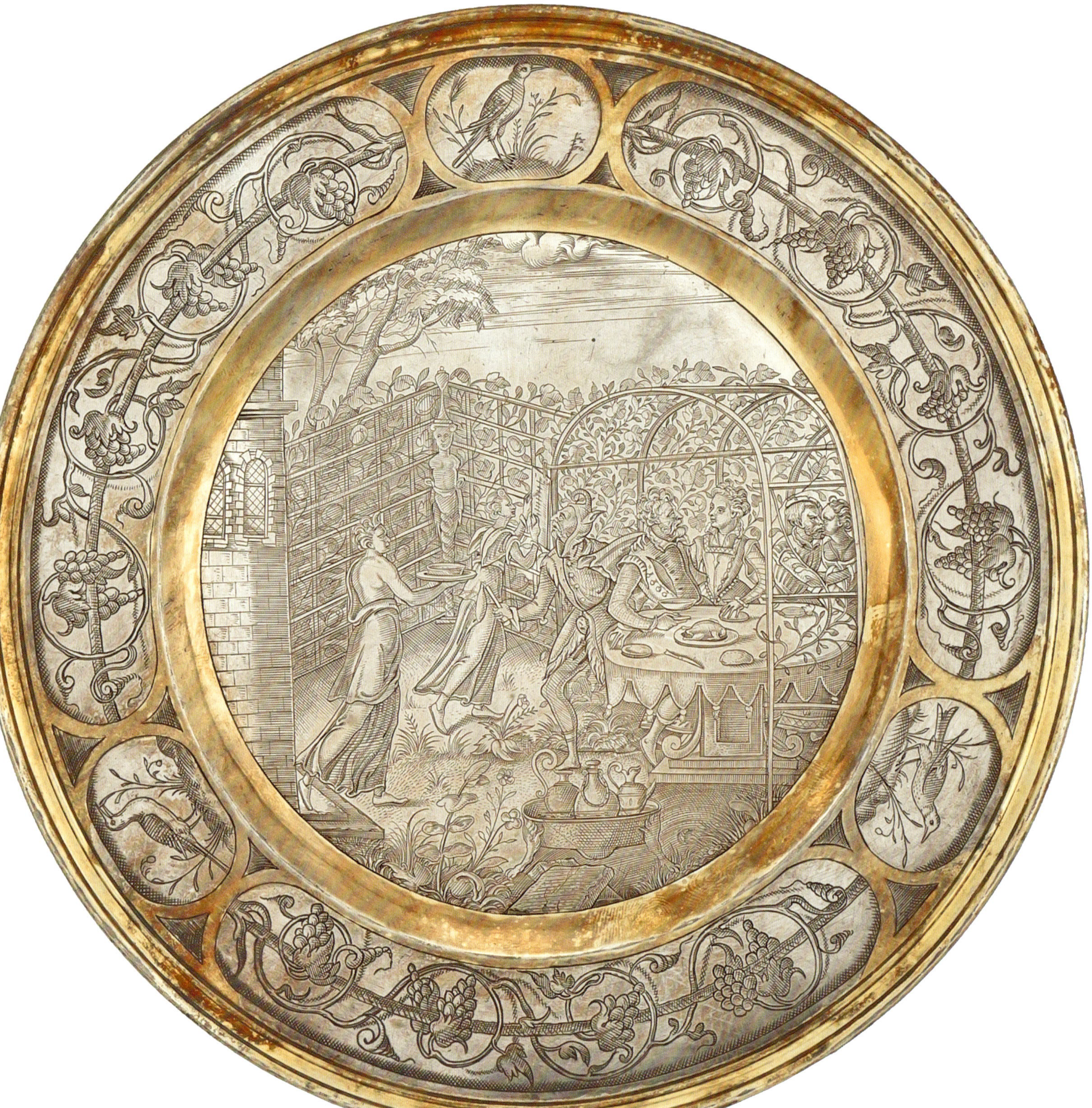

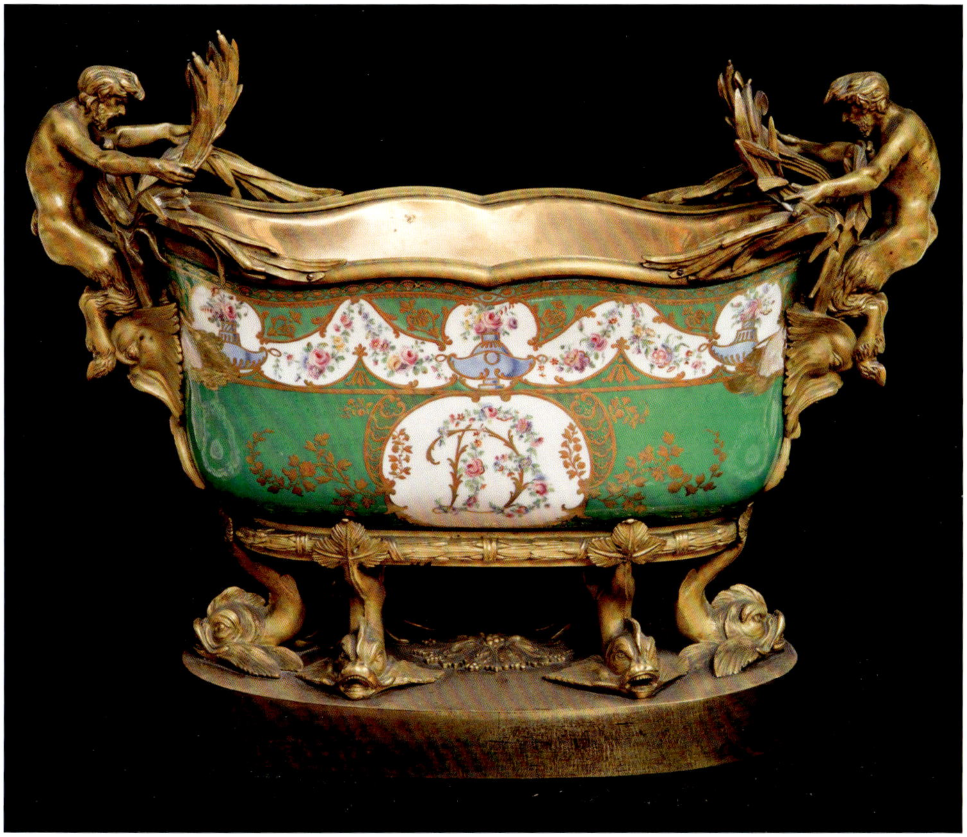

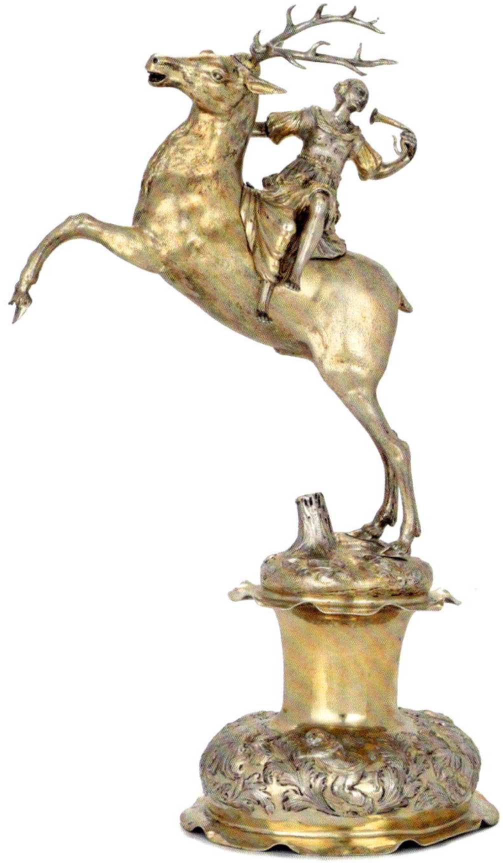

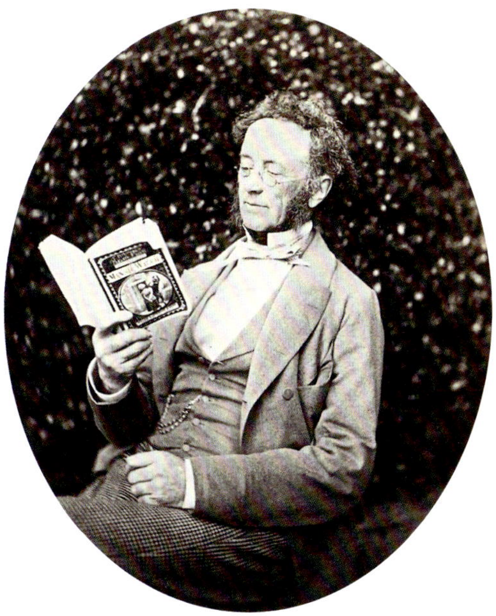

ABOVE *Seau-à-bouteilles from a Sèvres service made for Madame du Barry in 1771 and bought by the 5th Duke and Duchess in a buying spree in the 1830s. The green ground was probably added c.1820 by the London dealer Baldock, whose 'enlivened' Sèvres earned it the epithet 'Baldock Sèvres'*
ABOVE RIGHT *Parcel-gilt ewer of a huntress riding a stag by Heinrich Mannlich, Augsburg, c.1660*
RIGHT *The star of the Order of the Thistle, to which successive Buccleuchs have belonged. It bears the motto of the kingdom of Scotland, 'Nemo Me Impune Lacessit' (No one attacks me with impunity)*
LEFT *The 5th Duke reading a racy paperback, 1867*
OPPOSITE *One of 12 rare Elizabethan parcel-gilt and silver plates illustrating the Parable of the Prodigal Son. Inherited by Kitty, Duchess of Queensberry, they were bought by Horace Walpole and bought back by the family in 1842*

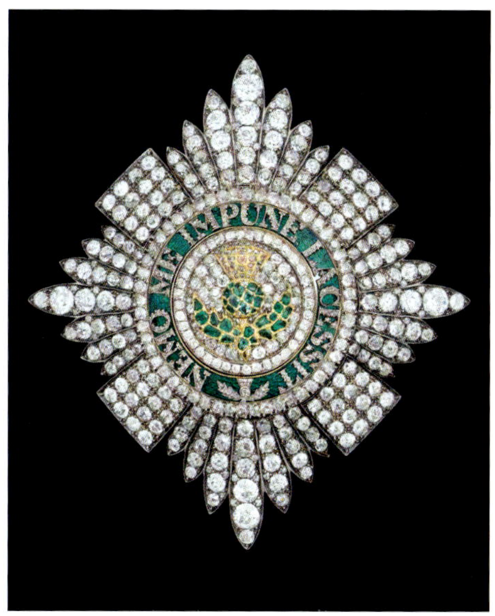

# The Old Kitchen

*The Old Kitchen, entered nowadays from the stables courtyard with its clock tower at the east end of the house, still reflects the almost industrial scale of Victorian catering. It was here that the chef Joseph Florence created medieval culinary fantasies for Sir Walter Scott*

Nowadays the main Bowhill kitchen is located in the basement in the centre of the house, but until it was badly damaged by a fire in 1937 this room had been the kitchen for almost a century – in a complex of buildings adjoining the east end of the main house. Burn had sought the advice of the upper servants on how to plan the rooms they would work in. Painstakingly restored by the late Duchess Jane, with the advice of a number of retired members of the household who could remember working in it, the kitchen contains almost entirely original equipment.

The array of saucepans, jam pans, casserole dishes, fish kettles, jelly moulds and so on, all made of copper, bring a wonderful gleam to the room. The sets on display today come from various family homes, as indicated by the stamped initials. They were kept clean with either a mixture of lemon juice and salt, or vinegar and white sand.

Today we can have no sense of the bustle or noise of the kitchen, let alone the heat, particularly when the house was full. The steward kept records of the number and names of family members and guests present for meals each day, and while there were certainly quiet times of the year, they were matched by hectic periods. In the week beginning Monday, 7th December, 1835, for instance, an average of 34 people were fed each day in the main dining room, and staff probably doubled the number.

Much of the food would have been fresh, local and seasonal. The larder, with its mesh netting to exclude flies, lay across the internal courtyard, in what is now the Theatre. Some food had to be imported, of course, though the block of sugar reminds us that it did not necessarily come in familiar forms.

Research is currently underway into the cooks and cooking staff who worked here. Perhaps the most eminent was Joseph Florence, chef to the 3rd, 4th and 5th Dukes. He was a big favourite with Sir Walter Scott. One account describes how 'the French artiste who presided over the ducal kitchen loved, when Sir Walter was a guest, to compliment him with medieval erections of pastry or marchpane [marzipan]', or with tableaux such as 'the hunt, cut out of toast, galloping over a landscape of boiled spinach'.

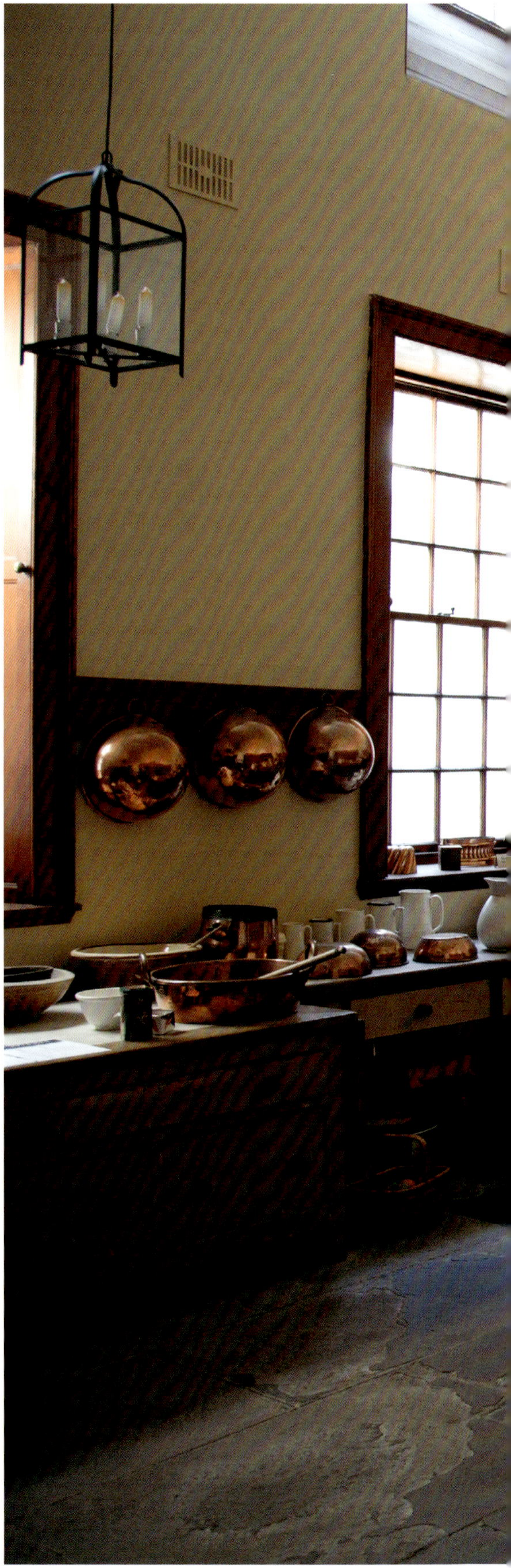

Cooking on a grand scale
*The stone-flagged kitchen, with its gleaming copper dishes, sturdy dressers and working tables. At the end of the table in the centre is a three-foot-high conical block of sugar weighing a stone*

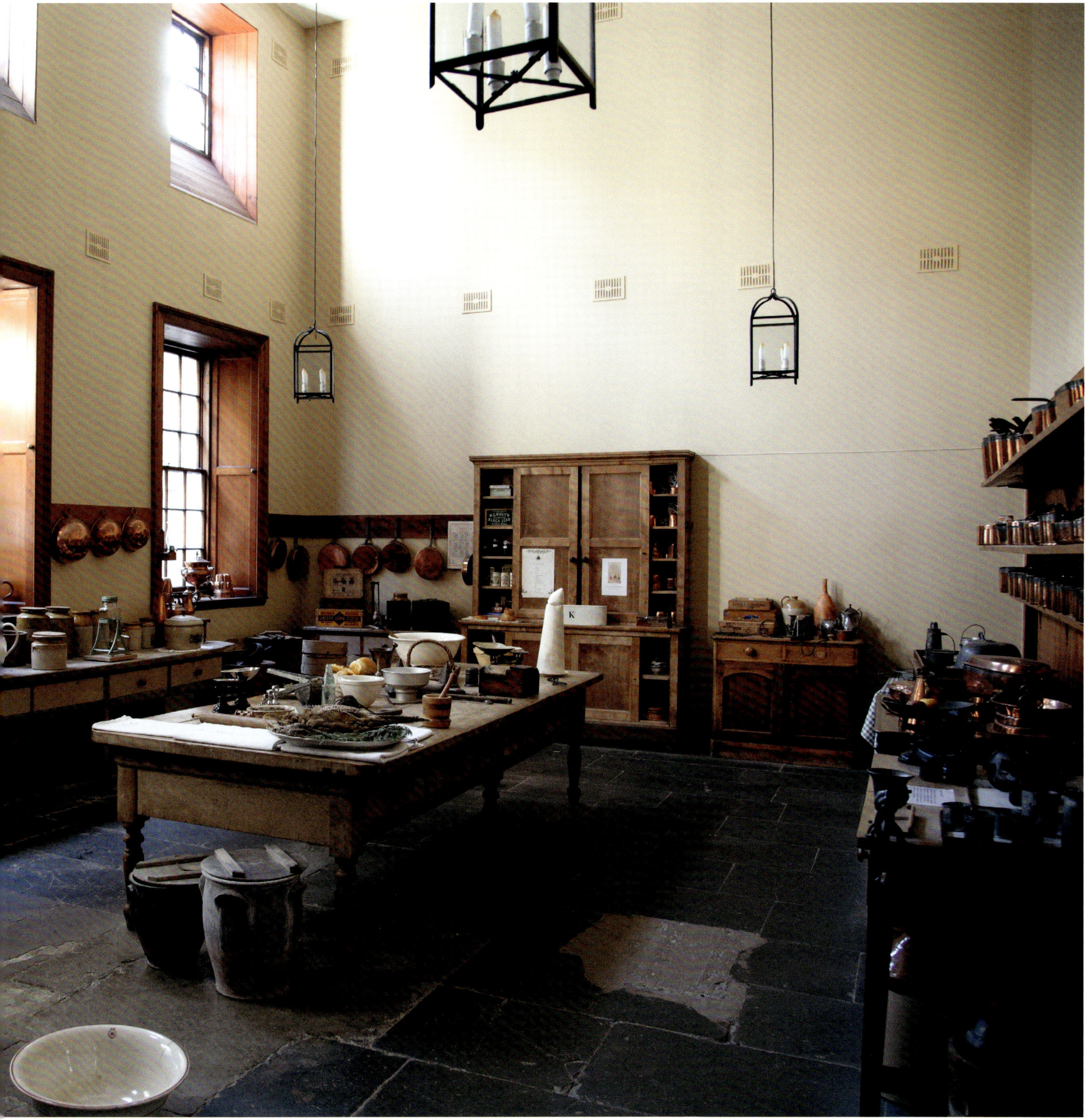

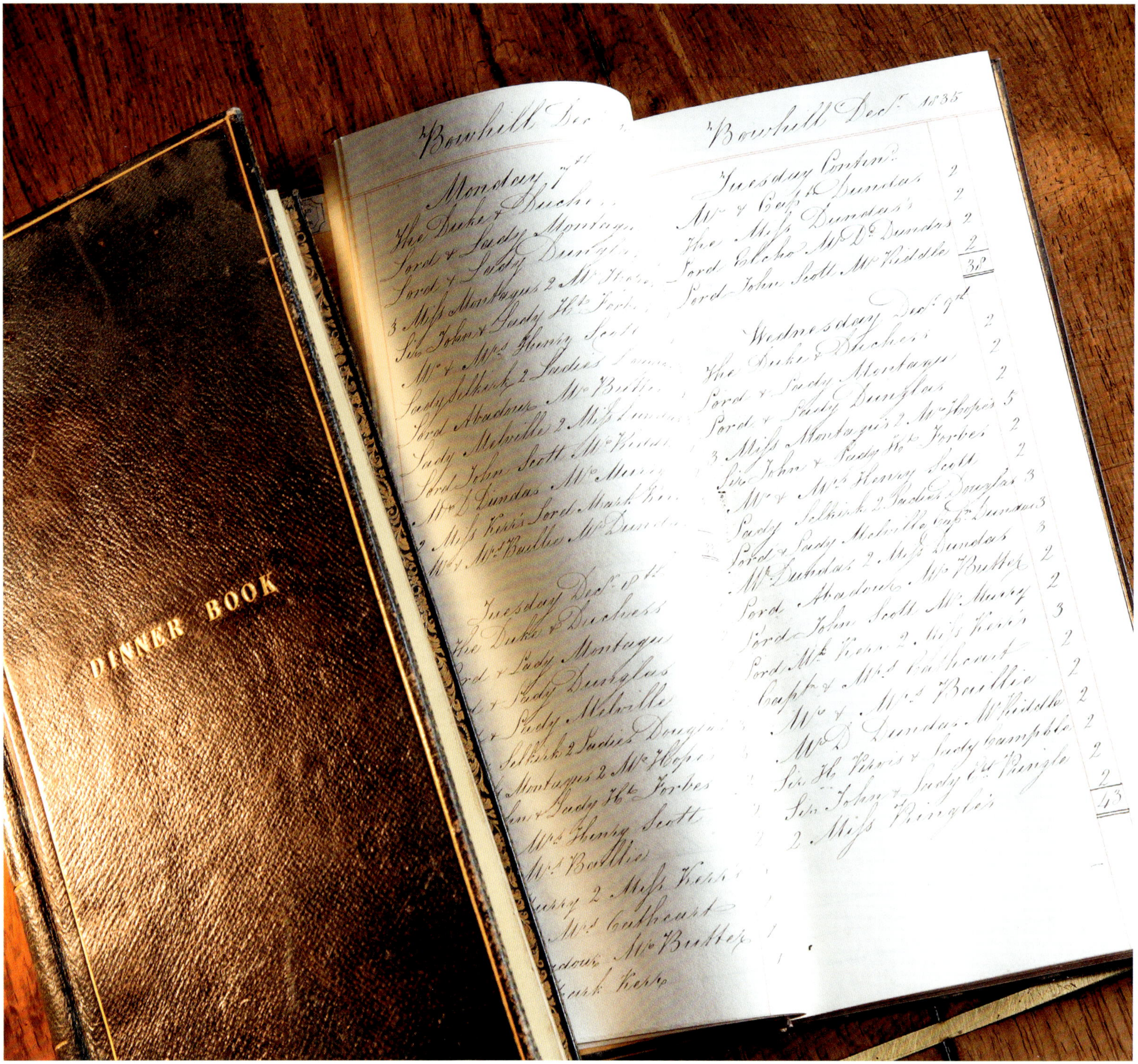
DINNER BOOK
Bowhill Decr 1835

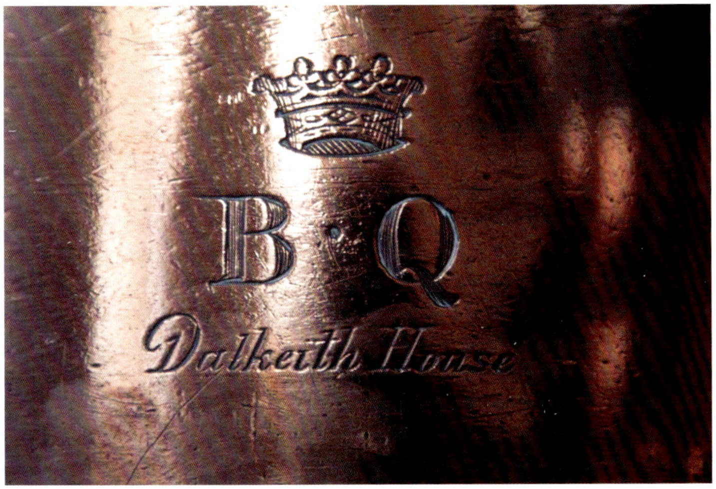


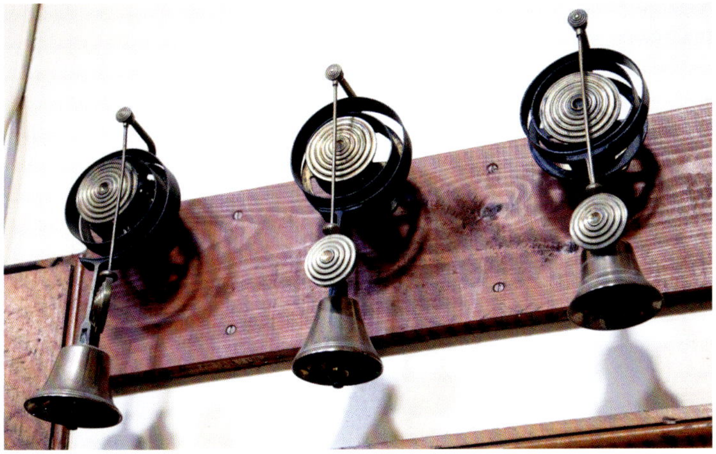

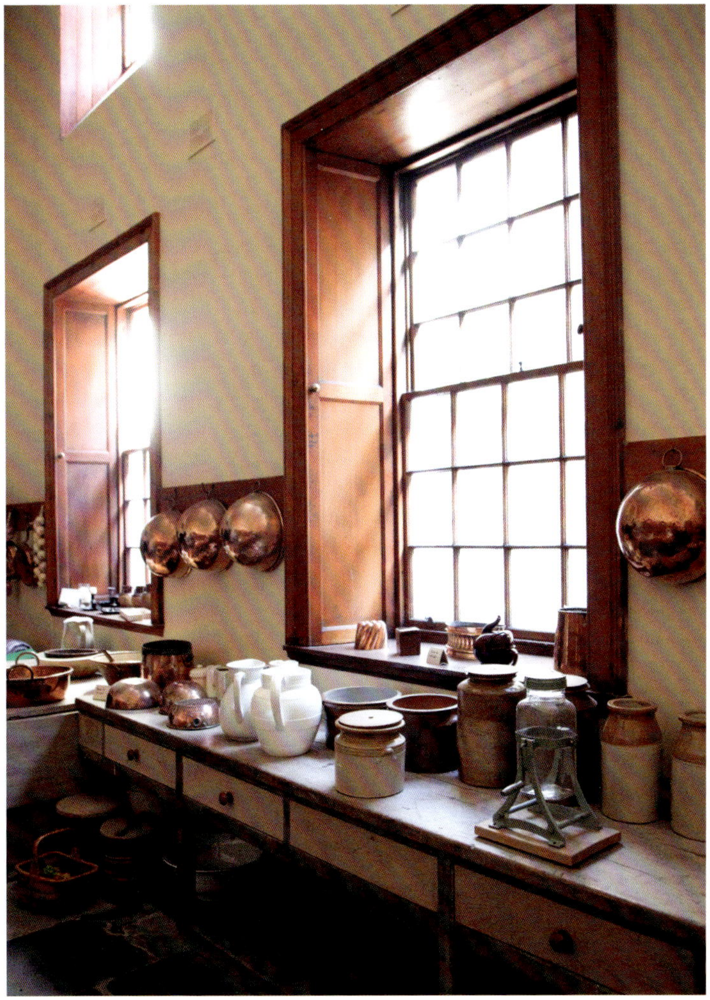

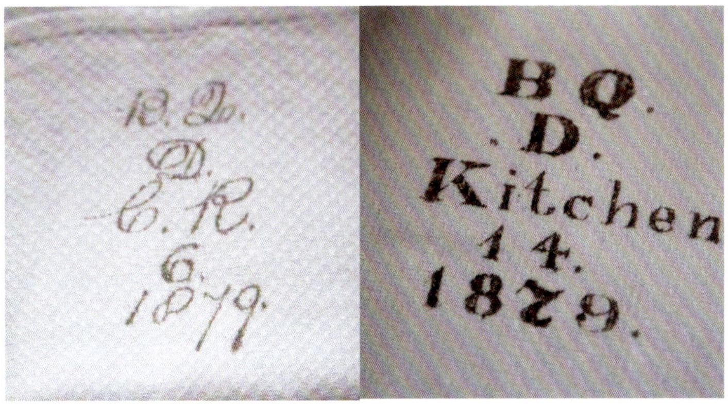


OPPOSITE *The steward's elegant and very detailed Dinner Book for the week beginning 7th December 1835. Forty-three people sat down to dinner on Wednesday the 9th, more than half of them family and clearly staying at the house. The list goes from the 5th Duke and Duchess down to the two Miss Pringles*

THIS PAGE *Burn created an enlightened environment for kitchen staff to work in (above right); two examples of linen from Dalkeith, both numbered and dated 1879 (right); an array of bells connected to the serving room next to the Dining Room (above); a huge pan from Dalkeith bearing the initials 'BQ' and the ducal coronet (top). The copper was brought from various houses during the late Duchess's restoration*

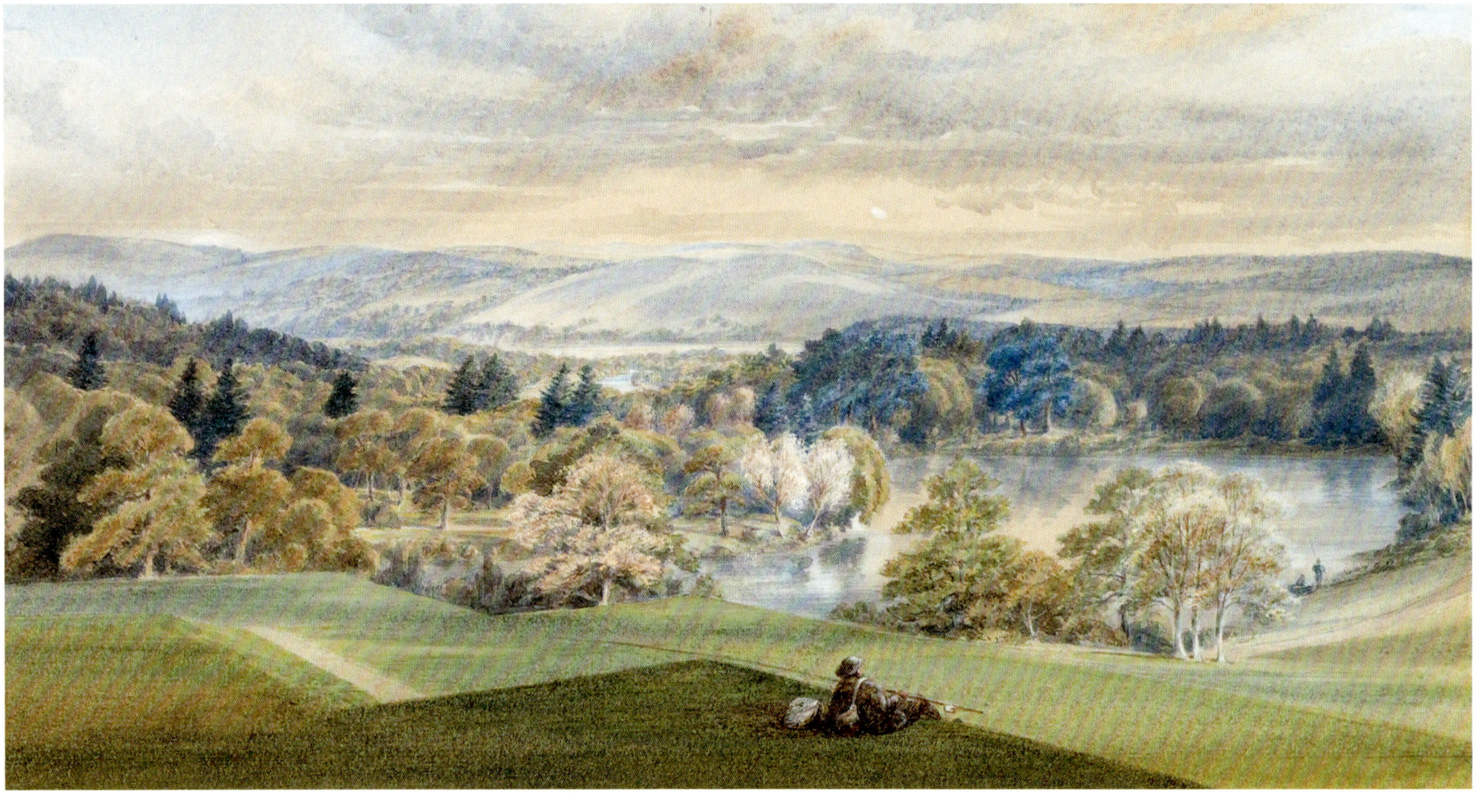

## The Gardens

*Bowhill's gardens, with their sculpted lawn terraces, were designed above all to enhance the pleasure of the view*

A subtle and easily overlooked aspect of Bowhill's landscape is the degree to which it has been shaped over at least three centuries by the hand of man. The setting, between two scenic river valleys, the Yarrow and the Ettrick, which rise to heather-clad hills with wonderful views over the Borders, has been gently tailored by the addition of rich woodlands and lakes and the simple grassy terraces on which the house sits.

Historic Scotland's official inventory of gardens and designed landscapes, reaffirmed in 2011, classifies it in every respect as 'high' or 'outstanding'. This is due in part to the 'picturesque improver' William Sawrey Gilpin (1761–1843), who briefly gave advice in the 1830s at the time of Burn's additions, and whose notes survive at Bowhill. His advice was certainly implemented on the north and south driveway entrances across the Yarrow, with their lodges by Burn, and on the visual enlargement of the small southernmost loch and the entirely artificial upper loch. Most important was the creation of the three sculpted terraces on the south side, which gave way to the tree-enclosed parkland known as South Bowhill, now with few remaining mature trees.

The woodland setting can be traced back much further. In about 1700 Duchess Anna is known to have ordered the enclosure of woodland, no doubt to protect it from the depredations of grazing livestock and timber-cutters. This perhaps explains the survival nearby of important areas of ancient woodland, including, not far from Bowhill, the Tinnis Ash, probably Scotland's oldest ash tree. Three generations later, in the 1770s, her

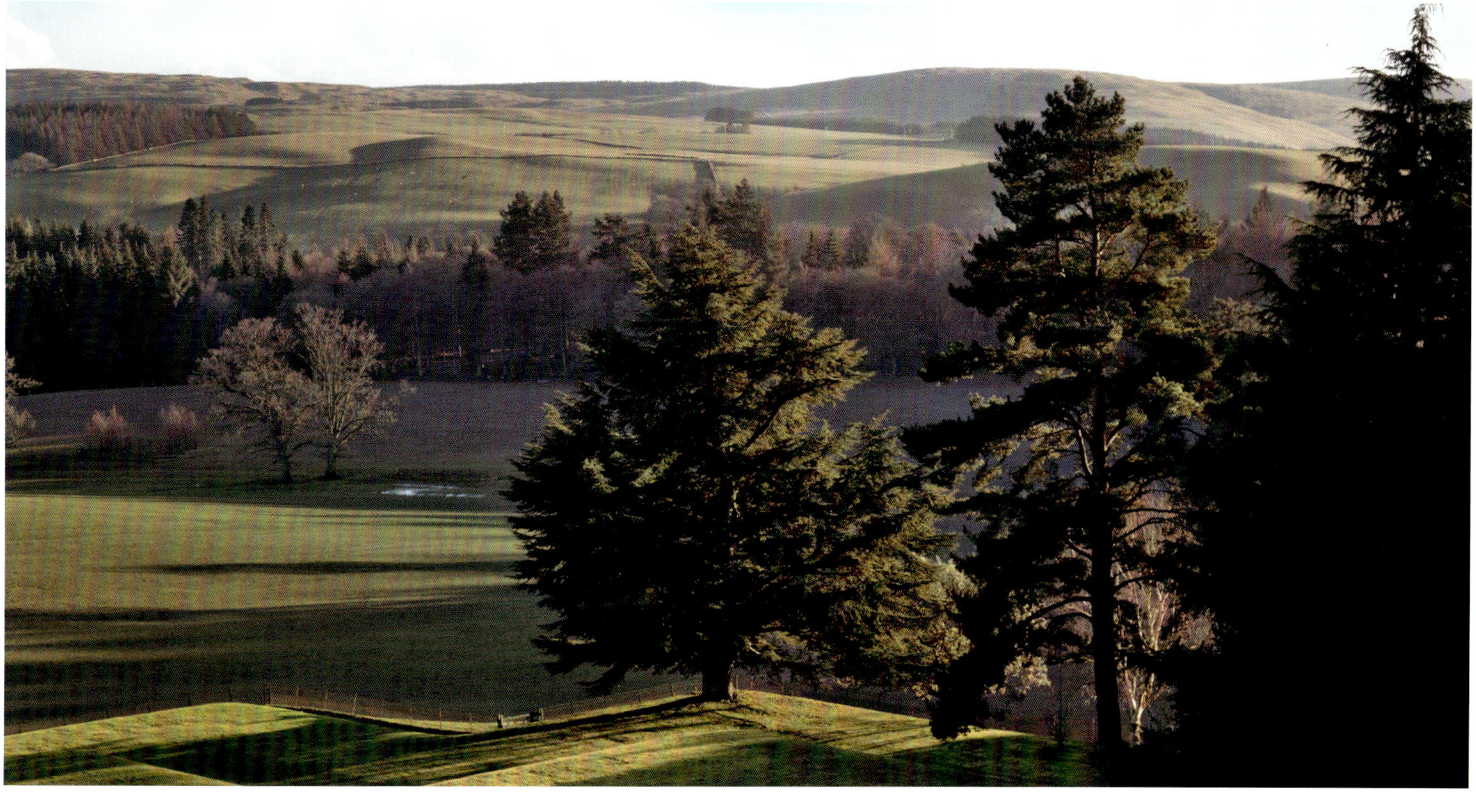

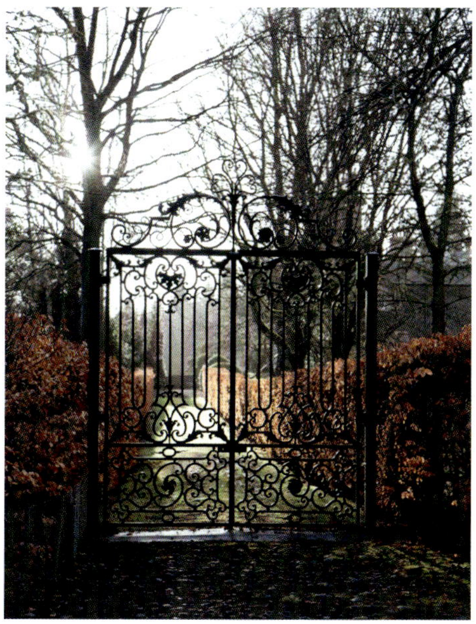

successor Henry is recorded as planting, at one time, 120 acres and, at another, 15,000 trees including oak, ash, elm, beech, chestnut, larch and spruce. Fine woodland takes decades, if not centuries, to mature, along with much patient management, and both the 8th and 9th Dukes were renowned as passionate foresters, the latter being for many years President of the Commonwealth Forestry Association.

Closer to the house are some interesting herbaceous borders, the creation of the 9th Duke's wife, Jane; on the north side, banks of azaleas and rhododendrons add seasonal colour that contrasts with the sombre greywacke stone of the house.

The approach to the old entrance on the south side is now more clearly delineated by beech hedges and fine 18th-century gates that once hung at Dalkeith.

ABOVE *The terraced lawns overlooking the park known as South Bowhill. The woods at the end of the field conceal the Lower Loch. In the early days of golf a seven-hole course was created here but it was later abandoned*

LEFT *Iron gates made for Dalkeith Palace mark the approach to the terraced gardens along the South Front, the original entrance to the house*

OPPOSITE *Lord Charles Scott, the future admiral, reclines on the lawn above the Upper Loch, dressed to go fishing, in a watercolour by his brother Henry, the future 1st Lord Montagu of Beaulieu, c.1870*

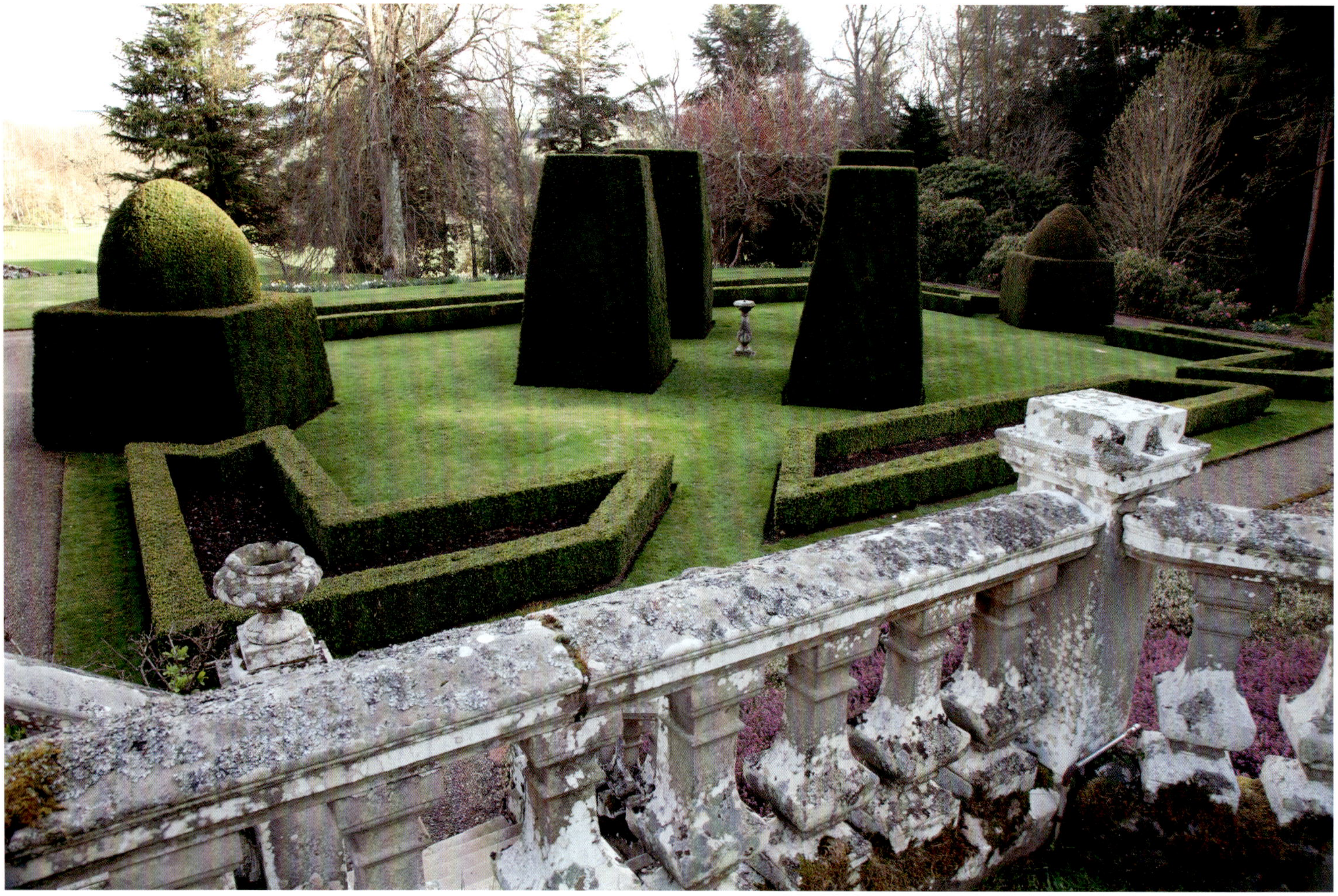

ABOVE The West Garden
*Lichen-covered balustrades screen the formal garden below the Duchess's Boudoir. Old photographs show the heather garden being used for picnics*

OPPOSITE Chinese wallpaper
*A bird with exotic plumage perches in the Morning Room*

INSIDE FLAP The South Front
*Bowhill in winter: the house looks out over the Ettrick Valley from a platform of frosty terraces*

BACK COVER
Bowhill inside and out
*The austere greywacke stone façade of the South Front, all 400 feet of it, belies the welcoming warmth of the interior. In the Drawing Room, the Scottish light has faded the crimson damask walls to a golden hue*

Bowhill House and Country Estate
Selkirk TD7 5ET, Scotland
Tel 01750 22204
blht@buccleuch.com
www.bowhillhouse.co.uk

First published in 2010.
Second edition 2018


Published by
Caique Publishing Ltd,
Hawick TD9 7YF, Scotland
www.caiquepublishing.com
ISBN 978-0-9957566-1-8

Printed by Ofset Yapımevi, Istanbul. www.ofset.com

Project editor John Scott
Colour editor Berrin Scott
Co-editors Susana Raby and Hilary Stafford-Clark
Editorial advice Charlotte Anne de Castellane, Damian Montagu Douglas Scott

Design Clive Crook

Archivist and historical adviser Crispin Powell
Collections & conservation Scott MacDonald

With special thanks to Helen Currie, Calum Flanders, Orhan Gündüz, Sandra Howat, Karen Howes, Colin MacIntosh

All photographs by Fritz von der Schulenburg unless otherwise stated.
Albums, miniatures and tapestries John MacKenzie
Paintings Richard Shellabear / Todd-White Art Photography. 'Braan', p103: John MacKenzie / National Gallery of Scotland
Porcelain Mark Usher.
Map Susanna Hickling

Related books
*Drumlanrig: The Castle, its People and its Paintings* (2nd edition 2016)
*Boughton: The House, its People and its Collections* (2016)